No. 635
$14.95

# PROFESSIONAL BROADCAST
# WRITER'S HANDBOOK
## by Stanley Field

 **TAB BOOKS**
Blue Ridge Summit, Pa. 17214

FIRST EDITION

FIRST PRINTING— APRIL 1974

Copyright©1974 by TAB BOOKS

Printed in the United States
of America

International Standard Book No. 0-8306-3635-8

Library of Congress Card Number: 72-97215

# *Preface*

Based on many years of teaching experience, I have found that the majority of students in writing classes are uncertain of their ultimate objective. Some are interested in becoming freelance dramatists, others are intrigued by the documentary, a few want to write quality scripts for children's programs, and some have a knack for catch phrases and believe they can outdo the current crop of commercial copywriters. That is why this text encompasses all these writing disciplines.

If you are planning to make a career of professional broadcasting, you will probably start at the smaller radio and television stations where staffs are limited and where writer's find it necessary to handle various types of scripts: public service announcements, commercials, news, possibly documentaries. Writers should be adaptable. You should be able to tackle every type of writing assignment and perhaps later, moving up the ladder, you may concentrate on the drama, or the documentary. To help potential writers, many of whom may never have seen a professional script, I have included many examples from current radio and television programs.

I wish to express my thanks to the copyright holders of the following scripts and other materials who have granted me permission to reprint their work in whole or in part:

MICHELANGELO: THE LAST GIANT, excerpts reprinted by permission of the author, Lou Hazam; produced by the National Broadcasting Company.

AMERICA, THE VIOLENT, excerpts reprinted by permission of NBC NEWS.

GUNSMOKE, excerpts reprinted from MILLIGAN by Ron Bishop; permission from CBS Television.

THE NEW DICK VAN DYKE SHOW, excerpts reprinted from THE BIRTH by Saul Turletaub and Bernie Orenstein; permission from the authors; © Cave Creek Enterprises, Inc., 1971.

TO ALL MY FRIENDS ON SHORE, excerpts reprinted by permission of the author, Allan Sloane; a William Cosby-Gilbert Cates Production.

THE LAST OF THE MOHICANS, excerpts from television adaptation reprinted by permission of the author, Harry Green, and the British Broadcasting Corporation.

ONE LIFE TO LIVE, permission to reprint Episode No. 1007 granted by Agnes Eckhardt Nixon; produced on the ABC network.

SWEET SMELL OF FREEDOM, permission to reprint granted by the author, Jerry Johnson; produced by WMAL-TV.

SIT DOWN, SHUT UP OR GET OUT, excerpts reprinted by permission of the author, Allan Sloane, and NBC NEWS; produced by the National Broadcasting Company in association with the National Council of Churches and presented on the NBC Television Religious Program.

THE JUNK BEHIND THE PICTURE WINDOW, excerpts reprinted by permission from WMAL.

My deepest gratitude is extended to all those members of the broadcasting industry without whose cooperation this book could not have been written. I am particularly thankful to writers Ron Bishop, Alvin Boretz, Howard Browne, Harry Green, Edward Hanna, Lou Hazam, Howard Jaffe, Jerry Johnson, Charles A. McDaniel, Agnes Nixon, Bernie Orenstein, Sol Panitz, Allan Sloane, Saul Turletaub; and to David Brinkley; L. T. Steele, chairman of the executive committee, Benton and Bowles, Inc.; Ted Bergmann, Herman Rush Associates; Irving M. Sloan, vice president, Wells, Rich, Green, Inc.; Ronald W. Mochak, D'Arcy-MacManus-Intermarco, Inc.; Bruce Lansbury, Paramount Television; Patricia A. Healy, Children's Television Workshop; Tom Paro, vice president, NBC; Bryson Rash and Tom Houghton, WRC-TV; Steve McCormick, vice president, Mutual Broadcasting System; Doris Ann, NBC NEWS; Pamela Ilott, CBS NEWS; Anne Nelson, CBS Television; Ted Landphair and Marc Kuhn, WMAL; John F. Hurlbut, WVMC; O. Leonard Press, executive director, Kentucky Educational Television; Hyman Field, WETA-TV; the Reverend William F. Fore; Robert Keim and Maxwell Fox, The Advertising Council; and to Stuart Finley. I am, most of all, indebted to my wife for once again giving untold hours to editorial suggestions and corrections and for her unswerving devotion.

Stanley Field
Falls Church, Virginia
1972

# Contents

# Chapter 1

## Formats

We are—all of us—accustomed to writing prose, whether it be a letter to a friend or a composition for an English class. So, if we were to attempt to write a novel or a short story, the format would present no problem. However, television is an electronic medium and its requirements for indications of visual effects and stage business pose the need for a specialized format.

It is necessary for aspiring television writers to acquaint themselves immediately with the proper formats. It would simplify matters if there were one accepted format such as the style almost universally employed for radio scripts. Unfortunately, a variety of formats are used in television, particularly for the documentary and the drama. We shall illustrate them in this chapter.

Presumably, every would-be writer owns or has access to a typewriter. In this computerized age, some technical genius may invent a typewriter which will respond automatically to the format for a television script. But as matters stand now, the writer can at least manipulate the margin and tabular setttings, readily enough, for the proper spacing.

### Television Formats

Let us consider first the formats for a documentary script. Some networks and local stations prefer the audio on the left and video on the right; others reverse the procedure. If you were employed as a writer on the public affairs staff of a broadcasting station, you would naturally follow the format used by that department.

Since many documentaries use stock footage (that is, film which is already in existence), the writer often indicates the reference numbers of the footage in the video portion. Also, you will notice that the video directions are in uppercase while the audio portion is in lowercase type. This is preferable, although some script writers use lower case throughout. You will observe these variations in the sample scripts reproduced in the various chapters. However, the formats illustrated in this chapter are based on actual scripts, and submissions for the documentary or drama utilizing any one of these formats will prove acceptable.

| VIDEO | AUDIO |
|---|---|
| 1. PAN STREET SCENES OF KYOTO | NARR:<br><br>This is Kyoto, third largest city of Japan. It was the capital of Japan until succeeded by Tokyo in 1868. |
| 2. PAN EXTERIORS OF KYOTO UNIVERSITY | However, Kyoto remains the cultural capital of Japan and a center of Buddhism. |
| 3. LONG SHOTS OF TEMPLES THEN MOVE IN FOR CLOSEUPS | |

Numbering the various scenes helps in editing the documentary. The writer or director can quickly identify any scene which requires revision, and the numbers are used as cues for the narrator. However, not all documentary writers use this method. The following format is the reverse of the previous example and is employed by the National Broadcasting Company.

| AUDIO | VIDEO |
|---|---|
| MUSIC: UP AND DOWN<br>NARR:<br><br>In October of 1541—<br>Already a morose old man of 66—<br>Michelangelo at last is done—<br>And stands aside for Rome—<br>Caught up in the throes of the Inquisition that followed the Protestant Reformation of Luther—<br>To be literally paralyzed by<br>What it sees! | PULL BACK FROM FIGURE OF GOD TO WIDE SHOT OF ENTIRE FRESCO |
| MUSIC: TRUMPETS TO BEGIN AS "LAST JUDGMENT" UNFOLDS | CUT TO SEVERAL SHOTS OF ANGELS BLOWING TRUMPETS |
| NARR:<br><br>As the angels sound their trumpets<br>Of doom, up from his throne rises<br>An angry Christ, his Virgin Mother<br>Turning away from what is to come... | CUT TO FIGURE OF CHRIST, RISING...AND VIRGIN MOTHER |

## Drama

The formats for television drama scripts are quite different from those of the documentary. The simplest format is illustrated below. The writer leaves the right half of the page blank. This is to enable the director to indicate the shots he wants. There is no precise division of audio and video as there is in the documentary script. In this format, the writer specifies, in the left-hand column, the stage business or action, which is visual, and an essential adjunct to the dialog. In a sense, this format is similar to that of the stage or legitimate play. Observe that the dialog is in the lowercase while all stage actions are in uppercase. Parentheses are generally used when describing the characters' emotions to distinguish such direction from stage business.

         MRS. ARCHER
        (SHE TRIES TO KEEP
        HER VOICE STEADY)

You are not on the senate floor, Hiram.

         ARCHER

Emily—first, you contradict me. Now, you are being facetious.

         MRS. ARCHER

        (SHE HOLDS HER
        COURSE DOGGEDLY)

You were beginning to make a speech, Hiram.

         ARCHER

        (CONDESCENDINGLY)

Well, well, perhaps you are right. The home is not a place for speech making.

HE DRINKS HIS COFFEE AND HIS EYE RETURNS TO THE NEWSPAPER

I'm still hopeful this story is a complete exaggeration. I shall investigate it as soon as I reach my office. If it's the truth, I am going to take it upon myself to warn Mrs. Lockwood that she is being both reckless and foolish.

FADE OUT

    When live presentations became the exception and filmed or taped productions the rule, the television drama moved from New York to Hollywood, where formats followed the pattern of the familiar film scenario. This format, illustrated below, is widely used by most Hollywood production agencies.

Notice that in the stage directions, the characters' names are capitalized. This enables the actor to quickly identify his direction for stage movements.

FADE IN:

1. INT. NIGHT. THE GREENSPAN STUDIO
It is a small square room with a sink at the back. Several racks hold paintings, rolls of canvas and stretchers. A palette and brushes lie on the counter space next to the sink. At left is a stairway which leads to the upstairs apartment. LOUIS places his mother's painting on an easel and examines it. His eyes light up with sincere admiration.

LOUIS                Mama—you did this!

MRS. GREENSPAN   Who else?

Aroused by the tone of his voice, she rises and joins him in front of the canvas.

LOUIS                Mama—it's wonderful—it's superb—it's lyric.

He throws his arms around her.

MRS. GREENSPAN   You think so? You mean it, Louie?

The dispirited look on her face vanishes into a smile.

LOUIS                Of course, I mean it. It's so wonderfully free and expressive. Look at those rhythms and those textures. Mama, how did you do it? If I paint for a hundred years, I'll never be able to do anything like it.

**Title Page**

Generally, you need be concerned with title page formats only for dramatic scripts. The one reproduced below is typical.

**THE NEW DICK VAN DYKE SHOW**

"The Birth"

| | |
|---|---|
| DICK | DICK VAN DYKE |
| JENNY | HOPE LANGE |
| ANNIE | ANGELA POWELL |
| MIKE | FANNIE FLAGG |
| CAROL | NANCY DUSSAULT |
| BERNIE | MARTY BRILL |
| DEBBIE GARRIMAN | PHOEBE NOEL |
| HEAD NURSE | RETA SHAW |
| NURSE 1 | KAREN CARR |
| NURSE 2 | ANN TAYLOR |
| MAN IN WAITING ROOM | BOB ANTHONY |
| 2nd MAN IN WAITING ROOM | BERNIE ORENSTEIN |
| MR. GARRIMAN | GORDON JUMP |

```
DR. NEAL_____BURKE RHYND
DAVID ROGERS_____BARRY VAN DYKE
PEOPLE IN WAITING ROOM
```

## SETS

INT. PRESTON HOME: LIVING ROOM & KITCHEN
BEDROOM

INT. DICK'S OFFICE

INT. HOSPITAL: ADMITTING AREA & WAITING
ROOM

## News

This excerpt from a WRC-TV newscast illustrates the usual format:

| VIDEO | AUDIO |
|---|---|
| METRO POLICE BADGE | RINKER: The metropolitan police department today released the crime statistics for last month. They show a decrease in every category...except homicide. Our reporter on special assignment, Al Johnson, has more on the story...Al? |

## Timing

Another problem the television writer faces is the question of timing. Time ℚ₃ of the essence in broadcasting and programs must be precisely timed, especially on commercial stations. The terms half-hour and hour are actually misnomers for the writer. A script for a half-hour sponsored program may run approximately 23 minutes, while the script for the hour sponsored program may run from 48 to 50 minutes. This is to allow for commercials, trailers, and local station identification.

On public (noncommercial) television stations and some sustaining programs on commercial stations, scripts more closely approximate the program time; that is, a script for a half-hour program may run 29:30 and a script for an hour program, 59:30.

The writer may time his dialog by reading it aloud to himself. A stopwatch is useful; if not available, a standard watch or small clock with a second hand will do. Timing the visual portion of the script is more difficult, particularly when you are writing a dramatic play which may include a great deal of action such as a western or crime drama. The visual action that is not synchronous with dialog must be estimated.

In writing the documentary, timing depends on whether the script is entirely narrative or whether there are inserts, such as interviews. Finally, it is experience that will enable the writer to accurately gage his timing.

## RADIO

Fortunately, one type of format, generally, is considered standard for radio. Most of the writing for radio today is for news programs or, in the case of "good music" stations, music commentary. Quite a few commercial radio stations produce documentaries. Public radio stations present both documentaries and contemporary radio dramas.

The following excerpt is from a radio drama. There is some similarity to the television format in that the dialog is in lowercase, the music, sound effects, and emotional responses in uppercase. However, you will note that the script is written across the entire page. Sound and music cues are underlined, and the script is double-spaced.

SOUND: AMBULANCE SIREN UP AND THEN FADING IN DISTANCE AS

MUSIC: COMES UP FOR TRANSITION AND UNDER

TOM: They rushed me into an oxygen tent. I guess there are more pleasant places to spend an evening, but when I felt life coming back and that cough fading away, I just kept thanking whoever invented that oxygen tent....Well, Janet learned the truth. I quess old Doc Starret must've found out all there was to know and told my wife. But there was worse news...

MUSIC:    UP AND OUT

DR. STARRET: I'm afraid we'll have to keep you here at the hospital for a few weeks for observation.

TOM: Good grief, Doc. I'm up to my neck in work at the office. I can't just lie around this hospital for a couple of weeks.

DR. STARRET: Tom, I know this is going to be hard to take. But I've just gone over the entire history of your case. I don't think you'll be able to work at a full-time job any longer!

MUSIC:   STING

### Timing

Radio scripts are much more easily timed than television scripts. Usually, a half-hour script runs 24 to 26 pages and a quarter-hour script, 12 pages. You can time your script fairly accurately by reading it aloud. You must allow time for music and sound effects which are "in the clear"; that is, not running simultaneously with the dialog.

# Chapter 2

## Technical Terminology*

As good craftsmen are aware of the capabilities of their tools, so writers for broadcasting should be familiar with the technical aspects of their craft. For example, they should have a working knowledge of the limits and the scope of the camera, the prime tool of the television medium. The technical knowledge is increasingly important when the writer is also producer or director. In the areas of the documentary and news programs, the writer is generally on the staff and so is in daily contact with the technicians. This is also true of the writer of commercials who is employed by an advertising agency or an independent producing company.

### TELEVISION

There are divisions of responsibility in television so that the final product, unlike the novel, is not the work of one person. In particular, the director vitally affects the script writer. In many instances, especially when writers are free-lancing, they have little or no say in the actual production of their scripts. The director of a television drama may decide to delete certain lines or possibly a scene if the program runs overlong in rehearsal, or may agree with an actor who suggests revision of some of the dialog. Documentary script writers, on the other hand, are so closely aligned with productions that they are almost always on hand to confer with the producer or director when any changes are required.

Our purpose in tracing this relationship of writer to director is to emphasize the degree of technical terminology writers may be required to include in their scripts. Actually, the writer need only utilize certain basic terms which we will define. In the drama, for example, the director determines the final shots; what is required of the writer is a precise definition of the action. If, in a dramatic script, the writer indicates profuse technical directions, it will not only prove annoying to the director, but will also be a sign of the amateur who has more academic than practical knowledge. The following are basic definitions and examples of television production terminology with which the writer should be familiar.

*The abbreviations used in the various scripts throughout this book are listed and defined at the end of the glossary, page 394.

ESTABLISHING SHOT: As its designation implies, the ESTABLISHING SHOT is generally the curtain raiser and, in essence, establishes the locale. We use the qualification "generally" because where a TEASER is employed, it is possible to begin the documentary or drama with vivid action before defining the locale.

### Example

ESTABLISHING SHOT: THE LAW OFFICE OF MRS. BELVA LOCKWOOD. WE SEE A LARGE MAHOGANY DESK ON WHICH A GREAT MANY PAPERS ARE FILED. A BOOKCASE WITH LAW BOOKS STANDS AT THE RIGHT WALL. BEHIND THE DESK IS A LARGE WINDOW HUNG WITH CRISP WHITE CURTAINS.

TEASER: A brief scene preceding the body of the drama or documentary. It may be a sequence taken directly from the play or documentary, or it may be a chronological episode actually preceding the basic events. It is used to capture the immediate attention of the audience.

### Example

FADE-IN THE CHAMBER OF THE UNITED STATES SENATE. WE HEAR A COMMOTION OF VOICES. ONE SENATOR IS ANGRILY GESTICULATING AT ANOTHER WHO EVIDENTLY HAS THE FLOOR. THE PRESIDENT PRO TEM BANGS HIS GAVEL. THE GESTICULATING SENATOR SEATS HIMSELF RELUCTANTLY. SENATOR HIRAM ARCHER, WHO HAS THE FLOOR, LOOKS ACIDLY AT HIS OPPONENT AND THEN PROCLAIMS:

ARCHER

My brother senators, do you realize that permitting this woman to practice before the bar of the highest tribunal in the nation is setting a fearful example for all womanhood? Mrs. Belva Lockwood—though I respect her widowhood—has already upset the bounds of decent convention many times. She has dared to oppose the members of the bar who did not believe it was proper for a woman to practice before the Supreme Court of the District of Columbia. But having won that victory, she was not content. I know that she has had the effrontery to persuade you, my brother senators, nay, to cajole you, to cast your votes for her bill. You may say she is a unique person. But I say she is a woman. And other women will be emboldened by her victory. I tell you, my dear colleagues, there may be an exodus from our homes. Women will want careers for themselves, and motherhood and the family will be destroyed. This year of 1884 will go down in infamy!

DISSOLVE TO CREDITS AND TITLE

**FADE-IN:** Connotes coming from a black or blank screen to an ongoing scene. It is similar, in a sense, to raising the curtain on a stage setting. It is always used for the opening of a program. The FADE-IN is often indicated during a program when commercials interrupt the action. The scene following the commercial will then FADE IN.

### Example

FADE-IN RECEPTION ROOM OF MRS. LOCKWOOD'S OFFICE. MRS. LOCKWOOD'S SECRETARY IS AT HER DESK BUSILY TYPING A LETTER. A VISITOR ENTERS.

**FADEOUT:** This is the reverse of FADE-IN. It is used to denote the end of a scene and, at times, is referred to as "going to black," that is, a blank screen. As the FADE-IN implies the curtain is going up, the FADEOUT refers to the curtain going down. The FADEOUT is also used during a program to punctuate a scene. For example, if a murder is committed, the camera may focus on the body and then the scene will FADEOUT to leave an impact on the viewer. There is also a FADEOUT before each commercial.

### Example

MARTHA

(WHISPERING) Are you afraid of me, John?

JOHN

No, I...I'm afraid of my own emotions.

MARTHA

You needn't be.

HE HESITATES FOR A MOMENT THEN EMBRACES AND KISSES HER.

FADE OUT.

**DISSOLVE:** The technique of immediate transition in television productions is termed the DISSOLVE. When a DISSOLVE is called for, the scene that is being viewed and the following scene appear on the screen simultaneously for a brief moment until the second scene completely supersedes the first.

### Example

MRS. LOCKWOOD IS PACING HER OFFICE ANXIOUSLY. THEN SHE SITS DOWN AT HER DESK, STUDIES THE BRIEF BEFORE HER, SIGHS DEEPLY

AND GIVES IT UP. SUDDENLY SHE BANGS HER FIST
DETERMINEDLY ON THE DESK. SHE CALLS OUT:

MRS. LOCKWOOD

Martha—Martha—

DISSOLVE TO RECEPTION ROOM. MARTHA IS
BESEIGED BY A HALF DOZEN REPORTERS.

There are several variations of the DISSOLVE: (1) The
LAP DISSOLVE is employed in order to sustain an effect; the
transition from one scene to another is accomplished slowly.
(2) The MATCHING DISSOLVE may be used to indicate a
lapse of time. For example, we may see a garden in
springtime with flowers blooming and then DISSOLVE to the
same garden covered by snow. The MATCHING DISSOLVE
may also be used in a FLASHBACK sequence.

### Example

WE SEE A CHARWOMAN ON HER KNEES SCRUBBING
THE CORRIDOR OF AN OFFICE BUILDING. SHE
WRINGS OUT THE MOP AND STARES AGONIZINGLY
AT HER WORN HANDS. AS SHE STANDS THERE
CONTEMPLATING HER HANDS, DISSOLVE TO PAIR
OF HANDS, BEAUTIFULLY MANICURED. AS THE
CAMERA PULLS BACK, WE SEE IT IS THE CHAR-
WOMAN AS A YOUNG DEBUTANTE.

**CLOSEUP:** As this direction implies, the camera moves
forward to obtain a view of an actor, interviewee or other
participant from the waist or shoulder high. Sometimes a BIG
CLOSEUP is used to focus on a particular feature of an
individual: If we were producing a television version of
"Cyrano de Bergerac," we could call for a BIG CLOSEUP of
his nose.

### Example

ALICE

A woman running for the Presidency will do more than any
other act to dramatize our cause. Will you accept?

MRS. LOCKWOOD

You must give me time to think about it.

ALICE

Very well. I will arrive in San Francisco in about two
weeks. Will that give you enough time?

MRS. LOCKWOOD NODS. MISS COLTON RISES.

Good. I expect your answer to be yes.

CLOSEUP OF BELVA LOCKWOOD'S FACE AS SHE PEERS THOUGHTFULLY INTO SPACE.

**LONG SHOT:** If you have ever taken a group photo with your own camera, then you know you must step back in order to focus the entire group in the viewer. This, simply enough, is a LONG SHOT. As the camera moves forward to take a CLOSEUP, so it moves backward to obtain a LONG SHOT. An advantageous use of the LONG SHOT is to reveal an entire setting. Many ESTABLISHING SHOTS are LONG SHOTS to permit the full view of a street, a village, a courtroom or wherever the action is taking place or going to take place.

### Example

DISSOLVE TO THE AUDITORIUM OF MONTGOMERY HIGH SCHOOL. LONG SHOT OF THE STAGE SO THAT WE CAN SEE THE BANNER STRUNG ACROSS THE BACK OF THE STAGE: "EQUAL RIGHTS PARTY— BELVA LOCKWOOD FOR PRESIDENT."

**MEDIUM CLOSEUP:** This camera direction indicates a shot midway between the LONG SHOT and the CLOSEUP.

### Example

FADE-IN THE DINING ROOM OF THE ARCHERS' HOME. WE SEE THE ENTIRE ROOM. SENATOR AND MRS. ARCHER ARE HAVING BREAKFAST. THE CAMERA MOVES IN FOR A MEDIUM CLOSEUP SO THAT NOW WE HAVE A FULLER VIEW OF THE SENATOR READING HIS NEWSPAPER AND MRS. ARCHER SIPPING HER ORANGE JUICE. THEN A CLOSEUP OF MRS. ARCHER'S FACE AS WE CATCH THE MIXED EMOTIONS OF HATE AND FEAR.

**SUPERIMPOSURE:** A special effect whereby the pictures from two cameras are focused onto a single scene. This effect is often used at the beginning of a program when the title may be SUPERIMPOSED over the ESTABLISHING SHOT or at the end of a program when the credits may be rolled over the closing sequence. The SUPERIMPOSURE can be a highly effective device in a television play to portray the thoughts of a person or it can be used to heighten suspense in a drama of the occult.

### Example

ALAN ENTERS THE OLD DECREPIT HOUSE. THE FLOORS CREAK. WE HEAR THE HOWL OF THE WIND OUTSIDE. SUDDENLY THERE IS A CLAP OF THUN- DER FOLLOWED BY A PIERCING SCREAM. SUPERIMPOSE A GHOSTLY FIGURE ABOVE ALAN'S HEAD. HE TURNS IN HORROR.

**PANORAMIC:** A horizontal sweep of the camera. We may PAN across a room or a sports stadium. Generally, panning shots are horizontal and a vertical sweep is referred to as a TILT. The PAN shot is used frequently, particularly to establish atmosphere: the tense faces of fans at a boxing match; the varied abstract paintings at a modern art gallery.

### Example

FADE-IN SMALL PLATFORM ON STREET CORNER WITH A SMALL CROWD OF MEN AND WOMEN. MARTHA DIXON IS ON THE PLATFORM ABOUT TO EMBARK ON HER MAIDEN POLITICAL FORAY. CAMERA PANS CROWD AND WE SEE THE EX- PECTANT FACES.

**INTERCUT:** A CUT is a rapid, staccato movement as compared to the smooth flow of the DISSOLVE. To INTER- CUT is to move abruptly from the image on one camera to the image on another. It serves as a technique to obtain simultaneous reactions or to give the effect of two people speaking to each other on the telephone.

### Example

MARY IS SEATED ON THE SOFA READING A BOOK, BUT IT IS EVIDENT HER MIND IS NOT ON IT. SHE KEEPS GLANCING UP AT THE TELEPHONE ON THE END TABLE. SUDDENLY IT RINGS. SHE DROPS HER BOOK AND HURRIES TO PICK UP THE RECEIVER.

MARY          Hello! Oh, hello, John! It's been so long.

INTERCUT

JOHN           I'm sorry, darling.

For the above scene, the SPLIT SCREEN device could also be used. In that case, we would see Mary and John simultaneously on the screen. The two cameras would be semimasked so that each image occupies only half the screen.

The terms included above are merely representative of those used in television scripting. A more comprehensive listing is included in the glossary. In the scripts incorporated in this book, taken from a diverse array of sources, a number of fairly standard abbreviations are used; these abbreviations are also explained and defined in the glossary.

## RADIO

Where the basic tool of television is the camera, for radio it is the microphone. Radio has only one element to work with—sound. But sound has its various components: voice, music, and effects. The following technical terminology will assist the writer in the preparation of his script.

**FADE-IN:** A gradual increase in volume of sound or music. This direction is used frequently; it may indicate a sound coming from a distance and then approaching closer.

### Example

DR. STARRET: Your husband is very ill, Mrs. James. I've called for an ambulance.

SOUND: FADE-IN AMBULANCE SIREN

**FADEOUT:** This is the reverse of FADE-IN and indicates a decrease in the volume of sound, music or voice.

### Example

SOUND: AMBULANCE STARTING. FADE OUT SIREN AS AMBULANCE DRIVES OFF

**UNDER:** Indicates music or sound effect that is to be heard beneath the dialog. Music UNDER narration or dialog heightens the mood of a scene.

### Example

MUSIC: IT SETS THE MOOD OF THE SUPER-NATURAL: UP AND UNDER

NARRATOR: It all began at the National Gallery, and it is as unexplainable today as the time it happened.

**SEGUE:** Denotes a transition from one type of music to another in immediate sequence. It comes from the Italian, meaning to follow, and is pronounced phonetically: segway.

### Example

MUSIC: BRING UP THEME THEN SEGUE TO BRIEF CHORUS OF "HAPPY DAYS ARE HERE AGAIN"—HOLD UNDER

**SNEAK:** Connotes music or perhaps sound which is heard very softly at first and then builds to a normal or, if necessary, loud level. It helps to establish a mood and is a form of dramatic foreshadowing.

### Example

NARRATOR: The old man stopped before a door which was securely padlocked. I waited breathlessly for the magnificent sight I was certain would greet my eyes.

MUSIC: SNEAK IN OMINOUS MOTIF AND HOLD UNDER

NARRATOR: I was not disappointed. There on a wall, in a huge gold frame, was the most glorious painting I had ever seen.

**STING**: Refers to a note or brief series of notes of music used to punctuate an exciting or emotional scene or as a musical accent to denote danger.

**Example**

MUSIC: UP SHARP . . . PREMONITORY . . . THEN UNDER

NARRATOR: My mind became a whirlpool of doubt. Now what was I to believe? What unearthly manifestation had taken on the aura of reality—for there on the front page, hauntingly vivid, was a picture of a house in flames—the house!

MUSIC: STING

**COLD**: Indicates that narration or dialog begins with no introduction. Sometimes a program, for effect, will open COLD, perhaps as a TEASER, preceding the announcer's introductory remarks.

**Example**

DR. NOLAN: (COLD) Stop worrying, Matt. It's your firstborn and it'll take time. And, Matt, I think you'll enjoy that cigar more if you remove the foil.

MUSIC: UP AND UNDER

ANNOUNCER: Tonight, we bring you another in our series of half-hour dramas.

**UP AND OUT**: Refers to music which has been held beneath narration or dialog and is then to be brought to a conclusion.

**Example**

MUSIC: UP AND UNDER

NARRATOR: I could not sleep that night. As soon as I closed my eyes, the walls of the hotel room became a screen upon which Linda and her father played out the tragic meeting. I told myself over and over again—it was a strange hallucination. I had become fascinated—bewitched. I turned on the light and reached for the book. Feverishly, I read: "The painting is believed to have been destroyed by fire." That was it!

MUSIC: UP AND OUT

**CONCLUSION**

The above technical terminology will generally suit a writer's requirements. There is a glossary at the back of the book, with a rather complete list of terms and definitions. However, as we have stated previously, the writer need not be overly concerned with directions.

# Chapter 3
## The Documentary

Newton Minow's condemnation of television as a "vast wasteland" was a great catalyst to documentary production. His castigation may be debatable, but the fact remains that in the intervening years there has been a tremendous upsurge in the scheduling of documentaries.

The documentary in television is presumed to be an enlightening force. If it does not add to the sum of man's knowledge, then it has little purpose in being. The documentary is the oasis of idealism in the electronic medium's desert of commercialism. Since television drama wove so brief a cultural spell, the documentary has filled the void with such creative productions as "The Saga of Western Man," "Shakespeare: Soul of an Age," "Greece: the Golden Age," and "Michelangelo: the Last Giant," among many others.

The pioneer documentary film producers, such as Flaherty, Grierson, and Rotha, had several characteristics in common: vision, a social conscience, and an instinct for creative composition. Our current crop of television documentary writers and producers must possess these qualities if they are to present successful productions. Sometimes, as in the case of Lou Hazam and John Secondari, the producers are also writers and can bring their multiple talents to the creative tasks.

Very often, the networks and local stations advertise upcoming documentaries with the self-defeating designation of "specials." The connotation is that the documentary is a rare bird which makes a very occasional appearance, and this in itself is an indictment of the industry's outlook on its creative life. The documentary should not be a "special" but a continuing, frequent presentation. It is a form particularly suitable to television and its possibilities for the revelation of truth are immeasurable.

Before the advent of television, documentary films were produced for theatrical presentation. In the 30s, when the "March of Time" formulated the news-documentary approach, its outlet was the motion picture theater. Today, television provides the major medium for the presentation of documentary films. However, the basic tool, even with the advent of video tape, remains the same—the camera. Documentaries for television are generally filmed, although some sequences may be video-taped. The film camera, at this writing, is still the most flexible tool for location shooting.

## CONCEPT

In the beginning, there is the idea. And so, for many productions, the first step for the writer is the **concept** This is a brief statement of the theme of the proposed documentary and the general area it will cover.

The concept may be as brief as one paragraph; usually, it will run to one page and seldom more than two. For an agency that produces many documentary films, concepts are valuable in determining which themes to choose. A writer may be asked to submit several concepts for various programs or they may be prepared by the producer or a member of the public affairs staff. The following is a sample of a concept:

### "Mapping in the 1970s"

"Most of the earth's land surface has not been accurately mapped and, at current rates of progress, the end is not even in sight. Indeed, some areas of the moon are better mapped. The growing world population, the pressure for optimum use of the earth's resources, the need for maps in economic development and military security make the classical time-consuming approach unacceptable. Methods are being developed to accomplish the task in a fraction of the time.

"In emerging countries, maps are being used for economic advancement. In the older, developed nations, growth in urban areas is creating a continuing need for very large-scale maps to help meet problems attendant to taxation, utilities, water resources, transportation, recreation and housing. And as the terrain changes, either through man's efforts or the capriciousness of Mother Nature, the maps will have to be revised and updated to meet the then current needs.

"This film will trace briefly the history of mapmaking from the use of the plane table and transit to today's satellite geodesy and tomorrow's even more sophisticated methods. It will demonstrate graphically how new equipment and techniques are being developed to cut production time while improving accuracy. The sharp contrast between classical mapping of the ages and modern advanced technology will be dramatically portrayed."

## TREATMENT

The writer may also be called on to prepare a **treatment** prior to script development. The treatment is a detailed outline of the documentary in which every scene is described. Obviously, this cannot be done until the writer has complete knowledge of the subject, gained by thorough research.

The treatment is generally quite lengthy and may run as many as 20 pages or more double-spaced. The producer should be able to ascertain from the treatment the scope of the documentary, the locations for shooting, the proportion of live footage to stock, and whether or not it meets the objectives of the program. The treatment is valuable to the writer in clarifying the structure of the documentary and in providing a blueprint for constructing the script. Several excerpts from a typical treatment are presented below:

### "The Power of Language"

"Language, as varied and complex and awkward as it is, is still the most basic and effective means that human beings have of conveying ideas to one another. So, to expand understanding, one essential would seem to be to expand our facility with the tools, the means of understanding. That means language training.

"Open on an establishing shot of the Language Institute. Then dissolve inside as narration explains that from here is directed a teaching activity, a language training effort of a scope and an effectiveness that has never been known before.

"There are shots of men in language-lab type work. Use an establishing shot, close shots, and face closeups of the men, with intercut shots of tape machines running. Pause for a moment for live sound as one of the students is repeating what he is hearing on the tape. The sound sequence is long enough to hear the intonation in his delivery.

"Dissolve to the outside of the building, where we see a small group of students walking. Narration brings out the fact that the Institute graduates several thousand students a year and has a curriculum that includes 25 foreign languages.

"Cut to a lounge where a number of faculty members are chatting over coffee. Narration points out that there are some 400 faculty members. Now, over individual shots of the faculty members, we take a moment to reflect on the quality of these people. For visual interest, perhaps one or two of the women faculty members can be dressed in the traditional costume of their native lands. As we look at their faces, as they chat, drink their coffee, smoke, and listen, each with subtly different ways of gesturing, narration brings out some interesting facts:

"To teach any given language at this school, the teacher must be a native speaker of that language. But, in fact, it is not uncommon for one of these instructors to be able to express himself in as many as six languages. Among their number are descendants of royalty, prominent artists, musicians, statesmen, educators, judges, and former government officials dislodged from their native countries by internal revolts.

"We dissolve to an extreme closeup of an instructor speaking phrases into a microphone. Then a shot which shows that he is sitting in a small studio, fully equipped. We see shots of the technician making the recording. Narration points out that for each student to be able to hear his homework, as well as read it, means many hours of painstaking work by the faculty in the school's recording studios. These give the student a clear, correct speech model to fashion his own lingual patterns from as he progresses in his learning. In our narration, we detail the extensiveness of the tape-copying setup and how it works, including an explanation of how the high-speed copying makes it possible to re-record a half-hour instruction tape in four or five minutes.

"Now we go to the area outside the Far East building where there is an attractive oriental gate and stairway, leading down to the level space in which the oriental garden has been created. We pan the camera to follow a group of two or three students as they come down this stairway and move into the garden area. We follow them as they walk through it on their way to class. Narration states that day by day, in class and out, the student is acquiring a whole new frame of reference and an additional dimension of understanding as he reinforces his learning of the spoken and written language with the daily experience of various facets of the culture and conventions out of which that language springs.

"Dissolve to a high angle shot of the splashing fountain in the Patio Ibero Americano. Again, there are students sitting in the patio, conversing and, again, with picture and narration, we point out the Spanish and Portugese flavor of the environment. Narration underscores that this is an organic part of the teaching philosophy.

"Dissolve to a class in progress. It is a Russian class. One member of the class reads aloud from a Soviet newspaper as another translates what is being read. Then we dissolve to the Russian store setting. We see students acting the part of sales clerks and customers. The products are Russian articles and the money is a copy of actual Soviet currency. We hear students discussing prices, making sales, changing bills, etc.

"Now we dissolve to a sequence of computer-assisted instruction. We explain how the student taps a key or combination of keys to notify the computer that he is ready. The computer types out the first question or problem, perhaps a sentence in English which the student is to translate into Russian. The student types the Russian translation. Immediately, the computer types back with the correct version. Each student can work at his own pace.

"Our final scene is graduation. We see the students receiving their certificates. Then we dissolve to an exterior shot. Students are standing around in groups, congratulating each other in various languages, speaking easily and fluently."

## SCRIPT

The final writing of the script depends on several factors. Many documentaries employ a single narrator who may be off screen for the entire documentary or whose lines may be divided with a portion off screen and a portion on screen. Where a narrator is used with no interposed sequences, the writer obviously has a great deal more to write than in the scripting of a documentary which may include interviews or ad-lib comments. In either event, there is one basic principle which should guide the writer: does the script add to the sum of knowledge of the viewer? It is pointless and redundant for the writer to define what the visual clearly explains. Many documentaries suffer from overwriting. While one picture may not actually be worth a thousand words, the writer should be concise.

Although writers of television drama have much wider scope than documentary writers, the latter should also make their writing dramatic. A pedestrian script will prove detrimental to even the finest of visual material. If we accept the old adage that truth is stranger than fiction, we may find that the documentary is often more dramatic than the fictional play. For the documentary deals with the stuff of life, with real people and real problems. Ergo, the terms often associated with documentaries: verity and actuality.

Writing procedure is also affected by other elements. When the documentary includes historic events, writers may be required to do a stock search and tailor their scripts to available footage. This is a necessary procedure, also, in coverage, let us say, of the recent Southeast Asian conflict. Footage is shot as the action occurs: no producer can stage a battle during an actual war! However, a producer can decide to make a film on drug addiction and the script can be written as a scenario for shooting. In this latter instance, the writer does his research among drug addicts, interviews government officials regarding narcotics control, talks to parents whose children are addicts. They will then proceed to write the script and the cameras will follow the guidelines of the script.

## OBJECTIVITY

Marshall McLuhan has perpetrated a phrase, "The Medium is the Message," and one can hardly deny the overbearing influence of television. However, we are more inclined to agree with Charles Steinberg's refutation of McLuhan (**Television Academy Quarterly**, "The McLuhan Myth") that "It is not media which create problems without precedent, but the way in which media are used. It is not the medium but the message which causes concern."

The cumulative hours spent before the home screen by American families amount to an astronomical figure. This imposes a burden on the conscience of broadcasters, or at least it should, when they consider the power for good or evil of the instrumentality they control. The question arises: how objective can broadcasters be? How far can they go in tackling a controversial issue? The dilemma of television is that it is a Goliath in dread of a David with or without a lethal slingshot.

Yet notwithstanding the wrath of a segment of the public, the timidity of a sponsor or the displeasure of the sales department, many compelling documentaries have been produced. Of course, when broadcasters do take a stand, they face the opposition cry of bias.

We do not believe it is possible for producers or writers of documentaries to be purely objective. They would have to be operating in a mindless vacuum. Witness: A producer may have to choose one or two thousand feet from some eight thousand feet of film, depending on whether the documentary will run a half hour or an hour. Producers may be objective in choosing footage on the basis of technical quality, but given two segments of equally fine footage, the choice they make is subjective. And in turn, this choice affects the writer, since the words must coordinate with the film. Perhaps the ultimate answer is the faith of the viewer in the integrity of the producer and the writer.

Industry, labor, government, or philanthropic institutions which contract for documentary films that may be shown on television, have a definite point to make and must take a positive approach to their respective organizations. Obviously, a labor union will not contract for a documentary film that derides the blue- or white-collar worker. Nor will a government agency produce a film which is derogatory of its operations. Nor for that matter, could anyone conceive of a network spending upwards of a hundred thousand dollars to produce a documentary film which purports to demonstrate that television programming is indeed a vast wasteland. Or the pharmaceutical industry sponsoring a documentary which decries the high price of drugs. Indeed, objectivity has its limits. Nevertheless, within those limits, controversy has had surprisingly wide play on the national networks and on many independent stations.

Until recently, the networks refused to present documentaries which were not produced under the aegis of their public affairs or news departments, presumably under the theory that many documentaries are, in essence, based on news events or contain editorial matter which reflects the policies of the networks. Management at the networks believed that any programs in the area of news and public affairs should be strictly under the broadcaster's supervision.

It was Wolper Productions which finally caused the withdrawal of the self-imposed restriction. Unable to obtain time on the networks for the documentary film, "The Race for Space," Wolper and his sponsor circumvented the networks by purchasing time on individual stations, many of which were network affiliated. Later Wolper documentaries, such as "The Making of a President" and "D-Day," experienced little problem in obtaining network time.

## RESEARCH

Since the documentary deals solely with facts, the more research a writer can do, within the deadline of the production date, the more informative the script will be. Research methods are largely twofold:

1. Contacting individuals and through interviews obtaining pertinent material for the documentary. For example, if a documentary were being planned on tax reform, writers might query tax experts, economists, lawyers, accountants, and the not-to-be-forgotten taxpayer. Unless they are devotees of shorthand, writers or researchers may find it helpful to carry a small tape recorder to record the conversations which then can be played back at will.

2. Library research involves the study of books, periodicals and newspapers covering the subject matter. It also includes stock search in film libraries.

Many writers prefer to do their own research. Some, however, who may be busy with several assignments, employ researchers. The size of the producing organization and budget also influences the methods of research. At the networks, with their large staffs, writers are assisted by research departments. On the local level, the independent station may not be able to afford a researcher and the writers will find it necessary to do their own digging to unearth the necessary background.

## THEME

In his comprehensive volume, "Documentary Film," Paul Rotha aptly stated: "Subject and theme must always come first. It is only for their full and lasting expression that good craftsmanship is necessary." And Rotha advised that "technique must never be permitted to play the most important part in documentary."

Although the above axioms, at first glance, appear to relate largely to the province of the producer and the director, they do affect the writer. In many instances, as we have pointed out, the producer and the writer are the same. There is a tendency among young filmmakers in the latter case to substitute technique for substance. We do not mean to imply that one should not attempt new approaches in the use of the camera, but that every technique should be an integral part of the production. The primary purpose of a documentary is to inform. Entertainment is the realm of the drama and, while the documentary should be "entertaining" in the sense of holding an audience, it does not have the same function as drama. Able dramatists will skillfully veil any message they wish to convey; documentary writers will be forthright about what they have to say.

The choice of theme may well be affected by the controversiality of the subject matter. A well rounded documentary will try to present both sides of the issue. However, since broadcasting stations may now editorialize, a television station may produce a documentary which presents management's editorial opinion.

Indeed, the choice of a theme is extremely wide-ranging. Any facet of life may provide the theme for a documentary, no matter how delicate the subject, provided the script is written with taste and produced with sensitivity.

## CATEGORIES

It is possible to catalog documentaries by type, but unless we use very broad categories, we may find a good deal of overlapping. In a previous work ("Television and Radio Writing," Houghton Mifflin), we identified three such categories: (1) Action, (2) Information, (3) Dramatization. These identifications are still valid—with modifications.

The dramatized documentary, per se, is now rarely presented. It was a genre exemplified by the Armstrong Circle

Theater, which based its productions on fact but used actors to portray the actual people. In many instances, the living protagonist of the documentary was presented in a summation at the close of the program. CBS' "You Are There" series utilized a documentary approach to dramatize history.

With the demise of the Circle Theater, the wholly dramatized documentary went out of fashion. Actuality and verity were the new banners waved by the documentarists. This is not to say that dramatization disappeared entirely from the documentary production. A new designation, "re-creation," was employed. For example, if a documentary were being produced about welfare recipients, and the writer or researcher had come upon an incident which required staging, the scene might be reenacted with the actual participants or, if this were not possible, staged with actors. This could also be the technique employed for historical sequences. But these types of dramatizations are only a small part of the overall documentary presentation.

We might point out that the documentary may utilize within its structure every known technique of television: interview, talk, discussion, drama, monolog, flashback, candid and random shooting, etc. The writer-producer may be circumscribed by facts, but there is no limit to the imagination that may be brought to play in the creative presentation of those facts.

Classifying the documentary as "informational" opens a very wide umbrella. Presumably, every documentary imparts information. This classification is used to differentiate the documentary of pure exposition from the action documentary where the purpose is to arouse in the viewer a desire to participate in a reform movement or donate to a cause. A documentary on child beating might exhort the audience to write to the local political officers to enact suitable legislation, or the United Givers Fund might present a documentary on its activities to stimulate donations during the annual fund drive.

Professor A. William Bluem in his book, "Documentary in American Television" (Hastings House), illustrates two overall categories which also provide a sound basis for study: (1) the news documentary, (2) the theme documentary.

The first, as its title implies, is based on news events. Its forerunners were the pioneer "March of Time" and the Ed Murrow-Fred Friendly series, "See It Now." The news documentary is pictorial journalism which may utilize for its subject matter events such as the sorry spectacle of the riots during the 1968 Democratic convention in Chicago or the tremendous excitement of the moon landing.

The theme documentary is divided by Professor Bluem into three production categories: (1) compilation, (2) biographical, (3) dramatic. The compilers use stock footage from film libraries to present their stories which may portray the glamor of Hollywood or the struggles of the battlefield. Living biographies describe the lives of prominent persons by the use of film clips. The dramatic technique is generally employed in the production of documentaries which lend themselves, obviously enough, to high drama. A documentary unit, for example, may decide to film the incidents occurring in a detective's daily skirmishes with danger.

As we have stated, it may be convenient to attempt to define the documentary by type, but it is is not always possible to do so. One of the sample scripts in this chapter is "Michelangelo: the Last Giant." It is biography, history and a comment on the social mores of the time. It may be said to have a theme: the conflict of man against man, or the struggle of genius to overcome the conventions of his contemporary society. It is also definitely informational and highly dramatic.Therefore, you will find that many documentaries fit into several categories and all we can safely employ are very generalized designations.

## "OF BLACK AMERICA"

Civil rights, racism, riots in the streets, and violence on the campus offer a fertile field for the documentary. It can mirror, as can no other vehicle, the problems that confront the nation, the "now" situation. The television documentary can let you see and hear the people who are directly involved.

The emergence of the term Black as a descriptive adjective for Afro-American (vis-a-vis its counterpart, White), and the righteous wrath of the Black man in demanding equality, furnished the theme for a series of documentaries produced by the Columbia Broadcasting System. They were written by Andrew A. Rooney and Perry Wolff; the latter was also the executive producer of the series. The narrator was television star Bill Cosby.

You will notice in the following excerpts from "Of Black America" the style of the narrative. In the very choice of a narrator, the writer's approach may be qualified. If a comparatively unknown professional narrator is employed for largely off-screen voicing, the writer has the greatest latitude. When a name star is the narrator and particularly when that star has developed certain well defined characteristics, the writer may find it advisable to emulate the actor's style. Of course, the writing is tempered by the subject matter. No writer will attempt a light-hearted approach to a documentary portraying the devastating effect of a hurricane in Mississippi.

Yet in any area of creativity, and this is a statement you will find reiterated throughout this volume, there are no hard and fast rules. Such rules would defeat the very essence of creativity—free expression and originality. Although we have mentioned tailoring narration to suit the idiosyncrasies of an actor, the truly talented performer should be able to assume a diversity of roles. However, for our particular study of this first episode in the documentary series, "Of Black America," you will observe that the style does suit the relaxed performance we have come to associate with Bill Cosby as an actor and comedian.

ANNOUNCER: CBS NEWS presents OF BLACK AMERICA: "Black History: Lost, Stolen or Strayed."

(CHILDREN SINGING "CHARLIE BROWN)

MRS. BILLUPS (TEACHER): Great! Very good. All right. We'll go to lunch now and this afternoon we'll continue.

BILL COSBY (TRYING CHILD'S CHAIR): No, I could never fit in that—never get in that at all. This is more like it.

Now, what's the whitest thing you know? Whiter than the driven snow, whiter than the whites of your eyes? Sugar. Nonintegrated, nonblack, sweet sugar. But you see there is a Black man in your sugar. His name is Norbert Rillieux. Norbert Rillieux in 1846 invented a vacuum pan that revolutionized the sugar refining industry. You have to dig to find that fact. I mean, it's not much history, but it's still history.

Now what do you stand in? In your shoes. Now, there's just you in your shoes, isn't there? Nope. See there's a Black man standing in your oxfords with you. Sharing your sole—and your heel—is a man whose name is Jan Ernst Matzeliger. In 1863—this is a drawing by the kids—Matzeliger invented the machine that made mass-produced shoes possible. Now you have to dig around for that fact, too. And again, it's not much history, but it's history. Am I coming in clear to California? I mean is this TV signal driving through a pass in the Sierra Nevada Mountains and slipping into San Francisco? Okay. Well, I want to thank you, Jim Beckwourth. Jim Beckwourth, out of St. Louis, hunter, trapper, and honorary chief of the Crow tribe of Indians. We had trouble finding you, Jim. Though you helped open the West, you didn't make the books. Chicago—right here where the Wrigley Building is—young fellow by the name of Jean Baptiste du Sable.

Jean Baptiste. He founded you, Chicago, when he traded with the Indians. And, of course, there it is right there. At that particular time it was called Eschikagou or "stinking onion" by the Indians, and du Sable, he didn't even change the name at all. Now you take the Lewis and Clark expedition here—right in there. You'll find a Black man named York helping to open the West. Those men are trying to wash the black out of York. That's what you might call historically significant because a lot of people think we ought to wash white—but we ain't gonna, you see.

Texas—coming down to you, Texas. Right down the Chisholm Trail, right here. Right down there with 5,000 Black cowboys who never made it to the Hollywood Western. Did you know that? In this same group, there was one Black outlaw—his name was Deadwood Dick—who claimed his soul brothers were Bat Masterson, Billy the Kid, and Jesse James. Deadwood Dick used to ride into the saloon, order two drinks—one for himself and one for his horse. And here's his horse, drinking a shot of red-eye with a straw.

And how about the 186,000 Blacks who fought on the Union side during the Civil War? Thirty-eight thousand died.

How about Teddy Roosevelt's charge up San Juan Hill? It wasn't just the Rough Riders who made it. Four Black regiments went right up with Teddy. They didn't get lost going up the hill. They got lost in the history books.

How about the North Pole? Snow white? Well, the first man there was Black. Matthew Henson. He spoke Eskimo, and he was Admiral Peary's navigator; and although he made it first to the pole, it never quite made it to the history books.

And how about your heart? Can we get there? All right. Daniel Hale Williams first performed open-heart surgery successfully. This list could go on forever. Blacks who made history, but who didn't get into the history texts at all. And the strange thing is, how little there is about us in the textbooks. Napoleon once said, "History is a fable agreed upon." And the fable agreed upon up to now is that American history is white on white.

The narration continues in this vein. But it is not entirely monolog. To verify his statements, Cosby introduces experts as you will see in the following excerpt. Cosby's narration is the responsibility of the writer; the expert's comments may be video-taped or filmed and then edited or the copy may be scripted by the writer after an interview with the expert.

BILL COSBY: But there is the scar of history running right through kids as young as these. It tears you up, if you know how to look at drawings kids make, because kids shouldn't know much about history and anything about discrimination. I mean, nobody hates little Black kids—but why do some of them cause so much trouble? If you ask Black and White children to draw themselves, or trees, or houses, some strange things happen. We asked some ordinary White kids from ordinary families to make some drawings for us. Like—well, let's call him John. John's White, and we asked him to draw himself. This is John. This is his house. This is his tree.

Then we asked a Black kid—let's call him Ralph—to do the same thing. This is Ralph's drawing of himself. This is his tree. Now why should two kids of the same age draw so differently? Enter the expert. This is Dr. Emmanuel Hammer, psychiatrist specializing in children's therapy.

DR. HAMMER: Let me illustrate it for you. Let's take these drawings. No matter what a child draws, he's really picturing himself. Ask a secure child to draw a tree, and he's likely to draw a bountiful, spreading tree. A Black child drew this tree. Cut off in its growth. Stark, bare, ungratified.

In the following sequence, Cosby analyzes the attitude of the motion picture industry to the Black man and its impact on society. To illustrate his points, the program inserts scenes from early and contemporary screen plays such as "The Birth of a Nation," "Green Pastures," and "Guess Who's Coming to Dinner."

BILL COSBY: In the past fifty years, 33,000 feature films have been made in the United States, and about 6,000 of them have had parts for Black actors. For the most part, the Black portraits have been drawn by White writers, White producers and White directors for a White audience.

Most Black parts were the way White Americans wanted them to be. The Black male was consistently shown as nobody, nothing. He had no qualities that could be admired by any man, or, more particularly, any woman.

(SONG: "Mississippi Mud")

White people didn't like to think much about them. Sort of like a relative you've got in a rest home. Happy Darkies dancing and singing was all they wanted to hear about. Being good Christians, the Whites out front liked to think the Blacks out back were kind of happy.

"Uncle Tom's Cabin" was one of the first movies made that tried to say anything about Black people. Uncle Tom was changed a little each time it was put on the stage and all the parts were played by White actors and by the time they made a movie of it in 1903, Uncle Tom was just the

White man's idea of "a good nigger." You might say he was what H. Rap Brown ain't.

The first really vicious anti-Negro film was called "The Birth of a Nation." And it was a honey. The second worst thing about it was that technically, in 1918, it was the best movie that had ever been made. A cat named D. W. Griffith produced it and he knew how. See? This film is 50 years old and it may look silly and out of date now, but it didn't look silly when it was made and seen. Several million Americans who saw it were propagandized to believe that this is the way things would be if they weren't careful. So they've been pretty careful.

(SCENES FROM "BIRTH OF A NATION")

The newsreels that were shown along with the feature films knew a good thing when they saw one. They helped keep all the Black cats in their place. Nobody Black ever did anything very newsy in a newsreel. They did things like eat watermelon in a watermelon eating contest.

(SCENES FROM NEWSREELS)

But things were getting pretty tough in the 30s. A good thing for a lot of Black actors was they made a movie called "The Green Pastures" with, like they say, "a cast of thousands." It gave a lot of people work, but it had all the old stereotyped characters. It was clever and funny and all Black, but it was a White man's picture.

(SCENES FROM "GREEN PASTURES")

Mostly Black actors aren't playing the old stereotypes any more. There are people who say they're playing a new stereotype. Sidney Poitier is always helping some little old ladies across the street, whether they want to go or not. Black people in this country got a bum deal for a long while, and it won't hurt much if we see a little of that now and then.

Stanley Kramer has let us use some scenes from "Guess Who's coming to Dinner." Look at these and remember "Birth of a Nation." This is the opening scene when Katherine Houghton is bringing Sidney home for the first time.

(SCENES FROM "GUESS WHO'S COMING TO DINNER.")

In the final scene, excerpted below, Cosby introduces an unusual approach to educating Black children; symbolic of what is happening around the country.

BILL COSBY: The message down here is coming in strong. It happens to be: Be yourself. Be Black. A new

34

generation of Black young Americans is asserting itself. What they're saying is: If you can't wash white, even if you have the money, if you can't wash white 'cause you're basically black, what you do is react, sometimes radically.

Here's a measure of the reaction to "White is beautiful." This is a storefront school in Philadelphia. The children here are being given a Black preparation before they enter the city's schools. They're not specially gifted children; they're just from the neighborhood. One Black man named John Churchville put it all together and financed it himself.

CHURCHVILLE: A number is a concept of quantity or an amount. Right. Do you understand that? All right. A number is a concept of quantity or an amount. That is wrong.

CLASS: No. No.

CHURCHVILLE: A number is a concept of quantity or an amount. That is dead wrong? Well. Yes or no? Is it wrong?

CLASS: No.

CHURCHVILLE: All right, then say it loud. You ought to be screaming me out of this room. A number ...

CLASS: No. No. No.

COSBY: He's not only teaching new math to children whose ages range from seventeen months to five years—he's decided to give them the emotional armor they need to protect themselves against the education he thinks they'll receive when they start kindergarten.

CHURCHVILLE: Anybody tells you something wrong, are you going to do it?

CLASS: No!

CHURCHVILLE: What do you want, Jenell?

JENELL: I want freedom.

CHURCHVILLE: When do you want it?

JENELL: I want my freedom now.

CHURCHVILLE: No, you have to wait until next week, Jenell, you can't have it now. Can you wait until next week?

JENELL: Yes.

CHURCHVILLE: Okay. Sit down. All right, young man, stand up. When do you want your freedom, young man?

MICHAEL: I want freedom now.

CHURCHVILLE: You can wait till next week, can't you?

MICHAEL: No.

CHURCHVILLE: Suppose I said that you have to wait until next week. Now you're gonna wait till next week, aren't you?

MICHAEL: No.

CHURCHVILLE: How are you going to get your freedom?

MICHAEL: I will use any means necessary to win my freedom.

COSBY: It's kind of like brainwashing. Or is it? Can you blame us for overcompensating? I mean when you take the way Black history got lost, stolen or strayed, when you think about the kids drawing themselves without faces and when you remember the fine actors who had to play baboons to make a buck, I guess you've got to give us the sin of pride. Pride. "Hubris" in the original Greek.

Three hundred years we've been in this American melting pot and we haven't been able to melt in yet. That's a long wait. Listen, we've been trying all kinds of parts to make the American scene. We've been trying to play it straight and White, but it's been just bit parts. From now on, we're going to play it Black and American. We're proud of both. Hubris.

"Of Black America" illustrates the documentary approach to the problems of our society. The script we are about to study portrays the culture in our civilization.

### "MICHELANGELO: THE LAST GIANT"

"Michelangelo: The Last Giant" was written and produced by Lou Hazam for the National Broadcasting Company. Hazam is one of the finest practitioners of the art of the documentary. He envisions the documentary film as an artist does a painting. His canvas is the television screen; his brush, the fervent poetry of his script; his paints, the vibrant visuals he has guided the camera to capture.

In treating historical material, it is not enough to accurately portray past events; the documentary, to provide impact, must go beyond what has already been said. As Rick Du Brow, television critic for UPI, commented: "So much has been said and written and repeated about Michelangelo that it required an out-of-the-ordinary treatment of the subject to stimulate the viewer."

For the original production of "The Last Giant," Jose Ferrer was the narrator with Peter Ustinov supplying the voice of Michelangelo. A cast of several other actors read incidental lines which added variety to the presentation. The superb camera work and the direction were under the supervision of Tom Priestley. In this latter respect, it should be noted that there was no dramatization on the screen; that is, no actors were used to portray historical incidents. The voices were all off screen and movement was achieved by the vivid manipulation of the camera for both internal and external shooting. We see Michelangelo's work; we do not see any actor in the guise of Michelangelo. If actors were used on screen, the end result would have been historical drama instead of the documentary effect "The Last Giant" achieves.

The program opens with the standard television technique of the teaser. Hazam and Priestley did not employ special effects unless they definitely served the purpose and the mood of the program. Because of the immensity of the subject matter, "The Last Giant" was presented in two parts, each one hour in length.

## TEASER

| AUDIO | VIDEO |
|---|---|
| MUSIC: IN TREMULOUSLY AND UNDER | FADE UP FROM BLACK ON MYSTERIOUS CU* OF SILHOUETTE OF MICHELANGELO IN NICODEMUS "PIETA"; ZOOM IN TO BLACK AREA OF FACE |
| NARR:<br>Who was he...<br>Whose stone face is hid, now,<br>By five centuries of time? | |
| MUSIC: ACCENT | |
| NARR:<br>Painter? ... | |
| MUSIC: ACCENT | FADE-IN SISTINE EKTACHROME AND PULL BACK |
| NARR:<br>Architect? | DISSOLVE TO DOME OF ST. PETER'S |
| MUSIC: ACCENT | |
| NARR:<br>Poet? | DISSOLVE TO CU OF WHEAT FIELD, WAVING IN WIND |

CU * CLOSEUP

MICHELANGELO:

"Ah me! Ah me! whene'er I pine,
For my past years, I find that none,
Among those many years, alas, was mine..."

MUSIC: ACCENTS

NARR:

Sculptor?

DISSOLVE TO STATUE OF DAVID

(PAUSE)

Truly, in the words of his contemporaries—as they laid him to rest after 90 long years on this earth—"This one, was four."

DISSOLVE TO MS, SILHOUETTE OF NICODEMUS PIETA

SUDDENLY THE SAD, BROODING, NICODEMUS-FACE OF MICHELANGELO IS REVEALED—BATHED IN LIGHT

MUSIC: FULL NOW FOR SALUTE, AND INTO TITLE THEME

DISSOLVE TO CU MICHELANGELO'S FACE

SUPER: NBC NEWS PRESENTS

PULL BACK TO REVEAL ENTIRE STATUE

SUPER: MICHELANGELO ... "THE LAST GIANT"

PETER USTINOV AS THE VOICE OF MICHELANGELO

JOSE FERRER AS NARRATOR

MUSIC: CURTAIN TEASER

FADE TO BLACK

The approach to the basic story is chronological. In keeping with the subject matter, Hazam's writing is poetic. The entire documentary is an appeal to the intellect. Yet there is emotion and there is exposition, skillfully combined.

The following excerpts from Part One and Two of "The Last Giant" should give you a comprehensive view of the scope of the documentary. Note how the narrative is interwoven with quotations from Michelangelo's biography and from his letters. The excerpts are presented in the precise format of the final production script. Observe how the very placement of the words connotes a visual poetic image and influences the reading by the narrators.

As you study the video directions, you will learn how the camera coordinates with the narrative and how, in almost all instances, the narrative adds information which the visual alone could not impart. If you had had the good fortune to see the production, you would have experienced the effect as Lawrence Laurent, television critic of the **Washington Post** described it: "static, immobile series of objects moving, delighting and exciting wonder."

| AUDIO | VIDEO |
|---|---|
| MUSIC: IN TO HAND UNDER TREMULOUSLY, PROPHETICALLY | UP ON CANDLE-LIGHT OUT OF FOCUS. BRING INTO FOCUS AND PULL BACK TO REVEAL LIGHTED CANDLES IN WINDOW OF M'S BIRTHPLACE AT NIGHT |
| BIOGRAPHER: | |
| "It was certainly a great birth. Mercury, a fateful and felicitous star ... and Venus ... were welcomed benignantly into the house of Jupiter... | |
| "And this promised exactly what turned out to be the case— a lofty genius, to produce by the art of his hand, marvelous and stupendous works ..." | |
| MUSIC: ACCENT AND HOLD | |
| NARR: | |
| So wrote his biographers. Wrote his father ... | DISSOLVE TO TREES, OUT OF FOCUS: COME INTO FOCUS AND PULL BACK TO REVEAL HOUSE AT DAWN |
| MUSIC: DOWN ALMOST TO FADE OUT | |
| FATHER: | |
| "I, Lodovico di Lionardo Buonarroti Simoni record that on this day, March 6, 1474, four or five hours before daybreak a male child was born to me at Caprese." | |
| SOUND: CHURCH BELLS | CUT TO CU, CHURCH BELLS TOLLING. |

FATHER:

"On the eighth of the same month, in the Church of Santo Giovanni, he was baptized ..."

MUSIC: BAPTISM

PRIEST: (IN LATIN)
(BAPTISMAL QUOTE)

CUT TO INTERIOR, LIGHT REVEALING ALTAR CROSS: CUT TO CU FACE OF CHRIST

FATHER:

"I gave him the name—Michelangelo."

CUT TO CU, URN POURING WATER; CU, BAPTISMAL FONT;

SOUND: BELLS UP TO PUNCTUATE

MUSIC: IN TO OVERCOME BELLS, DOWN UNDER

CU, BELLS RINGING

NARR:

High on this remote hill in Italy,
In the little Tuscan village of Caprese
Where his father was the Podesta, or Mayor,
Michelangelo,
Who is to pass most of his life in torment
To become the last—
Perhaps the greatest—
Of the giants in art bequeathed us by the 15th Century,
Begins that life peacefully.
Soon after,
His family moves to its home in Settignano.
Ripe with olives,
And rich with stone,
The hills of Settignano
Provide a livelihood to the people of the district,
Who work its outcroppings
With Chisel and hammer.
Amidst its rocks and quarries,
Michelangelo is put to wetnurse with a stonecutter's wife—
Not unlike this child in one of his drawings.
Years later, he jests...

DISSOLVE TO CU BERRIES IN FIELD AND PULL BACK TO FIND THE TOWN OF CAPRESE ON HILLTOP

DISSOLVE TO CU—PAN UP GNARLED TREE TO TOP

DISSOLVE TO BUCOLIC SCENE OF COUNTRYSIDE

DISSOLVE TO PAN DOWN OF M'S HOME IN SETTIGNANO

DISSOLVE TO PAN DOWN OF QUARRIES TO FIND SINGLE STONE. ZOOM IN AND DISSOLVE TO DRAWING OF CHILD SUCKLING MOTHER

MICHELANGELO:

"What good I have comes because I sucked in chisels and hammers with my nurse's milk!"

ZOOM INTO CHILD

NARR:

Not far away...
Indeed, within sight of Settignano ...
Lay Florence.
And here—
Perhaps before he is ten years old—
Michelangelo comes to live...
Live with his father and stepmother,
(His mother had died when he was only six)
And four brothers.
What a revelation is Florence...
The heart and the mind of the Renaissance!

DISSOLVE TO PULL BACK FROM OVERCAST SKY TO REVEAL FLORENCE, AND CATHEDRAL

CUT TO CLOSER SHOT OF FLORENCE CATHEDRAL

DISSOLVE TO TWO DIFFERENT ANGLES OF BUILDINGS IN ANCIENT FLORENCE

MUSIC: UP TO CARRY FLORENCE ESSAY AND DOWN UNDER

DISSOLVE TO AND PAN LUSH FLORENCE-ERA TAPESTRY

NARR:

It is the city of Botticelli,
Who painted "Spring"
And Ghiberti,
Whose golden bronze
Michelangelo later called...

DISSOLVE TO AND EXPLORE EK. OF BOTTICELLI'S "SPRING"

DISSOLVE TO TWO EXTERIOR SHOTS, GHIBERTI DOORS

MICHELANGELO:

"Fit for the gates of Paradise!"

MUSIC: UP AND DOWN TO CHANGE FOR MEDICI

EXPLORE CU OF DOOR DETAIL

NARR:

But especially is Florence
The city of its rulers...
The rich and powerful family of the Medici—
And its leader Lorenzo,
Painted here as a young man
In a fresco of the procession of the Three Kings.
In time,
Michelangelo's life will come to
        touch this man's ...
But that time is not yet.

DISSOLVE TO SEVERAL SHOTS, COAT OF ARMS OF THE MEDICI DISSOLVE TO EK. OF PROCESSION OF THREE KINGS AND EXPLORE

MUSIC: INTO LORENZO GARDEN SEQUENCE AND UNDER

NARR:

This—still intact—is a
                garden of the Medici.
Rich with ancient statuary,
It is similar, perhaps,
To the one in which
Michelangelo—
As one of the promising
students
        offered by Ghirlandaio—
Suddenly finds himself,
Giving up his painting ap-
prenticeship
To embark upon a totally new
                career—
Sculpture—
Destined to engulf his life ever
                after.
Under the old master, Bertoldo,
He studies in a school set up by
                Lorenzo
To encourage—
With the passing of the
sculptors
        Donatello and Verrocchio—
The rebirth of this ancient art
                in Florence.
Strangely drawn to stone
As a hungry man to food—
Michelangelo eagerly sets to
work...
In time fashioning a faun—
                since lost—
Which may have resembled
                this facsimile.
Let his biographer, Vasari,
                continue...

BIOGRAPHER:

"He was polishing the faun one
day when the Medici passed by.
The great man stopped to
examine the work and ob-
served: 'You have made this
Faun quite old, yet have left
him with all his teeth!'
Michelangelo took the hint and
knocked out a tooth from the
upper jaw. When Lorenzo saw
how cleverly he had performed

FADE UP FROM BLACK. SLOW PAN OF GARDEN OF LORENZO

VARIOUS SHOTS OF STATUES IN GARDEN

DISSOLVE TO CU, CHISEL CARVING STONE

DISSOLVE TO FACSIMILE OF BUST OF FAUN, TURN-ING FROM PROFILE TO FULL FACE WITH TEETH INTACT

DISSOLVE TO CLOSER SHOT OF FAUN, WITH TOOTH GONE

DISSOLVE TO PAINTING OF LORENZO

the task, he resolved to provide for the boy's future and take him into his own household."

CU, PAINTING MICHELANGELO
CUT TO MS, ENTIRE PICTURE REVEALING M. PRESENTING FAUN

MUSIC: IN AND UNDER SOMBERLY

NARR:

And now the time has come for death.
God chooses for His moment:
Michelangelo upon the threshold of his 90th year.
Weak and feverish,
But refusing to relinquish his chisel,
He continues his lifelong "duel with stone"
By carving on three different Pietas
Destined to be his last works...

FADE UP FROM BLACK ON PALESTRINA PIETA. START ON FEET OF CHRIST AND EXPLORE

NARR:

Growing each day weaker,
He sits before the fire on Sunday,
A day he planned to work—
Until reminded it was Sunday.
Now death, in truth, seemed tugging him by the cloak—
As he once put it—
And feeling it,
He burns in the fire many preliminary drawings
He wishes not to leave behind,
And asks that word be sent for his nephew to come.

FRIEND:

"I beg you to hasten. It is certain now our dear Michelangelo must leave us for good and all..."

MUSIC: UP AND DOWN

NARR:

Monday.
He makes his will—
Entrusting his property to his family...
His body to the earth...
And his soul to the hands of God.

MS OF CANDLE, QUILL AND DOCUMENT ON TABLE

CU OF CANDLE AS FLAME FLICKERS ON NARRATOR'S WORDS "HANDS OF GOD"

| | |
|---|---|
| MUSIC CHOIR SINGING | |
| NARR: | |
| Tuesday, February eighteen, In the year 1564— "In the attitude of a perfect Christian, And about the Ave Maria"— | DISSOLVE TO SANTO SPIRITO CRUCIFIX, ZOOM INTO FACE |
| MUSIC CHOIR FADES OUT | |
| MUSIC: RESUMES WITH LIGHT TOLLING OF BELLS | |
| NARR: | |
| Michelangelo... The Last Giant... Returned to the Master That had sent him... | DISSOLVE TO ECU OF FACE OF NICODEMUS |
| MUSIC: THE LAST CHIMES FADE AWAY | SLOWLY THE FACE DIMS TO BLACK, LEAVING ONLY THE SILHOUETTE OF FACE IN LIGHT—WHICH FINALLY GOES TO BLACK. |

## "THE EISENHOWER STORY"

The documentary film as "living biography" or "dramatic biography," as categorized by Professor Bluem, offers an additional area of visual exposition. The illustration we have chosen for study, "The Eisenhower Story," may fall into the classification of "living biography," since it was written and produced when the president was alive. It also comes under the heading of compilation documentary, since it was composed almost entirely of stock footage except for original shooting at the Eisenhower Museum.

Remember that the biographical documentary does not include dramatization per se. When Professor Bluem speaks of dramatic biography, he is concerned with subject matter that is dramatic; incidents, in the life of the man or woman portrayed, which are inherently exciting. For example, if a documentary film were to be written on the life of Wernher von Braun, it would be replete with drama culminating in the first landing on the moon.

In a seminar on the documentary film, Richard Hanser, script writer for many network productions, offered some pertinent comments on writing narration for the documentary, particularly the compilation documentary. "The basic peculiarity," Mr. Hanser said, "is, of course, that the words have to be tailored to footage." And he noted, "the right sentence with the right choice of words, planted at the right place, can, when combined with the right pictures, suggest whole areas of information and emotion in one quick stroke." Hanser is of the opinion that "the less narration the better," but he adds, "there is no known rule for gaging when precisely enough words have been written to clarify the pictures without cluttering up the sound track. It is a matter of feeling and instinct."

And so, in the final analysis, it is the artistry of the writer that prevails. That artistry is not lightly come by; its sharply perceptive edge is honed by experience. As you study the following excerpts from "The Eisenhower Story," you will find, generally, that the writing is understated. Much of the narration consists of simple declarative statements which blend with the visuals to become a coherent whole.

| VIDEO | AUDIO |
|---|---|
| NEWSREEL SHOTS OF EISENHOWER HOMECOMING | NARR: The time is June, 1945. The occasion, the return to his homeland of a war hero whose stature has seldom been matched in the esteem of his countrymen. The European phase of the greatest war America ever fought is over. And part of the warmth with which the people of Abilene, Kansas, greet General Dwight D. Eisenhower reflects the deep joy of a nation approaching peace again. Some of it is the kind of welcome any hometown might give a favorite son who has done a good job. But more than anything else, it is tribute. A gratitude felt in every corner of the allied world, no less than in Abilene, toward the man who stewarded a crusade to its |
| FOOTAGE OF D-DAY INVASION | victory. It was a crusade with many battles and many triumphs, but it found its symbol in one day above all others. D-Day—June 6, 1944. |
| PAN SHOTS OF ABILENE | Abilene, Kansas, today, a busy and proud town of almost 7,000 people living in the heart of the western wheatland, is typical of the kind of town that comes to |

| | mind with the phrase "grass roots America." |
|---|---|
| LONG SHOT OF EISENHOWER MUSEUM | One of its newest and proudest buildings is the Eisenhower Museum which carries forth the spirit and the history of the Eisenhower family of Abilene. |
| PAN MURALS | Inside the museum, the life of Dwight Eisenhower, boy and man, is depicted in a series of murals. |
| STILLS OF EISENHOWER'S PARENTS | Eisenhower was born in 1890, in Denison, Texas of parents whose families had migrated to Pennsylvania from Europe and thence to the American midwest. Young Eisenhower's parents had lived in Abilene before his birth and it was to Abilene—once the wild town at the end of the Chisholm Trail—now a peaceful village of the plains—that they returned when he was an infant. |
| STILLS: EISENHOWER AT WEST POINT | He was 20 when he left Abilene for the military academy at West Point. Many a great American has begun his march into history as a cadet on the plain at West Point. |
| GROUP STILL OF GRADUATING CLASS. CLOSEUP OF "IKE" | Eisenhower was graduated from the military academy in 1915 and commissioned a second lieutenant of infantry. |
| STILLS OF WEDDING SCENES | A new phase of life was beginning. In the summer of 1916, as a newly promoted first lieutenant stationed at Fort Sam Houston, Texas, he married Mamie Geneva Doud of Denver. |
| STOCK FOOTAGE OF LOUISIANA MANEUVERS | In the summer of 1941, Colonel Eisenhower became chief of staff to General Walter Kreuger whose newly organized Third Army was preparing to participate in the most realistic war maneuvers yet held by American troops. |
| | Soon after the maneuvers were over, Eisenhower was |

46

| | |
|---|---|
| STOCK FOOTAGE: PEARL HARBOR | promoted to brigadier general and within a matter of days— came the bombing of Pearl Harbor. |
| PAN MURAL | A mural covering the west wall of the Eisenhower Museum dramatizes the high spot of the next great sequence in the adventure involving the nation and the man, whose ability to rise to grave responsibilities brought him rapid promotions. |
| PAN MURAL | On the opposite wall of the museum, another mural depicts some of the major episodes in the great crusade which liberated Europe. |
| | The Supreme Commander's orders from the Combined Chiefs of Staff were quite simple—to land on the coast of France and thereafter to destroy the German ground forces. Between the order and its execution lay an agony of effort. |
| STOCK FOOTAGE FROM US ARMY REPOSITORY | Across the Channel, the heavy fortifications lining the coast of France bespoke the Nazis' belief that they could push the invading armies back into the sea. |
| STOCK FOOTAGE | D-Day, with the fate of the war hanging in the balance. Half a million troops, backed by millions more, faced outward across the stormy sea. |
| STOCK FOOTAGE OF NOR- MANDY INVASION | On beaches that dotted the French coast of the Channel, British, Canadian and American troops touched shore. The first fateful moment passed, and Allied troops were holding on French soil. |
| | One week after the landings, the Commander was able to say to the vast armies under him: "Your accomplishments in the last seven days of this campaign have exceeded my highest hopes." |

SCENES OF EISENHOWER INAUGURATION

History is recording today the story of Eisenhower the statesman. The stories may be separate, but soldier and statesman, they are the same man—Dwight D. Eisenhower, citizen of the United States—spokesman for and symbol of the free world—and son of Abilene—as rich a study as this nation has produced of the capacity for greatness which lies at its grass roots.

## THE LOCAL PRODUCTION

Due to comparatively low budgets which restrict the size of the staff, the writer on the local level is more apt to be a writer-producer. However, what the local production lacks in budget, compared with network expenditures, can be replaced by the use of imagination and ingenuity. The local production must set its sights on issues which affect the potential viewing audience of a single station. Nevertheless, the parochial viewpoint need not be confining. For example, pollution of our waterways is of national consequence. The local documentary production can attack the problem of pollution by demonstrating how the community is affected by the pollution of the river which courses through the city.

The script we are about to study is the work of one of the more creative and brilliant young documentary writer-producers, Jerry Johnson, now with Wolper Productions. Among the many documentaries Jerry Johnson wrote and produced for WMAL-TV in Washington, "The Sweet Smell of Freedom" is one of his most powerful. It deals with the District of Columbia Reformatory in Lorton, Virginia, and examines the life of prison inmates, the problems of correctional officers, the various phases of the prisoner rehabilitation program and the work-release program. The documentary won both an Emmy and an Ohio State Award.

Before we study the script itself, it is interesting and informative to peruse some of the pages of the diary which Jerry Johnson kept while filming was in progress. Johnson and the film crew lived for three weeks on the Reformatory grounds. This is literally living with your material, and, in a small way, reflects the tradition of the great pioneer of the documentary film, Robert Flaherty. Before he shot a foot of film, Flaherty often spent as long as a year or two living with the people whom he was to immortalize in his documentaries. Contemporary network writer-producers, like Lou Hazam, often spend many months in the location area to completely familiarize themselves with the inhabitants and their surroundings. This is a costly procedure, particularly when one considers Hazam's production, "Sahara." For the local writer-producer, who is bounded by a metropolitan area, living with his material should not present an economic problem, but it sometimes can prove hazardous as you will see from Jerry Johnson's production diary, excerpts of which are reproduced below.

"Monday: Arrived on location in Lorton, Virginia, at the Men's Reformatory of the District of Columbia. Project to be a half-hour color film documentary on life as it is for the 1200 inmates confined here for felony crimes. Also hope to focus on the newly established work-release program which allows a prisoner to work at a steady job outside the wall during the day and return each night to the reformatory. Promises to be an interesting assignment.

"Crew arrived late a.m. in high spirits. Equipment and vehicles all in good order. Set up office trailer next to gun tower nine at the south entrance. Trailer equipped with complete editing and screening facilities. Have arranged for a courier to pick up exposed film each day and return here with rushes next p.m. Plan to edit as we go since we will be living here during entire three weeks of shooting.

"Tuesday: Awoke to find 11 inches of snow covering the ground. Had to reshuffle shooting schedule. Sound unit was to have joined crew early this a.m. but didn't make it here until 11:30. Lost half a day making arrangements and getting clearance to shoot this afternoon.

"Recorded first roundtable session with the inmates we selected to do the film narration. Material exceptional, both technically and in content. Discussion of the problem of homosexuality with the reformatory very gutsy. Unlike anything we could possibly write. Depressingly impressive.

"Wednesday: Continued with inmate interviews today. Started at 10 a.m., finished at 11 p.m. Feel we have statements of fact and emotion never recorded on tape before. Dramatic beyond belief at times.

"Friday: Six inmates escaped. Nothing like being inside the wall when an escape is made. Probably never be so near such a story when it breaks again during our lifetime. Filming scheduled for tonight put off until Sunday at the request of officials here. Crew filmed stories for TV News on the breakout. Situation inside the wall tense, dramatic but orderly.

"Monday: Shot most of visitors day sequence this a.m. Large bare room with long wooden benches. Filmed the room empty of people, with subjective camera playing the part of the guards walking around the room looking over the shoulder of the visitors. Will record sound to match shot next visitors day. So that as guard (camera) walks around the room, snatches of individual conversations of an actual visitors day will be heard as the camera moves from one bench to another.

"Tuesday: Fantastic footage this a.m. (Filmed in foundry where they were casting large water pipe valves.) Long dark building, black sand dust four inches thick covers the floor, sweating black men with the orange glow of molten metal reflected in their eyes. White hot iron exploding from black sand molds. Black choking dust filled air. So hot it hurts to breathe. Almost clobbered by the gigantic crane as it passed over us by about two inches, wielding a 2-ton bucket of molten iron. Had the camera mounted 20 feet above the floor on a fork lift truck when we saw the bucket coming at us just in time to yank the cameraman out of the way. Beautiful footage though.

"Friday: Light snow early a.m. Down around 20 degrees, very windy. Good day for exteriors. Strapped camera, battery and tripod on our backs and head cameraman, Foster Wiley, and myself climbed the water tower at the reformatory. Entire ascent had to be made on an ice covered ladder welded to one of the legs of the tower. We used lineman safety belts to make the 145-foot climb. Wind really tried to blow us away. Severe vibration and buffeting on the top. Gear felt like a ton by the time we got to the top. Hairiest part of the climb was taking the safety belts off every time we had to climb past a girder. Completed most of the exteriors. Very cold. A real blue-nose day.

"Shot chapel scene this p.m. Dramatically realistic life-size crucifix, sculpted by inmate, hangs above altar. A fitting end to location filming here at the reformatory."

Now that we have gained a little insight into the preparations used by a local writer-producer to obtain the essential footage for a factual documentation of a social problem, let us examine the script itself. Because many, if not most, young script writers will begin their careers at local stations, we thought it would be advisable to reproduce this script in its entirety.

## "THE SWEET SMELL OF FREEDOM"

| VIDEO | AUDIO |
|---|---|
| | NARR: |
| CU: CRAWL, MOVES UP THRU FRAME IN SYNC WITH NARR. | The subject of this film is the rehabilitation program of the Men's Reformatory of the |

District of Columbia. For three weeks a film crew of WMAL-TV Public Affairs lived on the grounds of this institution in order to film the report you are about to see. It should be noted that the selection of officials and inmates who appear in this program was entirely at the discretion of WMAL television, and at no time was any censorship imposed by the District of Columbia Department of Corrections.

1 CU: SUN; ZOOM TO LS: GUN TOWER SILHOUETTED AGAINST SUNSET
2 MS: GUN TOWER; GUARD WALKS AROUND TOWER, STANDS FRAME RIGHT `

MUSIC: BLUES VOCAL BY JIMMY OWENS "I GOT SO MUCH TROUBLE"
(first and second lines)
(third and fourth lines)

DISSOLVE: 48 FRAMES

GUITAR BRIDGE BEGINS

3 CU: CELL BLOCK LOCK BOX AS KEY IS INSERTED, HANDLE TURNED

FX: KEYS IN LOCK (SYNC)

4 LS: CELL BLOCK DOOR SLIDES OPEN
    ACTION: GUARD ENTERS FRAME RIGHT, WALKS DOWN CELL BLOCK

FX: DOOR OPENS WITH SLAM

MUSIC: OWENS BEGINS TO HUM WITH GUITAR AS BG

NARR:

VOICE OVER:
AUTHORITATIVE,
SHARP, DICIPLINED
MANNER

For two hundred years the United States Government has been locking men in cages as punishment for crimes committed against society.

5 CU: GUARD (TRACKING SHOT)

Some fifty years ago the concept of rehabilitating the criminal was born.

6 MS: CELLS (TRACKING SHOT)

The purpose of this report is to examine one institution for correctional treatment of the convicted criminal...the Men's Reformatory of the District of Columbia Department of Correction.

| | |
|---|---|
| SUPER: TITLE CARD NO. 1: "THE SWEET SMELL OF FREEDOM"<br>SUPER: TITLE CARD NO. 2: "NARRATED BY TOM FINN"<br>SUPER: TITLE CARD NO. 3: "A PRESENTATION OF WMAL TELEVISION NEWS & PUBLIC AFFAIRS"<br>FADE SUPER: AS DOLLY COMES TO REST ON LAST CELL, GUARD ENTERS FRAME RIGHT, SLAMS CELL DOOR. | MUSIC: UP FULL LEVEL<br><br><br><br><br><br>FX: CELL DOOR SLAMMING<br><br>MUSIC: PAYS OFF AND FADES |
| FADE TO BLACK | |

FIRST COMMERCIAL BREAK

| | |
|---|---|
| FADE UP FROM BLACK TO<br>7 CU: GUN TOWER NO. 10; GUARD STANDING AT RAIL | FX: LOW WIND NOISE<br>NARR: |
| 8 MS: OVER SHOULDER OF GUARD AT TOWER NO. 1, DORM ROW BG | "We are ready to assist you in every way that we can, and, if you permit us, to make your stay here as profitable as possible. |
| 9 LS: GUN TOWER NO. 2 FG; TOWER NO. 3 BG | It is not likely that you ever intended to come here. |
| · 10 LS: GUN TOWER NO. 3 FG; TOWERS 4 & 5 BG | Neither you, your family, nor your friends ever thought that this would happen to you. |
| 11 LS: FORM COMPOUND EXERCISE YARD<br>12 CU: HORSESHOE PIT<br>13 ECU: HORSESHOE IN DUST<br>14 CU: GUN TOWER NO. 4 | In your childhood and youth you played, went to school, probably worked some, and dreamed, as all of us have. |
| ZOOM TO LS: PRISON WALL | As a man you made plans, and realized some of them, but incarceration and prison were never a part of this." Thus begins "A Guide Book of Adjustment," published by the |
| 15 CU: GUIDE BOOK<br>16 ECU: GUIDE BOOK | D.C. Department of Corrections. |
| | Each inmate receives this upon entering the Reformatory for men. The Reformatory is located 18 miles south of |

| | |
|---|---|
| 17  LS:  REFORMATORY (AERIAL) | Washington near Lorton, Virginia. |
| | **NARR:** |
| | It houses some 1200 inmates convicted of felony crimes. A chain link fence and brick wall surrounds the entire 71-acre compound. Though it is a penitentiary, separating the criminal from society is not its only purpose. |
| 18 LS: HARDY SUPER: NAME & TITLE (DIR. DEPT. OF CORR.) | **HARDY:** |
| | The mission of this department is twofold. |
| 19 CU: HARDY | First, we must maintain custody over those committed to us by law. Secondly, we must treat and train those committed so that they can be rehabilitated, hopefully, by the time of their release. |
| | **NARR:** |
| 20 LS: QUADRANGLE | To the casual observer, life in the reformatory appears to be not unlike that of a well ordered military post. |
| 21  LS: SHOP STREET, IN-MATES WALKING ACROSS 22 LS: CHOW HALL 23 MS: DORMS (PAN SHOT) | Prisoners move about from place to place unescorted by armed guards. They eat together in a large dining hall, and live in barracks-like dormitories. |
| 24 LS: WEAKLEY | There are, however, serious disadvantages to such a system. As explained by Kermit Weakley, Superintendent of the reformatory. |
| | **WEAKLEY:** |
| 25 CU: WEAKLEY | We do have our everyday problem of contraband with the inmates spread out throughout the compound itself and in addition the large volume of traffic, vehicle traffic, inmate traffic, personnel traffic, in and out of the compound. We're certainly watchful; we search, we shake down, continuously |

with respect to contraband and particularly we are mindful of narcotics, a serious problem, we feel. But with the shortage of personnel we're only able to do just so much.

HARDY:

26 LS: HARDY

Recently, at Lorton we had an escape involving six men. Now this was not a breach of the perimeter; that is, they didn't take wire cutters and cut through our anchor fence or take a sledge hammer and cut a hole through the wall in the penitentiary area. They went out under a disguise; that is, one was disguised as an officer and passed the other five in a truck. Of course, this points to a breakdown in our security measures, our count system, and certainly I intend to have this corrected.

NARR:

27 CU: OFFICER'S ASSEM-BLY ROOM SIGN, TRACK TO LOOK THRU WINDOW
28 LS: GUARDS AT ROLL CALL AS THEY TAKE OFF HATS
29 CU: CAPTAIN OF GUARD CALLING ROLL (SYNC)

Security within the institution is maintained by a staff of some 200 uniformed officers. Starting salary for a correctional officer is 4700 dollars a year.

GUARD: (BEGINS TO CALL ROLL) UP FULL, THEN UNDER AS BG

NARR:

30 LS: GUARDS

These are the men that come in contact with the inmates most frequently. Thus it is that many inmate complaints are aimed at the security force.

31 MS: TRACKING SHOT, GUARDS

INMATE: (VOICE OVER)

I used to see the officers coming in at 3:30, change shifts, and they would stop to talk to each other; how many you bust today, partner? Say, well I wasn't lucky today. I didn't get but one, so I'll get them that you didn't catch this afternoon. So this is the type of thing that you hear and see round here every day...not one day ...every day!

54

| | |
|---|---|
| 32 CU: CAPTAIN OF GUARD CONTINUES WITH ROLL | GUARD: UP FULL :05 THEN UNDER BG |
| | INMATE: |
| 33 LS: GUARDS BREAK UP AND EXIT | One of the main reasons that we have this lack of cooperation between the staff and the inmates I believe is probably because of the underlying factors of prejudice by the majority of the population on this reservation being Negroes and the reverse as being true as far as the staff. |
| DISSOLVE: 24 FRAMES TO | |
| 34 LS: GUARD WALKING DORM ROW STOPS, LOOKS IN DORM | FX: FOOTSTEPS OF GUARD (wild) |
| | INMATE: |
| | There's an awful lot of officers here that don't like colored people. I mean you see it...you can feel it when you're talking to 'em. The way they degrade you and the way they talk to you, that old thing they got, boy this and boy that, and they want you to say yes sir to them. |
| 36 MS: GUARD WALKING (TRACKING SHOT) | |
| 37 LS: GUARD WALKING THRU ARCHES | INMATE: |
| | You got some officers down here that you can carry a problem to them and they will do everything they can...just a few of these now...but they have some you understand. |
| 38 MS: CAPTAIN MORGAN SUPER: NAME & TITLE | CAPTAIN: (sync) |
| | Most complaints that come into this office by inmates are about officers making shakedowns. Shakedowns in the shops, in the dormitories, on the walks, lockers, and other places throughout the institution. |
| ZOOM TO LS: CAPTAIN TAKES WEAPONS FROM DESK | Let me show you something. |
| 39 MS: HIGH ANGLE OF WEAPONS | In shops, dormitories, things like this are always found. This is a chain with a taped handle, others are prison-made knives with taped handles. This is more like the punch type, dagger type. Others have |

homemade handles, are very sharp and very dangerous. This one is a fountain pen with a weapon made in the end of it.

40 CU: CAPTAIN

Many of these weapons are carried by younger inmates here who fear sexual assaults by some other inmate. Often inmates come to the captain's office with complaints they're being pressed into sex acts they do not care to perform in. They often times will say they intend to hurt or harm someone if they continue pressing them into such an act. It is then we often shake down lockers of men who have fear of such attacks and find such weapons as these.

NARR:

41 LS: DORMITORY

Although it is impossible to state with statistics the problem of homosexuality within the institution, it is generally agreed by both the administration and inmates that such acts do occur frequently.

INMATE:

42 MS: MAN ASLEEP

I think this homosexuality thing is a big problem and a frightening thing.

43 MS: MAN SITTING ON BUNK

Uh...When this thing first happen they might not like it but if they continue they become to like it...y'know.

INMATE:

44 MS: MAN ASLEEP

Well in all of these dormitories you have the opportunity to observe some things y'know...In the shower this is taking place, y'know. The man next to you may be mastur- bating, you see what I mean.

45 MS: MAN ASLEEP

46 CU: PINUP ON LOCKER

INMATE:

47 CU: PINUP ON WALL
48 CU: PINUP

49 CU: PINUP
50 CU: PINUP

Well, I tell you now...You see a man that's in a place of this kind, if he is a man he looks to get release some kind of way. He may tell you for a year in and year out that he won't mess

56

| | |
|---|---|
| 51 CU: PINUP (PERSONAL)<br>52 CU: PINUP | with a homosexual and he wakes up one night thinking about his woman or wife or who she may be...and can't stay in the bed...and it ain't no telling what a man will do when he get in that kind of fix. |
| | NARR: |
| 53 MS: DORM | Certainly dormitory life for many inmates is not a pleasant experience. Living space is at a premium. |
| 54 LS: BED & LOCKER WITH STOOL ON TOP OF BED | With each man having only his bed, a stool and a locker in which to put his personal belongings. |
| 55 LS: SHOWERS TRACK TO SHOW TOILET | Shower stalls are open and can be seen from anywhere in the dormitory. The same is true for toilet and sink areas. Privacy is almost unknown. At the end of |
| 56 MS: MEN PLAYING CARDS | the working day, most inmates pass the time playing cards or watching television. |
| 57 MS: MAN STUDYING AT BEDSIDE | And, it is difficult indeed for the man who tries to study in such surroundings. |
| 58 CU: MEAT CUTTER | FX: MEAT GRINDER BG |
| | NARR: |
| 59 CU: MEAT BEING CRAMMED DOWN GRINDER | The subject of food is always of paramount importance in any institution. And, whether a man is serving one year and a day or a life sentence, keen interest is |
| 60 CU: MEAT COMING OUT GRINDER | expressed in the quality and preparation of his meals. |
| 61 LS: KITCHEN | FX: kitchen sounds, wild BG |
| | INMATE: |
| | The food that they have here is fine...it's the preparin' of the food you know. |
| 62 MS: MAN STIRRING | You see the men that they have in there preparin' that food is |
| 63 CU: MAN STIRRING | doin' time just like I am. |
| 64 ECU: NOODLES POURING OUT SPOUT | FX: up full |
| 65 CU: ABOVE, STRAINER IS REMOVED | |

| | |
|---|---|
| 66 MS: CREASY | CREASY: |
|     SUPER: NAME & TITLE (CHIEF STEWARD) | Professional cooks? In the kitchen here the stewards do the best they can to supervise the cooking when they have time. There's other duties the stewards have to do such as locking doors, unlocking doors, checking groceries, taking inventory of meats, foodstuffs and so on and so forth. They |

67 LS: CHOW LINE
68 CU: PEAS BEING DIPPED
69 CU: BEEF AND NOODLES

just cannot stay in one spot at all times. Now if we did have any type of what we'd call a cook be assigned and don't do nothing but that, I'm sure they would improve the service a whole lot.

70 MS: CREASY (SYNC)

71 MS: MAN TAPING HOLE IN IRON FURNACE

FX: FOUNDRY SOUNDS, SYNC

72 CU: MOLTEN IRON RUNNING OUT TROUGH

73 CU: MAN WITH SAFETY SHIELD REFLECTING RUNNING IRON
74 MS: MAN AT FURNACE TILT TO IRON BUCKET

NARR:

Some 33 trades and skills are available to the inmate who is confined to the reformatory.

75 MS: CRANE OPERATOR SHIFTS INTO GEAR

76 MS: IRON BUCKET SWINGS AWAY FROM FURNACE

77 LS: IRON BUCKET TRAVELING

78 CU: MAN TILTING BUCKET, PAN TO SHOW MOLTEN IRON

These shops provide services to the institution and produce products for sale to other government agencies. Money received from products helps to defray the cost of operating the prison system.

Depending on the trade and his own skill level, an inmate earns from three to thirteen dollars a month.

79 CU: SPOUT OF BUCKET WITH MOLDS BG

80 MS: LINDSEY (SYNC)
    SUPER: NAME & TITLE

LINDSEY:

At the present time we have approximately 450 inmates assigned to industrial operations producing goods for district, federal, and other government agencies

| | amounting to some one million two-hundred thousand dollars per year. |
|---|---|
| 81 CU: LINDSEY (SYNC) | Inmates assigned to the industrial shops receive primarily on-the-job training from the paid supervisors; they also receive vocational training commonly referred to as related classes. |
| | MECHANIC: |
| 82 CU: MECHANIC UNDER TRUCK (SYNC)<br><br>83 LS: MEN WORKING ON TRUCK | All right number one's loose...pull it up (CONVERSATION BETWEEN INMATES WORKING ON TRUCK CONTINUES) BG |
| | INMATE: |
| | First of all, in the shops where we're supposed to be training, it doesn't have the modern equipment. |
| 84 MS: ABOVE<br>85 CU: WHITE MECHANIC<br>86 CU: NEGRO MECHANIC WITH CIGAR<br>87 MS: THREE-SHOT ABOVE<br><br>88 LS: ABOVE | I was assigned to the garage as a mechanic trainee and I never actually had an instructor there. I was assigned to a section to work with an officer and this officer made it clear to me that he wasn't there to actually give me the training that I was seeking. He was there to perform a job himself as well as for me to work along and this is the type training that they have. |
| 89 CU: SHIRT PASSING THRU SEWING MACHINE | FX: SEWING MACHINES (wild) |
| 90 CU: INMATES FACE, SEWING<br>91 CU: HANDS SEWING COAT | INMATE:<br><br>When I came here I was put in the industrial tailor shop. The offoicer in the shop introduced me to the other two assistants he had there. So the lead man threads the machine; after threading the machine he tell me...say now you try it. So I threads the machine for about ten times. After threading it for ten times he takes a rag, sews a pocket on; gives me the |
| 92 CU: INMATE<br>93 CU: INMATE | |

94 LS: TRACKING SHOT OF SHIRT LINE

machine, gives me a rag, gives me a pocket and tells me, "Now you sew it on." So I sew on about a hundred pockets. So he tells the supervisor, yeah, he's a damn good sewer. So after I'm in the shop for about 6 months they got eight fellows goin' upstairs to the tailor class, so I speak with the supervisor about goin' to the tailoring class, so he tell me I got too much time I can go later on. So I ask for a transfer out of there.

95 MS: SILK-SCREEN PROCESS

FX: SILK-SCREEN ACTION UP FULL THEN BG (SYNC)

INMATE:

96 CU: SIGN ON STACK; FOLLOW TO SPRAY-PAINT RACK
97 CU: SIGN ON STACK; HOLD ON STACK AS SIGNS ARE PICKED UP
98 CU: SPRAY PAINT RACK; HOLD AS SIGNS ARE PICKED UP
99 LS: TAG STAMPING PRESS
100 MS: OVER SHOULDER OF PRESS OPERATOR
101 CU: TAGS BEING PRESSED

I worked in the tag plant since 1958 and I'm a spray painter and while they do do spray paintings in the tag plants such as tags, signs, and they have a vocational class for the shop which consists of about four men and the shop foreman he runs the class and we just talk about the shop. There isn't anything to learn about it because the machines that they got to work on there are really out of date. All the machines here are good for is to hurt somebody.

102 MS: LINDSEY
SUPER: NAME & TITLE

LINDSEY: (sync)

It is true that some of our equipment is outmoded and outdated, particularly in the tag shop.

103 CU: TAGS BEING PRESSED

104 MS: OVER SHOULDER OF PRESS OPERATOR

DISSOLVE: 24 FRAMES TO 105 MS: TAG PRESS SAME AS ABOVE BUT WITHOUT OPERATOR

Not long ago we had an incident where an inmate lost his hand due to the malfunction of a press, even though it was equipped with safety devices. We have since ordered a new press which we'll be seven months obtaining. In the meantime the press is no longer in use.

DISSOLVE: 24 FRAMES TO 106 LS: FOUNDRY, TILT TO MANHOLE RINGS

FX: LOW WIND NOISE

107 MS: MANHOLE COVERS;
PAN TO STREET LIGHT
BASES
108 CU: WATER-METER
COVER

109 MS: CIVIL WAR CANNON

110 CU: LATHERED FACE
BEING SHAVED
111 MS: BARBER SHAVING
INMATE

112 CU: BARBER CUTTING
HAIR
113 ECU: BACK OF HEAD
BEING CUT
114 MS: TWO CHAIRS OC-
CUPIED

115 CU: INMATE TALKING
TO BARBER, TILT TO
BARBER
116 MS: ABOVE TWOSOME

117 LS: PAN OF SCHOOL

118 CU: FRACTION WRITTEN
ON BLACKBOARD
119 LS: CLASSROOM; IN-
MATE RISES, GOES TO
BOARD

120 MS: INMATE WORKING
PROBLEM

121 CU: INMATE LISTENING
122 CU: INMATE LISTENING

INMATE:

Under the trade training program if you dig deep enough you'll see it for what it really is...you'll see it as something to keep the institution in operation...you'll see it as being a type of production for the public and you'll see if you go even deeper where no one is really benefiting from it, except perhaps a few individuals.

NARR:

The goal of the vocational training program is to see that each inmate is an economically independent citizen when he is released from prison. Barbering is one profession where this goal appears to be realized. However, many jobs performed by inmates have little application outside the institution. This would seem to be the case in the license tag plant and broom manufacturing shop. Unfortunately, most inmates still leave the reformatory with 40 dollars, a prison-made suit and no job.

Academic schooling is also an important part of the treatment program of the reformatory. Last year, more than 300 inmates completed courses offered in this modern, well-equipped school.

TEACHER: (FINISHES WRITING FRACTION ON BOARD AND BEGINS DISCUSSION OF PROBLEM)

NARR:

Courses are conducted by professional teachers and must reflect the wide range of inmate abilities. The curriculum includes four tracts: literacy; elementary; high school; and special studies. Attendance is encouraged in vocational,

123 ECU: INMATE HOLDING CIGARETTE BUTT; INMATE RETURNS TO SEAT
124 CU: TEACHER CONTINUES DISCUSSION
125 CU: INMATE LISTENING
126 CU: INMATE LISTENING
127 LS: CLASSROOM
128 CU: BASKETBALL PASSING THRU HOOP

129 MS: CLOSE QUARTER ACTION OF BASKETBALL GAME
130 LS: TEAMS MOVE DOWN COURT
131 MS: LAYUP ACTION
132 CU: BALL THRU HOOP
133 LS: TEAMS MOVE TO NEAR END OF COURT

134 MS: CLOSE QUARTER ACTION

135 ECU: CRUCIFIX
136 MS: CRUCIFIX, TILT TO INMATE BUFFING FLOOR

137 LS: CHAPEL, CRUCIFIX BG

138 MS: LOW ANGLE, MAN BUFFING CRUCIFIX BG

139 MS: HIGH ANGLE, LOOKING DOWN THRU CRUCIFIX TO MAN

140 LS: CHAPEL

141 CU: CRUCIFIX

142 LS: PSYCHOLOGIST AND INMATE
143 CU: PSYCHOLOGIST NODS

academic and social adjustment courses with a pay incentive program. Although some inmates feel this forces them to attend, most men agree the pay incentive program is justified.

FX: BASKETBALL GAME (SYNE & WILD)

NARR:

For men who are confined for long periods of their life to a penal institution, physical exercise is a must. At the Men's Reformatory of the District of Columbia, the athletic program rivals that of a small college. Facilities and equipment are exceptional. Inmate participation is enthusiastic as reflected in the high number of intramural teams.

NARR:

This life-size crucifix was created by an inmate while he was confined to the Reformatory. It is prison policy to permit each inmate to participate in religious services according to his own faith. This includes those inmates who follow the teachings of Muhammud. The prison chaplain has an unusual position, because he is both a government employee and a carefully chosen minister of a religious society. The chaplin acts as counselor, advisor, and comforter. And he must listen with patience and interest to a man's problems and whenever possible help the inmate to find a solution.

ADDICT:

I come from southwest in Washington, D.C. I was raised in a vice area and I met my wife when I was about 16. She was a

| | |
|---|---|
| 144 LS: ABOVE | prostitute at that particular time. That's when I left home. I was smoking marijuana in school when I met my wife... |
| | (CONVERSATION BETWEEN THE TWO CONTINUES BG) |
| | NARR: |
| | Counseling by professional psychologists also plays a vital role in the reformatory rehabilitation program. It is |
| 145 MS: INMATE, HIGH ANGLE, LOOKING DOWN ON HANDS | through such services that many inmates are brought face to face with reality for the first time in their life. |
| | PSYCHOLOGIST: |
| 146 CU: PSYCHOLOGIST | You said something struck you, what did you mean? |
| | ADDICT: |
| 147 ECU: INMATE | Somehow or another during that six years something hit me and I wanted to get away from drugs. I did the six years and I went out...stopped using drugs and got involved in the traffic, and I was arrested in 1955 with a large quantity of heroin and I was sentenced to 80 months to 20 years. I came here to Lorton in June, 1956, and I've been here ever since. |
| 148 LS: HARDY SUPER: NAME & TITLE | HARDY: (SYNC) |
| | There seems to be much concern about our psychological services center, its operation, because it is expensive. We see an operation there of 11 staff servicing some 70 inmates with intensive treatment as opposed to a staff of about five social workers and two psychologists reaching out to 1,000 inmates. It's this proportion that I'm concerned with, but we have found from this experiment that we can save or help save the intractable person if he wishes to expose himself to deep therapy. In corrections |
| 149 ECU: HARDY | the administrator has to follow |

about the same road as the commanding officer on a battlefield. That is, in combat your casualties come back to the first-aid station and you only have so many doctors and corpsmen; therefore, they go to work on the hopeful cases they can save with limited staff. Likewise with corrections. I would feel with the limited staff we have we should place our emphasis on the hopeful cases, but you see with the psychological services operating we are shifting our emphasis to the more intractable inmate and working on him. But I don't want to discredit this operation. It's there to prove a point. And that is if you give us enough staff, we can give intensive treatment to the hopeful as well as the hopeless as long as the hopeless gain some insight or have some anxiety about himself and wants to get into the program.

NARR:

By definition, therapy takes many forms. Certainly a visit from a friend or relative should boost the morale of a man in prison. But, for some inmates such is not the case.

INMATE:

Well, the visit here is not too nice. First of all they have these hard benches and hard chairs to sit on and you have to sit there for an hour to talk and you be pretty tired in the rear.

INMATE:

Yeah, you can touch, you can kiss. If it's your wife you can hold her hand, but the worst thing about the visit is to have an officer stand up over top of you and look right down in your mouth while you're talking and

150 CU: VISITORS SIGN

DOLLY: TO LS OF VISIT HALL

151 CU: INMATE BENCH
152 CU: VISITOR'S CHAIR

153 MS: BENCH & CHAIR HIGH ANGLE

| | |
|---|---|
| DOLLY: TO END OF BENCH | constantly walking up and down behind you. |
| | INMATE:<br><br>The inmates that receive visits they really look forward to this. |
| | INMATE:<br><br>They live from visit to visit and after they receive their visit usually they're in very high spirits...morally I don't think that they could feel better under the conditions but five |
| DOLLY: STOPS ON LAST CHAIR | minutes later it's a different picture. |
| | INMATE: |
| DISSOLVE: 24 fr to<br>154 LS: SHAKEDOWN ROOM | After a man has received his visit he has to go in for a complete shakedown. This means a complete frisk. He |
| DOLLY: TO END OF ROOM, CENTERING ON INSPECTION TABLE | strips completely. He is asked to expose certain parts of his body which is very demoralizing. His clothes are turned usually inside out and he is really given the treatment. After this, regardless of how the visit went, it has a tendency to make the average person a little sorry that they had to go on a visit. |
| SLOW FADE TO BLACK | NARR: |
| 155 MS: DOOR OF PAROLE BOARD ROOM | When a man is near the end of his minimum sentence, the D.C. Board of Parole rules on his appeal for parole. The board is comprised of one professional and four part-time public citizen members. It meets one day a week and hears an average of 20 cases a day. |
| DOOR OPENS TO ROOM;<br>CAMERA DOLLIES INTO ROOM | INMATE: |
| | The first thing I was asked by the people on the parole board was what I come up there for. So I told them that I come up |
| 156 CU: INMATE'S CHAIR, HIGH ANGLE | there because it was my parole date and I came up to see about |

| | |
|---|---|
| 157 MS: INMATE'S CHAIR, LOOKING FROM BOARD MEMBER'S CHAIRS | getting paroled. Say boy have you ever been in any trouble? |
| 158 CU: INMATE'S CHAIR, HIGH ANGLE | Said no not since I been here. |
| 159 MS: INMATE'S CHAIR, LOOKING FROM BOARD MEMBER'S CHAIRS, TRACKING SHOT | So his next statement was you done got penitentiary slick. |
| | INMATE: |
| 160 CU: INMATE'S CHAIR, HIGH ANGLE | So I said what you mean penitentiary slick? He say you |
| 161 MS: INMATE'S CHAIR, LOOKING FROM BOARD CHAIR | been here long enough, I don't have to explain that to you. He said you go ahead on we'll talk |
| 162 LS: BOARD ROOM | with you later. So I get a slip back; parole denied. |
| | INMATE: |
| 163 CU: BOARD MEMBERS' CHAIRS, TRACKING SHOT TO LAST CHAIR | The parole board as I see it...it's a department created by Congress or the Commissioners' Office of D.C. It's not answerable to anyone. They are invested with power that no one can question. |
| 164 LS: SARD SUPER: NAME & TITLE | SARD: (SYNC) |
| | The inmates just don't understand. The board is under many controls. |
| | It's controlled by the law which created the board. Many cases have been decided by the courts which control the action of the board. The board is under control of the Board of Commissioners as to policy. |
| 165 MS: SARD | In the single area of decision-making; it could be said the board is not under control, but even then if the board should act arbitrarily or capriciously, their action could be reviewed by the courts. |
| 166 LS: BOARD ROOM, 300-DEGREE TRACKING SHOT | I know they say the D.C. Board of Parole is one of the toughest boards in the United States. The President's Crime Commission somewhat confirmed this in |

this recent report in which it pointed out the D.C. parole board had parolled only 22 percent of the cases coming before the board last year. I might say the board has recently been reexamining its philosophy on the parole and in the past two months it has paroled 41.5 percent of the cases coming before it.

DISSOLVE: 72 FR. TO
167 MS: SLOW PAN OF PRISON WALL

MUSIC: SLOW, LONELY GUITAR, "LEADBELLY"

NARR:

Correctional treatment...on-the-job training...vocational education...academic education ...social education...religious counseling... psychological guidance. Even with all of these, the fact remains that few men in today's prisons are ready to step back into the outside world. For prison is all too often an artificial and sheltered environment. In case after case, a man released with 40 dollars and a prison suit again turns to crime as a way of life. One solution to this traumatic step from prison life to the outside world is the so-called work-release program.

168 CU: GUN TOWER NO. 4, ZOOM TO LS WALL AREA

169 LS: WALSH
      SUPER: NAME & TITLE

WALSH: (SYNC)

Work release, not to be construed as another correctional panacea, nevertheless offers one of the major solutions to this problem. Work-release is a program whereby selected offenders, some 50 currently out of a population of 1100, work in the community by day and return to the reformatory at night. Eventually it is hoped one fifth of the Department's population can participate in such a program.

170 CU: WALSH

171 MS: WALSH

The fact remains that the job of rehabilitation is only half completed by institutional and correctional treatment and training programs such as work-release. The other half is the responsibility of the community to which the offender will return. The community must accept him as a rehabilitated individual and extend to him every opportunity to demonstrate this fact.

DISSOLVE: 48 FR TO
172 MS: GUN TOWER NO. 10
AT SUNSET

MUSIC: JIM OWENS HUMMING "I GOT SO MUCH TROUBLE"

INMATE:

173 SUPER: TRACKING SHOT
OF CHAIN-LINK FENCE

DISSOLVE: 48 FR TO
174 MS: TRACKING SHOT
BEHIND GUARD WALKING
BEAT AT NIGHT

SUPER: FENCE CONTINUES

Like I said before when I was doin' wrong I was doin' wrong and didn't need no help. My mind wasn't made up to do right then. Now I makes my mind up to, I makes it up my own self and I come to you and say well I wants some help, now I ain't never asked you for no help before but I'm ready to do right you say you can help me...all right?

SUPER: TRACKING
SHOT, STOPS, HOLDS ON
FENCE
DISSOLVE: 64 FR OUT
SHOT OF GUARD WALKING
BEAT

FX: CELL DOOR SLAMS
SHUT

MUSIC: PAYS OFF AND
FADES OUT

FADE TO BLACK

SECOND COMMERCIAL BREAK

FADE UP FROM BLACK
TO

175 CU: CELL BLOCK LOCK
BOX AS KEY IS INSERTED,
HANDLE TURNED (SYNC)
176 LS: CELL BLOCK DOOR
SLIDES OPEN: LOOKING
FROM OPPOSITE END OF
CELL BLOCK, GUARD ENTERS.

FX: KEYS IN LOCK (sync)

FX: DOOR SLAMS OPEN

MUSIC: JIM OWENS HUMS
WITH GUITAR "I GOT SO
MUCH TROUBLE"

68

| | |
|---|---|
| 177 MS: TRACKING SHOT OF CELLS, PRISONERS IN VARIOUS BORED POSITIONS | |
| SUPER: TITLE CARD NO. 1: "THE SWEET SMELL OF FREEDOM" | |
| SUPER: TITLE CARD NO. 2: "NARRATED BY TOM FINN" | |
| SUPER: TITLE CARD NO. 3: "A PRESENTATION OF WMAL TELEVISION NEWS & PUBLIC AFFAIRS" | |
| FADE SUPER: AS DOLLY STOPS ON LAST CELL, GUARD ENTERS FRAME RIGHT, SLAMS CELL DOOR SHUT | FX: DOOR SLAM |
| FADE TO BLACK. | MUSIC: PAYS OFF AND FADES |

## SPECIAL PRODUCTIONS

More than two decades ago, Stuart Finley was producing a public affairs series, for WRC-TV in Washington, D.C., with the ironic title of "Our Beautiful Potomac." The program focused attention on the fearful pollution that had turned a once beautiful river into an ugly brown sewage-strewn flow that was a disgrace to the nation's capital. In presenting this series of half-hour programs, the technique employed was to show a documentary film of the devastated river, leaving time for a discussion by public officials.

The U.S. Environmental Protection Agency has now been established to deal with ecological problems and Stuart Finley Productions contracted to produce several films describing the problems faced in solid waste disposal, aptly categorized as the "third pollution."

One of the problems tackled is that of recycling. A 21-minute documentary film was produced for showing on television and, following the technique employed by the "Beautiful Potomac" series, it permits time for discussion by local officials or concerned citizens, briefly for a half-hour program or extensively for an hour program.

The film, entitled simply and explicitly, "Recycling," presents a good example of writing against film footage. Because of the comparative newness of the subject, it was necessary to do all the shooting before a script could be written. It is true that some cities, like Los Angeles, were attempting to recycle solid wastes such as glass, metals, and paper many years ago, but the emphasis on environmental cleanup is, unfortunately, a recent issue.

A treatment was prepared for the "Recycling" script, but there were so many new methods being hurriedly developed which, presumably, were to make recycling a scientific reality that it was essential to determine whether or not there were projects in a sufficiently advanced stage to permit documentary film coverage. Highly experienced cameraman Ted Jones was entrusted with the responsibility for acquiring usable footage.

The challenge to the writer in this type of script is the ability to be at once concise and fully explanatory. You are dealing with a technical subject in a film which, largely, is to be shown to a lay audience. The newness of the subject matter meant a paucity of footage and the writer had to tailor his script to very tightly edited film, and also permit effective use of music. The procedure is to time each sequence precisely; then the narration must coincide with the visual.

Here, for example, is the brief teaser opening for "Recycling," and a portion of the first sequence.

| | |
|---|---|
| JUNKMAN DRIVING HORSE DRAWN CART PILED HIGH WITH SALVAGE | MUSIC: :07 : 00—: 07<br>In earlier times, there was the junkman.<br>He knew that one man's trash could be another man's cash! |
| SUPER TITLE: "RECYCLING" | We must learn that what we throw away today contains the resources we will need tomorrow.<br>: 16 : 07—: 23 |
| CART DRIVING OFF | (MUSIC) :04 : 23—: 27 |
| VARIOUS SCENES OF ALCOA COLLECTION CENTER | (MUSIC) :02 : 00—: 02<br>Today's "junkman" is often a member of the environmentally conscious younger generation who has joined a recycling campaign.<br>: 09 : 02—: 11 |
| YOUNGSTERS CARRYING STACKS OF CANS<br><br>CANS LOADED INTO TRUCKS | (MUSIC) :03 : 11—: 14<br>These young people are taking part in an innovative campaign against "contamination"—and to help conserve a valuable resource. |

(MUSIC)        :02:28—:30

YOUNG MAN PAYING FOR CANS

They are paid ten cents a pound for returned aluminum cans.

Collection centers for reclaiming cans are being set up wherever aluminum cans are used in large quantities.

:15:30—:45
(MUSIC)        :01:45—:46

Another sequence describes the process of turning junked cars into scrap steel.

(MUSIC)        :04:00—:04

CU OF CLAW

Junked cars can be turned into high-grade scrap steel. Processing plants—like this one on the West Coast—have been doing it for only a few years.

CLAW LIFTING CAR ONTO CONVEYOR

A huge claw lifts a doomed car onto a conveyor for its final journey. To misquote the bard, these cars are getting ready to shuffle off their mortal coils. They've come full round—from the assembly line to the disassembly line. These are stripped hulks. The auto wrecking industry removes motor, battery, radiator, and other salable parts before these bodies are chewed up by the shredder.

CARS ON CONVEYOR

:39:04—:43

VIEWS OF THE SHREDDER

Rube Goldberg might have designed this enormous shredder—with an appetite for a thousand cars a day—covering half a city block—costing several million dollars. Today's mechanical shredder is able to separate steel from all other materials in your old car—converting it into high-grade pulverized steel.

MAGNET LIFTING PIECES OF STEEL

:22:47—1:09
(MUSIC)        :07 1:09—1:16

71

And here is a short scene dealing with still another aspect of solid-waste disposal.

(MUSIC)  :02 :00—:02

SUGAR CANE HULLS

MAN FEEDING BAGASSE INTO MACHINE

PILOT PLANT EQUIPMENT

Bagasse—the remains of the sugar cane after the juice has been removed—is the basis for a reuse project. At Louisiana State University, research—sponsored by the EPA—is under way to convert cellulose waste into high-protein animal food—and possibly for human consumption.

WS OF MAN APPROACHING EQUIPMENT

PROTEIN    FIBERS EMERGING

The pilot plant should be capable of producing protein from bagasse at the rate of some 75 pounds a day. Some day you might be asked to please pass the bagasse—but at the moment, the prime objective of the LSU project is to produce protein for animal consumption.

:39 :02—:41

(MUSIC)  :02 :41—:43

One of the latest developments in solid waste management, a hydrasposal system, is described. Notice the relation of the narration to the visual; this is particularly essential when you are dealing with technical subjects.

(MUSIC)  :03    :00—:03

CU MUNICIPAL REFUSE

MAN SHOVELING REFUSE ONTO CONVEYOR

REFUSE    COMING    OFF CONVEYOR

New and better solid waste management systems must be developed. Here at Middletown, Ohio, a demonstration project tests the effectiveness of a wet grinding system. The input is ordinary municipal refuse—cans, bottles, everything.

:20 :03—:23

(MUSIC)  :04 :23—:27

REFUSE FLOWING INTO HYDRAPULPER

The objective is to recover useful material from trash—

HYDRAPULPER EQUIP-
MENT

FIBROUS MATERIALS

paper fiber, glass cullet, and ferrous metals. The method is to dump raw refuse into a hydrapulper which disintegrates the refuse. Fibrous materials from paper and cardboard are reclaimed with equipment similar to that used in the paper industry.

:23 :27—: 50

REJECT MATERIAL

This rejected material will be burned in the fluidized bed incinerator. Future large-scale operations could use this heat to generate electric power.

:09 :50—: 59

JUNK EJECTOR

The junk ejector removes heavy metallic objects. Further processing can segregate reusable ferrous metals.

:09 :59—1: 08

(MUSIC)          :02 1:08—1: 10

LIQUID CYCLONE

The slurry is pumped through a liquid cyclone which removes particles such as broken glass, sand and small pieces of metal.

:07 1: 10—1: 17

(MUSIC)          :03 1: 17—1: 20

FIBROUS MATERIALS

This pilot plant is a prototype for systems that could be established nationwide.

:06 1: 20—1: 26

(MUSIC)          :03 1: 26—1: 29

## THE RADIO DOCUMENTARY

When "Hear It Now," after a season's existence on CBS radio, transferred to the visual medium under the title of "See It Now," it also marked the end of the heyday of radio documentaries. But it was not, by any means, the death knell of radio documentaries. What has happened in radio is that the production of documentaries has left the aegis of the networks for the more parochial attack of the local station. Documentaries are still produced by the networks, on occasion, as, for example, Edward Hanna's "America The Violent" which won a Writer's Guild Award. It was part of the series presented by NBC under the overall title of "Second Sunday."

"American The Violent" is "an examination of violence in America—its history, its cultural and psychological causes." It opens with a compelling teaser.

("AMERICA THE BEAUTIFUL"; UP AND UNDER) (GUNSHOTS)

MAN: Police and National Guard are shooting with everything they've got—submachine guns, rifles, pistols...

MAN: ...were fired as President Kennedy's motorcade passed through downtown Dallas...

MAN: We have hydrogen bombs of five megatons, ten megatons, fifteen megatons...

MAN: ...wife and four of their children were found shot today...

MARTIN LUTHER KING: So I'm happy tonight. I'm not worried about anything. I'm not fearing any man. Mine eyes have seen...

MAN: ...have ended their 24-hour Tet cease-fire...

ROBERT KENNEDY: My thanks to all of you, and now it's on to Chicago, and let's win there.

MAN: ...it was seen that at least three students were dead and at least twelve...

(GUNSHOTS)
(MUSIC OUT)
(THEME MUSIC)

What writing there is for the script encompasses the narration of NBC News correspondent Edwin Newman.

EDWIN NEWMAN: Someone in the United States is going to be the victim of a violent crime within the next 48 seconds. That's how often violent crime occurs in this country now, according to the latest statistics—once every 48 seconds. In the last ten years, violent crime has increased more than 100 percent. That's according to reported figures, information collected by the Federal Bureau of Investigation. But it has been estimated by the National Commission on the Causes and Prevention of Violence that the true figures may be nearly twice as high. Here, we're talking about murder, rape, robbery, and aggravated assault. So, in other words, violent crime may be taking place about every 24 seconds or so, less time than it takes me to tell about it.

The chairman of the National Commission, Milton Eisenhower...

Or again, further on in the script...

NEWMAN: Television has come in for a good deal of criticism because of the portrayal of violence, as have movies, comic books, and paper books. But television, having by far the largest audience and the greatest impact, has come under the most criticism.

Spokesmen for the industry, in testimony before the National Violence Commission and congressional committees, have maintained that only a portion of programs broadcast are of a violent nature, or even contain violence, and that it is the policy to reject violence used only for its own sake.

The industry has also maintained that there is tentative evidence to indicate that children as well as adults bring their own conflicts to the medium, rather than take conflicts from it. Still, the broadcast industry has been continually under attack, not only for the violence portrayed on entertainment programs, but displayed on news programs.

Many people, some of them influential, feel that television—and radio, for that matter—should not report violence that occurs in the news, or at least should tone it down considerably.

The narration serves as a lead-in to taped statements by authorities including Margaret Mead, Lionel Tiger, Charles Frankel, and Frederick Wortham. The program is a sort of montage of comments, with the varied opinions focusing on the theme of the documentary. It is a valid approach to presenting enlightened analysis of a compelling problem.

Progressive radio station managers realize the potency of the documentary in helping their stations to assert themselves as a force in the community. Radio documentaries are very inexpensive to produce. Compact, self-powered tape recorders make it possible for reporters to obtain on-the-scene coverage anywhere. In many instances, the writer of the radio documentary is also the producer and reporter.

Basically, the radio documentary writer can follow the same precepts which guide the writing of a television documentary. Obviously, the impact of the visual is lacking, but through words, sound, and music, the radio documentary can stir the imagination of the listener, and often imagination may equal or even surpass what the eye beholds.

### "The Junk Beyond the Picture Window"

Every large city is faced with the terrible reality of drug addiction among its young people—rich and poor. The radio documentary series, "The Junk Beyond the Picture Window," produced by Ted Landphair, Director of the WMAL Public Affairs Division, and Marc Kuhn, presents this universal theme. WMAL had a booklet printed which includes a preface to this documentary series and a transcript of the final program. Here is an excerpt from the preface which describes the production of the series.

"Broadcast journalists are forever scolding drug educators for alarming young people with outdated, righteous, and simply incorrect information. Then the broadcasters themselves put together 'drug specials' filled with funeral music, moralizing accounts of junkies who have seen the light, and outright editorializing that paints a joint of marijuana as mankind's greatest scourge since Genghis Khan. The result is misinformation that reaches neither the young nor sophisticated adults.

So, in the formative stages of the WMAL series, 'The Junk Beyond the Picture Window,' an examination of the spread of hard drugs into the Washington suburbs, we first resolved not to be preachy. Many of our citizens are agitated about the drug problem. Others feel it should be taken in stride. Some young people think drugs are a perfectly reasonable alternative to a vapid suburban reality. We gave each viewpoint its due, trusting our listeners to winnow the worst and cull the best of all arguments.

Who could listen to Ada and Harry Berg, parents of a boy who died of a drug overdose; or to a 26-year-old speed freak who chose amphetamines over a successful corporate career; or to Fairfax County's prosecutor describing the bodies of young people stiffened on slabs in the morgue and not see the senseless tragedy of drug abuse. Yet, only an ostrich could listen to youngster after youngster decrying parents' hypocrisy and chase for a buck; or to treatment directors detailing the profound psychological cavities in their clients and not understand at least part of the motivation for suburban drug addiction.

We bombarded our listeners with information: 30 separate programs—more than 13 hours—over 15 days. If a theme emerged, and we saw to it that it did, it was that drug abuse is neither the ghetto's nor one's neighbor's problem alone.

Within the 30 programs we examined, among other things:

The lifestyle of the suburban junkie.

The suburban drug abuser's elaborate rationalizations.

The poignant—and bitter—recollections of parents who lost a boy to drugs.

The range of knowledge and attitudes on drugs of the average suburban parent.

The work, and criticisms, of the 'nark,' the undercover officer.
Approaches to drug education.
Encounter as a technique in treating addiction.
The struggles of a preaddict treatment program to get started.
The 'permissive' or 'people problem' school of thought on drugs.
The hard-line approach.''

And from the final script in the series we have culled these selections which will give you an insight into the writing and research that characterized the series and the use of music for point and counterpoint.

Mr. Henshen: This is Kurt Henschen, WMAL News. In a recent 3-week, 30-part investigation into the spread of hard drugs throughout the Washington suburbs, WMAL Radio Public Affairs Director Ted Landphair and I talked with junkies and judges, experts and ex-addicts, hard-liners, soft-liners, parents who have lost children to drugs and parents who think it can't happen to them.

Tonight, WMAL News recaptures the highlights of more than 13 hours of programming, "The Junk Beyond the Picture Window—A Summing Up.''

Captain Jack Bechtel: In 1963 we only had 13 juvenile narcotics arrests for the whole year. At this time, when we were out giving speeches to various civic clubs, we were trying to tell them at that time that we thought that our narcotic situation with juveniles was escalating and we should start to do something about it, start setting up some kind of programs. And of course people said, "No," it was only a fad and it would probably just blow over.

(Background Music: "Auld Lang Syne") "In 1970 in Montgomery County, there were 246 juvenile narcotic arrests. Also in 1970 there were 302 adult narcotic arrests. A sum total of 548 narcotic arrests for the year 1970. This total would be 285 more narcotic arrests in Montgomery County in 1970 over 1969.''

Mr. Henschen: In Montgomery County, as in the other suburban Washington jurisdictions, the 1963 style "pot party" is passe. But drugs were not hula hoops. The fad did not pass. LSD, amphetamines, and barbiturates soon caught the fancy of the bored or disenchanted suburban kid. More in vogue today are fruit salad parties. Everyone dips into his parents' pill supply in the medicine chest, tosses a few in a brandy snifter and in turn picks blindly and waits for the appropriate trip to set in. This "kicks" approach is the stereotype of the suburban drug problem. Or it was. Recently, a darker element, the bone of the ghetto, the symbol of frustration and hopelessness, has joined Washington's suburban drug scene: Junk. H. Heroin.

(Background Music: "Heroin" and Lyrics) "Our house was a horror house. For four or five years our house was a horror house."

(Background Music: "Heroin") "Stanley wasn't meant to live that long. Twenty-two years was all God gave him."

(Background Music: "Heroin") "I lured an old man into an alley and I jumped on him and, you know, beat him up."

(Background Music: "Heroin") "When they don't have that chemical you ought to see them some time. You should have seen me when I didn't have my dope."

(Background Music: "Heroin") "We really don't have a drug problem, we have a people problem."

Mr. Henschen: The sounds of a turned-on, tuned-out world. A suburban drug subculture that is thrusting upon us its own discomfiting vocabulary: Nark, barbs, chipping, cooker, strung out, main line—

(Background Music: "Auld Lang Syne") "In 1970 in Fairfax County there were 322 drug arrests; 175 of these arrests were adults, 147 were juveniles. Compared to the year 1969 when we had 226 arrests, 100 juveniles and 126 adults. Also in the year 1970 in Fairfax County, we had three drug overdose deaths, one from heroin, one from methadone and one from barbiturates. All these were under the age of 20."

Mr. Henschen: Grim figures? Obviously. But drug statistics can be deceptive, as WMAL Radio Public Affairs Director Ted Landphair found out in his investigation of suburban Washington's drug scene.

Mr. Landphair: Gallup has taken no poll on the number of split-level bedrooms, shopping-center alleys, or drive-in parking lots in which kids are shooting up. Surveys taken in schools miss the worst abusers, most of whom are dropouts. Only cold, harsh arrest and death statistics mean much, and they too can be misleading. For while they indicate a startling increase in drug offenses, they also reflect a concerted antidrug effort by the police.

(Background Music: "Auld Lang Syne") "In 1970 in Arlington County, the total arrests for drugs was 368. Of the 368, there were 78 juveniles charged and of the 78 juveniles, 28 were for heroin. Last year's figures against this year's are 209 against 368. And the overdose deaths last year were five."

Mr. Landphair: WMAL News will talk with junkies and judges, teachers and treatment directors, parents and police, hard-liners and soft-liners about the hard drug situation. They agree upon only one thing: Hard drugs are here, in the so-called "best of families," and communities are three to five years late in facing up to it.

(Background Music: "Auld Lang Syne") "In the year 1970 in Prince George's County there were 511 drug arrests. Of these 121 were juveniles and 390 were adults. Of the 511 arrests, 121 were arrests for the violation of possession, sale, and-or control of heroin. The 121 arrests for heroin violations is an increase of 53 arrests over the 1969 figure. This total of 511 drug arrests for 1970 is 170 more than in 1969."

Mr. Landphair: Two questions pervaded my investigation. Why would a kid who supposedly has everything, a kid who is smart enough to know the end product of heroin addiction, get into junk in the first place? And be addiction a drug problem or a people problem, a question of cutting off narcotic sources or changing society's attitudes, what can each county—and each parent—do about the problem? If the people you will meet don't have the answer, who does?

(Background Music: "Auld Lang Syne") "In the City of Alexandria, Virginia, we had a total of 101 drug arrests for the year 1970. On heroin possession, we arrested one juvenile, 21 adults. On the sale of heroin, eight adults were arrested, one juvenile. In comparison to the figure of 1969 versus the figure of 1970, we had approximately a 98 percent increase."

Mr. Landphair: A 19-year-old college boy wrote recently, "This generation was born into a world filled with leisure time and paved with wall-to-wall carpets. This world was the dream of our parents who, having experienced the horrors of the Depression and the War, had put their backs together to build a better America for us. They presented us with a complete prefabricated dream house, with those two long-wished-for cars and a precious television set. "What to our parents was the fulfillment of a beautiful dream was, to us, just two cars, a house and a television set." So wrote the student. Some suburban Washington youngsters today are presenting their parents with an unappreciated world, a world of fruit salad parties, speed, acid—and heroin.

(Background Music: "Auld Lang Syne") In 1970 in suburban Washington, there were 1850 drug arrests. 63 percent more than in 1969.

(Music and lyrics of, "Do you use it?") Suburban kids who do use the hard stuff, even those hooked on heroin, typically live at home in comfortable style complete with personal car, bountiful allowance, and an endless variety of deceptions for their parents. That car gives them incredible mobility. The Annandale boy who tells his parents he will be staying at Johnny's down the street overnight can easily be off to Baltimore to a drug party. Fairfax Commonwealth's Attorney Bob Horan tells me of four youngsters who pooled their pocket money—1300 bucks, incidentally—and sent one of their number to the West Coast to buy LSD. The next evening they were all on a trip, at home, their parents none the wiser.

There is an interesting distinction between the suburban drug abuser and the casual user. The experimenter is often above average in intelligence and outgoing. The abuser or addict below average, a lonely loner. One drug program director tells me the abuser is the weakest link in a weak family. Captain Jack Bechtel of the Montgomery County Police says most every kid arrested for heavy drug use comes from a broken home, broken emotionally if not literally. Whatever his pedigree, lower-middle to upper-upper class, the suburban drug addict caught short of money and a fix is every bit the classic dope fiend. Listen to three youngsters, the boy 16 and the girls 18, all from comfortable suburban Washington homes, and all presently in an abstinence program.

Debby: I used to have this thing, like me and three other guys, I would lure an old man into an alley and they would, you know, jump on him and beat him up, you know, or, you know, it was housebreaking, like in the middle-of-the-night type thing. I would open a window and go in and take somebody's bread.

Mr. Landphair: How did you feel about yourself when you were luring men into alleys?

Debby: I never thought about it. I didn't like to think about me or anybody else, I just thought about how much money he might have, or you know, how good it's going to be after we buy it with this man's money. But I never related it to me.

Greg: My dad and mom like had a lot of money lying around the house. Like, they had these envelopes every week or something that give five or six dollars to the churches. Like I'd just go in the envelopes, open them and like take all the money and leave a dollar in and close it back up and put it back. You know, or else I would go through my mom's purse or something, or like just rip off friends.

Peggy: I ripped off my friends all the time. My main thing was I guess housebreaking and breaking into cars for two-way radios or something. I had a fence for any type of guns or rifles I could get from houses, and I got into a whole thing with forging checks.

Mr. Landphair: You say, "Friends." That's a funny kind of friendship.

Peggy: Yes, well being a junkie, you know, the only way I can see it is that you can't trust, you know, anybody and you can't trust yourself just like—I didn't think I'd be ripping off my friends but I did, so I really couldn't trust myself, it's just a life style that I acquired.

Mr. Landphair: A life style she acquired. Were these young people psychopaths, misguided kids, victims of society or predators upon it?

Mr. Landphair: After a stint in a California mental hospital, John moved to Montgomery County to join his parents. And how did he find the suburban drug scene here?

John: **Very** far out, very far out because they are doing drugs in their homes, not on the streets. And it is quite a difference. You know, I never had any of that when I was on the Coast. You know, working every day relating with parents and at the same time using drugs. It's fascinating, it's very interesting; we are into all kinds of interesting games in the suburbs.

Mr. Landphair: What games?

John: "I am your father, as long as you are living here you do as I say." "Dad, I don't like your world. I'm trying to turn you on to my world, the one I created, which makes you my child."

"You are not listening to me." "Of course I don't listen to you. How do you expect me to listen to anyone that has long hair, is a Communist, and believes in anarchy and things like this."

And these are the types of games that are going on in suburbia on a very, sometimes hostile, sometimes comical, sometimes pathetic but still on a very high level.

Mr. Landphair: We have been at it for nearly an hour. John was getting edgy, his thoughts ramble. "How do you feel about the hobo life?" I asked him.

John: It's a trip. Three years ago it came to me in a flash what the problem was. It is that ultimately that each of us as individuals would be hopelessly trapped inside and around our own private universe and all that we had would be us and our children and they would all be just exactly like us. And they never get a chance to—

Mr. Landphair: The first of a few breakdowns. He recovered, then began a journey into philosophy.

John: The crime of history is that the poet and the artist have always been left far behind our regular time, and the shame of the world as everyone knows is that youth is wasted on children. So if we can change that around and make us get our thoughts...

Mr. Landphair: Laughter, tears, sighs in the same short paragraph. Sensing his strain, I asked John one last question. Speed-freaks, remember, like to play with words. "Where, John, do you see yourself going?"

John: (Laughter) Out. What we, Bob Dylan and I, are going to do is go back and become—to be the parents of humanity, you know, the God the Father that's him. I guess I will be Mother Nature, you know, the missing link, you know, everyone wants to know, everyone wants to know if Darwin is right, we can prove Darwin is right by the Bible.

Mr. Landphair: Reality is a painful place for many people who slip into addiction. Drugs dress up that reality. Soon unreality becomes fantasy, and fantasy at times tragedy. As John would say, "Speed-freaks do **that** too."

(Background Music: "One pill makes you larger")

Mr. Henschen: Stories like John's never really end with the telling. Since this interview was recorded, a Montgomery County drug-treatment director who has worked with John received a letter from him saying John's parents had forced him out of their house. The return address: Springfield State Hospital, Sykesville, Maryland.

(Music and lyrics: "Get up in the morning, get on the bus, drive to work like the rest of us...") Mr. Henschen: How much does the suburban parent know about drugs, and what is his thought on them? At Montgomery Mall, Ted Landphair talked to parents at random. This is Marv Kampsen, sales manager and father of four from Potomac, Maryland.

Mr. Landphair: Mr. Kampsen, are you familiar with the term "speed"? Do you know what speed is?

Mr. Kampsen: I believe that's an amphetamine drug. Precisely what reactions it has, I don't know.

Mr. Landphair: Do you know how a person who is taking heroin acts or what symptoms he shows?

Mr. Kampsen: No, I don't. I don't think I would be familiar with what symptoms he had.

Mr. Henschen: Fred Staten, insurance company vice president, father of an 11-year-old boy, from Rockville.

Mr. Landphair: Why would a child who in essence has everything turn to drugs in the suburbs?

Mr. Staten: Probably boredom and probably the need to identify with their peer groups. It's become a social stigma to children not to participate in this sort of thing.

Mr. Landphair: What do you tell your son about this problem then? Or haven't you yet had many discussions about it?

Mr. Staten: Not too many. He is getting a good fundamental education on drugs in school, I think. There are definite efforts being made. At this point I'm doing nothing other than hope.

Mr. Henschen: George Corbin, owner of an ice cream parlor, father of four, from Potomac.

Mr. Landphair: What are your thoughts as to some of the solutions or attacks that we can take to counter this drug scene?

Mr. Corbin: I think a harder line towards the parents of the kids. I think the parents should be made responsible for the children's actions. I think a stiffer penalty for pushing the hard drugs, by pushing I mean selling to minors. As far as the so-called soft drugs, I really don't know. I don't know that much about them.

(Background Music: "Heroin") Mr. Landphair: You've all heard the expression, "What can a mother do." Well, what **can** a suburban mother—or a father or a family—do, concretely, to keep the drug problem from being their problem?

(Music and lyrics of "How can I try to explain? When I do he turns away again, it's always been the same") Mr. Landphair: For one thing, ask the Metropolitan Washington Council of Governments about a publication called "Vibrations." It's a newsletter, published on and off because of a shortage of funds, that serves as a sort of monthly clearinghouse on drugs. You will be told that Vibrations is in short supply. The council prints only about 250. But if there is enough of a response, a way just might be found to print more. Most suburban families turn first to their physicians when a drug problem hits home, and the physician is scarcely better informed than the parent. A copy of Vibrations in every waiting room might improve that situation.

(Music and lyrics of "Teach Your Children Well") Mr. Landphair: You doubtless have an opinion on the need or lack of need for drug education in the schools, particularly at the elementary school levels. But do you know who is teaching what in your children's particular school? Drug education programs are popping up like spring flowers, with little direct evaluation from the public.

Music and lyrics..."Well we all need someone we can lean on") Mr. Landphair: Do you know what drug treatment facilities exist in your community? The Council of Governments can tell you. More to the point, do you know how these facilities are run and who is running them? Many suburban drug abusers I have talked with openly mock certain treatment directors and treatment programs and make a game of beating surveillance techniques like urinalysis. Public money—your money—supports most treatment agencies. Public review might improve their efforts.

(Background Music: "One pill makes you larger...") Mr. Landphair: In this series, suburban parents have been pilloried unceasingly for shortchanging the emotional needs of their youngsters. The old "ten dollars rather than ten minutes" argument has had full play. The message would seem to be that communication is a two-way process. That uptight, possession-conscious parents and bored or disillusioned offspring alike must relate on a human level, exposing hangups and honest emotion in the process. One concrete possibility: Some families are scheduling regular, free-swinging family rap sessions in which dialog replaces television and the evening paper.

(Music and lyrics..."God save the child, God save the child") Mr. Landphair: Ada Berg, mother of the boy who OD'd on drugs summed up the message of this series better than anyone:

Mrs. Berg: I was one of the smart alecky people too. Can't happen to me. But it did.

Mr. Landphair: The Bergs were one of suburbia's so-called "best of families." Now that Stanley Berg is dead, they are one of the wisest.

This is Ted Landphair, WMAL News.

# Chapter 4

## The Television Drama

The paradox of the television drama is that it may have reached its golden age in its infancy. In the 50s, there was hope that a new art form may have emerged; the one-hour and 90-minute TV dramas were neither one-act plays nor full-length legitimate theater productions, nor bore any relationship to motion picture productions. But "Studio One," "Playhouse 90," "Kraft Theater" were comparatively short-lived, and most of the television playwrights those programs spawned left for other fields. Sporadically, CBS revives a "Playhouse 90" production or NBC presents its Experimental Theater.

Yet the spate of drama continues unabated: situation comedies, westerns, anthologies, daily serials, motion pictures for television, etc. In a typical week, CBS presented 96 assorted dramas, from daily serials and reruns of situation comedies to original dramas and motion pictures. Multiply this by the other networks, independent stations and public television stations and the total number of programs requiring dramatic scripts is astronomical.

Good writers are constantly in demand, but we must emphasize **good**. The industry has as much run-of-the-mill type as it can handle and the beginning writer must not harbor the illusion that because there is so much mediocrity, any script he or she submits will be accepted. The exigencies of the marketplace are discussed in another chapter.

But why the avalanche of mediocrity? As in any creative endeavor, there are only a relatively few who have the spark of genius. The rest are adequate practitioners. The demands of the insatiable medium of television forsake quality for quantity. Often, the writer's well written script goes through so many changes by nonwriters that its original impact is lost. Too many times, the writer is low man on the drama pole, a necessary evil, whose poor handiwork must be molded by the director, the producer, the network executives and the sponsor. The fact is that when a dramatic series fails, it is almost always due to poor scripts, rarely to direction or acting.

The consistently excellent scripts for a program such as "All in the Family" can catapult comparatively unknown actors into great prominence. The inadequate scripts for "superstar" Shirley MacLain saw that series suffer an early demise. Yet the star system generally prevails and very few people among the millions of viewers can name the script writer of any dramatic series unless he is also in the unusual role of host, as, for example, Rod Serling and his "Night Gallery."

Professor David Boroff commented, "There is something about the elliptical, swift-paced style of television writing—the necessity to encompass a great deal in 50 minutes—which is inimical to the creation of genuine literature. The building blocks of literature are words, and imaginative, richly textured language is the most expendable thing of all on TV."

We agree with Boroff that the "Necessity to encompass a great deal in 50 minutes is inimical to the creation of genuine literature," but there have been television scripts and there will be scripts that are richly textured and imaginative. Perhaps they will come mostly from public television; surely the scripts for the "Six Wives of Henry VIII" and the beautiful narrative prose of Sir Kenneth Clark for the "Civilization" series are examples of "richly textured" writing. And Rod Serling's "Requiem for a Heavyweight" was an outstanding example of sensitive writing. What this implies is that the television writer faces the greatest challenge of all in attempting to create some form of literature against formidable obstacles. But it is possible.

In the ensuing sections of this chapter, guidelines are set forth. Basically, it is sound to have some principles to go by. As the writer develops, he may veer from those guidelines because the essence of creativity is the originality of approach. But some principles of drama stem from Aristotle and are as valid today as when he promulgated them. To begin with, let us examine the nature of one element of the drama .

## CONFLICT

There are three basic conflicts:

Man against man
Man against society
Man against nature

These conflicts may be subdivided infinitely. Man against man might provoke the eternal triangle: two lovers competing for a woman's favors. Or a domestic conflict: man against woman in a foundering marriage or man against man competing for a coveted executive position.

Man against society might be the draft card burner protesting involvement in a war; the rioters burning down a ghetto; the consumer advocate battling the giant corporation.

Man against nature might portray fortitude during a natural disaster or a struggle to climb a previously unconquerable mountain.

To build conflict within a play requires complications which lead to a series of crises and finally to a climax and resolution. The exigencies of writing a television drama necessitate precise planning, particularly under our current system of sponsorship. The hour TV drama might be likened to a 3- or 4-act play; the commercials act as curtains with the sponsor hoping, however, that the audience will find his intermission message as intriguing as the play, and sometimes this does happen.

The TV dramatist must write the play so that it reaches a crisis at the commercial break in order to pique the viewer's interest enough to remain with the program. Generally, the acts, so-called, of the TV drama should be of some comparable length. Some accurate timings, which may serve as guidelines for hour TV dramas, have run as follows: Teaser: 5:20; Act I: 13:45; Act II: 11:35; Act III: 10:10; Act IV: (The Resolution) 8:00. This adds up to a total of 48:50 which is typical for an "hour" sponsored drama. Notice the divergence between the teaser and the resolution and the body of the play. The three acts are roughly comparable, with the second and third acts somewhat briefer than the first. This is standard technique in television.

To pay for the great cost of scheduling motion pictures originally made for theater showings, or motion pictures made for television, the networks and individual stations find it necessary to saturate the time with commercials. The technique is to run the first part of the film at some length, enough to gain the interest of the viewers so that they are eager to see the rest of the film. As the motion picture progresses, the film segments become shorter and shorter and the commercials more numerous, with the announcer assuring us at several points that the station is merely pausing for identification which becomes some sort of euphemism for additional commercials.

There is a different approach for plays presented on public television. Since there are no commercial interruptions, a play moves to more natural crises in the sense that the drama does not have to conform to specific "curtain" scenes because of commercial breaks. In either case, complications or crises are essential to the development of conflict. A crisis may be defined as an obstacle that appears insurmountable.

### "The Andersonville Trial"

An example of a powerful conflict is portrayed in "The Andersonville Trial," originally written for the stage by Saul

Levitt and later adapted for presentation on public television. The drama is based on the actual trial of Captain Henry Wirz who was the commandant of the infamous confederate prison at Andersonville, Georgia. Forty thousand Union prisoners were packed into a filthy stockade; 14,000 of them died.

The indictment against Wirz charged him with criminal conspiracy to destroy the lives of soldiers of the United States in violation of the laws and customs of war. The prosecuting attorney was a lieutenant colonel representing the War Department; the attorney for the defense, a civilian lawyer from Baltimore.

As the trial progresses, witnesses who were former prisoners at Andersonville relate the horrors they faced; the blistering hot summers; the cold, freezing winters without adequate shelter or food; men dying at the rate of 70 a day; escapees pursued by ferocious dogs. And when the neighboring farmers offered to bring food to the prisoners, their offer was refused. Captain Wirz's defense was that he was acting under orders from his superior officer and that, as a soldier, he was trained to obey.

The prosecuting attorney raises the issue of morality versus obedience and finds himself—a military officer— bringing up the ominous question of whether an officer may disobey his military superior; a particularly touching point since it is a military tribunal which is judging the case. The issue is raised: Is a military superior also a moral superior?

Here then is the crux of the conflict. The parallel has been brought home to us vividly in our contemporary society by the My Lai incident.

The resolution of "The Andersonville Trial" is the conviction and sentencing to death of Captain Wirz, even though there appears to be evidence that the witnesses for the prosecution may have been exaggerating or even lying. Captain Wirz, in a final scene, pleads that he is a soldier and performed his duty as a soldier, but the sentence is invoked.

## PLOT STRUCTURE

Lawrence Langner in "The Play's The Thing" (G. P. Putnam & Sons) stated, "The kind of subject for which the play form is best suited is one in which there is a major situation or situations involving conflict between characters or groups of characters or between characters and their destiny which build in conflict, interest or intensity throughout the play to some sort of conclusion." Mr. Langner, of course, is speaking of the legitimate theater, but his observation is equally pertinent to the television play.

In structuring your plot, you must first consider the problem involved in your story. Is it universal? Is it unique? You have the two ends of the spectrum here. A universal problem should attract because it is familiar to the viewer. He may have faced the problem himself and so he is curious as to how the playwright will handle it. Or the plot may be unique, far removed from the ordinary man's life experience but intriguing to him: a spy drama, for example.

The familiar plot of star-crossed lovers—the Romeo and Juliet theme—has been repeated in different forms countless times. Shakespeare himself borrowed the plot from a narrative poem by Arthur Brooke, "The Tragical Historye of Romeus and Juliet." It was the basis for a highly successful musical on Broadway: "West Side Story." And it formed the plot for a 90-minute "made for TV" movie, under the title of "If Tomorrow Comes."

The writer of the television movie in searching for a background that would permit a contemporary retelling of the famous love story chose a very adaptable time period: immediately preceding and following Pearl Harbor day, December 7, 1941. His "Juliet" was the daughter of an American family that had just moved to California. His "Romeo" was the son of a Japanese farmer.

The Shakespearian plot was followed almost to the letter, except for one or two twists. It is "Juliet" who takes a walk in the neighborhood and comes upon the Japanese holding a celebration. She meets "Romeo" and they fall in love. They are both senior high school students. They confide their love to "Juliet's" neighbor, a spinster high school teacher who represents the nurse character. The three of them convince a minister (Friar Laurence) to marry them secretly. The couple are about to reveal their marriage to their parents when Pearl Harbor is bombed. The tranquil California city where Japanese emigrants and native Americans have lived together peacefully for years turns into a hotbed of suspicion and hate. The Japanese men are sent to relocation camps ...the American version of concentration camps.

The boy and girl cannot reveal their marriage now, particularly since the girl's father is incensed against the Japanese. And so the couple meet surreptitiously. But they are seen by a friend of the girl's brother who hastens to inform the brother of the lovers' rendezvous. The brother (Tybalt) and his friend hurry to surprise the lovers, but on the way they meet a friend of the Japanese boy. An argument ensues and the girl's brother fells the Japanese (Mercutio) with a baseball bat.

"Romeo" discovers his dead friend and then does battle with his brother-in-law who, during the fight, is hurled against a rock and is killed. "Romeo" is tried and acquitted, but the town is up in arms against him. He tells "Juliet" that he is leaving for Bakersfield to find a job and will come back for her. She tries to bring herself to tell her father of her marriage but, in a heated discussion about the current war situation, he warns his daughter that he would rather see her dead than consorting with a Japanese.

"Juliet" conceives the idea of shocking her father into realizing the tragedy his hatred can spawn. She leaves a note that she is going to commit suicide and prepares a trail of circumstantial evidence at the neighboring shore line. Then she proceeds to Bakersfield to look for her husband.

However, her young husband is on his way back home. When he returns, he immediately visits the school teacher's home which has been one of their rendezvous shelters. The teacher is in tears and informs him of his wife's suicide. The shock drives him to kill himself. In the closing scene, we see the girl returning home only to find that her loved one is dead.

Professor David Boroff in his commentary on "Television and the Problem Play" stated, "One of the more tenacious notions about our culture is that theater is 'serious' while television—the land of the fadeproof smile—offers mere entertainment." He goes on to say, "Since television is ubiquitous and immeasurably powerful, educators ought to pay attention even to the most trivial shows, for even triviality does not exclude attitudes and points of view. But there is another level of television program—the serious drama— which invites comparison with the theater."

"If Tomorrow Comes" was hardly a masterpiece of writing, but the choice of plot and the handling of the conflict does invite comparison with the theater.

## THEME

How important is it to have a theme in mind before beginning your play? The writer who feels impelled by social consciousness, by a drive to get a message across, will have a theme in mind: the poison of prejudice, the perils of pollution, the disaster of divorce, the anguish of abortion. But since the prime goal of television playwriting is entertainment, any message must be woven into the fabric of the plot. It cannot be overt because people dislike being preached at. But the aspiring playwright will want to express an opinion, to get an idea across to the viewer. It must be done subtly so that the audience is not aware of the message until the play is over.

Ray Bradbury, the famous author of many books and screenplays, related at a writers' symposium that he had once asked a cab driver whether he had seen anything good on TV lately. The driver said he really liked the "Twilight Zone" series and when Bradbury inquired why, the driver responded: "Because when it's over, it makes you think."

There are too few television dramas that make you think. The reason may have been honestly defined by an anonymous advertising executive who was quoted as saying that sponsors veered away from thoughtful dramas because there was a tendency on the part of the viewer to savor the play's message and not the sponsor's.

The probability is that most TV playwrights think solely in terms of situation rather than theme and if a theme should emerge, well and good. Their philosophy is, let the story intrigue you and the theme will take care of itself.

Perhaps the most lucid definition of theme was expressed by Lawrence Langner in "The Play's The Thing" (G. P. Putnam & Sons): "By 'theme,' I mean some illumination of life so that the audience does not take away with them upon leaving the theater merely the story of a group of characters but also an important comment on them or their behavior or a point of view or philosophy of living."

## CHARACTERIZATION

When you are planning your play, the ancient query about which came first, the chicken or the egg, may be applicable. For you may well ask yourself: which does come first, the situation or the character?

The answer is: either one. This is not to be ambiguous. The point is, if you are writing a murder mystery, the situation is paramount. If you are writing a play about a mother's relationship to her children, then character is the prime concern. Situation may be developed because of the protagonist's qualities or lack of them; or the realization of the protagonist's character may come about because of the situation he or she faces.

What is important is that within the scope of the play, we must have some insight into the character of the hero-heroine or antihero-heroine. Naturally, the hour or 90-minute drama will permit much more character development than the half-hour play. But it is interesting to observe how much can be said in so little time.

A basic principle is to know your character thoroughly. If you do not, you will not be able to project his or her image believably. There is an exercise we have given to our students which we have found very helpful in developing a major character: write a brief biography of your protagonist, not more than two double-spaced pages. But in that short space, you should prove to yourself that you know your protagonist. Where was he or she born? How well or poorly educated? What about economic status? Relationship with parents, friends, men, women? Hangups?

Ask yourself what makes your characters act as they do. Why do they have their specific problems? Are they responsible for their actions or are outward forces compelling their responses? Professor Alvin B. Kernan ("Character and Conflict"; Harcourt Brace Jovanovich, Inc.) tells us that "characters are a dramatist's primary images of human nature; they are his statements in speech and gestures about the elusive creature, man."

There are several steps the playwright can take to effect realistic characterization:

1. **Outward appearance**: The playwright describes the physical appearance of the characters, particularly any unusual physical bearing or markings. The type of clothes they wear may also be indicative of a time period, an age group or a cult.

2. **Movement**: Do they move about lethargically or animatedly? Do they gesture exuberantly or lackadaisically?

3. **Emotional reactions**: Quick to anger or controlled response? Cool in the face of danger or flustered?

4. **Speech**: Speech idiosyncrasies; regionalisms; verbosity or taciturnity. Straightforward responses or circumlocutions.

5. **Through the dialog of other characters**: People in your play discussing the protagonist. The problem with this device is that, realistically, people's prejudices color their opinion of other people and so their appraisal may be suspect. Still, this is an ancient and honorable technique, used by playwrights through the ages.

6. **Through the character's thoughts**: Contemporary TV drama generally avoids thought sequences. The monolog in which the character expressed his innermost feelings or the use of asides was a favorite device of the Elizabethan playwrights. The technique was revived with telling effect by Eugene O'Neill in "Strange Interlude." Occasionally, a television playwright will use the device: for example, we see the character staring into space or contemplating a letter or a portrait and we hear his voice, usually filtered, expressing his thoughts.

## EMPATHY AND SYMPATHY

In the well written play, the viewer will identify with the protagonist, will suffer his pangs, enjoy his triumphs, shed a tear when the heroine cries, smile or laugh at her comic antics. Empathy must embody sympathy. If your audience is indifferent to your protagonist, it will probably tune to another channel or fall asleep.

The unsophisticated audience may accept a protagonist who is a shining example of good and has no evil qualities or a villain with no redeeming features. But sophisticated viewers will reject such characterizations and rightly so because humans are multidimensional. One-dimensional individuals are apt to be boring.

## MOTIVATION

Professor Kernan defines a motive as "the force that moves a person to seek the satisfaction of some need." It is this driving force that compels your character to the satisfaction of elemental needs or the fulfilling of esthetic desires. A hungry man may be driven to steal; a heroin addict to murder; a businessman to go into debt for a luxury he cannot afford.

Playwrights must be able to plumb the innermost emotions of their characters, and know why they are impelled to act as they do. The concept that behavior is motivated is as ancient as philosophy itself. But it is only recently that psychologists have given the study of motivation scientific status. Playwrights have tended to side with the philosophers, but today the playwright should study psychology because it is the psychologists who are attempting to explain human drives.

Professor Floyd L. Ruch ("Psychology and Life"; Scott, Foresman and Company) tells us that "Motivated behavior depends not upon a single stimulus but rather upon a complex pattern of stimuli even when a single stimulus triggers the response. Thus, motivation varies greatly on different occasions and among different individuals." As Professor Ruch illustrates this theory, a young man as a soldier may awaken in the morning very hungry but with the knowledge that he is to stand inspection before breakfast. He will be motivated primarily by the necessity to be ready for the inspection and inhibit the hunger drive. That same young man at home, awaking hungry, will immediately act to satisfy the drive.

In this author's previous volume ("Television and Radio Writing"; Houghton Mifflin), we stated that there are certain basic drives which affect all of us: physical drives, such as hunger, thirst, sex, and physical needs such as shelter and clothing. There also are the social drives of love, hate, fear, anxiety, ambition, pride. Whereas the physical drives are more or less universal, social drives will vary with environment. Changing mores affect our outlook. The generation that lived through the Great Depression of the 30s was motivated by a drive for security. When the youth of that day grew to middle age, many of them were obsessed by the drive for material wealth. Conversely, many of their offspring spurned the goal of affluence; a hippie society arose, communes sprang up. When that generation reaches its middle years, what will its motivations be? Romantic love and marriage appear to be outdated conventions to many young people. Chastity seems to have been transformed from a virtue into a vice. Writers, more than anyone, have to have a penetrating perception of contemporary mores because the bulk of their writing will be on contemporary themes.

## DIALOG

Dialog is basic to the drama. In the theater of the absurd, dialog may be minimal but so is comprehension. Max Wylie, in his latest volume on "Writing for Television" (Cowles), put it caustically but aptly: If something isn't understood in television, it's tuned out. If something isn't understood in the theater, it's celebrated."

Unless they are writing for the experimental programs that the networks rarely present, television writers must always bear in mind thay they are reaching a mass audience. Hopefully, the mentality level of the television audience is higher than that generally accorded it by critics of the medium. Still, any play that is to reach millions of viewers must contain dialog that is readily comprehensible. There is no time for the viewer to stop to contemplate abstruse dialog. This is not to imply that television playwrights cannot express ideas; on the contrary, they are continually dealing with ideas. It is all a matter of how clearly they define their concepts.

There may be a tendency on the part of students to espouse reality and have their characters presumably tell it like it is. All well and good. But the pitfalls of dullness must be avoided. The dialog we hear in daily contacts is often too full of routine formalities: "How are you?" "Fine, how are you?" "Looks like it's going to rain." "Yeah, if the clouds don't break up." "Haven't seen you in a while." "Yeah, haven't seen you either." Realistic but tedious.

Dialog, particularly in the television play, where time is of the essence, should be pithy and must be relevant. Keep amenities to a bare minimum. Viewers realize that people normally exchange meaningless greetings and they will forgive you for eliminating them; more than that, they will thank you for not boring them.

Dialog should perform a dual function: inform; arouse emotion. Your characters' conversation should contain information and move the story. After you have written a scene or an entire play, check the dialog. See what happens if you eliminate a line here and there. Is the meaning still clear? If so, the chances are the dialog is unnecessary.

This does not mean that you are going to get down to bare bones. You may have humorous lines which create enjoyment for the viewer. They may not seem essential to the movement of the play, but they may add to characterization. Therefore, that particular dialog would have significance.

A writer once defined fiction as friction. The point is well taken. To maintain interest, there should be friction in your dialog. The dialog of disagreement, if you will. No one is more apathetic than a yes man. When you write your dialog, see that it expresses differing viewpoints. Let there be a duel of words; emotions ripping emotions. Even with a star like James Stewart and a very knowledgeable producer like Hal Kanter, the "Jimmy Stewart Show" suffered from deadly dull dialog. The shock of interchange was rarely ever ignited.

Again we underscore the necessity for the beginning writer to watch TV plays critically, to observe where the dialog crackles and where it fizzles. Try to analyze why the one is good while the other is poor.

From the excellent television play, "To All My Friends On Shore" by Allan Sloane, we have chosen three examples of effective dialog.

1. Dialog as characterization (an insight into the character of the father):

After a moment, the door opens again, and VANDY reenters. He goes over to his mother's bedroom door.

| | |
|---|---|
| VANDY | Mamma? |
| SERENA (voice OC) | Yes? |
| VANDY | Sumpin' I forgot. |
| SERENA (voice OC) | What is it? |
| VANDY | They havin' the last church picnic tomorrow. |

After a moment, the door opens. SERENA is buttoning the blouse of a nurse's-aide uniform.

VANDY          Can I go? It only cost five dollars for the whole trip.

SERENA         You ask your daddy.

VANDY          No, you ask him.

SERENA         Why can't you?

VANDY          He always says no to me.

SERENA catches the boy as he is about to take off.

SERENA         Now that's not so.

VANDY          Well it seems like. Every since he got the idea of that old house.

SERENA         That house is your daddy's dream.

VANDY          Dreams is for sleepin'.

2. Dialog of conflict:

TEMPO          Oh, that's all right. I'm takin' the kids to Playland. How's about Vandy comin' along?

VANDY looks to his father, then to his mother.

SERENA         Ask your daddy.

TEMPO          Be no bother, Blue. Love to have him.

VANDY          We goin' in the Cadillac?

TEMPO          All the way and back again!
               What do you say, Blue?

BLUE           Well...there's work to be doin'
               on the house—

TEMPO          Aw, you can't work all the time.
               Matter of fact, why don't you come on along.

               (a beat)

               We could talk, Blue.

BLUE           No...no, I got things to do.

               (a beat)

96

                    And I was figurin' on Vandy helping.

TEMPO               Oh sure. Well, catch you next time, Vandy.

VANDY is about to cry. The door closes on TEMPO.
VANDY turns to BLUE and cries—

VANDY               I hate you!

SERENA grabs him and urges him toward and out the
door.

SERENA              Go on, Vandy—catch 'em!

VANDY roars out the door. SERENA slams it behind him,
and as BLUE speaks, goes to the table. She grabs a pencil
and an envelope and starts writing on it in big letters.

BLUE                Why'd you do that? It's a waste of money—and
                    he always gets sick on them trips!

SERENA              Money ain't good, money ain't bad; it's what you
                    do with it. Fun for a kid's no waste.

She looks up from her writing, burning angry.

                    There's something you left out of your system of
                    livin' out of envelopes, Blue. You and your whole
                    life all wrapped up inside of an envelope!

She proffers the envelope to him. He brushes it aside.

BLUE                I got all my dreams in that envelope!

SERENA              And no room in it for Vandy and me.

She literally slaps the envelope into his hand and we can
see what she has printed on it in big block letters. It says
START LIVING NOW.

                    It's a long time since you put anything in this
                    one, and you better start. Or you move in, when
                    you do move, alone.

BLUE looks at it and at her. Suddenly, loud rock music
breaks out off camera. BLUE, in frustration, goes over to
the wall and bangs on it.

BLUE
(yelling)           Turn it down, turn it down!

                                              DISSOLVE

3. Dialog that expresses the theme of the play:

He opens the gate and they start up the walk. BLUE climbs the steps and sits down at the top. VANDY stays at the bottom. BLUE beckons toward him, until VANDY reaches a step where his head is on a level with BLUE's and BLUE holds him between his knees.

BLUE          Vandy—

VANDY         Daddy, I don't want to talk about this old house.

BLUE          (he pushes the kid's face in affectionately)

That's my line! 'Cause I don't either. I want to talk about people. Three kinds of people.

He lifts the boy up and sits him down next to him. For a moment, the urge to hang on to the child is strong—and he holds him. He all but chokes on the next line.

BLUE          You—you're gettin' strong!

VANDY         **What** kind of people?

BLUE          Well—yesterday, today, and tomorrow people. Now yesterday people—**my** daddy was one of them.

(he imitates his father)

Oh, you can talk about your cars—but ridin' the wagon home from the harvestin', them was the days.

(drops the imitation)

And then, when he come up from the country, and we kids was all workin'—

(he imitates)

"Oh, you don't know what a dollar is till you chop cotton in the sun. For me, a nickel was a great big deal!"

Now that was your grandpa. Everything was better yesterday. Now **your** daddy—

VANDY         That's you.

BLUE          That's me. What kind of people you think I am?

VANDY         Mamma says you one of the crazy kind.

BLUE          She's right. 'Cause I am crazy enough to do my living in some tomorrow some day.

|   |   |
|---|---|
| | (a pause) |
| BLUE | I am a tomorrow people. Always on tomorrow. Some day. |
| | (a pause) |
| | Dreams in an envelope—my life in this house. |
| (quietly) | Gardens, chickens, workshop, schemin' and dreamin', cravin' and savin'—no more, Vandy. No more. |

VANDY looks at him. He reaches out and takes his father's hand.

|   |   |
|---|---|
| VANDY | No more what, Daddy? |
| BLUE | There is going to be no nice front porch **tomorrow**, and there is going to be no banty hens, and no workshop—there is going to be no more bein' so afraid—living in the spirit of fear for someday, instead of love for now, where everything is. |

He takes the boy's hand.

> We are all going to be today people, you and Mamma and me.
> Because that is all there is to grab in your hands right now. That is all I can take in my hand today. Everything else is nothing. All that is is what I can take in my hand today.

And he places his other hand over VANDY's.

> This is all there is. **Now** is all we got.

We should add, as a footnote, that "To All My Friends On Shore" is actually a vehicle which deals with the dread ethnic disease, sickle cell anemia. But while it portrays Vandy, the boy, as a victim of the disease, and there are hospital scenes showing how doctors cope with it, Allan Sloane has woven a highly sympathetic story about a father whose dream is to have a home of his own and take his family out of the ghetto. We are wrapped up in this basic story so that the play does not become an obvious preachment for action to conquer an incapacitating disease. "To All My Friends On Shore" is, after all, a drama, not a documentary.

## TEASER

Competition for the viewer has led to use of the device known as a teaser. As its name implies, the teaser's function is to entice the audience to want to see more of the program. Since the audience has its multiple choice of channels by a simple switch of a dial, it is extremely important for the play to gain immediate attention.

The teaser may be chronological in that it is the opening of the drama or it may be taken from the body of the play. In this teaser sequence from an episode in the "Medical Center" series, "Circle of Power" written by Alvin Boretz, the central conflict is foreshadowed:

FADE IN:

INT. WAITING ROOM OUTSIDE SURGERY
PAVILION—DAY                                                1

CLOSE ON SIGN reading: "Surgery Pavilion—No Admittance."

CAMERA PULLS BACK and ESTABLISHES the isolated pools of waiting RELATIVES and FRIENDS. A NURSE emerges from behind the pavilion doors and respectful looks follow her as she crosses and goes out. An OLDER WOMAN rises and crosses to window, staring out. Her THIRTYISH SON follows her, puts his arm around her shoulder and speaks softly to her.

GANNON enters from a main corridor and strides across the Waiting Room. He appears intent on some irritating errand. As a doctor, the looks cast his way are both anxious and deferential.

INT. SURGICAL CORRIDOR—DAY                                  2

As Gannon enters, he moves purposively down the corridor, past O.R. doors, behind which several operations are in progress. A FEW STUDENTS pass into a gallery entrance...a DOCTOR hurries into a Scrub Room.

NURSING STATION                                            3

as Gannon comes up to it...

GANNON          Doctor Benson still in surgery?

NURSE ADAMS     Yes, Doctor.

GANNON          When did they begin?

NURSE ADAMS     About fifteen minutes ago.

He glances impatiently at his watch.

GANNON          Tell her I'd like to see her, please. The moment she's free.

NURSE ADAMS   I'll tell her, Doctor Gannon.

He turns away abruptly and CAMERA FOLLOWS him down the corridor. As he passes an O.R., he decides to stop and look in through the door. Should he go in? He is deciding. Then, he turns and goes toward the exit doors.

INT. WAITING ROOM—DAY                                    4

As he emerges into it: Absorbed, he fails to glance at the people. But then...the old woman whom we had seen being comforted by her son, looks up to see him.

MRS. BRODY       Doctor Gannon?

He stops and turns to see who has called. Now, he crosses to her.

GANNON           Hi.

MRS. BRODY       You remember me. Mrs. Brody?

GANNON           Of course. Nice to see you again. Now don't look so worried. I'm sure everything's going well.

MRS. BRODY       He's not a young man any more, Doctor.

GANNON           Hardly anyone is any more. But you know that Mr. Brody has one of the best surgeons around.

MRS. BRODY       I had such confidence in **you.**

GANNON           Thanks. I appreciate that. But will you feel better if I tell you Doctor Sangford was one of **my** teachers?

MRS. BRODY       Thank you, Doctor.
(reassured)

INT. OPERATING ROOM—CLOSE—DR. RALPH SANGFORD—DAY                                      5

CAMERA PULLS BACK with below to establish the team.

Expecting Sangford to be the primary surgeon, we are in for a surprise for we see that DR. CARRIE BENSON is wielding the scalpel and that Sangford is assisting.

SANGFORD         How's it look now?

CARRIE           Seems clean, Doctor Sangford.

SANGFORD         Make sure.

A slight beat, then...

CARRIE          Fine.

SANGFORD        Let's be on our way then.

She appears ready to step back for him.

SANGFORD        No, no...you finish up. Watch that small
                bleeder...

He holds the clamp...

                                                    CUT TO:

INT. SURGERY CORRIDOR—DAY                        6

Sangford comes out with Carrie from O.R.

SANGFORD        Carrie, that was a first class job.
                Very nice, indeed.

CARRIE          Thank you, Doctor Sangford.

SANGFORD        I'd better go see Mrs. Brody

Sangford walks off. Carrie is about to start off when an
INTERN who has stepped out of O.R. walks up to her.

INTERN          Hey, Carrie—what gives?

CARRIE          What do you mean?

INTERN          The maestro claims you're a great assistant, but
                more and more it's you who's playing the
                number one scalpel man.

CARRIE          He always gives me a good road map.

INTERN          Yep. Sangford gives you everything but the
                credit.

He walks off as she is about to make an angry defense of
Sangford.

                                                    CUT TO:

INT. THE WAITING ROOM—WITH SANGFORD—DAY 7

He enters and the Brody family turns to him. We see
clearly now. He is sixty, strong in appearance,
distinguished. A man of quality.

SANGFORD        No problem at all, Mrs. Brody. He came through
                it like a bull.

MRS. BRODY      He'll be all right?

102

| SANGFORD | It's customary to say a few weeks of recuperation and he'll be good as new. I'm afraid I can't improve on that. |
| --- | --- |
| MRS. BRODY | Everybody said you were the best doctor here. And they were right. |
| SANGFORD | I see you've been talking to my friends. Will you excuse me, Mrs. Brody? I have to see to another patient. |
| MRS. BRODY | Thank you, Doctor...for saving him. |

He pats her shoulder and crosses back to the pavilion doors.

INT. SURGICAL CORRIDOR—DAY                    8

As he enters: He goes quickly to a door...pushes it open.

INT. LOCKER ROOM—DAY                    9

It is empty. The moment he is inside, and having made sure no one is present, he sinks slowly onto a stool. He holds out his hands, stares at them.

CLOSEUP—HIS HANDS                    10

They are trembling as he opens and closes them. A perceptible twitching of the small muscles can be seen.

CAMERA GOES TO his face as he stares down at them...a sickening awareness that something is wrong with him... no longer concealed.

                    FADE OUT.

## FLASHBACK

It is sometimes essential in a drama to re-create a scene of the past. The device for doing so is called the flashback and is generally a method of exposition. However, it presents a dichotomy of approach since it is both abnormal and normal. Abnormal in the sense that we cannot physically go back in time and yet a flashback in a drama does just that. Normal in the sense that we possess memory and can recall incidents that have occurred to us day, weeks, or months ago.

The camera may be used effectively in preparing the viewer for a flashback by the method of defocusing. Since it is normal for us to see a clear picture, it is abnormal to see the picture suddenly going out of focus and, in the viewer's mind, it means something out of the ordinary is occurring. If you use a defocus to begin the flashback, it should also be used to return to the chronological action.

Matching dissolves are also employed to effect the transition into time past. For example, a woman returns to her hometown after an absence of many years. She visits her birthplace; it is old, shingles have come off the roof, a window pane is cracked, the unpainted clapboard looks ancient. As she stands staring at the old house, there is a dissolve to the same home, spanking new.

It is possible to write your drama using a series of flashbacks, but most plays are written chronologically. If you do use the flashback, it should be fairly brief; otherwise, the viewer begins to accept the scene as current action and returning to the actual, forward thrust of your play will prove a wrench to your audience.

In his TV play, "Sit Down, Shut Up or Get Out," Allan Sloane used a series of flashbacks to portray the character of his youthful protagonist. His device was to use dialog to prepare the listener for the flashback sequence.

BOLTON          I mean to say—I.Q.-wise, he relates to my subjects in the top grouping.

                      (he taps his head)

                      Plenty schoolhouse upstairs. But one big mouth. That's the main problem. Take this morning in math.

SCENE TWENTY-TWO: MATH CLASS:

Chris at desk. Chris is reading a book. BOLTON voice continues over.

BOLTON         My rule is, when you finish your assignment, you
(voice OC)     put your pencil down across your work and wait. But not Chris.

BOLTON comes into frame and takes the book away, glances at it and puts it into his pocket.

CHRIS           Hey—that's mine!

BOLTON         You can come back after class and get it.

                      (he scans Chris's work)

                      How'd you finish so fast?

CHRIS           It was easy. I factored up there and I combined
(indicating)    terms down there—

| | |
|---|---|
| BOLTON | You can't do that— |
| CHRIS | Well it checked, so it has to be right— |
| BOLTON | But you didn't follow process— |
| CHRIS | I know, but I figured— |
| BOLTON | Simmer down. I see what you've done—but you can't do it that way. |
| CHRIS | Why not? |
| BOLTON | A, you haven't learned that procedure yet— |
| CHRIS (getting upset) | But I **figured**— |
| BOLTON | And **B**—there are two ways to do things in this class. My way—and the wrong way. |
| CHRIS | But I got the right answer! |
| BOLTON | My way—and the wrong way. |

CHRIS stands up. BOLTON pushes him down firmly, speaking reasonably.

| | |
|---|---|
| BOLTON | Chris, I'm trying to teach **process**—**method**—not just answers. Process, method, structure, logic, math is the gateway to logical thinking! |

and he leans over and proceeds to work out the problem in his way as—

| | |
|---|---|
| CHRIS (voice OC filter) | If process is supposed to be the way to get correct answers, and if I get the right answer with my process—why can't I use my process? Isn't that only logical? |

SCENE TWENTY-THREE: "COURTROOM"

| | |
|---|---|
| BOLTON | Now let's take science. Today was the blow that killed father— |

The line, "Take this morning in math," is the preparatory device. With Bolton's voice off camera, we maintain the continuity of the transition and carry the viewer back into time smoothly. The same device of using dialog off camera is used to return us to the current action.

**ADAPTATIONS**

Many dramas produced for television anthologies are adaptations, much in the same manner as motion pictures are often based on novels and plays. Most adaptations are taken from already successful vehicles: a best selling novel, a hit play, a musical, or a short story in a mass circulation magazine. On the surface, it would appear that adaptations provide a simple task for the writer. However, many years ago when Paddy Chayefsky was concentrating his talents in television, he remarked that he tried to avoid adaptations. He was always torn between his own creative impulses and a desire to maintain the integrity of the original work. Therefore, he always preferred to do his own thing, as it were.

This brings up the question of how much liberty the adaptor can take. There is no defined limit. Some adaptors follow the original story line faithfully: others leave practically only the title intact.

Of course, it is simpler to translate a legitimate stage play into a TV drama than a novel or short story. The play is already presented in a totally visual medium and is entirely written in dialog. Such an adaptation may require merely judicious editing. Most stage plays today are written in two acts with a major crisis at the end of Act One and reach a climax towards the close of Act Two. Adapted to an hour or an hour and a half on TV, there may be anywhere from four to six commercials so that the adaptor finds he needs to develop three to five crises for curtain scenes. Also, the TV play almost always opens with a teaser. The writer can lift a teaser sequence right out of the body of the play, or perhaps the very opening scene lends itself to a teaser; otherwise, he will have to add one.

Another problem the adaptor faces is that many plays, for reasons of economy, are written with all the action taking place in one setting. This is very acceptable on the stage, but it makes for a static presentation on TV. Therefore, the adaptor has to manipulate the action to occur in several different settings. The reverse is generally true in adapting novels. In the print medium, there is no problem of physical settings. A novelist can have action take place, literally, at a hundred different locations. In this case, the adaptor has to be able to compress the locales; otherwise, even with the tremendous flexibility of the camera, costs would be astronomical.

Again, in stage plays, the casts are comparatively small, although musicals do require large casts, and stage plays are held to some sort of time limit, usually two hours. But in novels, the number of characters are limitless, and page lengths may run anywhere from a hundred to a thousand, so they present challenges in either compression or expansion. Additionally, some novels may be written with an abundance of prose and a minimum of dialog so that the process of adaptation is indeed a difficult one.

Then there is always the inexorable time element of the broadcast media. This author was on assignment to write adaptations for NBC's "Great Novels" series and it was indeed a feat to compress a 250-page book into a half-hour or hour time slot. It requires very careful reading, an analysis of the plot structure and the characterizations, and a decision as to whether plot changes are essential for transference to the visual medium. It has always been our method to hew to the major plot line. There would seem to be little point in undertaking an adaptation if you are going to wind up with an original story of your own.

Adaptations are usually written on assignment; they are not vehicles for free-lance writers to try to market on speculation. First of all, a contemporary story will require obtaining rights and few writers will assign such rights on a speculative basis. Books in the public domain are available to anyone and you are probably wasting your efforts to try to market such adaptations, plus the danger of having some production agency deciding to do its own version against which you would probably have no recourse. However, if you are a student at a university which has its own radio or TV station or are on the staff of a commercial or noncommercial TV station, the possibility may arise for you to write an adaptation of a public domain book of your choice.

### "The Last of the Mohicans"

The British Broadcasting Corporation (BBC) has produced many excellent adaptations of classic novels; including a series based on Galsworthy's "The Forsyte Saga," Dostoevski's "The Possessed," Stella Gibbon's "Cold Comfort Farm," and more recently a series devoted to the famous American classic by James Fenimore Cooper, "The Last of the Mohicans."

The BBC has been kind enough to let us have one of the "Mohican" scripts. In this instance, the writer, Harry Green, did not have to face the problem of trying to compress a long novel into one hour or 90 minutes. With the commendable policy of the BBC to give full scope to these adaptations, "The Last of the Mohicans" was dramatized in eight episodes. This enabled the writer to follow the course of the novel rather faithfully and to give the viewer a full-bodied production. Also, since the BBC is noncommercial, the hour-long episodes were just that. In the United States, "The Last of the Mohicans" was presented on public television stations so that the series was shown in its entirety.

We cannot assume that every one of our readers has read the Cooper classic, so we will very sketchily outline the involved plot. It deals with the trials and tribulations of Cora and Alice Munro who have come from England to join their father, Colonel Munro, Commandant of beleaguered Fort William Henry. The time is 1757, during the French and Indian wars. The girls are escorted by Major Duncan Heyward, but their Indian guide, a Huron named Magua, proves treacherous. The girls and the major are captured by the Hurons and a number of hair-raising incidents occur as their rescue is attempted by a frontier scout known as Hawkeye, his Indian friend, Chingachgook, and the Indian's son, Uncas, the last of the Mohicans. The story ends on both a tragic and happy note. Cora must accompany Magua to be his wife as the price for the release of the others. Uncas trails Magua and is killed in trying to rescue Cora. Magua, in turn, is killed by Hawkeye, but Cora is slain by the Hurons before she can be rescued. Alice, however, arrives safely; Major Duncan and she are in love. Hawkeye returns to the forest to remain with his friend, Chingachgook.

In Episode 7 of the dramatization, we are, of course, reaching the climax of the story. The episode opens with a scene of Hawkeye and Chingachgook planning to rescue the captives. Although the writer has followed the plot line rather faithfully, he has also inserted some of his own philosophy.

2. INT. SMALL HURON CABIN. NIGHT.

UNCAS bound to a stake. MAGUA enters, very sombre. He looks at UNCAS, then away again.

UNCAS: A cloud darkens the brow of Magua. There is no more joy in his heart that I am soon to die?

MAGUA: (LOW, SADLY) Tonight the Great Spirit came to Magua in a dream. He showed me the days past of the red men—in the land which He gave to them as He has made it, covered with trees and filled with game. Then the tribes of His children were happy. The wind made their clearings; the sun and rain ripened their fruits, and the snows came to tell them to be thankful. If the Great Spirit gave them different tongues, it was that all animals might understand them. If they fought among themselves, it was to prove that they were men. In that time the red men were happy.

UNCAS: Why speak to me of things gone? Does not the egg become the worm—the worm a fly—and perish? Why tell me of good that is past?

MAGUA: The days of your race are short, Mohican. Do you not care that the days of all the red men may be short?

UNCAS: Magua talks in riddles.

MAGUA: In the dream Magua saw more through the eyes of the Great Spirit. He saw the days to come of the red men. And what he saw made his heart sick with shame.

UNCAS: What did Magua see?

MAGUA: The white men, sick with their gluttony, their arms enclosing the lands and goods of the red men, from the shores of the salt water to the islands of the great lake. The white men, more plentiful than the leaves on the trees, with their black slaves. All this Magua saw. But of the red men he saw only their shadow in the still waters. (PAUSE) This need not come to pass, Mohican. As I watched there came to my ears a roaring as of a great wind. It was the voices of our dead fathers of all the ages, calling on me to gather all the warriors of the red men. "Drive out the white dogs!" they cried. "Turn the salt lake into a sea of blood—the blood of a million palefaces."

UNCAS: If there be truth in Magua's dream, hatred of the white man will not change it.

MAGUA: What would the brave Mohican do?

UNCAS: Only in friendship with his white brothers is there hope for the red man.

MAGUA: (SNEERING) Fool! It is well you die. The false tongues and the cunning of the white men have already destroyed you.

The writer has also taken liberties with the rescue sequence. In the book, Hawkeye disguises himself in a bearskin. It is the type of costume worn by Indian conjurers and so he is undetected. Hawkeye enters the tent where the captives are bound and frees them. Also, in Cooper's narrative, Hawkeye battles with Magua, the Huron, and subdues him in order to effect the rescue. Harry Green, however, has preferred his own version of the action. There is no disguise in the rescue scene. The action is much more gripping in the dramatization.

69. LOW CU UNCAS. AS HE LOOKS L., PAN TO CS WALL.

7. INT. SMALL HURON CABIN. NIGHT.

UNCAS BOUND TO STAKE. EXT. SOUNDS TO BE HEARD, BUT MUTED. UNCAS IS SUDDENLY ALERT. LOOKS TOWARDS BACK WALL.

70. CS WALL PAN L. & ZOOM OUT TO 35 DEGREES. 2S. CHING. PROFILE— HAWKEYE.

8. EXT. BACK OF CABIN. NIGHT.

HAWKEYE AND CHINGACHGOOK CROUCHED AGAINST THE BACK WALL, WHICH IS OF BARK ON TIMBER FRAME. CHINGACHGOOK IS SCRATCHING THE BARK AS A SIGNAL. HAWKEYE WATCHES ALL ROUND.

71. CU UNCAS LOOKING L. HE LOOKS R.

72. LOW 2S. HURON BRAVES GUARDING DOOR.

INTERCUT FOLLOWING WITH INT. OF HUT AS APPROPRIATE.

| | |
|---|---|
| 73. 2S. CHING. CUTTING, HAWKEYE. AS CHING. GOES THROUGH, CUT: | CHINGACHGOOK TAKES OUT A KNIFE AND CUTS AWAY AT BARK TILL THERE IS AN OPENING BIG ENOUGH FOR HIM TO LOOK THROUGH. HE DOES SO. |
| 74. MS CHING. COMING THRU WALL. | |
| | 9. INT. SMALL HURON CABIN. NIGHT. |
| | GRAMS. BIRD NOISE & VILLAGE. |
| ....PAN HIM R. & ZOOM OUT TO C2S.<br><br>CHING. — UNCAS<br><br>THEY FREEZE | UNCAS AT THE STAKE. CHINGACHGOOK CUTS HIS BONDS. WHEN UNCAS IS FREE HE MANIPULATES HIS MUSCLES TO GET THE BLOOD RUNNING. AS HE DOES SO, CHINGACHGOOK, HAVING WIDENED THE OPENING, COMES THROUGH LIKE A SNAKE. THEN HAWKEYE PUTS IN HIS ARM WITH A KNIFE IN THE HAND. |
| 75. THEY LISTEN, AND ARE SATISFIED | CHINGACHGOOK GIVES ONE KNIFE TO UNCAS AND IN DUMB SHOW TELLS HIM TO GET BACK INTO HIS BOUND POSITION. CHINGACHGOOK TAKES A STANDING POSITION NEAR THE DOOR. HE NODS TO UNCAS. |
| 76. CHING. RELEASING UNCAS.<br><br>SEE CHING. GIVE KNIFE TO UNCAS, WHISPER & EXIT R. | |
| | UNCAS: (LOUD) The Huron warriors are brave, when the enemy is bound. |
| TRACK IN TO LOW MCU UNCAS | |
| | INTERCUT THE FOLLOWING WITH EXT. OF CABIN |
| | Let Uncas be bound, and the Hurons may safely spit in his face. |
| 77. CU HURON (RH BRAVE) REACTION | THE HURONS DON'T LIKE THIS AT ALL. |

111

| | |
|---|---|
| **78. CU UNCAS** | But let Uncas be free...and the Hurons will run like hinds. They will run like Reed-That-Bends. Uncas saw him run. He would not face Uncas. The Hurons forget Reed-That-Bends. He is dead and his name forgotten. But the Mochicans do not forget. Uncas does not forget that he ran before Uncas. The Huron cannot face Uncas. |
| **79. C2S. HURON'S REACTION** | |

| | |
|---|---|
| **81. SEE RH HURON ENTER HUT** | ONE OF THE HURON GUARDS IS GOADED AT LAST. HE COMES IN WITH TOMAHAWK IN HAND. NOT QUITE READY TO STRIKE BUT LONGING TO. |

| | |
|---|---|
| **82. (AS HE ENTERS) C2S. UNCAS L. FG, HURON COMING FWD.** | THE OTHER GUARD LOOKS IN. UNCAS ADDRESSES THE TOMAHAWK MAN. Greeting,  Reed-That-Bends! |
| **SEE UNCAS TURN & STAB & AS HURON FALLS, SEE 2ND HURON ENTER BG. AS HE STEPS FWD:** | THE TOMAHAWK COMES UP, AND UNCAS GOES FOR THE UNDERBELLY WITH HIS KNIFE. THE OTHER GUARD LEAPS IN. CHINGACHGOOK KNIFES HIM. HE DIES INSTANTLY. |
| **83. HIGH 3S. UNCAS—HAWKEYE—CHING EN-TERING FROM R. FG. AS HE STABS, SEE HURON FALL TO R.** | THE FIRST GUARD, CRUMBLING, GROANS. CHINGACHGOOK STRIKES HIM MORTALLY. CHINGACHGOOK: That was badly done. My son should know how to bring death silently. |
| **84. AS HURON CS FALLS) HURON L, GROANING. PAN UP TO MCU CHING. AS HE KNEELS & STABS** | UNCAS SAYS NOTHING. Tonight, my son, we have fresh scalps at our belts. |
| **85. LOW 2S. UNCAS FAV—CHING. R. FG. LET THEM GO L.** | |
| **86. HIGH 2S. DEAD HURONS, NOT SEEING HEADS. PAN UP TO LOW 2S. HURON (JAMES), MAGUA TRACK IN TO LOW MCU MAGUA** | 11. INT. HURON CABIN. NIGHT. MAGUA LOOKS DOWN AT THE DEAD HURON GUARDS. MAGUA: Their scalps have not long been taken. Two more in the woods are dead. Four scalps in all hang at their belts. |

For those of their brothers who have died, the Huron will be avenged! Go — summon all the warriors!

In order to more explicitly illustrate a method of adaptation, we are reproducing a passage from Cooper's book and its transference to the television screen. You will notice that, where he can, the writer has used the precise dialog from the novel. First, Cooper:

"Would the Yengees send their women as spies? Did not the Huron chief say he took women in the battle?"

"He told no lie. The Yengees have sent out their scouts. They have been in my wigwams, but they found there no one to say welcome. Then they fled to the Delawares—for, say they, the Delawares are our friends; their minds are turned from their Canada father!"

This insinuation was a home thrust, and one that in a more advanced state of society would have entitled Magua to the reputation of a skillful diplomat. The recent defection of the tribe had, as they well knew themselves, subjected the Delawares to much reproach among their French allies; and they were now made to feel that their future actions were to be regarded with jealousy and distrust. There was no deep insight into causes and effects necessary to foresee that such a situation of things was likely to prove highly prejudicial to their future movements. Their distant villages, their hunting grounds, and hundreds of their women and children, together with a material part of their physical force, were actually within the limits of the French territory. Accordingly, this alarming annunciation was received, as Magua intended, with manifest disapprobation, if not with alarm.

"Let my father look in my face," said Le Coeur-dur; "he will see no change. It is true, my young men did not go out on the warpath; they had dreams for not doing so. But they love and venerate the great white chief."

"Will he think so when he hears that his greatest enemy is fed in the camp of his children? When he is told a bloody Yengee smokes at your fire? That the paleface who has slain so many of his friends goes in and out among the Delawares? Go! my great Canada father is not a fool!"

"Where is the Yengee that the Delawares fear?" returned the other. "Who has slain my young men? Who is the mortal enemy of my Great Father?"

"La Longue Carabine."

The Delaware warriors started at the well-known name, betraying, by their amazement, that they now learnt, for the first time, one so famous among the Indian allies of France was within their power.

"What does my brother mean?" demanded Le Coeur-dur, in a tone that, by its wonder, far exceeded the usual apathy of his race.

"A Huron never lies!" returned Magua coldly, leaning his head against the side of the lodge, and drawing his slight robe across his tawny breast. "Let the Delawares count their prisoners; they will find one whose skin is neither red nor pale."

Now Green's dramatization:

DELAWARE CHIEF: Would the Yengees send their women as spies?

MAGUA: The minds of the Delawares are turned from their Canada father.

DELAWARE CHIEF: Let the Canada father look me in the face. He will see no change. My young men did not go on the warpath—they had dreams which said 'Do not go.' But they love and venerate the paleface chief, Montcalm.

157. LOW MCU MAGUA

MAGUA: He is not a fool. What will he think when he hears that his greatest enemy is fed in the camp of his children. When he is told a Yengee smokes at your fires. That a paleface that has killed so many of his friends, goes in and out among the Delawares. No, my great Canada Father, is not a fool.

158. PROFILE MCU CHIEF & BRAVES BG.

DELAWARE CHIEF: Who is this that a Delaware may fear?

159. CU MAGUA
160. MCU CHIEF REACT.

MAGUA: La Longue Carabine! A Huron never lies!

# Chapter 5
# The Series Plays

A staple of television fare is the drama series, including situation comedies, westerns, science fiction, adventure, crime, and soap opera. Its progenitor was conceived in the very early days of motion picture production when on Saturday mornings youngsters would queue up at the local movie house in eager anticipation of seeing the current episode of that silent thriller "The Perils of Pauline." Radio abounded in series dramas and it was natural for the visual medium to follow the trends of its predecessor.

The series plays differ from anthologies. The series plays establish a set of characters about whom the plot revolves each week or each day, whereas anthologies present a different play with new characters each program. Some of the series plays enjoy extremely long runs and reruns. In checking through our previous book on television and radio writing, which was published in 1958, we noted that several of the series plays we analyzed, "I Love Lucy," "Gunsmoke," and "Dragnet," are still very much to be seen at this writing. However, the majority of the series plays we discussed at the time have long since disappeared from the airwaves. But the formulas remain the same, year after year, except that television has become somewhat more emboldened in scheduling a series such as "All in the Family." There is also emphasis on the recognition of minority groups in the presentation of such programs as "Julia" and "Sanford and Son." Other series plays, including "I Spy" and "Mission: Impossible," have brought stardom in highly sympathetic roles to Bill Cosby and Gregg Morris.

There is no question but that the elimination of the stereotype is beneficial. With the tremendous influence of television, the continual sight of a minority group actor in subservient positions could perpetuate an unfavorable image. The temper of the times has changed radically since the advent of television. "Amos 'n' Andy," a phenomenal success on radio, was a failure on TV. "The Rise of the Goldbergs," even though Gertrude Berg insisted that she used an intonation rather than dialect, would probably not have succeeded in a transference to the small screen. Still, the placement of a minority character in a very favorable situation, sans dialect, does not insure success. Witness the "Julia" and the Bill Cosby situation comedy series. However, "Sanford and Son," at this writing, appears to be drawing a substantial audience.

### "Marcus Welby, M.D."

One of the most popular of the weekly series plays is "Marcus Welby, M.D." on the ABC network. With all due respect to its fine cast, headed by Robert Young, the primary reason for the success of this series is its consistently good scripts. We believe one of the outstanding scripts in the series is "In My Father's House" by Charles A. McDaniel. There is an interesting footnote to this script. McDaniel felt that his first draft was by far the best "Marcus Welby" script he had written. It deals with a highly controversial subject: how far should a doctor go in maintaining life when the patient's survival means an incurable "vegetable" existence?

As is almost always the case, particularly when a network is intent on reaching a vast audience, controversy is devoutly avoided. And so, undoubtedly with much head shaking and finger crossing, the script was rewritten.

This matter of rewriting poses a problem for television writers. They do not control their manuscript in the same manner as the playwright for the stage. Once they have fulfilled their obligation of writing the script and turning it in to the producer, they no longer have any control of the material. Further decisions about script changes are made by the director, the producer, and network officials. In only rare instances can television writers insist on the integrity of their scripts and win their points. Again, the stage playwright stays with the production until it is fully launched. TV writers are generally deep into other script assignments and, therefore, find little time for pleading their case even if they were invited to be present at rehearsals or rewrite sessions. Nevertheless, "In My Father's House" carries a great deal more impact than the usual run of series of plays and we are happy to reproduce the following excerpts.

The play opens with the traditional device of the teaser and immediately develops the situation: the problem father and his relation to his children. The curtain scene precipitates a family crisis.

FADE IN

EXT. SAN DIEGO—DAY—SERIES OF SHOTS—STOCK

Enough to establish the city, then:

INT. A BALLET SCHOOL—DAY—SHOOTING PAST DANCERS AT THE BARRE TO ELLEN.

As a ballet teacher, Ellen, attractive, early thirties, and dressed in a severe, businesslike leotard is very much in command of her three ten-year-old dancers. There is the sound of adagio piano music (Mozart 12 German Dances K.586) coming from a record player in BG.

ELLEN                    Plie'...and up. Glissade—assemble' Rib cage, Gloria. Stretch the back.

She moves over to the child and straightens her as the music continues. The kids are doing well enough—Ellen is a good teacher—but we'll get a sense of dissatisfaction from here, nonetheless. The music and ballet terms continue over as we:

CUT TO

INT. DOOR TO THE CLASSROOM—DAY—TWO SHOT— KILEY AND MIKE KILEY

Kiley has his helmet in his hand; Mike Kiley, his younger brother, has a small suitcase; it's obvious they've just entered. They stand watching for a moment and smiling.

ANGLE—ELLEN

She sees them at the door, smiles and crosses over to the record player, shutting it off.

ELLEN                    That's it for today. Wednesday at three we'll start floor work.

The kids applaud (a ballet tradition at the end of a class) and then dash for the door. We hold and pan with Ellen as she crosses over, following the kids, and embraces Mike.

ELLEN                    Mike—oh, Mike....

MIKE                     Hi, big sister.

ELLEN                    How did you two—

KILEY                    I came on down from L.A. and picked him up at the airport.

ELLEN                    My brother the doctor—

(to Mike)                My brother the physicist—

MIKE                     Well, not quite yet. How's it going here?

**117**

| ELLEN | (hesitates, then with a shrug of truth) |
| | You saw my beginners' class...all three of 'em. |
| KILEY | We'll worry about it later. |
| ELLEN | That's the best time. |
| KILEY | We've got ourselves an idea for Dad's birthday party. |

There's a beginning chill in Ellen's reaction.

| ELLEN | He's having a birthday party? |
| MIKE | He is now. We're going to throw him a real blast. |
| | (aware of her displeasure) |
| | What's the matter? He'll enjoy himself. |
| ELLEN | Who were you planning on inviting? |
| MIKE | All his friends. |

As she starts shaking her head:

| KILEY | What is it, Ellen? |
| ELLEN | Since you got him to AA, he's been sober. That's three months now and it hasn't been easy on him; or, frankly, on me. Most of his 'friends' are old drinking buddies. I just don't think it's fair to tempt him that much. |
| KILEY | I think she's right, Mike. |

Mike gives a "whatever's fair" shrug.

| KILEY | So we'll make it dinner out for him then—just family. |
| ELLEN | All right. Family. Family and Herb. |
| MIKE | Herb? |
| KILEY | She's going to get married again. |
| MIKE | Hey, that's wild—why didn't you write— |
| ELLEN | Because it's not signed and sealed yet. Herb's met Dad, but I haven't told him anything about...the problem. |
| KILEY | Then a birthday dinner seems a good time to let 'em get together, doesn't it? |

118

Ellen nods and we:

INT. SAN DIEGO RESTAURANT—NIGHT—CLOSE SHOT—PANNING A BIRTHDAY CAKE INSCRIBED "HAPPY BIRTHDAY DAD"

We pan with the cake as a waiter carries it to the table. As the cake is set down, we pull back to:

GROUP SHOT—FAVORING DAN KILEY—NIGHT

It would be an indulgence to describe Dan as anything other than the stock Irishman. However, there is a difference about him in that he is sober; a fact which, we'll feel, still astonishes him. In the group are the three Kiley children, plus Herb Bayliss, a quiet, steady type who is most attentive to Ellen. By now they have finished the song and there are ad-lib cries of "Speech, speech," etc. Dan rises and acknowledges the greetings. He has a glass of apple juice in his hand:

DAN                 I thank you. Thank you. You'll say to yourself that it's an odd thing indeed for an Irishman to be celebratin' his birthday with apple juice—

(breaks off, a mock bow to his youngest, Mike)

—beggin' your pardon, Mike—even **organic** apple juice...

(reprising)          Yes, indeed...it's an odd thing...you'll say it to yourself 'cause I'm sayin' it to myself.

They laugh, and then Dan gets serious for a beat.

DAN                 But it's a good thing. I know you won't believe it, but I'm grateful for it....

Now, as Dan continues, we begin to notice a slight slurring of his words—a hesitancy; the "apple juice" bit becomes increasingly suspect, so that his family begin to exchange uneasy glances (Ellen's future may be riding on the impression Dan makes on her intended—Herb Bayliss).

DAN                 (makes a small toasting gesture mainly toward Kiley and Ellen)

You helped me and I...thank you.

(now to Herb)       And to you...Herb...I'll make my toast as I under...understand you might be joinin' this family.

Herb reacts, smiling it off; Ellen could have done without the remark quite nicely, thank you.

DAN    May the wind be forever at...at your back, Herb boy. And may...may the Devil not only lose your ad—address....

Again, briefly, he hesitates, stumbling over the word.

REACTION SHOTS—KILEY—MIKE—ELLEN

as his sons react concerned; Ellen with growing suspicion.

DAN    But may you be a half hour...in Heaven before the man knows...you're dead.

He drops his glass and falls forward onto the table.

REACTION SHOT—ELLEN

filled with angry disappointment.

ELLEN    He's drunk.

ANGLE FAVORING KILEY

He glances sharply at his sister, then moves quickly to his father. With eyelid and pulse he makes a fast examination. Mike stands over him, staring down at his father in puzzled concern.

MIKE    How could he be?

Kiley looks up, his face grave.

KILEY    He's not drunk. I think he's had a stroke.

On their shocked reactions—Mike's, Herb's—and Ellen's; she may not believe it—we:

FADE OUT

Act One deals largely with the treatment given to Dan Kiley for the stroke he suffered. At Steve Kiley's insistence, Dr. Kingman, a noted neurologist, is called in. Steve also wants his father transferred from the local hospital to Lang Memorial, even though the expense may be more than he is able to bear. He is determined to do everything he can for his father. In this scene, just before the conclusion of Act One, Steve is discussing the situation with his father:

KILEY    You miss the drinking?

| | |
|---|---|
| DAN | Like I miss my left arm. |
| KILEY | We can do something about that. You'll use that arm again. We're going to move you up to Lang Memorial and we're going to see to it. |
| DAN | Lang Memorial, is it? |
| KILEY | That's right. |

A change of tone: the bantering is gone.

| | |
|---|---|
| DAN | Are you that afraid of my dying? |
| KILEY | Who said anything about your dying? |
| DAN | You didn't, but you should have—don't you know that patients listen very hard to what a doctor doesn't say? |
| KILEY | Dad—you've had a stroke. A mild one. You've got some stiffness in the left side of your body which is completely normal after what's happened. But we can fix that. Dad—you're going to be fine. |
| DAN (not convinced) | Then why Lang Memorial? |
| KILEY | Because it's got Kingman and he's the best. |
| DAN | Ummm—and just why do you need the best? |
| KILEY | Because you're my father. |
| DAN | Come on, boy...what kind of father was I to you? As I remember it I took you to only one baseball game in my whole life. And then I got drunk on the beer and you had to help me home in the fifth inning. What kind of father is that? |
| KILEY | The only one I had. |
| DAN | It's a shame you didn't have a choice. |
| KILEY | I never wanted one. |

A dissatisfied sound; Dan doesn't believe him at all.

| | |
|---|---|
| DAN | The day you get me to believing that is the day I'll start calling you 'Saint Steven.' Son, I was never very responsible for you...so you're not responsible for me. Now I've been in the V.A. hospital before—dryin' out, I grant you—but they're good people and I'm sure they've got |

|       |                                                                                           |
|-------|-------------------------------------------------------------------------------------------|
|       | everything there that they've got at your Lang Memorial.                                   |
| KILEY | I'm sure they do, but they don't have Doctor Kingman. He's the man I want for you, and he's the man you're going to get. |
| DAN   | For all the money it's going to cost? Steve—you don't owe me that.                         |
| KILEY | It's not a case of owing. You're my father and I'm going to do the best I can for you.     |

Dan is touched, but he covers it with a disapproving glare, as we

FADE OUT

END ACT ONE

In Act Two, we have a very perceptive sequence as Dr. Welby enters Dan Kiley's room and the two men, who have played so important a part in Steve Kiley's life, meet for the first time.

INT. DAN KILEY'S HOSPITAL ROOM—DAY—TWO SHOT—DAN—WELBY

Welby has just entered. Dan looks up to him—just a bit apprehensive. These two men have heard a great deal about one another but they have never met before. So this first moment of meeting is important to each of them.

|                   |                                                                    |
|-------------------|--------------------------------------------------------------------|
| WELBY             | Mr. Kiley...I'm Doctor Welby.                                       |
| DAN (nods)        | I think I'd've known.                                               |
| WELBY (warmly)    | And you look like Steve's father—there's a family resemblance.     |
|                   | (a pause as he glances at chart, then)                             |
|                   | I hope you got some sleep on the way up.                           |
| DAN               | Too much. I'm wide awake now and there's nothin' to do.            |
| WELBY             | You'll be busy enough when we start to work.                        |
| DAN               | Steve said something about a physiotherapy thing. What is that exactly? |
| WELBY             | Massage, exercises, maybe some whirlpool baths—whatever Dr. Kingman decides. |

122

| | |
|---|---|
| DAN | Kingman—who is he mad at all the time? |
| WELBY | Nobody. It's just the way he is. |
| DAN | He'd make a terrible Irishman. |
| | (Welby laughs) |
| DAN | This is a very fancy room you got me in. |
| WELBY | It's a very nice hospital. |
| DAN | I've got an idea what these things cost a day. |
| WELBY | You're not to worry about that. |
| DAN | I don't want the boy payin' for it. I wanted him to take me to the V.A. and he wouldn't do it. |
| WELBY | Then he made a decision and we'll have to respect him for it. |

Another pause. Dan looks at Welby almost defiantly, then he softens.

| | |
|---|---|
| DAN | I was resenting you. I apologize for it. |
| WELBY | Resenting? |
| DAN (nods) | When Steve came down to San Diego he'd talk about you. 'Course there were a lotta times I wasn't in the kind of shape to remember much of it—but enough got through. Marc Welby's teachin' me this, Marc Welby's showin' me that...he'd go on and on. I'd get to thinkin'...what did I every teach or show my boy. And it wasn't much. |
| WELBY | Why do it to yourself, Mr. Kiley? It doesn't accomplish anything. |
| DAN | No, I know it doesn't. But I just wanted you to know how I felt...and how silly I feel now for feelin' it. |
| WELBY | I don't think you were resenting me. It was probably just a case of not being very happy with yourself. |
| | (beat) |
| DAN | No drunk is happy with himself—if he were, he wouldn't need the drink. Glorious stuff that it is... |
| | (directly to Welby) |
| | You were more of a father to my son than I ever was. Instead of resenting you for it—for whatever reason—I should have appreciated it. |

| WELBY | Mr. Kiley—none of that matters. Your son became a doctor, and a good one. That's something to be proud of. |
| --- | --- |
| DAN | But I didn't help him do it. I never gave him a dime toward medical school. His sister helped him—the rest he did on his own. He's not a doctor because of me. And now look what he's done...this room, this care and all the money he'll be spendin'... |
| WELBY | And you think you don't deserve it. |
| DAN | Do you think I do? |

The words are hard, but Welby, playing against them, is being very gentle with him.

| WELBY | All right. Let's say that I don't think you do. Let's say that I concur with your own opinion of yourself...that you were a bad father, that you never did anything for your son—that what he's doing for you now is the right thing only for the wrong reasons: Guilt as opposed to love. Let's say that I think he's being very foolish indeed to bear the financial, not to mention the emotional, burden of your care after what you've done to him. Just for argument, let's say I believed all of that. What could I possibly do about it? |
| --- | --- |
| DAN | You could tell him to stop. |
| WELBY | By what right? I'm not family. |
| DAN | You're more family to him than I am, man. You're more father to him than I ever was! |
| WELBY | Okay, let's accept that argument, too. As a member of the family—I will not advise him to do any differently than he's doing now. |

Dan starts to protest, but Welby stops him with a gesture.

| WELBY | A few months ago Steve learned to accept an alcoholic as a human being with a disease. Instead of something to be ashamed of—and he was ashamed—but he learned better; and when he did, he went down to San Diego, he talked to you. Perhaps it was for the first time, but he talked to you not as son to father, certainly not as doctor to patient, but man to man. The result of that talk was that you went to AA. Steve didn't take you there by the hand; you went yourself. You got sober and you stayed sober. Steve respected you for that. |
| --- | --- |

| DAN | A few months sober doesn't make up for 40 years drunk. |
|---|---|
| WELBY | Steve thinks it does—if he even thinks in those terms, which I doubt. There are a lot of good doctors around, but unfortunately, not that many good men. Your son is a good man—whether you accept it or not—you had a part in making him so. And whether you like it or not, he's going to see to it that you're very well cared for. |

There is a pause as Dan thinks this through; then, very quietly, as camera begins to move in closer on the two men:

| DAN | Have you ever been to an Irish wake? |
|---|---|
| WELBY | As a matter of fact, I have. |
| DAN | They make for quite a party. The kind I'd like to have for myself. |
| WELBY | There's no reason to start planning for it right now, Dan. |
| DAN | You're sure of that? |
| WELBY | Sure? No, I'm not sure. Nobody is in this business. All I know is that with treatment, there's a very good chance of your walking out of here—perhaps not completely recovered, that will take a long time; but with improvement. Huge improvement. |

Dan nods, believing him. The camera is very close on them now, over:

| DAN | I want to live as much as the next man—maybe more. These last months sober have shown me just what a man can do if he wants to bad enough. I'd like to keep on tryin'. But I'm not afraid of death. The Irish aren't, generally—they accept it. That's why they have such riotous wakes. What I am afraid of is being alive without bein' able to live. Layin' here in a bed with just your heart beatin'—that's life, but it's not living. I don't want that. I'd rather be dead and have the wake than that. It'd be a whole hell of a lot more fun. Do you understand me? |
|---|---|
| WELBY | Of course I do. |
| DAN | Good. Good.... |

Later when Steve returns for his vigil in his father's room, he is shocked as his father suffers a second massive stroke. This is the big crisis that rings down the curtain on Act Two.

In Act Three, Dr. Kingman, the neurologist, gives his frank estimate of Dan Kiley's condition to Steve.

KINGMAN        I'm sorry, Steve. It's a massive bilateral CVA. The condition is inoperable.

KILEY          I'm aware of that, Doctor.

KINGMAN        I want you to be.

WELBY          I don't think Steve's looking for any miracles.

KINGMAN        Good. Because there aren't any.

KILEY          But there is a survival rate, Doctor. Even after a second episode like this—even with an EEG like this.

KINGMAN        Yes, there's a survival rate.

KILEY          What is it exactly?

KINGMAN        To survive—a little less than two percent. To recover—a lot less than one percent.

KILEY          But it happens.

KINGMAN        It happens.

There is another beat, and for a moment Kiley loses his professional restraint.

KILEY          Only right now my father is very little more than a vegetable being kept alive by a machine.

WELBY          Steve—

KILEY          It's all right, Marc. It's a reality I have to face; I might as well use the real words.

(to Kingman)    I've heard you speak on this subject before —I know your views: As physician of record, if I tell you to use your best professional judgment, you're going to turn that machine off.

KINGMAN        I didn't say that.

KILEY          Doctor—I don't want you to turn off that machine.

| | |
|---|---|
| KINGMAN | I understand your personal feeling, Steve. But I also remember that when you attended my lectures, you were a pretty good student. You have to know that we're simply not at a decision-making point yet as to whether or not that respirator should be turned off. |
| WELBY | You'll give him time to challenge the respirator. |
| KINGMAN | Of course we will. He may start spontaneous breathing any time. But even if he doesn't for awhile, we still may not be at a decision point. It'll depend on the EEG and other criteria. |
| KILEY | We're not going to get to decision time. I want my father kept alive. |
| WELBY | By whose definition of life, Steve? Yours or his? What does he mean by being alive? Have you ever discussed it? |

Despite the gloomy prognosis, Steve is determined to keep his father alive. Expenses are mounting tremendously and he is forced to obtain a bank loan. His brother, Mike, gives up his studies at M.I.T. to take a job and help pay the bills. Steve decides to talk things over with his sister, Ellen, in San Diego.

| | |
|---|---|
| ELLEN | Steve, you asked me to think about it and I did. I'm not going back to Los Angeles with you. |
| KILEY | You sound like you don't even want to. |
| ELLEN | That's right, I don't. |
| KILEY | Okay. Why? |
| ELLEN | Very feminine, practical reasons: This is my home, my work; this is where my children are...and this is where my man is. There's a good chance that Herb and I are going to be married. My children need that—I need it. I'm not going to do anything to jeopardize it. But you want me to go up there, sit by Dad's bedside and play the dutiful daughter. Well, I don't feel very dutiful. |
| KILEY | Did he treat you that badly? |
| ELLEN | Yes, as a matter of fact, he did. But I told you I was being practical, so that's not even the main reason. You're a doctor, Steve. Give me the mathematics—what are his chances, not of being cured, but just of regaining consciousness again. What are they? |

(Kiley looks away from her)

He could lie there, just like he is now for years—couldn't he?

KILEY       We don't know yet.

ELLEN       I don't believe it, Steve. Because you don't believe it.

KILEY       Let's hear a little bit more about how badly you were treated.

ELLEN       Teary stories about a woman alone trying to raise two children, who has to share the same house with a drunk? You've got a pretty good imagination, so I'll spare you the details...the same way you spared 'em for yourself.

KILEY       I spared what for my—what are you talking about?

She looks away from him, softening a bit.

ELLEN       Something I was responsible for in a lot of ways, so I shouldn't be attacking you for it. I'm sorry.

KILEY       I still want to know what you mean.

ELLEN       Those times when you'd come home from medical school, I wanted to make it as easy as I could for you. And you knew I was doing it. We both did. It was as if we'd made a pact with one another—a silent and unsigned thing—we both agreed our father didn't exist, or if he did, he was not a problem. Remember all the times we didn't speak of him? Even when he was right there in the house, sleeping one off? We kept our pact very well because we were ashamed, not only of

KILEY       All right. I was ashamed, I'll admit it. And now I've got a chance to make it up to him and I'm going to do it.

ELLEN       No. You can't make it up to him; you're trying to make it up to yourself. It's nice to tell yourself you're going into debt and giving up what you're giving up out of love—but you're not. You're doing it out of guilt, and it's wrong.

KILEY       Ellen...I love my father.

ELLEN       Well, believe it or not, so do I. I've seen more of him. The good and the bad. But I don't love him

|       |                                                                 |
|-------|-----------------------------------------------------------------|
|       | to the exclusion of my children, or my chances of knowing a real home again. |
| KILEY | That's pretty selfish, isn't it?                                |
| ELLEI | All right, it's selfish. But name me something more selfish than guilt! |

Kiley stands and looks at her for a moment. There's a temptation to fling bitter words...but what's the use? Two years, or even two days ago, he might have slammed back; but he's learning, he's growing—and on its deepest level, that's really what this whole thing is all about. He simply nods to his sister in recognition of the fact that there is nothing significant to say; then he turns and exits.

Mike, on his part, tries to force Dr. Welby into a decision concerning his father's living death.

|       |                                                                 |
|-------|-----------------------------------------------------------------|
| MIKE  | Let me put it this way: Say you didn't know me—or Steve, but you had a patient in Dad's condition. What would you tell his family? |
| WELBY | Mike—please....                                                 |
| MIKE  | Wouldn't you tell them that there was no hope and the decent—the merciful—thing would be to just let him go? |

Welby takes a long beat.

|       |                                                                 |
|-------|-----------------------------------------------------------------|
| WELBY | Yes, I would.                                                   |
| MIKE  | Then why don't you tell that to Steve?                          |
| WELBY | I can't. I'm neither your father's doctor nor a member of your family. I haven't the right. |
| MIKE  | Doctor Welby, in a way, I feel closer to you than I do my own father. I know Steve does. You're family. |
|       | (beat)                                                          |
|       | So as long as that would be your decision, then there's nobody who has more of a right to speak to Steve. And you do really believe it, don't you? |
| WELBY | Yes, I do.                                                      |

We push in and hold close on Welby..."Let thy haste commend thy duty." And:

FADE OUT

END OF ACT THREE

In Act Four, Steve Kiley returns to Lang Memorial. He is still adamant about keeping his father alive. He confronts Dr. Kingman.

TIGHT SHOT—OSCILLOSCOPE

A softly wavering line seems to rest across the center of the scope—but every now and again a very faint impulse is seen to break the pattern.

KILEY (OC)      There's electrical activity there. Something is going on in his brain.

ANGLE—OVER KILEY TO KINGMAN

Again, Kingman is as gentle as we'll ever see him.

KINGMAN      Not very much, I'm afraid.

KILEY      But something.

KINGMAN      Something.

KILEY      He's a man alive, and I want him kept that way.

He turns and exits, crossing Welby.

TIGHT TWO SHOT—WELBY AND MIKE

Welby watches Kiley off then turns back to Mike. There is no nod or sense of agreement between them. None is needed.

CUT TO

EXT. THE ESPLANADE ALONG SANTA MONICA'S OCEAN PARK—DAY—TRACKING TWO SHOT— WELBY AND KILEY

We see them first at a great distance, then slowly zoom in to hold them as they take, at a deliberate pace, a very long walk indeed.

WELBY      This is a better place to talk than Lang Memorial.

KILEY      Yeah, I guess so.

WELBY      Your sister coming up?

KILEY      Not right now. She thinks I'm being very selfish.

WELBY      Don't resent her for it, Steve.

KILEY      It's Ellen's idea that what I'm doing for Dad I'm doing out of guilt, not out of love.

| | |
|---|---|
| WELBY | That could hardly have been a new idea to you. |
| KILEY | No. |
| WELBY | So you're aware now of a certain ambivalence in what you feel. |
| KILEY (nodding) | I took a very strong position: keep my father alive at all costs. Now I have to question that. I don't want to question it—there are other people involved—yourself, Mike, Ellen— |
| WELBY | Forget the other people, Steve.<br>The questions you have to ask of yourself are **for** yourself. No matter what you decide to do about your father, and I mean that literally—no matter what— in the course of making that decision you're going to learn an awful lot about Steve Kiley. |
| KILEY | I'd like to try getting very impersonal for awhile...scientific. |
| WELBY | All right. |
| KILEY | There's a patient, victim of a massive, bilateral CVA. That patient is as near death as a human being can be, and yet he's still alive. And for all realistic purposes, his chances of recovery just don't exist. Is that a fair evaluation of the case? |
| WELBY | It is. |
| KILEY | All right then, as a doctor, keeping in mind his condition, and all the other 'practical' things...would you let him go? |
| WELBY | Yes, Steve, I would.<br><br>(on Kiley's reaction)<br><br>But that's not really how you think of it. In your mind it's not 'letting him go'—it's ending his life. You're trying to be impersonal and you're not making it. I'm glad you're not making it—if you could remain impersonal, I'd worry about you.<br><br>(beat)<br><br>You're a doctor and you know as well as I do, the concept of taking a life—doesn't enter into this. What we're talking about is a legitimate procedure whereby doctors occasionally, when forced by medical criteria, allow the patient the dignity of his own death. |

**131**

| KILEY | Who are we to control death? |
|---|---|
| WELBY | The same doctors who, when we deliver a baby, control life. |
| (looks at Kiley) | All you have to decide is whether or not you authorize Bill Kingman—your father's doctor—to use his professional judgment. |
| | (Kiley is silent) |
| | About five years before I met you, I used to play golf quite regularly with a man named Bob Burroughs. We were good friends. I was his doctor. One night—it was very late—his wife, Carol, called me and said that he'd had a heart attack. I arranged for the ambulance to be sent and I met it at the hospital. Bobby's heart had stopped beating. It was a classic case for the use of heroic measures, and I used them. Thumper, respirator, direct cardiac injection—all of it. And it worked, Bobby's heart started beating again. Then I checked with the ambulance crew and discovered that for a period of some nine minutes, his heart hadn't beaten— |
| KILEY | Nine minutes!—his brain damage would have been— |
| WELBY | Steve, for all...realistic purposes—Bobby didn't have a brain any more. He'd been dead. I went back into the room, there was the resident on emergency, three nurses and myself. We reviewed the medical criteria—pupils were fixed and dilated—his respiration and blood pressure were being maintained by artificial means. He was areflexive, and he had a flat EEG...I told them to turn off the machines. |
| | (beat) |
| | And when I had to go and tell Carol what I had done—and why. And she thanked me. |
| KILEY | And that made you feel you'd done the right thing. |
| WELBY | It cost me a lot of sleep before I realized there was no right nor wrong. I'd simply done the only thing there was to do. |

There is a pause with Kiley thinking as they walk along.

| KILEY | You think I should let my father go, don't you, Marc? |

WELBY          Yes, Steve. I do.

A moment of silence, then:

                And Steve, no matter what you decide, don't
                think that it's over. Five days, six months 12
                years, from now—you're going to have to make
                other decisions—because you're a doctor...and
                they don't get any easier. Granted they won't be
                about your own family, but they may be about
                people close to you—as Bob Burroughs was to
                me. I think I'll leave you alone for now.

KILEY          Thanks.

                (a grave nod)

No heroic exit; Welby simply smiles a bit and leaves. We
push in and hold on Kiley as he thinks, and thinks...and thinks.
thinks.

                                                FADE OUT

                  END OF ACT FOUR

                      EPILOGUE

FADE IN

EXT. CEMETERY—DAY—FULL SHOT—ANGLE ON A
GRAVESITE—GROUP

The graveside service for Dan Kiley is over. There are the
pallbearers—old drinking cronies of Dan's, we may assume,
and a few elderly ladies decked out in their best bonnets;
they're chatting together in little groups, while the priest says
a few last words to the members of the family, Ellen, Steve
and Mike Kiley. Welby and Consuelo stand to one side, a little
apart from the others. As they start to walk away from the
gravesite, Ellen and Mike move after them, but Kiley remains
behind at the grave.

ANOTHER ANGLE

as Ellen and Mike catch up with Welby and Consuelo.

ELLEN          You'll have time to come back to the house for a
                drink, won't you?

WELBY          (a smile, remembering Dan's words)

                The Irish wake?

ELLEN          Something like that, I guess.

MIKE           Well, I'm not going to see the old man out with
                apple juice. I don't think he'd approve.

**133**

CONSUELO        I don't either

Mike glances back at his brother:

MIKE            I'd better wait for Steve.

CONSUELO        He'll be along.

She takes his arm, and they walk on toward the limousines, in BG, but Welby nods to Mike 'he's going back for Steve.' He starts back toward gravesite, where Kiley now stands alone.

MED. CLOSE—KILEY, WELBY—AT GRAVESITE

The other mourners have begun to disperse in BG, the two men are alone at the grave. They stand in silence for a moment, then:

WELBY           Ellen's asked us to go back to the house...want to
(quietly)       drive with me, Steve?

KILEY           Thanks.

                (beat, then)

                I was thinking about Kingman. When I went to him, he said...the same things you did...about there not being any right or wrong. In the two years I studied with him, I never heard him talk like that. He came across as a very—human—man.

WELBY           He is.

Kiley thinks about this for a moment, absorbing the fact, then Welby puts a gentle hand on his arm—

WELBY           Come along, Steve....We're going to do what your dad would've wanted—We're going to hoist one to Dan Kiley.

Kiley takes a breath—then nods. They turn and walk away together—

                                    FADE OUT


    The strength of McDaniel's script is in tackling an extremely touchy subject and carrying it through. There is no miraculous, sudden cure, no "happy ending" to placate the audience. Instead, it leaves the viewer contemplating the very meaning of humaneness.

All of the components of the script have been integrated into the main story line. We observe the relationship of the father to his three children and the effect of his stroke upon them: Steve plunging into debt to give his father the best of care, Mike having to sidetrack his education and possibly negating his future; Ellen, who has played mother to her parent, and is now demanding the right to pursue her happiness. These elements lead to the building of sympathy, or, if not sympathy, understanding of the children's plight. If Dan Kiley remains to vegetate, it is not he who will suffer but his children. In making his point McDaniel gathered all the forces in his play to justify his resolution: not as a preachment but within the dramatic structure.

## SITUATION COMEDY

Probably the most unexpected situation comedy success is "All in the Family." It was hardly anticipated that an anti-hero, a self-proclaimed bigot named Archie Bunker, would win the plaudits, or at least attentive viewing, of a large segment of the American television audience. The fact is the networks shied away from scheduling the program series for many years even though its predecessor in Great Britian had attained a remarkable success. The networks generally prefer to play it safe with new versions of tried favorites.

Yet there is a stirring among both intellectuals and blue-collar workers to repudiate Archie Bunker. John Slawson, writing in the **Educational Broadcasting Review** (April 1972), is opposed to the Archie Bunker concept. "Of course the ethnic digs made by Archie Bunker are funny," he admits, "and of course the millions of viewers laugh. However, these derogatory thrusts, enjoyable as they seem, do not sublimate prejudicial impulses toward the 'other' group and thus help relieve suppressed hostility toward it. As a matter of fact, there is every indication that the laughter is a sadistic response, vocally expressed, and symptomatic of submerged hostile attitudes. The laughter is a response to ridicule of an ethnic group. The viewers are not laughing at Archie, but at what this 'almost lovable' man is saying."

Slawson goes on to contemplate that "It is conceivable that the producers of "All in the Family" were of the opinion that bigotry might be dealt a severe blow through satire. However, effective satire would require holding up to censure the bigotry of Archie Bunker by means of ridicule, derision and irony. I fear it is, instead, the member of the ethnic group who is ridiculed and satirized."

If intellectuals like John Slawson, who is a fellow of the American Psychological Association, protest and if blue-collar workers are critical of the Archie Bunker portrayal as a reflection of their mentality, how does this reaction restrict the television writer? Would not white-collar workers be equally critical of Archie as an office worker? Ideally, we should divest ourselves of class symbols: blue-collar or white-collar. A worker is a worker is a worker. Or is every protagonist to be a nebulous creature belonging to no ethnic group, of no particular religious faith, nor any identifiable occupation so that eventually the most successful situation comedy series will be some program called "Anonymous Incorporated."

But there is also a danger in reaching a point where we can no longer laugh at ourselves; it may be equally as invidious as perpetuating a stereotype. When men and women take themselves so seriously that they can no longer brook a jibe at themselves, then they are surely insecure and on the road to fear that may end in disaster. We are aware that Slawson can and does point to history to indicate that jibes at Jews in the Hitler regime led to the most monumental catastrophe in the annals of civilization. But that was the calculated diabolicism of a man and a nation gone stark, raving mad. During the horrendous Nazi regime, it was governmental policy that inspired the jibes and not the jibes themselves that led to the political machinations.

It is noteworthy that no one in Nazi Germany dared, publicly, to poke fun at the regime. Imagine the fate of any playwright in the time of Der Fuehrer who tries to present a satire called "MacHitler!" And it is unnerving to discover that, in 1972, an Italian comedian was hailed into court in Italy because during his act he satirized certain heads of state. The law under which he was arrested was promulgated by the fascist regime under Mussolini and, somehow, is still on the books.

Well, on to lighter moments and the consideration of a more typical situation comedy series, 'The New Dick Van Dyke Show." As its title implies, this program series centers around the protagonist, Dick Preston, a successful performer, played by Dick Van Dyke. The characterization permits sequences in which Van Dyke can use his many talents. Settings are almost always interiors and include the Preston home and office. In the episode we are studying, there are three sets: the Preston home, the office, and scenes in a hospital admitting area and waiting room.

The "Dick Van Dyke Show" always pursues a fast tempo and is generally written in two acts, preceded by a conventional teaser and resolved by a closing tag. In the following episode, "The Birth," by Bernie Orenstein and Saul Turteltaub, the teaser is chronological and sets up the plot.

FADE IN

INT. PRESTON LIVING ROOM—NIGHT. DICK COMES IN THE FRONT DOOR, TAKES A BRIEF LOOK AT THE DAY'S MAIL, AND NOTICES A GUITAR. HE CALLS QUIETLY FOR HIS WIFE.

DICK          Jenny. Honey.

There is no answer and he heads for the bedroom.

CUT TO

INT. PRESTON BEDROOM—NIGHT. THE RADIO IS PLAYING SOFTLY AND WE HEAR THE LATEST ROCK TUNE AS "JENNY" IS ASLEEP ON THE BED. HER HAND IS COVERING HER FACE BUT HER NINE-MONTH STOMACH IS IN FULL VIEW. DICK ENTERS.

DICK          Hi, honey.

REALIZING SHE IS SLEEPING, HE CROSSES TO THE SIDE OF THE BED TO TURN OFF THE RADIO. AS HE DOES THIS, "JENNY" ROLLS AWAY FROM HIM AND IS NOW FACING THE CAMERA. WE SEE, AS HER ARMS DROP, THAT IT ISN'T JENNY BUT A VERY YOUNG PREGNANT GIRL ABOUT NINETEEN. DICK, STILL THINKING IT IS HIS WIFE, REACHES INTO THE CLOSET, TAKES OUT CASUAL CLOTHES, TAKES OFF HIS JACKET, TAKES OFF HIS PANTS. CASUAL TROUSERS IN HAND, HE LOOKS AT THE FIGURE ON THE BED AND CAN'T RESIST MAKING THAT GREAT HUSBANDLY ACTION: PATTING THE BELLY. STILL NOT SEEING THE FACE, HE DOES SO, AND GIVES HER HEAD A GENTLE KISS. LOOKING LOVINGLY AT HER, HE IS INTERRUPTED BY HIS DAUGHTER, ANNIE, WHO ENTERS THE ROOM IN HER PAJAMAS.

ANNIE        Hi, Daddy.

DICK          Hi, baby.

              (kisses Annie)

ANNIE        You're not going to be able to call me baby for very much longer.

DICK          Oh, yes, ma'am, I am. I'm always going to call you baby...I'll call the baby something else...

| ANNIE | What? |
|---|---|
| DICK | (thinks. stuck) |
| | Oooh—Popcorn! |
| | (Annie giggles) |
| | C'mon, we better be quiet now. Mama's asleep. |
| ANNIE | No she's not... |
| DICK | (looks again) |
| | Yes she is, honey. C'mon. We gotta get out of here. |
| ANNIE | (realizing Dick's mistake and thinking it's the funniest thing that's happened all day) |
| | Oh, Daddy, Mommy's not sleeping. |
| DICK | Listen, I know her better than you do. |

JENNY ENTERS THE BEDROOM. HE LOOKS AT JENNY AND THEN AT THE FIGURE ON THE BED. HE MOVES TO SEE THE FACE AND, IN THAT INSTANT OF REALIZATION, WHIPS HIS PANTS ON TO COVER HIS EMBARRASSMENT, MISSES, TRIPS, FALLS, SCREAMS, GETS UP, LIMPS OUT OF ROOM COVERING HIMSELF.

| DICK | Who is that? Who is that? |
|---|---|
| | FADE OUT |

Mistaken identity is a tried and true technique that has served playwrights from the time pen was laid to papyrus. It is used logically here since Dick's wife, Jenny, is also about to give birth. In Act One, Jenny tells her husband that, in a fit of compassion, she picked up the girl, Debbie, on the highway. Debbie is not married. Dick wants to send the girl home, but Jenny says that Debbie has been on the road for three nights and must have some rest. She tells Dick to make himself a sandwich while she readies the guest room for Debbie. As Dick is preparing his sandwich, Debbie enters and we discover her background in this expository scene.

DEBBIE HAS HER MILK AND SITS WITH DICK WHO EATS HIS SANDWICH.

| DEBBIE | Ya know, your wife's really great. |
|---|---|
| DICK | (sees opening) |
| | Yeah—oh—well, yeah she's a ... |
| | **Great** wife and—and a mother...in that order. Uh—where you from, Debbie? |

| | |
|---|---|
| DEBBIE | San Francisco. But I've been in L.A. for the past year. |
| DICK | Oh, and David? |
| DEBBIE | Oh, he's in New Mexico. That's where I'm heading. I want to be with him when the baby's born. |
| DICK | When is he expecting you? |
| DEBBIE | He doesn't know I'm coming. I thought I'd surprise him. |
| DICK | Oh, well, that's some surprise all right. ...I'd like to see the look on his cardiogram!!! |
| DEBBIE (smiles) | Well, he knows about the baby...he just doesn't know I'm coming. |
| DICK | Oh. I...I see. |
| DEBBIE | Oh, he didn't want me to travel. He was supposed to come back to L.A. and get me when I had the baby. |
| DICK | You know, he's right. |
| DEBBIE | Oh, I know, but I wanted to have the baby in our new home. |
| DICK | Do—do your parents know about the baby? |
| DEBBIE | Uh-uh. No. |

(she shakes a "no")

JENNY ENTERS.

| | |
|---|---|
| JENNY | Debbie? Oh, there you are. Did you get something to eat? |
| DEBBIE | Well, I was having a glass of milk here before I went to bed. |
| JENNY | Ah. Well, your room's ready. When you are. |
| DEBBIE | Thank you, Mrs. Preston...thank you both. You're really just good people. Good night. |
| JENNY | Good night. |
| DICK | Sleep well. |

DEBBIE EXITS

| | |
|---|---|
| JENNY | Isn't she lovely? She's bright, too. |

| | |
|---|---|
| DICK | Yeah...make somebody a great wife...soon I hope. |

Dick and Jenny retire to their bedroom and are discussing the attitudes of the younger generation when they hear someone singing in the living room. They find Debbie strumming a guitar.

| | |
|---|---|
| DEBBIE | I'm sorry. I didn't mean to disturb you. I couldn't sleep and I didn't want to wake Annie. |
| JENNY | You didn't disturb us; it sounded beautiful. |
| DEBBIE | Thank you. I know you're uncomfortable about me being here. |
| DICK | Ooooh—will ya cut it out, Debbie? |
| DEBBIE | Ya know—actually...David and I **are** married. |
| JENNY | You are? |
| DICK (thrilled) | Are ya? |
| DEBBIE | Uh-huh. Oh, not like you two...but David and I have made a commitment to each other. We wrote our own ceremony—things that we really wanted to say—and David's brother officiated. |
| JENNY (relieved) | Is he a minister? |
| DEBBIE | No. He's a saxophone player.... |
| DICK | A saxophone player... |
| DEBBIE | We love him and he loves us. We didn't want some stranger to say all those pat words, so we had someone who was important to us. |
| DICK | Well—that...that makes sense. |
| DEBBIE | You see, David and I in our own way are as involved with each other as you are. I just hope we turn out to be as nice. I should be able to sleep now. |
| DICK | Yeah. Talking to me will do that for you. |
| DEBBIE | Good night. |
| JENNY | Good night. |
| DICK | Good night. |

140

DICK AND JENNY SAY GOOD NIGHT, AND DEBBIE EXITS.

DICK
Honey, I'm going to have Mike call her father in the morning.

JENNY
Oh, Dick...

DICK
I don't care. Honey...I'm sorry...but that girl is about to have a baby any minute. Now you're right—we can't throw her out of here...but if I'm going to make my house into a maternity ward, then somebody on her side of the family is going to at least have to boil some water!

FADE OUT

END ACT I

Act Two opens in Dick's office. He has told his sister, Mike, to phone Mr. Garriman, Debbie's father. Mr. Garriman is out and Mike leaves a message to have him call Dick. The call is returned while Dick is doing his show and Bernie, Dick's writer, answers.

SOUND: PHONE RINGS. BERNIE ANSWERS IT.

BERNIE
Hello...no this isn't Mike Preston...no, no. **She** will be available in about an hour or so...can I take a message? Yeah. Mr. Garriman. She called you about what??? Ohhh...well, I know what it's all about.. she just called to tell you that your daughter is all right..and that she's going to have her baby any day now. Oh...well, I'm sorry. I thought you knew. Well, you know now. Yeah...and you've got Dick Preston to thank for everything.That's right...it isn't every man that would accept the responsibility. Well, right now she's staying at his house. Uh-huh, yeah, get a pencil....I'll give you the address....

CUT TO

The following scene takes place in the Preston bedroom. Debbie awakens the sleeping Prestons to inform them that her baby is coming. Simultaneously, Jenny Preston is timing her own labor pains, which catapults Dick into a state of pandemonium.

There is a CUT to the hospital receiving area where Dick, with trepidation, watches both women being taken to delivery rooms. Afterwards, the head nurse has a few pertinent questions to ask Dick.

HEAD NURSE CALLS TO DICK.

| | |
|---|---|
| HEAD NURSE | Mr. Preston?... |

DICK CROSSES OVER TO ADMITTING DESK. HEAD NURSE HAS ADMITTING FORM ON A CLIPBOARD.

| | |
|---|---|
| DICK | Yes? |
| HEAD NURSE | I have to ask a few things. |
| DICK | Yes. Certainly. |
| HEAD NURSE | Now, one of those is your wife. |
| DICK | Yeah. Jenny. Jenny Preston. |
| HEAD NURSE | And the young girl? |
| DICK (not sure) | Well she's just—a fr—a friend. |
| HEAD NURSE | Uh—that—that would be Debbie. |
| DICK | Yes. Yes, I g—I guess this doesn't happen very often. |
| HEAD NURSE | Well, we get to see everything in a hospital. Now, umm, about Debbie's account. Who's gonna be responsible for that? |
| DICK | Oh, well, me. Yeah, I guess, I — I can take care of that. |
| | (trying to lighten the conversation) |
| | Do you have a group discount? |
| (sobering) | |
| HEAD NURSE | You have hospitalization insurance? |
| DICK | Yeah. |
| | (feels for his wallet) |
| | Oh — I didn't — I didn't bring anything. |
| HEAD NURSE | That's understandable. You have been rather busy. Well, we'll take care of that later. Why don't you join the men over there in the waiting area? Dr. Neal's upstairs. He'll let you know when anything or anybody happens. |

As Dick waits anxiously at the hospital, Debbie's father arrives.

INT. HOSPITAL—NIGHT (ADMITTING ROOM) SEVERAL HOURS LATER.

WE SEE A MAN (DEBBIE'S FATHER, MR. GARRIMAN) ENTER THE BIG DOORS AND HEAD

TOWARD THE NURSE. WE FOLLOW THE ACTION. GARRIMAN IS SO ANGRY HE HAS TROUBLE SPEAKING.

GARRIMAN (very uptight)    Uh — my name's Garriman. I wonder if my daughter's here.

HEAD NURSE    Is she a patient here, sir?

GARRIMAN    Yes.

HEAD NURSE    And what was the last name?

SHE LOOKS.

GARRIMAN    Garriman — she could be using Garriman...or Preston.

HEAD NURSE    Preston — oh yes. Why don't you join Mr. Preston over there in the waiting room.

HE TURNS WITHOUT A WORD AND WE FOLLOW HIM AS HE STRIDES TO THE WAITING MEN.

GARRIMAN    Preston!!

DICK WAITING FOR NEWS, PERKS UP AND STANDS.

DICK    Yes, sir. Right here!

GARRIMAN TAKES ONE STEP FORWARD AND KNOCKS DICK RIGHT OVER THE BENCHES AS WE

DISSOLVE TO

INT. WAITING AREA, MINUTES LATER. DICK IS LYING ON A BENCH WITH A COMPRESS TO HIS CHIN. MR. GARRIMAN IS WITH HIM.

GARRIMAN    I'm really very sorry.

DICK    Why, that's all right.

GARRIMAN    How's your jaw?

DICK    Aw, it hurts a little bit. Actually, you know, I think you straightened my back out. You know — you, you pack quite a punch there.

GARRIMAN    Well, that gentleman on the phone led me to believe the worst about you...Actually, I'm very grateful.

DICK    That daughter of yours, Debbie — she is some girl...my wife and I both just loved her.

A NEWCOMER ARRIVES IN THE WAITING ROOM.

| | |
|---|---|
| GARRIMAN | Well, believe me, Mr. Preston...she and the baby can come home and live with us...yeah, we're not going to turn our back on her. |
| DICK | Well, I — I don't think she wants to do that. I think—I think she wants to be with David. |

ANOTHER NURSE ENTERS AND APPROACHES.

| | |
|---|---|
| NURSE NO. 2 | Mr. Preston |
| DICK (flinching) | Yes... |
| NURSE NO. 2 | Mr. Preston, it's a girl...a very healthy girl. |
| DICK | Oh...which one???? |

THE NEWCOMER LOOKS UP AND WILL CONTINUE TO BE AMAZED BY ALL OF THIS.

| | |
|---|---|
| NURSE NO. 2 | Which one?? There was only one...a six-and-half-pound girl... |
| DICK | I mean wh—not which baby, which mother? |
| NURSE NO. 2 | Which mother? |
| DICK | Yeah. |

DR. NEAL COMES INTO THE ROOM.

| | |
|---|---|
| DR. NEAL | Mr. Preston... |
| DICK | Doctor Neal.... |
| DR. NEAL | Congratulations! You have a son. |
| DICK | Aaaa—Jenny? |
| DR. NEAL | (a little surprised) Yes, of course, Jenny. |
| DICK | A boy! Hey... |
| (to Garriman) (to nurse) | she got a girl, and I got a boy. |
| NURSE NO. 2 | You are a very generous man. |

The TAG scene finds everybody happy.

FADE IN: DICK'S BEDROOM—NIGHT. DICK IS IN BED. JENNY HAS JUST PUT THE BABY IN BASSINET. **WE HEAR A VERY TINY BABY** THAT JENNY HAS JUST FED.

144

| JENNY | You know, I forgot how much I hated getting up for the two o'clock feeding. |
|-------|-------|
| DICK | I'll do it tomorrow. |
| JENNY | No.... |
| DICK | Okay. |
| JENNY | You're some fighter. |
| DICK | I really hate it, honey. |
| JENNY | But you're always wide awake when I get back to bed. |
| DICK | Well, there's a big difference between giving a two o'clock feeding and being up for it. |
| JENNY | Oh, listen, honey, I got a letter from Debbie today. |
| DICK | Oh, no kidding...how is they? |
| JENNY | How is they? |
| DICK | Oh, I was going to just say how is she...and then I thought of David and Rachel and I didn't want to go back for the "ARE." |
| JENNY | They is fine. They got married married. |
| DICK | Married married? |
| JENNY | Uh-huh. In a civil ceremony. |
| DICK | Well isn't that against their beliefs? |
| JENNY | No, not really...they said as far as they're concerned they're already married, but they did it to please their folks....look, here's the announcement. |
| DICK (reads) | Miss Rachel Rogers announces that her parents, Debbie and David, were married on Saturday, the fifth of May.... |

FADE OUT

Most situation comedies attempt simple polt structures that skirt the realm of probability unless they are outright farce like the "I Love Lucy" series. They are usually zany, try hard to be laugh provoking and to leave viewers feeling they have spent a pleasant half hour in a completely relaxed mood.

**145**

Although many situation comedy scripts seem thin and to be straining for laughs, the fact of the matter is that writing humor is a difficult craft. Of the many hundreds of students who have attended our classes, we have found only a rare few who could evoke humor successfully. The writer of humor seems to possess an innate quality which appears to be rather elusive, judging from the rapid demise of so many situation comedies.

## ADVENTURE/CRIME

The "Mission: Impossible" series exemplifies both the crime and adventure genres. Its locale varies from any city in the United States to foreign nations. Several of the scripts have dealt with pseudo-political situations in foreign countries where an American is involved. This highly popular one-hour series is very fast paced, suspenseful, and employs many ingenious devices in outwitting the adversary.

The protagonists, Phelps, Barney, Casey, and Willy, appear in every episode and form a team of crime fighters. Ostensibly, they are always under assignment from some anonymous government source. The format of having a black-and-white team—Barney and Phelps—as protagonists is now prevalent.

The "Mission: Impossible" series is highly formularized. There is a teaser opening which thrusts the audience immediately into the core of the plot and then winds up with its standard device of Phelps uncovering a deftly hidden tape recorder with its message of the mission for the week. Here is the teaser from the episode by Howard Browne entitled "Stone Pillow."

FADE IN:

EXT. BROWNSTONE FRONT STREET—DAY

The POV is from across the street, favoring a brownstone. A MAN is exiting from it. A moment later VINCENT VOCHEK comes out. Each man ignores the other, the first man crossing to a parked car as Vochek passes a newsstand. As we MOVE IN, both faces are clearly recognizable, plus the headlines on the displayed papers. FREEZE FRAME. (Except for a barely audible CLICKING, all this is MOS.)

INT. VOCHEK'S PRIVATE OFFICE—DAY

As the film ends and the lights come on, we learn Scene 1 was a screening of a 16 mm color film. The projectionist is LARRY EDISON, 36, powerfully built, street smart, and completely crooked. In the desk chair in the richly furnished room is Vochek, 50, medium height, 20 pounds overweight and with eyes the color and opacity of wet gunmetal. His faintly bored expression suggests he's just seen the third reel of "Rebecca of Sunnybrook Farm." seated nearby is a tough-looking henchman called CLIFF and a middle-aged MAN who looks like a lawyer and is a lawyer. Edison flips the rewind lever. As the film WHIRRS softly:

VOCHEK          So?
(harshly)

EDISON          It puts you there, Mr. Vochek. At the time Morrie
(mildly)        Krohner was shot.

VOCHEK          Who says it was that day?

EDISON          Those papers on the newsstand.
                Blowups will show the date—
                and late editions go on sale
                between 11 and 11:30.

VOCHEK          Why were you tailing me?

EDISON          Not you, Mr. Vochek. The other man. He had a
                girlfriend at that address. His wife wanted
                proof. I got the proof—and you along with it.

During this the reel FINISHES rewinding. Edison removes it from the spindle, drops it on the desktop as:

EDISON          You understand this is a duplicate print.
(continuing)    Anything happens to me, the D.A. gets the
                negative. Take my word for it.

LAWYER          Take the word of a cheap con artist?
(angrily)       You think we don't know you're going
                to jail tomorrow?

EDISON          Sure. I got three to five and I'll be out in two
                years for good behavior.

                (beat)

                And I'm not a con artist. The word is **extortion**;
                it's spelled e - x - t—

VOCHEK          A hundred grand, cash on delivery. Take it or
(a growl,       leave it.
interrupting)

EDISON          Sorry, sir. Way I see it, the price has got to be as
(regretfully)   big as the man. And according to the Senate
                Rackets Committee you're...

| | |
|---|---|
| (groping for the exact quote) | ...the most powerful underworld figure west of Chicago. |
| (humorless smile) | That alone should run the price up to a million. |
| (sobering) | But I wasn't hatched yesterday, Mr. Vochek. All I'd have to do is let you get hold of that negative and I wouldn't live long enough to buy myself a bag of popcorn. |
| LAWYER (sharply) | Mr. Edison. Do I understand you want something from my client other than money? |
| EDISON | No sir. I'm simply saying that negative is buried and will stay buried. |
| | (a beat) |
| | As long as I get five thousand a month. Every month. |
| VOCHEK (harshly) | For how long? |
| EDISON (small smile) | I'll put it this way, Mr. Vochek. Let's both hope that I outlive you. |

CLOSE ON VOCHEK, furious, but helpless.

EXT. COUNTRYSIDE—DIRT ROAD—DAY

A Forest Ranger truck is parked by the dirt road. Beside it, a RANGER is scanning the hills for signs of fire with a pair of binoculars. Phelps drives up in his car, gets out and approaches the ranger.

| | |
|---|---|
| PHELPS | Any sign of fire? |
| RANGER | No. But it's the weather for it. Hot... |
| PHELPS (nods) | Low humidity...winds from the desert. |
| RANGER | (he looks at Phelps) |
| | Sure hope folks are careful with their campfires. |

The ranger moves into the brush. Phelps watches him leave, then goes to the truck cab, opens the glove compartment, takes out the tape machine and an envelope.

| | |
|---|---|
| TAPED VOICE | Good morning, Mr. Phelps. The pictures are of Vincent Vochek, head of a powerful West Coast syndicate family, and Larry Edison, a |

148

former private detective presently awaiting sentence on a confidence-game conviction. Vochek is suspected of murdering one Maurice Krohner, a police informer, six months ago. It is known that Edison holds a roll of film linking Vochek to Krohner's death, using it to blackmail Vochek. Conventional law enforcement agencies have been unable to locate this film and are helpless to proceed against the gang leader without it. Your mission, Jim, should you decide to accept it, is to learn where Edison's film is hidden, and turn it over to the proper authorities. This tape will self-destruct in five seconds. Good luck, Jim.

CLOSE ON RECORDER as the tape smokes and shrivels.

GO TO BLACK

Phelps' team is a versatile, extremely talented crew, whose ability, if it could be translated into reality, would surely minimize the crime statistics in our fear ridden cities!

In Act One, the "Mission: Impossible" team has discovered a link to Larry Edison, the ex-private detective turned con. Her name is Leona Prescott and she has just been discovered killed in an auto accident. However, a photograph of her is available and a mask has been made to exactly duplicate her features. It will be worn later by Casey, the lovely feminine contingent of the team.

Since Edison is to be imprisoned, Barney has had the governor's office install him as acting warden of the prison while the actual warden is presumably on emergency leave. In that capacity, Barney is able to thwart the plan of Joe Fort, a prison guard who in in cahoots with Vochek, the racketeer. Fort wants Edison placed in solitary. But the warden (Barney) orders Edison confined in a cell with Phelps, who is disguised as a convict.

The Scene

Phelps, in convict garb and wearing horn-rimmed glasses, is seated on the lower section of a two-tiered bunk bed. He looks up from the chessboard as Edison, now in prison wardrobe, enters the cell. They eye each other silently and without expression till Willy locks them in and moves off. Then Phelps smiles, indicates the upper bunk.

PHELPS          The penthouse suite is yours. Unless, of course, you're afflicted with acrophobia.

EDISON          It's okay with me.
(absently)

149

He crosses, eyes the chess set.

PHELPS          Do you play chess?

EDISON          I never even got around to checkers.

PHELPS          Pity. Losing constantly to oneself can result in
                a certain amount of ennui.

EDISON          I'll bet.
(vaguely)

PHELPS          I'm Derek Quayle. Known to my peers as the
  ˙             Professor.

EDISON          Larry Edison. Known to **my** peers as Larry
                Edison.

He turns, crosses to the cell door, grasps two of the bars
and gives them a brief, angry shake. From behind him:

PHELPS          First time, eh?
(sympathetically)

EDISON          Yeah ..

(bitterly)      And you wanta know something, Professor?
                Two hours in this iron palace and already it's
                getting to me.

(turns)         After two hours! What shape will I be in after two
                **years?!**

PHELPS          Keep looking at it that way and you'll end up stir-
                crazy.

EDISON          How else am I supposed to look at it?
(hotly)

PHELPS          By not thinking of it as years. A smart con does
                his stretch one day at a time. No yesterdays, no
                tomorrows—just today.

(gestures)      Then you put on a thirty-dollar suit, the warden
                gives you a short speech and a twenty-dollar bill,
                and you walk out the gate a free man.

(smiles)        And only one day older than when you walked in.

Edison smiles crookedly, begins pacing the cell. Then:

EDISON          What're you in for, Professor?
                Cheating at dominoes?

PHELPS          Nothing that exotic, I'm afraid.
(smiles)        It seems I broke a car window.

150

At Edison's incredulous reaction:

PHELPS
(continuing)

It happened to be in the new panel of an armored car containing eighty-four thousand dollars.

Edison laughs briefly. Noticing several books stacked on a small table, he idly picks up the top one, glances at the title, then incredulously at Phelps.

PHELPS
(continuing;
mildly)

Tastes vary, Mr. Edison. Some prefer magazines with pictures of girls in them; I prefer textbooks on calculus.

EDISON
(harshly)

I hope you're not gonna turn out to be one of these—

PHELPS
(overriding;
smiling)

Please, Mr. Edison. Don't make the mistake of equating intelligence with a lack of masculinity.

Edison eyes him expressionlessly for a beat, then smiles with a kind of grudging admiration.

EDISON
(dryly)

I wouldn't think of it, Professor.

During an afternoon exercise, a shot barely misses Edison. Fort storms into the warden's office and demands that Edison be placed in solitary for his own protection. But the warden has a visitor, Casey, disguised as a psychiatrist. She insists that Edison requires psychiatric treatment and the warden agrees with her, leaving Fort badly frustrated.

The plot begins to simmer when Edison, who is being brought back to his cell, observes Phelps surreptitiously sliping a piece of paper into a book he is reading. Again, we notice that Willy, one of Phelps' team, has assumed the job of a prison guard.

EDISON'S POV

A brief glimpse of Phelps as he hastily pushes the paper under the book's spine.

BACK TO SCENE

as Willy reaches the door, unlocks it. Edison steps in, Willy looks up and moves off. Edison, obviously deeply disturbed about something, begins slowly pacing the cell. After a beat:

PHELPS
(surprised)

They find out who took that shot at you?

EDISON

No.

PHELPS          You have any idea?

A beat; then almost as though thinking aloud:

EDISON          One man I know of could be behind it.
                But with what I've got on him, he'd
                be nuts to have me hit...Then **who**?

PHELPS          Do me a favor, will you?
(wryly)

As Edison looks at him questioningly:

PHELPS          Don't tell me about it.
(continuing)

He rises, casually drops the book he's been holding on top
of the others.

PHELPS          I've enough on my mind as it is.
(continuing)

As intended, both the action and the words remind Edison
of what he caught a glimpse of while outside the cell. He
eyes Phelps searchingly.

EDISON          Like what?

PHELPS          Nothing that would ineerest you.
(casually)

A beat as their eyes lock, hold. Then:

EDISON          You could be wrong about that.

He takes two smooth, quick steps, snatches up the book
Phelps has been holding. Phelps involuntarily starts
toward him, then stops short as Edison pulls the strip of
paper from the book's spine.

INSERT—THE PAPER

as Edison's hands unfold it. It is a topographical sketch of
a section of the prison yard, showing a manhole cover and
its relationship to the prison wall and nearby buildings.
OVER this:

EDISON'S VOICE  Figure on pulling a bust-out, Professor?

TWO SHOT
as they stare at each other. Edison's expression is
thoughtful; Phelps is wooden-faced. As Edison hands
Phelps the paper:

                                        GO TO BLACK

                    **END OF ACT ONE**

152

Act One ends on a note of suspense—a crisis. The planned prison break is a development anticipated by the viewer, but the suspense is heightened in Act Two by the opening scene in which Fort, the prison guard, brings a letter he has stolen from Edison to Vochek. It is addressed to Leona Prescott. Vochek has it opened, then resealed and mailed to the addressee. Neither Edison nor Vochek is aware that Leona is dead.

Meantime, back at the prison, Casey, as the disguised psychiatrist, holds a group therapy session at which Phelps and Edison are attendees. The prison break is about to take place. In the following excerpt, notice the sequence of action shots, minus dialog. Action—movement—the chase—essential ingredients of adventure and crime dramas. From the writer's standpoint, this calls for much less dialog than, let us say, a domestic drama or high comedy or any play where characterization is emphasized above situation. The script of "Stone Pillow" runs to 50 pages where the script for other types of hour dramas may run to 75 pages.

Phelps slips a hand inside his prison shirt, yanks out a small automatic pistol and levels it at Casey.

PHELPS
(continuing;
quietly)
Sorry, Doctor. Just do as you're told and nobody'll get hurt.

CASEY
(firmly)
There's a guard posted outside this room.

PHELPS
(cheerfully)
Plus twenty feet of corridor and two barred and locked doors. That's why you're coming with us.

CASEY
(coldly)
I'll do nothing of the kind. Furthermore—

Edison grabs her by the arm.

EDISON
(savagely)
You'll do it, lady. On foot or dragged by the hair.

The other two prisoners are following all this with fascination, making no effort to interfere.

FIRST
PRISONER
(hopefully)
How 'bout the rest of us?

PHELPS
Sorry.

(smiles)
Maybe next time.

Casey and the two men go to the door, stop there.

PHELPS          Call the guard.
(to Casey, softly)

> She starts to refuse, but Edison's fingers biting into her
> shoulder change her mind in a hurry.

CASEY          Guard!
(up)

> The door opens, the man starts in—and a judo chop by
> Phelps drops him, unconscious, to the floor. As Phelps and
> Edison, pushing Casey in front of them, exit:

EXT. THE PRISON YARD—DAY

> The area is deserted. Only one watchtower overlooks this
> particular section of the grounds.

ANGLE ON CELL BLOCK

> as a side door opens and Phelps, Casey, and Edison step
> out. The two men give the area a sweeping glance, then,
> each holding Casey by an arm, race across the open
> ground.

INT. WATCHTOWER—POV SHOT—DAY

> In a DOWN ANGLE we see the three figures running
> toward the metal cover of a drainage pipe set flush with
> the ground. The muzzle of a repeating rifle appears at the
> bottom of the FRAME, draws bead on the escapees.

ANOTHER ANGLE

> We now see that the guard with the rifle is Willy. The gun is
> still leveled at the group as they reach the drainage-pipe
> cover.

EXT. THE YARD—ON THE GROUP—DAY

> Together, Phelps and Edison manage to yank the heavy
> cover loose and to one side. The pipe underneath is large
> enough for their purpose. As Edison enters it feet first:

INT. PRISON WATCHTOWER—CLOSE ON ALARM
BUTTON—DAY

> As Willy shoves it home, a shrill eerie WAILING tears
> apart the silence.

OVER-SHOULDER SHOT

> Willy begins firing rapidly. The bullets rip into the ground
> a foot or two from Phelps; Casey and Edison have
> disappeared into the drain. As Phelps drops into it:

EXT. SHALLOW RAVINE—ON SECTION OF DRAIN
PIPE—DAY

protruding slightly from the bank. A beat, then Edison appears in the mouth of the pipe, works his way out. He is closely followed by a badly disheveled Casey, then quickly by Phelps. From the top we've heard the continuing WAIL of the prison siren.

PHELPS          This way!

The two men scramble to the top of the ravine, forcing Casey to accompany them, and disappear from view.

EXT. PAVED ROAD—ON A CAR—DAY

It's parked and unattended at one side of the narrow roadway. Trees and bushes block the view on both sides. A beat; then Edison, Casey, and Phelps enter to the car at a run. The siren continues to BLARE in the distance.

ON THE GROUP

panting from their exertions. As they stop at the car:

PHELPS          You're free to go, Doctor.
(to Casey)
(smiles)         You've been a big help.

Casey, relieved, turns to go, but Edison grabs her arm.

EDISON          Don't be a fool! Without her, we don't make it!
(to Phelps, angrily)

PHELPS          Let her go! I know what I'm doing.
(sharply)

EDISON          So do I, Buster!
(savagely)

He yanks open the car door, tries to shove Casey inside, and Phelps hits him with a judo chop. As Edison slumps, unconscious:

PHELPS          Go ahead. And stall them as long as you can.

As Casey takes off at a run along the road toward the prison, Phelps begins dragging the unconscious man into the car's front seat.

Casey, running along the road, is picked up by Fort and two other guards who are pursuing the escapees. She tells them in which direction the prisoners have fled. Phelps turns off onto a dirt road and then employs one of those ingenious devices "Mission: Impossible" is noted for.

EXT. HIGHWAY—DAY

It is bisected by a dirt road flanked by trees. Phelps' car comes along the highway. Just before it reaches the dirt road:

INT. CAR—ON PHELPS—DAY

as he pushes a button set into the dashboard.

EXT. MOVING CAR—CLOSE ON UNDERSIDE OF TRUNK—DAY

as brushes are lowered from the bottom of the car, covering any tire marks in the road.

ANOTHER ANGLE—THE CAR

as it follows a bend in the dirt road and disappears behind trees.

CAMERA WHIP PANS to the highway as Fort's car comes along it, stops. Fort jumps out, looks along the dirt road, then crosses to the point where Phelps' car entered the unpaved road and bends to look for tracks.

POV SHOT—THE ROAD

The surface is unmarked.

BACK TO FORT

He straightens, goes quickly back to the car, gets in.
He starts up the paved highway and speeds off.

EXT. STRETCH OF UNPAVED ROAD—DAY

A passenger car is parked on the shoulder near the edge of a deep ravine. Phelps' car comes quickly along the road, pulls onto the shoulder. Phelps gets out.

CLOSER ANGLE—PHELPS' CAR—DAY

Edison is still unconscious. Phelps takes a hypodermic from the glove compartment and injects a drug into Edison's arm. Phelps throws the hypodermic into the bushes, then pulls Edison out, shoulder lifts him and carries him to the other passenger car. He deposits him on the back seat floorboards, covers him with a blanket.

ANOTHER ANGLE

From the rear floor Phelps now takes a 5-gallon gas can, the carton of ashes, and two sets of prison uniforms. He splashes the contents of the can around the car interior, soaking the uniforms. Then he sprinkles the ashes on the front seats. Finally, he starts the motor, puts it in gear and releases the handbrake. It starts to roll. Phelps watches, as:

HIS POV

a WHOOSH of flame engulfs the first car as it rolls over the edge of the ravine.

ON THE BURNING CAR (STOCK)

as it cartwheels down the incline and EXPLODES.

Having eluded his pursuers, Phelps takes Edison to his apartment. After recovering, Edison is frantic and wants to make an urgent call to Leona.

INT. ND APARTMENT—NIGHT

Edison, waiting for an answer, is close to sheer panic.
He slams down the receiver, tries to stand up, as—

EDISON   I gotta get over there!

Phelps eases him back onto the couch, as—

PHELPS   You can't make it across the room. If you want to
(sharply)  tell me what's so important, maybe I can help.

Edison starts to blurt out the answer, stops short and eyes Phelps with a kind of suspicious cunning.

EDISON   Forget it, Professoer. For all I know, Vochek
      could have set this whole thing up!

CAMERA MOVES INTO Phelps' worried face, as—

CUT OF BLACK

And so the curtain falls on Act Two: a deepening crisis. Act Three opens in Vochek's office. He orders his henchmen to watch Leona's apartment on the assumption that she has the hidden negative of film which is the sole evidence of Vochek's guilt.

At the same time, Barney, Willy and Casey drive up in their electronically equipped van and stop near the Prescott apartment. Casey is now wearing Leona's mask and enters the building, stopping to take a letter from the mailbox. It is Edison's note and as she reads it, she is deeply disturbed. As she walks into the Prescott apartment, she is accosted by two of Vochek's men who threaten her with death if she does not turn over the negative. When they leave, she immediately communicates with Barney in the van via walkie-talkie, another favorite "Mission: Impossible" device.

The scene switches to Phelps' apartment. Edison insists on going to Leona's flat and Phelps accompanies him. Vochek and his men are now watching the apartment and Vochek is shaken when he sees Edison, who was supposed to have died in the auto accident. Edison confronts Casey (Leona).

### INT. PRESCOTT APARTMENT—DAY

as the BUZZER sounds. "Leona" crosses and opens the door slightly—then jumps back in alarm as Edison crashes in. Edison, his face a cold mask, kicks the door shut and comes deeper into the room as "Leona," apparently frightened, backs away, stopping near the escritoire.

EDISON            You lousy little tramp! You lied to me!
(thickly)

"LEONA"           No, Larry. I **did** send it. I swear it! The minute I
(badly scared)    heard—

EDISON            Send it how?
(overriding)

"LEONA"           By...messenger.
(flustered)

EDISON            Save your breath! A phone call was made. To the
(contemptuously)  D.A. He never got that film. In fact, he doesn't
                  even know it exists.

                  (a beat)

                  Get me that key.

This is the first any of the IMF group has heard of a key, and "Leona's" expression almost betrays the fact. Recovering quickly—

"LEONA"           Get it yourself.

EDISON            And turn my back on you? Not for a second.
(sullenly)

                  (takes a menacing step toward her)

                  Get it!

"Leona" starts toward the bedroom, Edison following.

### INT. BEDROOM—"LEONA"

As she enters, crosses to bed, and, in one swift movement, snatches up the handbag, yanks out a gun, levels it. Edison, just entering, stops short.

EDISON            Oh, come on! You're not gonna use that thing.
(annoyed)         Not on me.

"LEONA"           Why wouldn't I? There's no law against shooting
                  a dead man.

(goading smile)      The key's right where you left it, Larry. So is the film. But with you behind bars, why shouldn't I be the one to collect from Vochek?

EDISON
(coldly savage)      Somebody took a shot at me while I was in stir. Who set me up, baby? Not you; you don't have the brains or the guts. Not Vochek; he'd have nothing to gain, everything to lose. So, you brought in somebody else.

(a beat)

**Who is he?**

"LEONA"      Does it matter?
(impatiently)

She lifts the gun slightly, aims it squarely at his head.
As her finger tightens slowly on the trigger—

"LEONA"      I'm...sorry, Larry.
(continuing; quietly)

Edison, suddenly terrified, can only goggle at her. There is the curiously flat SOUND of a gunshot—and "Leona" drops the gun, stumbles backward through the open bedroom door, and out of sight of the two men. The SOUND of her body falling heavily to the floor comes over from OS.

ANOTHER ANGLE

to include Phelps. He is standing in the corridor doorway, holding a small black pistol. As he pockets it, in explanation—

PHELPS      I got worried.

(smiles)      Just protecting my investment in that fair shake you promised me.

Edison gives him a long, searching look.

EDISON      I'm beginning to get a feeling about you, Professor. Like maybe you've been pulling the strings all along.
enemies, he's headed for a straitjacket. I just
PHELPS      A man starts thinking his friends are his
(calmly)
saved you from —

Suddenly, from the OS bedroom—

"LEONA'S"      It's me darling! He knows! You've got to get that
VOICE (thickly)      film before he...

During this, both Phelps and Edison run toward the bedroom door. Phelps gets there first, stops short, blocking Edison.

THEIR POV

"Leona," on her knees beside the nightstand, lets the phone drop from her nerveless fingers and pitches forward, "dead" before her body hits the rug. Edison turns swiftly from the bedroom doorway, goes to the room's single lounge chair, tilts it sufficiently to remove the Shepherd caster from one of the legs. A thin key slides out of the hole and into his hand. He scoops up "Leona's" gun, levels it at Phelps.

EDISON                Give me your car keys.

Phelps takes out his key folder, tosses it over.

EDISON                This time, Professor, stay put—or the only fair
(continuing;          shake you'll get is a bullet.
grimly)

He goes quickly to the door, and out.

Now ensues the classic chase. Vochek and his hoods pursue Edison; Phelps and his men trail both. The denouement takes place in an abandoned warehouse. And here again action, shall we say, speaks louder than words.

EXT. ABANDONED WAREHOUSE—DAY

It's an ancient building, badly run down. Protective iron gratings over the windows and a solid, heavy door make the place a fortress. Over the entrance is a faded sign reading: ACME EXOTIC METALS, INC. Edison drives into the shot, stops near the entrance, goes to the door.

ON THE DOOR

It's secured with one of those heavy-duty padlocks that are almost impossible to force. Edison uses the key from the chair leg to unlock it, looks guardedly along the narrow street. No one around. He opens the door, enters. As the door closes—

INT. WAREHOUSE—DAY

It's cluttered with packing boxes, piles of rotting lumber, huge metal tables, empty racks for storing long lengths of metal rods, a huge anvil and, over everything, eight acres of dust. Edison stands just inside the door for a long beat, looking slowly around the big room and listening to the ten-ton silence. Finally, he walks past a pile of packing cases near the door, crosses to the anvil.

## ANGLE FAVORING THE ANVIL

It's not one of the type used by ordinary blacksmiths; this one appears to weigh a quarter-ton. Edison kneels beside one of the bolts securing the anvil to the concrete flooring.

## CLOSE ON BOLT NUT

Caked with rust and obviously impossible to remove. Edison's fingers close around it, give it a twist. There is a faint CLICK—and both the nut and bolt are lifted easily out of the cement.

## ON EDISON

He rises, dusts his knees, then puts both hands against the anvil and pushes. It slides askew easily on hidden rollers for a foot or two, revealing a hole in the floor. As he reaches into the hole, brings out the film, the SOUND of a gunshot comes from OS and a bullet RICOCHETS with an angry whine off the anvil. Instantly, Edison dives behind the anvil, yanks out "Leona's" gun.

## ANGLE FAVORING CLIFF

He and the two hoods from Vochek's car are standing just inside the warehouse door, half concealed by the packing crates near it. Cliff FIRES again; then he and the hoods instinctively duck down as Edison FIRES at them. There is no sign of Vochek himself.

The action that follows is TO BE ROUTINED ON SET. While the two hoods separate and attempt to outflank Edison while maintaining cover by use of packing cases scattered about the room, Cliff holds his original position to keep Edison where he is. Finally, one of the hoods, after narrowly avoiding one of Edison's bullets, dives behind a stack of lumber at a a point where he has a clear shot at Edison's crouching figure.

## OVER-SHOULDER ANGLE

As the hood slowly levels his weapon, a karate chop drops him. CAMERA BACK to disclose Willy, as he catches the slumping body, eases it to the floor.

## ON THE SECOND HOOD

crouched behind a heavy table. If he can reach a pile of c tes ten feet away, he'll have an unobstructed shot at E son. He takes a sprinter's position, leaps across the op ɔ space as a bullet narrowly misses him, reaches the sheltering crates—and finds himself staring into the muzzle of Barney's gun.

ANGLE FAVORING EDISON

peering off at the pile of boxes protecting Cliff. He catches a flicker of motion there, snaps off a SHOT, ducks as a BULLET ricochets off the anvil, tries to fire again—gets a dry CLICK. Slowly he lowers the gun, his expression showing bitter resignation.

EDISON          I quit!
(up)

CLIFF'S VOICE    Get rid of the gun and come out!

Edison tosses the gun into the open, picks up the can of film, takes a deep breath, rises from behind the anvil—and freezes, slack-jawed, as Cliff, hands lifted in surrender, comes out from the shelter of the packing cases. Behind him, gun in hand, is Phelps. As they reach Edison, Phelps puts out a hand.

PHELPS          I'll take that, Edison

As Edison wordlessly hands him the can of film—

EXT. WAREHOUSE—DAY

as the door opens and Barney, Willy and Phelps, carrying the film, come out. Two police cars are now on the scene. Vochek in handcuffs, is being shepherded to one of them by two policemen. Three policemen are entering the warehouse, guns drawn.

ANOTHER ANGLE—IMF TEAM

as they walk briskly off.

                                    CUT TO BLACK

And so "Mission: Impossible" has once more taken us on a suspenseful ride and we have seen the criminals foiled.

TV crime and adventure dramas are, largely, light on characterization and heavy on plot. Some of them, like "Dragnet" and "The FBI," are based on case files, but, of course, extensively fictionized. Romantic interest, if any, is generally underplayed in the half-hour and hour series. Action is the keynote, not sentiment. There is a single, straight-line plot. The 90-minute versions, such as "Columbo," may inject a sub-plot and attempt to flesh up the protagonist of the series; its hero, Peter Falk, plays the part of a bumbling detective who is actually extremely clever, an ancient but successful device. Or "McMillan & Wife"—a prototype of the successful motion picture series of the 30s, "The Thin Man," with the love interest kept in the safe bounds of matrimony and the mystery and action laced with comedy.

# WESTERNS

The western is another staple of television drama. It is an excellent vehicle for the visual medium: rampant action, outdoor vistas, picturesque towns. One of the most endurable western series is "Gunsmoke," which began as a radio program almost two decades ago and made an effective transition to television. By studying one of the "Gunsmoke" scripts, we will be able to discover the ingredients of a successful western.

## "Milligan"

As in any series, the writer must be familiar with the running characters. In the case of "Gunsmoke," they are Marshal Matt Dillon played by James Arness, Doc by Milburn Stone, Kitty by Amanda Blake, Festus by Ken Curtis, and Newly by Buck Taylor. The plot either revolves about the central characters or they are an integral part of the story—as in "Milligan," written by Ron Bishop.

The period of the series is the American West in 1873 and "Gunsmoke" strives for authenticity. This is a filmed one-hour series and because of its locale and type of action, the majority of the scenes are usually exteriors.

In a western, action builds quickly as you will observe in this excerpt from Act One of "Milligan." Notice Scene 2, particularly, and the writer's colorful description of Norcross. "Gunsmoke," through the years, has not only striven for authenticity but has attempted some depth of characterization to avoid the former stereotyped westerns with their one-dimensional characters. Norcross is, of course, a Robin Hood: an outlaw with compassion and style.

FADE IN:

EXT. DODGE STREET—FIRST MERCHANT'S BANK—DAY

A spring-wagon is pulled up before the bank:

JANET MILLIGAN, early 30s, a pretty, well-groomed woman of patrician heritage. Relatively new to the West. Yet receptive, sensitive, and intelligent.

WENDY ("Muggins"), 12, a buoyant, but well mannered and respectful girl, radiant, and, although of complete devotion to her mother, exhibiting that slightly deeper dimension which exists between father and daughter. Well groomed, regardless of stark circumstances, and the product of her mother's attention and love. Wendy holds an old battered tomcat she calls Jim Grim. She strokes Jim Grim.

PICK UP FIVE MEN slowly and unfettered riding down toward the bank.

ANOTHER ANGLE—MEN, FAVORING SPRING-WAGON (JANET AND WENDY)

The leader is a large, capable, amused and amusing man in his 30s—almost rakish; would be if he gave half a damn about facades: life's the way you look at it; and the way to look at it is from each new hill; leave your worries behind you like your horse does, clumped in the dirt and only important to flies. This is JACK NORCROSS, handsome in the way of cliffs, scar down one cheek that enhances rather than detracts. If this isn't a near man complete of this time, there aren't any. All the men are trail dusted. The four men who ride with Norcross are, by contrast, mirth-less, watchful; obvious self-reliance: hunting hawks. As they come to the bank tie-rail and dismount, Norcross, noticing Janet with a practiced eye, dismounts and takes a packet from his saddlebags. And as he passes the wagon on his way INTO the bank:

CLOSER ANGLE—NORCROSS, JANET, WENDY

Norcross tips his hat, the wide smile—to Janet's discomfort, and to Wendy's honest appreciation.

NORCROSS        Ladies.

WIDER ANGLE

as Norcross gives Wendy a wink. Saunters with the others for the bank.

INT. BANK—DOFENY AND MILLIGAN

Dofeny, bank officer, is well enough dressed, 50s, jowly, but not the prototype of the miser. Simply a man devoid of humor and overemployed with facts as the business of money demands. Milligan is plain and strong—plow strength that rarely knew another use.

MILLIGAN        Just enough to see me through to
(pleasant)      crop time, Mr. Dofeny.....

DOFENY          And when would that be, Mr. Milligan?
(flat)

MILLIGAN        Oh, no time at all, Mr. Dofeny. First rain. I can
                smell rain. I can always smell rain. Mr.
                Bodkin...he always saw me through...

DOFENY          Mr. Bodkin is on business in Hays,
(inhaling)      Mr. Milligan, and I'm here.

## ANGLE TO INCLUDE NORCROSS AND MEN

as they ENTER: the men positioning themselves casually; Norcross waiting, amiable by expression, packet under arm.

DOFENY          I'm not doubting your nose...and I know what
(flat)          they say about a banker's heart, but the facts,
                Milligan, are that it hasn't rained in seven
                months and even if your nose was right, this late
                you'd have a harvest that wouldn't fatten a range
                rabbit.

Milligan turns in deep dejection. Then turns to try a last time.

MILLIGAN        You're sayin' no.

DOFENY          No, I'm saying that at this time, I simply can't
                loan the bank's money on such a risk. Perhaps
                later...when things are better...

                (beat)

                I **mean** it when I say I'm sorry, Milligan.

An awkward moment, then Milligan EXITS in defeat.

## ANOTHER ANGLE

Norcross steps up. Dofeny is moving away to more important business.

NORCROSS        Oh, banker man....
(very politely)

Dofeny turns but doesn't come back. Norcross pats the packet on the counter. Dofeny still observes, unsatisfied, what must seem a most itinerant man.

NORCROSS (CONT'D)   Like to do business, banker man...
(kindly)            oh, a few thousand I'd say.....

Dofeny comes back slowly, an eye arched, but maintaining aplomb.

DOFENY          ...did you say...a few thousand...?

NORCROSS        Oh, I don't know what it'll be, 'xactly, till we
                count her.

                (starts unwrapping packet)

DOFENY              ...why, The First Merchant's would be most
(a smile blooming)  happy to serve you.

NORCROSS          Good! I do appreciate that...
(wide smile)

Unties the neat packet. Unfolds the paper: neatly folded
canvas sacks.

DOFENY          Where's the money...?

Norcross casually draws a gun, as:

NORCROSS          It's you oughta know...fill 'em up..
(sweetly)

CLOSE—DOFENY

Slow wrath.

NORCROSS

Wide smile.

FRESH ANGLE

The other men have guns out and placidly cover all personnel.

NORCROSS          Well...fill 'em up...
(politely)

DOFENY          You can't get away with this!

Norcross turns to another man.

NORCROSS          Now why is it you ole boys is always sayin' "you
(politely)          can't git away with this?" 'n us ole boys always
                  does...don't make you ole boys sound like much
                  as businessmen...now fill them bags up, banker
                  man.

Intimidated now, Dofeny turns stiffly, eye down the
muzzle, to a traumatized TELLER.

DOFENY          Ferguson, fill the bags.

                  (Ferguson is glued)

                  Fill the bags, man!

                  (now he moves to it)

NORCROSS          Thanks.
(smiles)

CLOSE SHOT—NORCROSS

Wide, pleasant smile as he looks at us (Dofeny).

NORCROSS          Now...you want me to sign somethin'...?
(ingratiating)          ...h'mm...?

CLOSE ON FERGUSON

stuffing bags with money.

EXT. BANK AND MILLIGAN—JANET AND WENDY IN
BG.

Milligan sits in the wagon: thorough dejection. Janet
forces a brightening smile.

JANET          Now, John, it's...it's not like the earth opened up
or something...We'll get by, we always have.

ANOTHER ANGLE

as Norcross & Co. comes banging OUT of the bank to the
horses. Vault up. Spur OUT. Norcross jumps his horse
over to the spring-wagon. Showers the wagon with bills
from the sack he lugs.

NORCROSS     Git that chin off your feet, plowboy, and pray for
rain.

Now comes a very basic element of almost every adventure drama: the chase. This is implicit in the western. A posse is gathered, led by Festus, Marshal Dillon's deputy. Milligan is part of the posse, riding a plow horse and carrying an ancient gun. He is a farmer and manhunting is foreign to him.

As Norcross and his gang flee from Dodge City, one of them, Power, is wounded in the back. The posse, after a chase, loses the trail. The following dialog becomes dramatically foreshadowing.

ANGLE ON THE POSSE

Newly is ahead, crosses the river and is checking for signs.
The rest of the posse draws UP. Newly inspects the
ground, then:

NEWLY         No more tracks, Festus, trail ends here.

MATTIS, a rangy man, 30s, wheels UP his horse.

MATTIS        Then I'd guess as we's done our chores an' can
git back to town.

FESTUS        You stay put, ain't none of us goin' back yet.

POTTER        Festus, it ain't as if Norcross is some barnyard
bobcat—got him a thought for others. Ever'body
knows he ain't all bad.

AD-LIB agreement from half of the posse.

| FESTUS | And them same ever'bodies knows a crime's a crime, Potter. |
|---|---|
| REEVES | I ain't all that fired up ta catch him, tell ya that. I heard about a widda woman he helped over Cimarron way... |

MORE AD LIB agreement.

| NEWLY | He helped her with stolen money, Reeves. |
|---|---|
| MATTIS | He only steals from rich banks an' insurance companies. Gives a lot of it ta folks what ain't got it so good. |
| NEWLY | You forgetting that poor people have their money in banks too, Mattis? |
| FESTUS | Like it or not, you're all deputized and we're gonna keep goin'. |

ANOTHER ANGLE

as Milligan COMES UP to the group.

| BURKE | Milligan, you best get you a cactus switch. |
|---|---|
| MILLIGAN (goodnaturedly) | What this old horse needs is a plow behind 'im. |
| FESTUS (to Milligan) | Take your time, Milligan. And don't worry on the horse. Ridin' late you'll see 'im if they circle back on us. Fire three shots 'n we'll come a'runnin'... |

Norcross sends his men ahead as he takes the wounded Power to a hidden shack. This is a sequence designed to win some sympathy for Norcross. Milligan, who has fallen behind the posse, accidentally comes upon the shack. He enters it and finds Norcross, with his back to the door, tending Power, who is breathing his last. Milligan, quaking, shoots Norcross. Study the reaction description and dialog as we come to the end of Act One.

EXT. SHACK—DAY

Milligan, gripping the gun, white-knuckled in both hands, squirts a cloud, and Norcross is blasted flat. Milligan yanks back the hammer again and WHAMS away at the general concern, LEAD ZINGING at random.

EXT. TRAIL—BACK TO FESTUS, BURKE AND MEN—DAY

as they react to the distant shooting.

FESTUS          Somebody's done found somethin'!

(to looter, of prisoners)  Get them back in town. Let's ride.

He wheels Ruth, followed by Newly, Burke, Mattis, Reeves
and Potter.

EXT. SHACK—SHOT OF MILLIGAN—DAY

He's squirting off his last SHOT at nothing. Eyes squeezed
shut. The gun CLICKS dry several times. He opens his
eyes slowly.

POV SHOT—NORCROSS

Out flatter and colder than New Year's in a mine shaft. He
lies over Power.

INT. SHACK—ANGLE ON NORCROSS AND POWER
FROM MILLIGAN—DAY

as Milligan APPROACHES, wholly uncertain; Milligan
walks toward him, matches for legs.

CLOSER ANGLE—MILLIGAN, NORCROSS, POWER

Milligan stands looking down at them, emotional ping.
Then he sits down and begins to shake. A beat, as we watch
a semishattered man; so long as instinct prevails, the body
functions as a machine—for good or bad reasons; employ
the exploration of reason with instinct and you have internal revolution, which is occupying Milligan at this
moment of moments. We watch Milligan in his throes as
we begin to HEAR HORSES APPROACHING. Long beat,
then:

EXT. SHACK—FESTUS AND POSSE—BURKE FAR TO
REAR

as they come over the rise and ride up. (NOTE: The other
outlaws are in custody.) Dismount, eyes searching. Burke
is APPROACHING, endeavoring wearily, and by all
axioms known to Newton, to keep his scrotum off the anvil.
Festus sees Milligan's horse. Cautious:

FESTUS          Milligan's ole horse.

               (beat)

               An' some others...

Quickly, they dismount and move to the outlaws' horses
and Festus spots the shack.

FESTUS (CONT'D)  Move around ta the back...
(gesturing)

(the men deploy)

Festus and Newly cautiously ENTER the shack.

EXT. SHACK—FESTUS, NEWLY, MILLIGAN—AND NORCROSS-POWER CLUMPED

FESTUS          Ya got 'em both.

(Milligan nods, eyes vacant at the ground, nods)

MILLIGAN        I ain't sure...I...guess...so...
(in a fog)

(then Festus nods, quietly before the sight of death)

NEWLY           That's Norcross, all right. I've seen just about
                every poster on him.

ANOTHER ANGLE

as Burke and others come IN. Milligan, sick to his stomach, rushes OUTSIDE.

EXT. SHACK—DAY

As Milligan EXITS, gulping down the bile.

INT. SHACK—ANGLE ON BURKE AND NORCROSS— DAY

as Burke probes around.

SHOT OF BURKE

as his face drains. He looks down a beat. Then quickly up.

BURKE           He's been shot in the back, Festus! They've...
(clarion)

                (looks up)

                ...they've **both** been shot in the back...!

FESTUS AND NEWLY

They, too, turn in drained reaction.

INDIVIDUAL SHOTS—POSSE MEN

as they ENTER and instantly stop in awed reaction.

ANGLE FROM BURKE AND NORCROSS

as Festus, Newly and posse men come slowly forward: spokes to the hub. Then in BG, we can HEAR Milligan puke. The men continue toward the body, unmindful, the larger incident (the back-shot deaths) the center of this frontier attention.

170

HOLD, then—

END OF ACT ONE

The build-up in Act Two revolves about the 19th century code of the West: you don't shoot a man in the back even if he is an outlaw. One of the posse, Mattis, who had been extolling Norcross' virtues, now stirs up his Dodge City cronies against Milligan for shooting Norcross in the back. This becomes the major plot line: man against society, even though Milligan had no intention of breaching the peculiar code. In the surgeon general's study of "The Impact of Televised Violence," there is a section on the definition of violence. The researchers have found that "The ethics of violence may be blunt: line-of-duty violent acts of soldiers and police may be acceptable." Also, "The ethics of violence may be more subtle: it may be acceptable to hit back, but not in the groin or in the eye." And so, at least for some citizens of Dodge City, it may have been acceptable for Milligan to shoot Norcross but not in the back.

The subplot runs in counterpoint; the desperate need for money by the Milligan family to see them through until harvest time. Janet (Mrs. Milligan) convinces her husband that he ought to approach the banker again for a loan, particularly since he has killed the bank robber. Milligan acquiesces. It is night but Dofeny, the banker, is still at work. Dofeny admits he is grateful that the robber was shot, but. . . .

DOFENY          ...but I can't give you the loan, Milligan. I turned you down this morning and if I gave it to you now, folks might think I was rewarding you for shooting a man in the back. And Jack Norcross was a hero to some folks. Of course, to some folks, a fire-snorting devil riding a dragon down their chimneys would be a hero.

                (beat)

                Personally, I don't care if you had shot him in quicksand, the point is you shot him. But the **double** point is you shot him in the back. And for some silly reason, people think that makes a difference. I'm sorry, Milligan, but I do business with you, and I go under. That **happens** to be the way of it...I'm sorry...I **am**...

Hesitantly, Milligan rises, a crushed (confused) man again. Turns, EXITS slowly.

ANGLE FROM DOFENY—MILLIGAN EXITING

Dofeny watches him go.

| DOFENY | Come see us again in a few months, Milligan. |
| (means it) | People around here will forget—they always do. |

| MILLIGAN | What do we eat till then, Mr. Dofeny? Crow? |

And he GOES. HOLD, then—

DISSOLVE TO

### EXT. DODGE STREET—NIGHT

A warm summer night; CRICKETS chatter idly and somewhere in the distance a DOG BARKS. Milligan walks listlessly along, lost in his own troubles. There's MUSIC coming from somewhere far down the street and a WOMAN LAUGHS—all of this counterpoint to Milligan's dejection.

### ANOTHER ANGLE

Milligan trudges along. Then, just as he passes the dark mouth of an alley, two figures materialize, grabbing and shoving him into the alley.

### EXT. ALLEY—NIGHT
Milligan is hurled to the ground. He pulls himself up, looks to see.

### HIS POV—FOUR HOODED MEN

encircling him.

| VOICE | Get on your feet, coward. |

### ANOTHER ANGLE—FAVORING MILLIGAN

| MILLIGAN | Who are you? What do you want from me? |

| VOICE (MATTIS) | Gonna show ya what we thinka backshooters... |

Milligan, pressed flat against the wall of the building, is terrified: Suddenly a fist slams out, knocking Milligan into one of the hooded men. Milligan grabs out, clutching the hood; it comes off, revealing Mattis. Milligan reacts, just as:

### SERIES OF QUICK SHOTS

Milligan is knocked flat and the SCREEN is FILLED with flailing fists and kicking feet. Milligan fights as best he can but he's badly outnumbered and is quickly unconscious. And as the fists pummel him...

FADE OUT

END OF ACT TWO

172

In Act Three, Milligan's wounds are dressed by Doc. Milligan steadfastly refuses to reveal the identity of his assailants. Doc discusses the situation with Kitty, who, like Marshal Dillon, has a comparatively small part in this episode.

The writer now introduces an element of the plot guaranteed to win abundant sympathy for Milligan: the children in the village begin taunting Milligan's daughter, Wendy, for her father's 'sin.' Milligan resolves to see the school teacher.

INT. SCHOOLHOUSE—CLOSE ON MILLIGAN—DAY

Milligan's face registers the pain of an honest man's shame. He stands a long moment, his eyes blinking, bewildered with his own emotions, then steps in a bit further:

ANOTHER ANGLE

The schoolmaster, MR. PANDY, is going about the business of starting up for another day. He is a sturdy, sour, middle-aging bachelor who is going comfortably to fat and his personality is tainted by the kind of snide, picayune, waspishness that often creeps into the dedicated celibate. He looks up when Milligan, awkward and deferential, COMES IN, his battered hat in his hand.

PANDY          Yes?

Milligan clears his throat.

MILLIGAN          Name's John Milligan, sir...

Pandy blinks, wondering what that means, then,

PANDY          Milligan...You'd be...

MILLIGAN          Wendy's father...she's my girl...

Now Pandy realizes, is somewhat embarrassed.

PANDY          Yes. Well...was there...something I could do for you?

Milligan shuffles closer, unsure how to begin, beginning anyway.

MILLIGAN
(looking around)          Ain't never been in one of these, Mr., ah...

PANDY          Pandy. Gerald Pandy is my name.

MILLIGAN          Mr. Pandy. Never had a good chance to get me any schoolin'.

He smiles shyly.

MILLIGAN      'Course I never took to 'er, see, or I guess I'd'a
(CONT'D)      done 'er, some way...

Mr. Pandy fails to see the humorous aspect of this con-
fession, stands waiting for the point and Milligan goes on.

MILLIGAN      My wife, now. She went t' school...
(CONT'D)

Mr. Pandy shifts his feet, closes his book bag, takes a
breath.

PANDY         That's good. Now, was there anything I could
              help you with, because if not, it's about time for
              class to begin.

Milligan settles to his subject.

MILLIGAN      Well, me not havin' the learnin', I been one to
              look up to it, Mr. Pandy. Hopin' my little girl
              could touch to finer things.

Milligan searches Pandy's face.

MILLIGAN      Mr. Pandy...you know my Wendy. She always
(CONT'D)      done good in her studies. Had her good reports
              since she started in. You ever have cause t' be
              trouble over Wendy?

This is becoming embarrassing.

PANDY         Ah, no...no, nothing at all that I can think of.

MILLIGAN      Reckoned not. Meanin' she done her part here,
              sir.

He takes a deep breath and turns a corner in his argument.

MILLIGAN      Now, my girl come home last night too sick t'
(CONT'D)      eat an' full a' shame fer a thing she ain't to
              blame for...

Pandy turns away and hastily re-erases an already clean
blackboard. Milligan gets to the hard part.

MILLIGAN      Mr. Pandy, I kilt a man an' I done it in what folks
(CONT'D)      seem ta think is a shameful way, I know that.

Pandy is in an excess of nervous discomfort and he turns
back sharply.

PANDY         Mr. Milligan, do we really have to go into...

174

Milligan cuts in, dogged, forceful.

MILLIGAN  Yes, we do. 'Cause it's all a part and piece of Wendy's trouble. Right's right, Mr. Pandy, and when a man's done wrong it's fair to punish him. The law does it when what he done's ag'in the law; folks'll do it theirselves if it ain't, and I can testify t'that...

Pandy is increasingly impatient.

PANDY  Excuse me, Mr. Milligan, but what is the point you're getting to?

MILLIGAN  Point is, sir, it ain't fair to punish them that's innocent, 'er see 'em punished, neither. Much less a little girlchild without one ounce a' sin in her whole soul and body!

Pandy is taken aback, or so he affects to be.

PANDY  I beg your pardon, sir, if you're accusing me, let me tell you I have never raised a hand...

And Milligan cuts in.

MILLIGAN  No, it ain't that. I know you never hurt her. But she's **bein'** hurt. And you're the **man** here. You're the one set over all the young'uns t' see their learnin's right an' proper...

Pandy is stung by the implications.

PANDY  And you actually think I set them on to pester Wendy, is that it?

Milligan shakes his head, trying to find the words.

MILLIGAN  You let 'em, sir. And she ain't pestered, Mr. Pandy: my little girl is dyin' inside.

Pandy turns away, his eyes roving nervously to avoid contact with Milligan's. There is an awkward silence.

MILLIGAN  I can bear whatever I got to bear for what I done,
(CONT'D)  sir. But I'm just a ordinary man with ordinary feelin's: I can't stand t'see my baby sufferin' for me.

His eyes are gentle and moist with a father's determination to take his child's part at any cost. He speaks softly, very low.

| MILLIGAN (CONT'D) | Mr. Pandy, you got to tell me if I can keep her here, or if we got to go... |
|---|---|

Pandy stops in his tracks, blinks, turns toward Milligan, who is waiting, his big hands hanging at his sides. Pandy removes his spectacles.

| PANDY | Mr. Milligan, I run a school here, and I try to keep a decent degree of discipline over the children. But I am not and cannot be a tyrant. |
|---|---|

Milligan is watching him hard, going for the meaning beneath the words.

| PANDY (CONT'D) | I can maintain a modicum of order in the classroom, and I do. But these children have parents, and the parents are the ultimate authority. |
|---|---|

Having polished his glasses to high gloss, he replaces them precisely.

| PANDY (CONT'D) | The town knows of...well...your recent unhappiness. I don't have to tell you that there are many who...condemn you for it. |
|---|---|

He raises his hands in a gesture of protest.

| PANDY (CONT'D) | Not I, sir, no! I judge not, lest I may be judged, that is my rule. |
|---|---|

He pauses again, thinking fondly of his excellent system of rules.

| PANDY (CONT'D) | But those who **do**, influence the thinking of their children; oh, my, yes. And, Mr. Milligan, I ask you: who am I to take the formation of these children's values out of the hands of their true and rightful parents? |
|---|---|

Again silence, a long, palpable silence. Milligan studies his hands which work together awkwardly in front of him, then turns and goes toward the door. When he is there, Pandy's voice stops him.

| PANDY (CONT'D) | Mr. Milligan. I am doing my best. |
|---|---|

Milligan turns again, looks at the teacher.

| PANDY (CONT'D) | Surely you understand my position? |
|---|---|

Milligan stares into his eyes a long moment, then nods.

MILLIGAN          I understand it, Mr. Pandy...do you...?

As he goes OUT ON Pandy's look of confusion, we PUSH
IN and—

FADE OUT

### END OF ACT THREE

Act Four brings Matt Dillon into the action. He appears at
the Milligan home with the reward for the apprehension—dead
or alive—of Norcross. It neatly takes care of the Milligans'
financial plight. But the irate posse members are incensed
that, on top of breaking the code, Milligan is rewarded for
what they have come to consider a misdeed rather than an
heroic deed. Mattis, the ringleader, decides to take steps to
force Milligan out of Dodge City.

One night, Wendy goes into her yard to bring in her pet
cat, Jim Grim, and finds the creature hanged. This cowardly
act arouses the slow moving Milligan to wrath. He rides into
the city and confronts Mattis. There ensues another staple
element of the western: the big fight. Milligan is badly battered until Matt Dillon enters the fray.

ANOTHER ANGLE

Milligan is battered and bruised; he's climbing up as Matt
comes INTO SCENE:

MATT             What's going on here...

He reacts to the sight of Milligan who's gaining his wobbly
feet.

MATT (CONT'D)    You boys out to teach Milligan a lesson, are you?

MATTIS           You know what he done. We don't like it an' the
                 town don't like it!

MATT             You speaking for the town now, are you, Mattis?

MATTIS           Any man'd shoot a man like Jack Norcross in the
                 back, we reckon he's a coward an' deserves what
                 he's got comin'.

MATT             Well...if you've got a lesson in courage to teach,
                 you'd better include me.

And without ceremony, Matt slams out a block of knuckle
granite that knocks Mattis stiffer than a February fence
post. Milligan, who had been feeling poorly up to then, lets
out a WHOOP like a locomotive's mating call, and the mix
is on for sure.

SERIES OF SHOTS:

to cover the fight. A champion brouhaha which covers the street with Matt and the battered but unbeatable Milligan finally cleaning the last clock in front of most of Dodge, in awe assembled and then, panting and cut up, turning to face each other. Matt smiles at a man who, for the first time in his life perhaps, has proved he doesn't have to apologize to anybody if he isn't wrong, no matter what kind of force is brought to bear.

ANOTHER ANGLE

MATT          I don't think you'll have any more trouble from
(to Milligan)  them...

MILLIGAN      Has anything changed, Marshal? **Really?**

CLOSE ON MR. PANDY

reacting, then:

LONG HIGH SHOT

as Matt and Milligan move AWAY and the crowd starts to disperse. Everyone that is except Mr. Pandy. HOLD, then

                                           DISSOLVE TO

EXT. COUNTRY ROAD—DAY

A wagon piled high with belongings—driven by Milligan. His wife and daughter sit alongside; they're leaving town.

A TAG (the resolution) brings a happy conclusion—and so, right finally triumphs. Although Matt Dillon appears only briefly in this episode of "Gunsmoke," he is the hero of the series.

In response to a researcher's query ("Television and Social Behavior), some of the writers for the series commented:

"Consider the fifty million people a week who watch a dedicated, intelligent Dillon risking his life to protect society, and you'll have to conclude that more good is done than evil"..."I identify with the hero who goes through danger and survives—if he does, maybe I will"..."The western is a fairy tale of every man getting back at whatever's bugged him all these years. It's a release.."

Perhaps that last statement best sums up the average viewer's reaction to the drama of adventure, action, suspense: "It's a release." Escapist drama is just that. It permits viewers to remove themselves from their everyday cares and to enjoy a vicarious experience, to picture themselves as rugged heroes triumphing over evil in roles they could never attain.

# THE DRAMATIC SERIAL

Daytime television for the networks is generally a combination of game programs and dramatic serials or, as they are more popularly known, soap operas. Both types of programs cater to the housewives who find a release in the never ending problems of the serial character, and are able to fantasize themselves as winners of prizes ranging from a color TV to a trip to Hawaii.

The daytime serials are an economic bonanza for the networks. Les Brown ("Television, the Business Behind the Box," Harcourt Brace Jovanovich) reveals that it costs less to produce five half-hour episodes of a typical soap opera than a single half-hour prime-time program. The revenue from one episode of a soap opera covers the production costs for a week, and it does not require a mathematical wizard to realize that the profit to the network on the daily serial is enormous. Therefore, it is obvious why this form of drama was such a staple on network radio and now is a fixture on network television. For the writer, it can provide a stable source of income. The serial writer is aware that he is not writing deathless dialog, but there is nothing to prevent him from climbing the literary ladder. As a very young man, Irwin Shaw, the noted novelist and playwright, earned his living writing radio soap operas.

In terms of longevity, no program series is comparable to soap operas. It is not unusual for such a series to run 20 to 30 years. This is a remarkable span when you consider that so many series, such as situation comedies, are scheduled once a week and many of them last only one season.

The problem the creator or writer of a soap opera faces is the manipulation of plot to sustain a program over so many years, especially when it is broadcast five times a week. The tendency has been to run a plot line for about six months during which time a number of subplots are interwoven. One of the subplots may become the next major plot and so on ad infinitum.

In order to maintain interest and hold viewers over a 5-day period, one aspect of the major plot is played up during the week, building to a crisis on Friday that will impel viewers to return on Monday. Action usually moves very slowly so that the viewer who was forced to miss an episode on Tuesday would find she had not lost the thread when she tuned in on Wednesday.

However, Agnes Nixon, one of the most successful practitioners of the dramatic serial, has a different approach. She is the creator and chief writer for ABC's "One Life to

Live" and "All My Children"; the former, at this writing, is already in its fifth year. Mrs. Nixon designs each episode to end with a crisis which piques the viewer's interest to an extent that will induce her to tune in the next day. Therefore, the Nixon scripts embody a faster pace than most competitive soap operas, although the other networks are now increasing the tempo of their own serials.

Writers of soap operas might be termed "dialogticians." Generally, they follow the formula dictated by the program's creator. The plot is outlined for them, divided and subdivided by the week and by the day. They are told what is going to happen in each episode and their task is to fill in the dialog to fit the plot. Their problem is to write as well as they can within very tight boundaries. They must tailor their dialog to preconceived situations and to rigidly defined characters.

The soap operas deal with contemporary situations; they never enter the realm of history. They are almost always written chronologically and rarely, if ever, use flashbacks as a device. They are always moral in tone; characters who live beyond the pale of convention are unhappy. A good marriage is the ultimate goal. Social problems are discussed only in a personal sense. In a study of daytime television serials for graduate work at Georgetown University, Jennifer Greene Sullivan illustrated the foregoing point. "Although drug abuse has become a national social problem," she observed, "one young woman (in a daily serial) who is addicted is a personal problem to her family and friends. In soap operas social responsibility is no larger in scope than personal responsibility to those one loves."

It is probable that the mass of viewers to the daily serials are—if we must employ some sort of class symbol—from the lower or lower middle class. And it is interesting to note, as Ms. Sullivan has discovered in her study, that whereas the majority of characters in soap operas come from good homes, wear fashionable clothes and are engaged in respected professions, "their deepest concerns are equated with those of the lower middle class: family insulation, personal well-being as a goal irrelevant to national welfare, suspicion of politicians." Ms. Sullivan comments that 'The most likely explanation for this is that the audience wants vicarious association with well-to-do people, but it wants its own problems and concerns dealt with."

Perhaps that concept could be carried a step further. The viewers receive a great sense of satisfaction in seeing that the affluent not only suffer the same vicissitudes they do, but their problems are even more intensified. Wives having strained relationships with their husbands discover that the women with expensive homes, lovely clothes, and financially successful husbands suffer even greater strains in their marital alliances. If ever the sine qua non for writing fiction, "the suspension of disbelief," is achieved, it is in soap operas, for the avid viewers, almost to a body, forget the fiction while they watch the plot unravel. Perhaps this has its tranquilizing effect and, therefore, creates an aura of receptivity for the sponsor's products.

Many of the characters in the soap operas are lawyers and physicians. Probably, there are very few, if any, members of these professions in the immediate family of the typical dramatic serial habitue. But they are professions she is familiar with, particularly doctors, so they have relevance to her. Indeed, she may have dreams that some day one of her offspring will become a member of those respected professions. Soap operas inspire few Tevyas to sing, "If I Were a Rich Man," because the very wealthy are generally depicted as being extremely unhappy or obviously corrupt.

Ms. Sullivan raises the question in her thesis: "Why is it that in an era when viable alternatives to marriage and raising children in an overpopulated world are being explored, marriage and families (in daytime serials) are the most highly valued goals?"

There appear to be two answers. One is that the sponsor who may associate his products for the life of the soap opera insists that highly controversial subjects be avoided, lest irate viewers refuse to purchase his soap or detergent. The second is that the vast majority of soap opera viewers are still living traditionally; i.e., the husband is the breadwinner and the wife is the homemaker. Indeed, in so many of the dramatic serials, it is the woman who solves the problems, which creates a great deal of empathy for the viewer.

In the heyday of the radio soap operas, recapitulation was employed before the opening of each episode. Their television counterparts have generally avoided this device, preferably opening with a prolog or teaser and repeating plot exposition within the body of the episode.

Settings are almost always interiors, and action occurs most often in the leading character's residence or place of business, so that new sets are kept to a minimum, which is a factor in economy of production.

### "One Life to Live"

This very successful dramatic serial was created by Agnes Eckhardt Nixon. It usually employs three writers. From a production standpoint, episodes are video-taped about a week before the air date. Because of the ongoing major plot and the various subplots, it will be to best advantage to study a script in its entirety. The following is Episode No. 1007.

| | |
|---|---|
| PROLOG | (SIEGEL KITCHEN, NOONTIME. DAVE SITTING AT THE COUNTER, EILEEN MAKING A SALAD. EILEEN VERY SUB-DUED.) |
| DAVE | This is the life...coming home for lunch... watching my wife make the best chef's salad anywhere in town... |
| EILEEN | You want it with strips of cheese? |
| DAVE | Sounds perfect. |
| EILEEN | Good. I've already put them in. |
| DAVE (fondly) | That's my Eileen. |
| | ( then: ) |
| | Have you been outside yet today? The weather's really glorious. |
| EILEEN | No...but I've been thinking of doing some gardening... |
| DAVE | Well, you should...in fact, I'd say this is just the day for gardening...I'm almost tempted to play hooky from work for the rest of the afternoon and join you... |
| EILEEN | Not reacting as she normally would, bringing the salad to the table) |
| | Oh? Here you are...now, I'll just get the rolls and butter... |
| | (LOOKS AT HER A BEAT, THEN: ) |
| DAVE | Sweetheart, what's the matter? |
| EILEEN | Nothing. |
| DAVE | That's what you said this morning at breakfast when I asked you. But I just can't believe it. Something's bugging you... |
| EILEEN | It's nothing... |
| DAVE | It's something...please tell me. |
| EILEEN | Well...you promise you won't laugh if I tell you? |

DAVE
(very distressed;
very serious)     Of course I won't laugh. What is it?

EILEEN            Well...last night I had this dream...it seemed so
                  real, Dave—so real and frightening...

DAVE              What was it about?

                  (pause, then:)

EILEEN            It was about Joe. He was alive—and he was in
                  terrible trouble. You promised not to laugh!

                  (TAKE DAVE, AND DISSOLVE TO JOE IN
                  WANDA'S ROOM. HE IS SITTING ON THE
                  EDGE OF THE COUCH, ALONE, AND LOOKS
                  VERY HAGGARD AND SHAKY...HIS HEAD IS
                  IN HIS HANDS AS HE MUTTERS)

JOE               I've got to get to a doctor...it's been a long time
                  now, and I can't go on kidding myself. I need
                  medical help badly.

                  and he shakes his head as we FADE OUT.

MUSIC: BRIDGE TO:

## 1st COMMERCIAL
## ACT I

(SIEGEL KITCHEN, CONTINUATION)

DAVE              (trying to comfort her)

                  Honey—it was only a dream...

EILEEN            But Dave, it was so vivid—I tell you, I saw Joe—
                  just as real as I see you sitting there—and he
                  needed help—but I didn't know what to do to help
                  him—

                  (pause then:)

                  Why would I dream something like that if there
                  weren't something to it?

DAVE              You want to know why? Because we dream
                  about the things that are on our minds a lot...
                  didn't you tell me you'd been thinking about Joe
                  throughout the trial...even praying to him for
                  help?

EILEEN            Yes...but this isn't the first time I've thought
                  about him since he died...

DAVE              No...and I'm sure it isn't the first time you've
                  dreamed about him either...it's just the first
                  time you remember.

| | |
|---|---|
| EILEEN | But it was so vivid... |
| DAVE | Dreams often are. Sweetheart, stop worrying about it. It was a dream. That's **all**. |
| EILEEN (unconvinced) | Oh I know you're right. Dave—but— |
| | (just shakes her head, then:) |
| | But why should it happen now? |
| DAVE | Just one of those things. |
| EILEEN | (still shaking her head) |
| | I don't know...I guess maybe deep down I'll never really believe that Joe is dead... |
| DAVE | What do you mean? |
| EILEEN | Well...on one level I know he must be dead, because his car went over that cliff and no one could've survived that. But Dave, they never found his body...there was nothing...well, **final** about his death...do you see what I mean? |
| DAVE (gently) | Yes...I do. His death was never...formalized for you. |
| EILEEN | Formalized? |
| DAVE | Honey—your trouble is that when someone dies, you expect to hold a real Irish wake for two days, go to a requiem mass and then go to the cemetery and see the person buried. But that was impossible with Joe. |
| EILEEN (relaxing) | Yeah, you're right... |
| | (then) |
| | I remember when Uncle James died we had a wake that—well, you wouldn't have believed it. The only thing bad about it was that Uncle James wasn't around to enjoy it—but—well, when it was over, and all the prayers had been said...at least we knew for sure that he was gone—we could accept it. |
| | (beat) |
| | I still thought about him a lot afterwards...but not the same way I think about Joe. |

| | |
|---|---|
| DAVE | That's understandable. Didn't your Uncle James die in a bed at home, surrounded by his family? |
| EILEEN | Yes...and I guess that made a real difference, because the last memories I have of Joe were of the way he was before he left—so vital and **alive**—you remember? |
| DAVE | I'll never forget. |
| EILEEN | I remember how he looked just before he went away that last time—to California. He was wearing that crazy loud orange sportshirt we gave him for Christmas...and the farthest thing from any of our minds was that he'd never come back... |
| | (beat) |
| | I guess that's what I can't quite believe—that he's gone—forever. |
| DAVE | Sweetheart...everybody feels that way when they lose a loved one. |
| EILEEN | I suppose...you know, I often think about families who are notified that someone they love has been reported missing in the war...and presumed dead. But they never really know for sure—do they? And sometimes the person turns out not to be dead after all—he was a prisoner, or had amnesia or something... |
| DAVE | That doesn't happen very often. |
| EILEEN | But it happens often enough that—I'm sure the wives and mothers of those boys will always believe deep down that their son or husband will come back some day. |
| DAVE (gently) | Do you believe that about Joe? |
| EILEEN | (THE MIXED EMOTIONS SHOWING ON HER FACE) |
| | Oh...no...not really... |
| DAVE | (A GENTLE ARM AROUND HER) |
| | He's not going to miraculously come back...you do know that, don't you? |
| EILEEN (smiling sadly) | Yes, I know it. |
| DAVE | There's nothing more natural than for you to dream about him. He was your brother and you |

**185**

|  |  |
|---|---|
|  | loved him very dearly...but dreaming or thinking about him won't bring him back, honey. |
| EILEEN | I know. |
| DAVE | His spirit is still alive, though...and always will be as long as you and the other people who loved him still remember him...and that's what's really important. |
|  | (begin poss cut) |
| EILEEN | Maybe...that's all my dream meant...that...Joe's spirit is still alive in my mind...when I think about him... |
| DAVE | Yes...I'm sure that's what it meant. |
|  | (beat, then:) |
|  | You aren't planning to tell anyone else about the dream, are you? |
| EILEEN | Heavens, no. I wasn't even sure I should tell you—but now I'm glad I did. |
|  | (and they exchange a very warm smile.) |
|  | (END POSS CUT) |
|  | (dissolve to Joe in Wanda's room as he mutters) |
| JOE | I can't pretend any more...I'm too sick! I've got to get to a doctor—soon. |
|  | (and he gets up very shakily and gets himself a glass of water, then goes back to the couch and takes a pill from the bottle Wanda got for him. Shakes his head to clear it, then his eye falls on the newspaper back issue and he picks it up again, and very concerned, starts to read) |
| JOE (reading) | "Mr. Burke? Were you with your wife and son at the time they died?" |
|  | (beat) |
|  | "Yes—we were all out together—out in the sound. A storm came up and the boat capsized." |
|  | (beat) |
|  | "Couldn't they swim?" |
|  | (beat) |

186

"Yes, but I told you there was a storm! The waves were six feet high! They didn't have a chance."

(beat)

"I see. Then how did **you** manage to survive?"

(now Joe stops reading and puts the paper down, obviously still very disturbed)

JOE          I think Wanda's right...this guy Burke could be a fortune hunter...and...maybe even a killer.

                                                    FADE OUT

MUSIC: BRIDGE TO:

### 2nd COMMERCIAL
### ACT II

CARLA'S OFFICE, SAME TIME. CARLA IS WORKING ALONE, AND AFTER A MOMENT BERT COMES IN

BERT         Carla?

CARLA        (looking up, surprised and very pleased)

             Why, Bert. Come on in.

BERT         Thank you...how are you?

CARLA        Just fine...and you?

BERT         Couldn't be better. Jim asked me to drop by the office this afternoon if I had time—and of course I said I did since that meant a chance to see you too.

CARLA        Well, thank you.

             (looking at her little telephone buttons)

             Jim's on the phone just now...

BERT         I don't mind waiting and talking to you—unless you're too busy.

CARLA        Don't be silly.

BERT         Well, did you have a nice dinner last night?

CARLA        What?

|        | (then, remembering) |
|--------|---------------------|
|        | Oh. Well, the food was quite good. |
| BERT   | That's all? |
| CARLA  | Bert...I'd really rather not talk about it if you don't mind. |
| BERT   | (beat) |
|        | I take it you and the good lieutenant clashed again? |
| CARLA  | Mmm...something like that. |
| BERT   | You two just don't get along, do you? |
| CARLA  | Perhaps it's what they call a personality conflict. |
|        | (smile) |
|        | Shall we not spoil a beautiful afternoon by talking about Ed Hall? |
| BERT   | All right. |
|        | (a little laugh) |
|        | (then: ) |
|        | We'll talk about you and me—and a quiet dinner tonight. |
| CARLA (smiling) | Is that an invitation? |
| BERT   | It is. |
| CARLA  | I accept. |
| BERT   | Good. How about the Mirador? |
| CARLA  | Perfect. |
| BERT   | And I hope you haven't forgotten about our date later in the week? |
|        | (she looks momentarily puzzled) |
|        | Steve and Viki's wedding. You haven't changed your mind about going with me— |
| CARLA  | Oh, no, of course not. I'm looking forward to it. |
|        | (Jim's door opens and he comes in) |
| JIM    | Carla, did you— |

|          | (stops, seeing Bert) |
|----------|----------------------|
|          | Well, Bert. I'm glad you were able to make it... |
| BERT     | No problem at all, Jim. |
| JIM      | (A SMILE) |
|          | Well—if you can tear yourself away from my secretary for a minute—come on in. |
| BERT     | I'll see you later, Carla... |
| CARLA    | Right... |
|          | (and she goes back to work. As Jim and Bert go into his office, we follow them) |
| JIM      | So—how are things in Washington? |
| BERT (smiling) | Hectic... I've been spending all my free time on a committee working on specific antipollution legislation. |
| JIM      | I'm glad to hear that. |
| BERT     | I think we're really going to accomplish something, though it may take years to work its way through the wheels of government... |
| JIM      | Well, it's a start. |
| BERT     | Yes...and a very good one, especially in the field of industrial pollution of streams and lakes... |
|          | (then:) |
|          | But I'm sure you didn't ask me here to discuss the trials and tribulations of a congressman... |
| JIM      | No...not exactly...though I'm always interested. I just wanted to thank you in person for the contribution you made in congress to the national VD campaign. |
| BERT     | Jim, all I did was insert the facts and figures you gave me into the Congressional Record... |
| JIM      | But that was a tremendous help, because one of the first goals of the campaign was to make the statistics as widely available as possible. And, Bert, the fact is, more and more people are now waking up to the problem. There's been a tremendous response to Cathy's article in the Banner— |

189

| | |
|---|---|
| BERT | I'm glad to hear it—it was quite a public service for the Banner to reprint that and offer it free to its readers...how many copies have been sent out, do you know? |
| JIM | I don't have the actual figures, but the article is in its third printing—and will probably go to several more. |
| BERT | That's marvelous. |
| JIM | And public health services all over the country are responding in a very big way to the national campaign...did you know there's now a national VD hotline? |
| BERT | No, I didn't—you mean that can be called from all over the country? |
| JIM (NODS) | A central number which anyone anywhere in the country can dial absolutely free of charge—to get information or advice about VD. The phones are being manned by unpaid volunteers 24 hours a day, seven days a week. |
| BERT | What about the problem of a caller having to identify himself? That could keep a lot of people from calling in— |
| JIM | No, Bert—no problem at all—a person who calls in for help is under no obligation to identify himself. |
| BERT | Jim, I'd like to make that number available at my headquarters.. |
| | I have it right here... |
| JIM (looking) | It's area code 800...523...1885. |
| BERT (writing) | 800...523...1885. Thanks a lot. |
| | (a look at him and a warm smile) |
| | You're really excited about the progress you've made in this campaign, aren't you? |
| JIM | Well, remind me not to get too excited. We still have a long way to go—and it's always possible the problem could get worse before it gets better. |
| BERT | But as we were saying a little earlier about pollution—it's a start. |
| JIM | Yes...and a real one. |

**190**

(then, a smile:)

BERT
(laughing)
You know, I'm almost beginning to believe that congressmen have no private life—that you spend all your time working for the public good.

I believe that myself sometimes.

JIM
Do you have time for much social life in Washington?

BERT
Not too much so far. I try to make up for it when I'm back in Llanview...with a little help from your secretary.

dissolve back to Carla, working away, then Ed Hall comes in

ED
Carla?

CARLA
(looking up)
Yes?

and then we see the screen of reserve descend as she sees who it is

Oh...hello.

ED
May I come in?

CARLA
Of course. What may I do for you?

ED
Well...for starters...you can agree to join me for dinner tonight.

GO TO CARLA, nonplussed

MUSIC: BRIDGE TO:

**COMMERCIAL**

**ACT III**

continue. Hall very calm, CARLA flustered and still quite cool

CARLA
I must say I never expected you to ask me to dinner again.

HALL
Oh? Why is that?

CARLA
Because we didn't exactly hit it off the last time we were together...or don't you remember?

ED
I remember very well...that we still have a lot of getting acquainted to do...

**191**

|  | and he smiles at her...it is this that upsets CARLA more than what he says...his supreme self-confidence and this should come across clearly |
|---|---|
| CARLA | I think we're already quite well acquainted. |
| ED | I'm sorry—but I don't give up that easily—you and I are going to become friends. |
| CARLA (controlling herself) | Mmm...perhaps. In time. |
| ED | Right. And that's all I'm asking for—a little bit of your time...I enjoyed myself the other night. |
| CARLA | I'll just bet you did. |
| ED | And I think you did too—just a little—even if you won't admit it. After all—when we weren't arguing, we found quite a lot to laugh about. |
| CARLA | You certainly are persistent. |
| ED | Maybe that's the cop in me. Anyway—will you join me for dinner tonight? |
| CARLA (very cool) | Thank you very much, but I already have plans for this evening. |
| ED | Oh. Well, then, how about tomorrow night? |
| CARLA | Ed, please...this is all very flattering...but I'm just not interested in having dinner with you...tomorrow night or any other time. |

(a joke)

Then how about a movie?

|  |  |
|---|---|
| CARLA | (in no mood for joking) |

No really. I'm perfectly willing to try to be friends with you—but I am not interested in going out with you. All right?

| ED (smiling faintly) | Well—you'll change your mind... |
|---|---|
| CARLA (rankled) | What's that supposed to mean? |
| ED | Just that I'm quite sure...you **will** go out with me again. |
| CARLA | (now her cool is gone) |

|  |  |
|---|---|
|  | Oh, I see! And just what makes you so sure—lieutenant! |
| ED | Carla—we may not have known each other for very long— |
| CARLA | Correction! We don't **know** each other at all! |
| ED<br>(calmly) | You're speaking for you—not for me. I think I read you pretty well— |
| CARLA | (the very phrase infuriates her) |
|  | You think you read me pretty well!!! Oh, I like that!! Tell me, is that rare bit of insight another sign of the cop in you! |
| ED | (another maddening little smile, he shakes his head) |
|  | We're going to have to do something about that hair-trigger temper of yours— |
| CARLA | We are not going to do anything—because we are not going to see each other again— |
|  | (AND SHE'S QUITE LOUD HERE WHEN JIM'S DOOR OPENS AND JIM AND BERT COME OUT. CARLA STOPS ABRUPTLY. THERE IS AN AWKWARD SILENCE,. THEN:) |
| JIM | Well—lieutenant—how are you? |
| ED | Hello, Dr. Craig—Mr. Skelly— |
|  | (uptight) |
| BERT | Nice to see you, lieutenant. |
|  | (they shake hands. There is an awkward pause, then:) |
| CARLA | (RISING, QUICKLY) |
|  | Jim—I'd like to see you in your office—we...uh...have to discuss your appointments for this afternoon— |
|  | (tapping her appointment book) |
| JIM | Oh, of course, Carla... |
|  | (she rises quickly leaving the book) |
|  | Bert, thanks again for stopping by— |
| BERT | My pleasure— |
| JIM | Lieutenant? Did you want to see me about anything? |

| | |
|---|---|
| ED | No...I was just in the neighborhood... |
| | then, with a faint smile, not having missed anything |
| | Carla...your appointment book... |
| CARLA | (furious and trying to control it) |
| | Oh, I—that's right, I—thank you. |
| | and she goes back to her desk and snatches it up. Then she and JIM go into JIM's office. There is an uncomfortable beat as BERT and HALL size each other up, then: |
| ED | Well, how are things in congress these days? |
| BERT | Busy...the way they were here when I was D.A.... |
| ED | Yes, we still miss you down at the department. |
| BERT | Well, I miss the department...and all my friends...I don't see them as often as I used to. |
| ED | No, I suppose not. |
| BERT | (beat, then:) |
| | I think Carla's been working too hard lately...didn't you think she seemed a little on edge just now? |
| ED | Mmm...now that you mention it. |
| BERT | I've noticed before that you and she...seem to rub each other the wrong way...why is that? |
| ED (cool) | Why don't you ask Carla? |
| BERT (cool as well) | Maybe I will...I'm having dinner with her tonight. |
| | and as they look at each other...dissolve back to EILEEN and DAVE...DAVE at the door about to leave |
| EILEEN | I'm so glad you came home for lunch, honey...you've cheered me up about a thousand percent. |
| DAVE | I'm glad. |

**194**

| | |
|---|---|
| EILEEN | (kisses him) |
| | Have a good afternoon... |
| DAVE | Thanks... |
| | and he opens the door...then steps back as STEVE comes up. Very surprised) |
| | Why, Steve... |
| STEVE | Hello, Dave...Eileen...I thought I should use the kitchen door. |
| EILEEN | What a nice surprise. Come on in. |
| STEVE | Thanks. I called Dave's office and when they said he was here...I decided to come over and say hello to the two of you. |
| EILEEN | Well, we're so glad you did! Dave, you can stay just a little longer and have a cup of coffee with Steve, can't you? |
| DAVE | Of course. |
| | coming back and getting settled, then: |
| | So tell us, Steve—how's the bridegroom? Nervous? |
| STEVE | Not a bit...I'm calm...and happy...and the luckiest man alive. |
| EILEEN | Of course you are. Because everything's going just perfectly, right? |
| STEVE | Right! And the reason I'm here—I wanted to confirm something with Dave... |
| DAVE | Sure, what is it? |
| STEVE | |
| | Well...once upon a time...you agreed to be my best man...and I just hope you're still intending to be. |
| DAVE (smiling warmly) | Of course I am— |
| | holds out his hand...they shake...EILEEN watches them, tears in her eyes |
| | Eileen and I are both so happy for you and Viki, aren't we, honey? |

|  | turns to her |
|  | Eileen? |
| STEVE | (also noticing) |
|  | Eileen—what's wrong? Why are you crying? |
| EILEEN | I'm...oh, it's nothing...and it's everything... |
|  | and smiling at them through her tears... |

FADE OUT

MUSIC: BRIDGE TO:

**COMMERCIAL**
**ACT IV**

(CONTINUE. EILEEN GOES TO STEVE AND
IMPULSIVELY HUGS HIM)

| EILEEN | Oh, Steve, I'm so happy for you and Viki. |
| STEVE (moved) | Thank you, Eileen... |
| EILEEN | I want you to have all the best things in life, and never have any problems... |
| STEVE (a little laugh) | I doubt if things can be quite that rosy, but thank you. |
| EILEEN | When I think of what the two of you have been through...and now that you're finally going to be together...oh, Dave, it's so beautiful, don't you think so? |
| DAVE (warmly) | Yes, I do. |
| STEVE | Well, I owe it all to you, Dave..if it weren't for you and the sacrifices you made for me...I doubt if I'd be here today. |
| EILEEN | Oh, don't even say that. |
| STEVE | Well, it's true. If your husband hadn't had faith in me all along and defended me...Dave, I've said it before and I'll probably say it again...I'm deeply grateful to you. |
| DAVE (embarrassed) | Steve...I defended you because I believed in you...and because you're my friend...it wasn't anything special. |

196

| | |
|---|---|
| STEVE | On the contrary...it was very special. And that's why I'm doubly glad that you're going to be my best man. |
| EILEEN | Oh, well, there was never any doubt of that. Just as there was never really any doubt that things would turn out the way they did...I prayed all through the trial—and my prayers were answered. |
| DAVE | Yes...I believe that's true...your prayers were answered through our anonymous man...who turned up the evidence at the last minute. |
| EILEEN | Yeah—Hey, don't you wish you knew who he was. |
| STEVE | Yes...but there still hasn't been any answer to my open letter...and I'm quite sure now we'll never know who he is. |

dissolve back to JOE still sitting alone, still feeling rotten, trying to work himself up to some course of action. He has the paper open to the trial transcript again...and we hear his thoughts:

| | |
|---|---|
| JOE (VO) | There's so little time now till the wedding...till Viki marries this Burke guy. If there were only some way I could find out more about him...if there were somebody I could ask...so I could be sure... |

shakes his head, then:

I'd sure like to talk to Eileen—if anyone could give me the lowdown on Burke, she could...

pause, then a reflective smile

It'd be just a little after lunchtime now...she'd be in the kitchen, cleaning up after lunch...maybe humming to herself the way she used to...and she'd be **alone**...I could just go over, knock on that old back door...

and he goes into a pretaped fantasy as follows:

siegel kitchen...this should look fairly surrealistic. Scene is in progress, JOE having already revealed himself

| | |
|---|---|
| EILEEN | Joe, I don't believe it! I see you standing there, but I don't believe it! |

| | |
|---|---|
| JOE | I'm sorry...I know it's a shock, honey...but I had to see you... |
| EILEEN | (impulsively hugging him) |
| | Oh, but what a wonderful shock! I've never been so happy in my life! My brother alive—with me—and—and Viki! I've got to call Viki! |
| JOE | No! I don't want anyone to know you've seen me—including Viki! |
| EILEEN | But—but—why not? |
| JOE | Nobody must know I'm back...you've got to promise me you'll keep our meeting a secret— promise me, Eileen! |
| EILEEN | All right, I promise...but...but why? Joe, don't you love Viki any more? |
| JOE | I love her more than ever...and that's why she mustn't know about me. I'm a sick man, Eileen...I'm very sick... |
| EILEEN | Joe—no—what is it? |
| JOE | Never mind...but I'm sick, I'd only be a burden to her...but before I leave...I have to know that she's happy... |
| EILEEN | She'll be happy when she finds out you're alive. |
| JOE | No. I may be dying— |
| EILEEN | Oh, no! What're you saying, Joe! You're alive and back with us— |
| JOE | Eileen, I'll explain everything later— |
| EILEEN | Joe, if you're sick, we'll take you to Jim Craig— we'll get the best doctors in the world... |
| JOE | No! Eileen, listen to me! The only reason I came here is because I knew **you**—of all people—would be able to give me an honest opinion about the man Viki's to marry, Steve Burke. |
| EILEEN | (her face changing) |
| | Oh...Steve... |
| JOE | I have to know, Eileen. If Burke is a good, honest man, then I can go away...at peace with myself, and never come back... |
| EILEEN | Joe...no...you can't do that—I won't let you— |

| | |
|---|---|
| JOE | Just tell me, Eileen? Is he the man who can make Viki happy? |
| EILEEN | (shaking her head) |
| | No, Joe...no, he's not. I've never for a moment believed that Viki was really in love with Steve...not the way she was in love with you...she could never love anyone the way she loved you... |
| JOE | But what do you think of him as a man? Do you believe the story he told about how his first wife and child died? |
| EILEEN (frantically) | Joe, I only know he couldn't love her as much as you did...he'd never begin to make her as happy as you did— |
| | the fantasy abruptly ends and we see JOE with his hands to his head having an argument with himself |
| JOE (aloud:) | What am I doing! What the devil's happening to me! I've got to start being objective about this! How do I know Eileen would react that way! Maybe she'd tell me Burke is a great guy and he and Viki will be happy together? |
| (beat) | |
| | Come on, Joe—you were a pretty good reporter at one time—do you suspect this guy because there's good reason to—or because you want to? Think about it! |
| pause, then: | |
| | Victor Lord obviously likes the guy—Victor may be a stinker...but he's no dope! He'd have had Burke checked out from top to bottom before he gave the green light to his marrying Viki...You know that! So maybe Burke's okay. |
| then, another pause | |
| | But still...there's that whole story about his wife and child...and the boat overturning...and only Burke being saved... |
| stops, just shakes his head, then speaks aloud again | |
| | There's only one way I can be sure...only one way. I've got to see Burke myself. |
| | FADE OUT |

MUSIC: BRIDGE TO:

**COMMERCIAL**

SUGGESTED BEAUTY SHOT: EILEEN,
DAVE AND STEVE IN A WARM SCENE.

The prolog is, in essence, a teaser preceding the first commercial, and its purpose is to capture the viewer's immediate attention. There are actually six commercials during the half hour. The episode is divided into four acts and the prolog. Each act concludes with a small crisis; the big crisis comes at the end of Act Four to stir the viewer's excitement and assure her tuning in the next day.

Predictability is an asset in a soap opera script, not a liability. Viewers are rarely shocked or disappointed by the outcome of a situation. The use of truisms is also a satisfactory device for the dramatic serial. When Eileen, in Act One, asks "Why would I dream something like that if there weren't something to it?" Dave replies, "Because we dream about the things that are on our minds a lot." You can almost see ten million viewers nodding their heads in agreement.

Notice the opening lines of the prolog. Dave says, "Coming home for lunch. . .watching my wife make the best chef's salad. . ." This dialog immediately identifies the locale and the relationship of the characters. They are all too well known to the constant viewer, but in the vast audience that television reaches, there are always newcomers to a program. Perhaps this may seem as if we were belaboring a point, but actually a good TV writer uses normal dialog to convey exposition. The opening line may well have been "Say, you make the best chef's salad. . ." Also normal dialog but no information.

Act One is a dialog between Eileen and Dave largely devoted to Eileen's dream and the supposed death of Joe. It puts the viewer into a very sympathetic mood because she knows Joe is alive. Therefore, she not only feels sorry for Eileen but at the same time achieves a sense of superiority in possessing knowledge the heroine lacks. The curtain scene brings us back to Joe. His reading of the newspaper is, in actuality, a recap, and informs the viewer of an important element of the plot. Act One winds up with a strong crisis and develops a suspense motif.

Act Two takes us into another plot line. This time it involves the romantic problems of Carla and her relationship to Congressman Bert Skelly and police lieutenant Ed Hall. We might take note of the economic status of the male characters: Dave, an attorney, Bert, a congressman, Jim, a doctor, and

Ed, a lieutenant of police. All rather well up in the middle class ladder.

This particular episode of "One Life to Live" has added interest for the script writer. Act Two interweaves a public service message regarding VD. This was evidently done in response to a request from a governmental or social agency to assist in its anti-VD campaign. Soap operas often cooperate with such public service campaigns. However, it places an additional challenge on the writer to integrate the message into the framework of the story. The congressman also mentions antipollution measures which gives the episode an added feeling of currency.

The potential writer should be aware of another requirement for the scripter: the inclusion of stage directions and emotional qualifiers: for example, CARLA: (NOW HER COOL IS GONE); JIM: (HE RISES QUICKLY, LEAVING THE BOOK). There are rarely any camera directions since this is the province of the director. However, the writer may indicate a few basic directions: DISSOLVE BACK TO EILEEN AND DAVE , and at the end of every act: FADE OUT .

The curtain scene for Act Two is comparatively a small crisis. This may be because Act Three is in immediate sequence. The greater crisis at the Act One curtain is strong enough to hold the viewer, while the secondary plot line is developed.

Act Three heightens the conflict between Lieutenant Hall and Carla. Although she tells him, in no uncertain terms, that they are not going to see each other again, the viewer is left with the feeling that this is hardly the end of the affair. A triangle situation is developed in the scene between Ed and Bert, and we are given additional background information when Bert says, "Busy...the way they were when I was DA ..."

This act brings us back to the major plot as we return to Eileen and Dave's home and meet Steve Burke and his fiancee, Viki. The curtain scene leaves the viewer with the premonition that Eileen's tears are not solely for joy.

In Act Four we learn, if we are a new viewer, that it was Dave who defended Steve. And it is Steve, of course, about whom Joe is suspicious. The concluding scene of this episode employs a device rarely used in soap operas: fantasy. Generally, soap operas, as we have mentioned, eschew flashbacks and fantasy, preferring straightforward story telling. The chronological trail is much simpler to follow. That "One Life to Live" does use such a device is definitely to its credit. The artifice does permit a heightening of suspense and rings down the curtain on a Big Crisis. The viewer eagerly anticipates tomorrow's episode.

In the final analysis, we find that this episode does contain a good many elements of conflict and a variety of action: Eileen's troubled dream about her brother who is presumed dead; Joe's suspicions of Steve Burke who is about to marry the girl he, Joe, was in love with; Carla's conflict with Ed Hall and the intrusion of Congressman Bert Skelly; and, finally, Joe's determination to discover the truth about Burke. As a writer of dramatic serials, you may not be involved with literature, but you will certainly be inundated with plot.

# Chapter 6

# The Radio Drama

Radio dramas are rare happenings today, but there are some stirrings. In 1968, the Radio Drama Development Project was initiated under the auspices of WGBH-FM in Boston. The project was supported by grants from the National Endowment for the Arts, Old Dominion Foundation, and WGBH Educational Foundation. Some of the objectives of the project were to reinvigorate radio drama as a theatrical form, to give promising playwrights a chance to have their work produced, and to convey the excitement of radio drama to the public. A radio drama script contest was held, offering prizes totaling $10,000.

The prize-winning play, awarded $5000, "portrayed the lynching mentality in graphic poetic imagery." The second prize-winning play was a "a satirical fable dealing with paternalism in civil rights." And the third prize-winning script was a fantasy "wherein the cool telephone sparks a hot love across space, real and psychic."

In 1972, the cudgels for radio drama were taken up by EARPLAY, with joint sponsorship by the University of Wisconsin Extension and the Corporation for Public Broadcasting. This project is specifically designed to produce radio dramas for distribution over the public radio stations in the United States, a network of some 500 outlets. The objectives of EARPLAY are outlined in its prospectus for acquiring scripts.

"There is no present market for drama on radio in this country. Further, it's fair to say that there never was a consistent market for plays of literary quality. It's our attempt, through the EARPLAY project, to create such a market. A basic assumption of the project is that because of the nature of radio listening in this country today, plays must be short—30 minutes is the absolute maximum; 15 minutes is much better; and five to ten minutes has the best chance of being heard by significant numbers of people. This is a serious limitation but, in our opinion, not a fatal one. The fatal mistake would be to ignore the limitation.

"Another limitation we must acknowledge is that most people listen to the radio on small monophonic receivers of only standard quality. The implication of this to the writer is that delicate sound fabrics or very soft focus treatment will tend to be lost in ambiance and low quality receiver pickup. Therefore, we are primarily interested in pieces with strong character treatment, bold sound backgrounds, and clear plot lines. This does not mean, however, that we will not consider pieces which are impressionistic in treatment or create purposeful ambiguity. Though we are attempting to reach a significant audience, we are aware of the need for a place for playwrights to try new ideas and new techniques. We hope that the EARPLAY project and National Public Radio can provide such a training ground.

"The EARPLAY project is a new project. It is not an attempt to bring back 'the good old days of radio.' It is an attempt to reawaken in playwrights and in listening audiences the interest and excitement in radio drama which has been dormant for so long. EARPLAY provides a production capability using the best radio acting talent in a thoroughly up-to-date production setting. It is the hope of this project that public radio, via the Corporation for Public Broadcasting and the University of Wisconsin Extension, will be able to provide this country with a writer's market modeled on that of the BBC in England where as many as 75 new dramatists are introduced every year on radio."

It is interesting to note the strict limitations placed on script lengths by EARPLAY. In contrast, the WGBH-FM project accepted scripts of much longer length: 45 minutes or more. We have scripts from two of the top prize winners of the EARPLAY competition and the excerpts we have chosen should give you an indication of what is being considered as contemporary radio drama.

"The Telephone" is a 15-minute play written by Carol Adorjan. It is, in essence, a characterization by dialog or, more precisely, monolog; a portrait of a psychosis. The opening sequence thrusts you immediately into the verbal disjointedness of the protagonist: the woman.

SOUND:   FOOTSTEPS:   MAN'S AND WOMAN'S ON WOOD FLOOR

WOMAN: It's right this way. You'll have to excuse the way everything looks—not that I could've done much about it, just moving and all—but, frankly, I didn't expect you today.

MAN: They didn't tell you I'd be here today?

WOMAN:  Oh, yes, they told me—one of those telephone company voices—but I didn't believe it for a minute. I mean how can you believe a voice like that? Smooth and clear—like ice, you know?—not a ripple. Have you noticed how they all sound exactly alike?

MAN: No, ma'am, can't say I have.

WOMAN: Oh, yes, it's very distinctive. Like an accent you might say. I was at this party recently. Just before we moved as a matter of fact. And there was this girl—woman really—and she had one of those voices. She had a couple of other things too, which shall remain nameless if you know what I mean. Anyway, someone said, "Where's she from?" And I said, "From the telephone company."

SOUND: MAN AND WOMAN ASCENDING STAIRS

WOMAN: Remember that movie? Oh, you know the one: where everyone lives on the other side of some mountain in Tibet or somewhere, and they all look beautiful and healthy and young. Very young. Some of them are hundreds of years old, but to look at them you'd never believe it. Oh, what is the name of it?

MAN: I don't know, ma'am.

WOMAN: No. You're too young I suppose. I myself was a very young girl when I saw it. It's been on TV since.

MAN: I don't watch much TV. Sports is all.

WOMAN: It wasn't the same. Neither was the book. Anyway, the leading lady—you'd know her if I could remember her name: a very prominent person; star of one of those series that ran forever. Of course, in the movie she was much younger. Anyway, she decides to leave this place—this...paradise on the other side of the mountain so to speak, because she's in love with Ronald Coleman or someone. I forget. He's from another world you might say, stumbled into the place by accident. Right down here. The room at the end of the hall.

The verbal diarrhea and the nonsequiturs flow from the woman as the man attempts to keep his mind on his task.

WOMAN: You know, I am truly amazed at the service here. When that girl said, "We'll send a man right out," I didn't believe it—not for a minute. They all tell you that: "We'll send a man right out." That's what they tell you. To put you off. You're not going to believe this, but—where we were before?—you couldn't get a phone unless you were pregnant or psychotic.

MAN: Is that so, ma'am?

WOMAN: Absolutely. Pregnant or psychotic. Limits the choices, you'll have to admit.

MAN: Yes, ma'am, I'll admit that.

WOMAN: It was months before I got one. Talk about discrimination. What's a person in his right mind going to do? I mean his hands are tied. Tied! Without a phone, he can't even organize! And quiet? You have no idea how quiet quiet is, until you can depend on it staying that way. I mean a phone is never quiet—is it?—if it can ring any time it gets the notion.

MAN: I guess not, ma'am.

WOMAN: There was this cartoon—did you see it?—where every time the phone rang it grew—actually grew!—until at the end it took up all the space and the man...he was on the inside.

MAN: I didn't see it, ma'am.

WOMAN: I don't like cartoons very much either, but that one...that one I could understand, because it said a very true thing if you know what I mean. I myself had a dream very much like that once. There was all this trouble out on the streets. Right in front of my window, all this...trouble? I couldn't make out what was happening exactly, except that there was shouting—oh, a lot of shouting—and I ran to the phone—you know, to help—to get help. Only the phone...it was very large and different—strange—and I couldn't get hold of it. I managed to knock the receiver off somehow—I remember that—and I could hear the buzzing—the dial tone?—but that was all. And then—then! What did happen then? Oh, yes. I woke up. The buzzing? My alarm.

The crux of the situation revolves about the placement of a shutoff on the new telephone.

SOUND: RECEIVER PICKED UP AND REPLACED

MAN: All set, ma'am.

WOMAN: And the shutoff?

MAN: The shutoff. You want it shut off, ma'am?

WOMAN: You mean you didn't put on a shutoff? They didn't tell you I wanted a shutoff?

SOUND: DISMANTLING PHONE

WOMAN: You see? Just like I said. I told that girl. Made a special point of it as a matter of fact. "We'll take care of it," she said. In one of those voices—one of those telephone company voices.

MAN: Probably an oversight, ma'am. I don't think there's much call for shutoffs.

WOMAN: No. Of course not. Who knows there is such a thing? I myself didn't know there was such a thing until after the doctor bills. They keep it very quiet—confidential!—like a secret weapon or something. Heaven forbid a person should ask for one! Un-American. Because you want a little privacy, you are un-American.

MAN: Wouldn't it be easier to have an unlisted number?

WOMAN: But they'd still have it, wouldn't they? An unlisted number. I mean there's a special list for unlisted numbers, isn't there?

MAN: Yes, ma'am, but—

WOMAN: Besides, it's the ringing does it. "Get more exercise. Drink more water. Eat green vegetables..fruit! They all said the same thing, those doctors, but it was the ringing did it. I mean I had very serious physical problems if you know what I mean, because of the ringing.

MAN: Do you want the downstairs phone shut off, too, ma'am?

WOMAN: Yes. Yes. Both phones.

MAN: But...you won't hear it ring then, ma'am.

WOMAN: Isn't that the whole idea? I mean what good is a shutoff, will you tell me, if it doesn't shut anything off? It's the ringing, don't you see? I used to leave my house—go out—because of the ringing. You know, I'd forgotten that. I'd wander around—shop, do anything!—to avoid the ringing, and I used to wonder: did it ring if I wasn't there to hear it. You know, like the tree falling in an empty forest. Does it?

MAN: Ma'am?

WOMAN: Ring when no one's there.

MAN: No, ma'am, not if it's shut off.

WOMAN: You don't understand. I mean **before**. I didn't know about the shutoff until **after** I had all that trouble—all those doctor bills. I've never been—well, regular, if you want to know the truth, since.

The WOMAN continues to harangue the telephone installer until his work is completed, but as he leaves she has another neurotic reaction.

SOUND: TRUCK PULLING AWAY

WOMAN: He shut off the phone.

SOUND: DOOR CLOSING

WOMAN: The phone!
SOUND: QUICK FOOTSTEPS

WOMAN:   That's it. I'll call them. That's what I'll do.

SOUND:   FOOTSTEPS OUT. RECEIVER PICKED UP

WOMAN: I'll tell them.

SOUND DIALING O

WOMAN: They'll take care of it.

SOUND: AMPLIFIED RINGING

WOMAN: They don't answer. Why don't they answer? My God! I can't call out. I can't even call out!

SOUND: CLICK AS OPERATOR ANSWERS

VOICE: Operator.

WOMAN: Oh, Operator. Thank heaven! I thought you weren't there. I thought no one was there.

VOICE: May I help you ?

WOMAN: Yes. Yes. Please. My phone? I think there's something wrong with my phone. I just moved in, you see, and this young man—the telephone company man?—well, it was his first day and he didn't know about the shutoff. I myself didn't until after the doctor bills.

VOICE: One moment please.

SOUND: AMPLIFIED RINGING

WOMAN: No, operator. Wait, please. Operator?

SOUND: CLICKING CRADLE

WOMAN: You don't understand. Operator!

SOUND: CLICK AS VOICE ANSWERS:

VOICE:   Good afternoon. This is your service represen-tative. May I help you?

WOMAN: I just told you, operator, it's my phone. There is something wrong with my phone.

VOICE:   I am sorry but you have not reached the operator. This is your service representative. May I help you?

WOMAN:  You're not the person I was speaking with?

VOICE:   This is your service representative. Would you like me to connect you with your operator?

WOMAN:  No. No. Please. It's just that your voices...they sound so much alike. It's very distinctive—like an accent you might say.

VOICE: May I be of any assistance?

WOMAN: Yes. It's my phone. I think there's something wrong with my phone. The young man?—he shut it off. He was new, you see—a very nice young man. I don't mean he wasn't a nice young man. But he shut it off from the...inside? And I can't get at it.

VOICE: We'll send a man right out. Just give me your name and—

WOMAN: No. No. You don't understand. This one—the phone I am talking to you on—this phone is not shut off and—

VOICE: Your name and number please, and we'll send—

WOMAN: No. Please. You don't understand.

VOICE: You don't want a shutoff. Just give me your—

WOMAN: A shutoff. Yes. I want a shutoff. Two! But this phone—the one I'm talking to you on?—it isn't off, don't you see?—because he didn't know how to do it except from the inside. The inside! And I don't want that, because I have to be the one, don't you see?

VOICE: We'll send a man right out to install ringer shutoffs. Now, that's on two phones?

WOMAN: Both phones. Yes. But that is not why I am calling, operator.

VOICE: This is your service representative.

WOMAN: Yes. Forgive me. But you see I am calling because I want someone to check the line—to ring me, don't you see?—because this phone...this phone has been on—I don't know how long!—and it hasn't rung. Not one ring. And I'm sure there must be something wrong with it, because they always ring—don't they?—when they're on. Even if a person isn't home, they ring. And I can't just sit here, can I?—waiting.

VOICE: If you hang up, Ma'am, I'll have the operator ring you.

SOUND: <u>CLICK FOLLOWED BY DIAL TONE WHICH GRADUALLY INCREASES IN VOLUME THROUGH FOLLOWING</u>

WOMAN: My number. Wait, operator.

SOUND: <u>FURIOUSLY CLICKING CRADLE</u>

WOMAN: You don't have my number. Answer me please. Operator, I've been cut off. Operator. Operator! (FADING) There is no way to get through—no getting through to them. Operator! (DISTANT) Someone! Please.

SOUND: DIAL TONE UP, MUSIC IN AND BLENDING. OUT.

Before we offer any additional comments, it may be advisable to examine another of the top prize winners. This radio play is called "Tweet" and was written by Harvey Jacobs, who is also a short story writer with credits in **Esquire, Cosmopolitan, Playboy** and many other magazines and the author of "The Egg of the Glak" (Harper & Row). His script runs approximately ten minutes. The story line is highly imaginative, although the vehicle for relating the drama—confessional on the psychiatrist's couch—is hardly that. Nevertheless, the involvement with a psychiatrist is a contemporary situation. The format Jacobs uses is actually that of the stage play rather than the radio play and indicated directions are minimal.

(The sound of a young man, Jordan Freeley, clearing his throat. The clearing is answered by a cough from Dr. Miermier, his psychiatrist.)

JORDAN

You coughed when I cleared my throat, Dr. Miermier.

DR.

Thus...?

JORDAN

The cough took you at least ten seconds. Why should I pay for that?

DR.

You feel you should not pay for the time I took coughing?

JORDAN

Or for the time spent discussing it. I want a readjusted statement for this session or 20 extra seconds.

DR.

No.

JORDAN

Oh.

**DR.**

Can you proceed now, Mr. Freeley?

**JORDAN**

You won't call me Jordan, will you?

**DR.**

No. Thus...?

**JORDAN**

Thus...thus...nobody says thus any more.
This is pointless.

**DR.**

This is without point? An interesting image.

**JORDAN**

I get your...meaning. Without point. The broken lance. And
I was free-lancing when I met her.

**DR.**

Yes.

**JORDAN**

You could applaud once in a while.

**DR.**

No.

**JORDAN**

I was free-lancing, right. I was working on a nostalgia
book for Purvin Press. The Tens.

**DR.**

The tens?

**JORDAN**

The 1910s. Fascinating decade. And virtually unknown.
Everything else, milked; not the tens.

**DR.**

Milked?

**JORDAN**

Milked. Of course. Zowie. I fell into that one. I **was**
drinking when I met her. At a party. But not milk. Vodka.

It was vodka martinis. It was. I remember Dick Figgie asking me what I had against olives. Olives...

(Fade in sounds of party, music, talk, etc.)

The author employs the flashback technique throughout the play. This is a natural device since he is describing past events to his psychiatrist. In the first flashback scene, Jordan is at a party where his friend, Dick, introduces him to a beautiful girl. She is Betty Royce who has recently had a polyp removed from her throat and, temporarily, can communicate only by whistling. Betty and Jordan reach an immediate understanding and fall in love. Jordan explains the unusual situation to the doctor.

JORDAN

Thus we made love. Dr. Miermier, you must know how rare true response is. How amazingly unusual. I mean, true response. Not just so much breathing. Response.

DR.

Response, yes.

JORDAN

Well, believe me when I tell you—true response.

DR.

Ah.

JORDAN

And no darkness. No silence. We made love with the lights on and we kept on talking.

DR.

Talking? All during?

JORDAN

All during.

DR.

You said Miss Betty whistled. You said she did not speak.

JORDAN

And that is how it was. That is how. I used clumsy, stupid words. She whistled. Whistled with the liquidity and fluency of the rarest bird in the greenest forest of the mind.

DR.

So? She whistled as you copulated?

JORDAN

Don't make it sound like I was making out with a tea
kettle.

DR.

Hostility, Mr. Freeley?

JORDAN

Look, doctor. It's hard enough to talk about this. Like, who
the hell are you to know so much? Who the hell are you to
write this down? It's my material.

But it is a love that comes to an abrupt ending. We
discover this bittersweet conclusion in the final scenes.

(Sound of radio playing soft music. Wine is being poured.)

BETTY

(Whistles)

JORDAN

You know, I can't explain any of this...but so much understanding has grown between us...

BETTY

(A few whistles)

JORDAN

And you haven't spoken a solitary sentence. Not in the
conventional sense. But soon your voice will be back.

BETTY

(Three whistles)

JORDAN

Three days. It's like knowing someone blind who suddenly
regains sight. I mean, dearest, what will you say?

BETTY

(Whistles)

JORDAN

Oh, it is important even if you don't think so.

BETTY

(Whistles)

JORDAN

You could say, Jordan, I love you. Or you could say, Jordan, I hate you.

BETTY

(Calm quizzical whistle)

JORDAN

Or you could say nothing. Just stand there, not whistling, not speaking, nothing. You could kill me, Betty. I'm not ready for this.

BETTY

(Whistles)

JORDAN

Danger signs are flashing. I know you feel it too. I mean, you've never heard me silent. You know what I mean?

BETTY

(Whistle with a question mark)

JORDAN

We are like bombs in each other's hand. Who defuzes who? Okay, Betty, alarms are going off.

BETTY

(Whistles)

JORDAN

We cannot see each other again.

BETTY

(A mild whistle)

JORDAN

I knew you would agree! I knew it. We have a perfect understanding! Wait until Dr. Miermier hears about this. What progress I've made.

BETTY

(Wan whistle)

JORDAN

You would love him. He's a wonderful older man.

(Tapping of the pencil and a ripping of paper.)

#### DR.

Your time is up, Mr. Freeley.

#### JORDAN

So you see, doctor, I gave you a good review. And don't tell me about the word "older." I know it connotes jealousy. I must admit, I thought we were at a stalemate. But after last weekend, I see light gleaming at the end of this dark corridor of the mind.

#### DR.

You're talking to get back the 20 seconds you think I owe you, Mr. Freeley.

#### JORDAN

Forty seconds. You coughed twice. Are you sick? Don't die on me. Not now.

#### DR.

Next Friday, Mr. Freeley.

#### JORDAN

Take care of yourself. This could be the breakthrough. I mean, I was right to stop seeing her, wasn't I? All things considered. It will never end now...never. It will last forever for both of us. (Whistles.)

#### DR.

The session has ended, Mr. Freeley.

#### JORDAN

Oh. I see the juxtaposition. Lord, the mind is a fantastic device.

#### DR.

Good night.

(The door to the Dr.'s office opens and closes. We hear Jordan whistling in the corridor, lower, lower, fade and out.)

And so we have in a brief episode a meeting of lovers in a very bizarre situation. The resolution is like a nonobjective painting: you read into it what you will. This is also true of "The Telephone." To continue our analogy with abstract painting, it is not what meaning you absorb from these plays but do you like them. In other words, they arouse a completely subjective response.

Neither of the plays has a beginning, middle, nor end in the classic sense. Interestingly enough, although they are very contemporary creative efforts; they are more closely allied to the slice-of-life school that categorized the early days of TV drama. That is, life itself is merely a series of incidents and no one's existence is precisely packaged.

However, with today's generation in total rebellion against old forms, we believe that EARPLAY is correct in not attempting to bring back "the good old days of radio." One station we know of, in Washington, did attempt just that by scheduling some of the radio dramas of yesteryear but with no success. The EARPLAY prospectus mentions the viable radio drama situation in England; radio drama is also ably represented in Canada. Yet both these countries have extensive television facilities, public and commercial.

In the United States, the music-and-news format has come to be the accepted pattern as if radio listeners in our country only tuned in on the run. A majority of listeners are literally rush-hour patrons: this is the time most of our adult working population does its listening while driving to and from work. At other times, radio listening is highly personalized: teenagers and their tinny transistors blaring out the newest rock or soul or underground or, at the other end of the scale, there are the few but intensely loyal classical music lovers and their fine stereos. It was in Washington, too, that these loyal longhairs saved the city's only AM classical music station from being turned into another proponent of pop.

Public radio stations may succeed in establishing a new form of radio drama, but it will be necessary to make imaginative use of basic tools. The pitfall the radio dramatist faces is comparable to that of many young filmmakers who substitute technique for substance. We have listened to several of a new breed of radio dramas whose only innovation was to have the narration put to music and sung to the accompaniment of a guitar. This is, of course, the technique of the ancient troubadours. Still, if an old and honorable technique will serve a modern purpose, why not use it. But while you are concentrating on how to say it, be sure you have something to say.

## PRECEPTS AND PRINCIPLES

The basic elements essential for writing television drama are equally applicable to radio drama. But radio has no camera to create visuals; therefore, radio dramatists must rely upon three tools: dialog, sound, and music. With these three tools, they can play upon the imagination of the listener to evoke any scene they wish. And they actually have more latitude than the TV playwright. The latter has to consider settings and locations. The more locations, the more expensive the production. In radio, a description by a narrator or a line of dialog or the use of sound effects can transport the listener in moments from place to place.

In the following study of the prize-winning play (Writer's Guild Award for 1971) by Sol Panitz, "A Walk with Two Shadows," we will observe how a skilled craftsman uses the tools of his trade. Panitz has written many excellent radio dramas during his long career, both for commercial networks and independent stations and for the Voice of America. "A Walk with Two Shadows" is an hour drama based on a little known incident in the life of General George Washington. It required extensive research.

The dramatist has used a narrator for commentary and transitions. The narration itself is poetic, philosophic, perceptive. The words flow easily, tonefully. In the prolog, there are compelling, suspenseful lines: "I am ordering the execution of an innocent man." There is an additional suspense element in that we are not apprised of the protagonist until the close of the prolog: "It is signed...George Washington."

MUSIC: SNEAK. INDECISION & MIXTURE OF GUILT, CONSCIENCE:

NARR:

Poised beneath the sprouting feathers,
The quill is wet and waiting.
But the hand that holds the pen
Is uncertain.
All that's required is his name,
A signature, no more.
Two words and a man will die.

MUSIC: LEAKS A LITTLE

NARR:

But the fingers recoil.

SOUND: PEN DROPS ON WOOD TABLE

NARR:

As if the pen had drunk
Of the red heat
Dancing in the fireplace.
He is a solider,
And he walks with two shadows,
His own and death,

As does every man in uniform.
Is it any different for a general?
What is so unique about a single life
When the quiet green meadows
Are dotted with the obscene hulks
Of what had been men?

WASH:

I am ordering the execution of an innocent man. He has committed no crime, no act of atrocity, no violation of the Articles of War. Yet he must be chosen and he must die.

NARR:

The eyes wander off, unseeing.
The fingers,
Driven by a duty
That is at once ugly
And shameful,
Drown the pen in the pot of ink,
The stain creeping
Onto the white feathers.

WASH:

It would be more fitting if the ink were red.

NARR:

The point touches the parchment.

SOUND:   LIGHT SCRATCHING UNDER:

NARR:

And he signs the warrant of death.
He looks at his signature
As if seeing it for the first time,
Appalled.

NARR:

Is this his mark,
Which he has burnished with pride
And honor?
It is.
It is signed...
George Washington.

MUSIC:   RESOLVES OUT

ANNCR:

In a matter of months the American War For Independence will come to its end. But first, a man and his principles wage a battle that is not confined to the 18th century, to this particular time and place. For General George Washington, it is among the most important decisions of his life, as he takes A WALK WITH TWO SHADOWS.

The conflict is developed in the dialog between General Washington and Major Wilson. Exposition is handled simply but naturally in the dialog: "As I remember, you are related to him in some way, Major Wilson?" "He was married to my sister."

WASH:

I don't wish to doubt you, Major, but are you certain that your information is accurate?

WILSON:

Yes, sir. Captain Joshua Huddy is dead.

WASH:

I knew he was a prisoner, of course, but...perhaps he died of his wounds.

WILSON:

Your pardon, sir, but Huddy wasn't even scratched when he was captured.

WASH:

Still...you know how wild tales are spread in wartime...

WILSON:

General Washington...it was murder!

WASH:

As I remember, you are related to him in some way Major Wilson?

WILSON:

He was married to my sister. **Was**, sir.

WASH:

And who is responsible for the act, do you know that, too?

WILSON:

They were led by a Richard Lippincott, one of the refugees. After Huddy was captured, he was confined aboard a vessel in New York harbor.

WASH:

A prison ship. Yes, we were advised of that.

WILSON:

Lippincott and the others in his party took him from his guards on a pretext. They said he was to be exchanged for a refugee prisoner we hold. They took him to shore, gave him a few minutes to write out his will, and stood him up on a barrel...

WASH:

Then the regular British forces were deceived...it was not of their doing?

WILSON:

It would appear they had no part of it.

WASH:

A terrible business. You will kindly give my expressions of sympathy to your sister.

WILSON:

And there the matter ends?

WASH:

I'll address myself to General Clinton who commands in New York. This act must be as repugnant to him as it is to me. He'll take steps against Lippincott, if indeed he's the one responsible.

WILSON:

A letter. Joshua Huddy is murdered and a letter will pass across the river!

WASH:

What would you have me do, Major? Go Lippincott one better and hang ten of our prisoners? Will it restore life to your brother-in-law and bring happiness back to your sister? What satisfaction would there be in acting like a brigand beyond the immediate discharge of emotions? Answer me, Major, suppose we hung one or even ten of our British prisoners...will it make us any better than Lippincott...will you sleep better because of it?

WILSON:

With all due respect, sir...

WASH:

Say what you will.

WILSON:

If we don't set an example, I'm afraid the refugees will commit other outrages.

WASH:

Sir Henry Clinton controls New York, not the refugees.

WILSON:

They outnumber his men and they are armed too. Sir, if you move now...select just one man in reprisal.

WASH:

Add another wrong and you get a right, is that your suggestion?

WILSON:

You make it sound unnecessarily harsh.

WASH:

What other way is there? You suggest I become a hangman and then you wince at the word!

WILSON:

The general's pardon, but it is...murder.

BIZ:   "MURDER ON ECHO WITH OVERLAPPING REVERB, BEHIND:

In the following sequence, the writer uses a flashback technique to point up the conflict within Washington's mind.

BIZ:   FOLLOWING SEQUENCE PLAYED ON LIGHT ECHO

WASH:

(TRYING TO CONTROL HIS ANGER)

General Nathaniel Greene. Your uniform denotes your rank, which I gave to you. But when you received your commission, it was not a license to murder! You're quite correct, General, I've ridden all night and I'm tired, so very tired. But more than fatigue troubles me now. I think I see my old friend Nathaniel, and yet I'm not certain it is Nathaniel. I see a uniform, resplendent in its blazing colors. The uniform covers my friend. No, it overwhelms him with its importance and status! I also see a hanging platform. This is to be used, I have been informed, to murder a British officer who is an honorable prisoner, because his Commanding Officer has hung one of your officers without provocation! (BEAT) Your intention is to stop this vile practice by performing in a manner as vicious as your opponent! Whereupon he is likely to do the same thing again! Then what, General Greene? Will you retaliate again and again? Will you outdo the Romans who crucified the thousands led by Spartacus? Do you have sufficient numbers of carpenters or do you wish to borrow some from my command? (BEAT) Now, General, you may provide for your commander's sustenance with a little music. I will sit here while the melody of destruction is worked on that scaffold. When it is gone completely, we will repair to your tent where you may offer me some other evidence of your hospitality.

MUSIC: FADING

WASH:

(FADING)

It grieves me, Nathaniel, to have spoken in such a manner to you, of all people. But you must understand how deeply this matter has affected me.

BIZ:    REMOVE ECHO WHEN WASHINGTON HAS FINISHED

WILSON:

(FADING IN)

Think of it as an execution, brought about by the necessities of war. I don't want blood for blood, but if Huddy's death goes unavenged we will have more trouble out of it than we contemplate now.

MUSIC: OUT ON COMPLETION OF WILSON'S SPEECH

Music and voice are combined to create mood and make the most of the aural medium.

MUSIC:   A SARDONIC STRESS, BACK UNDER FOR:

NARR:

Sorrow and pleasure
Often share the same bed.
The sadness of a burial,
It seems,
Can be erased by the death of another.
So they raise their voices...
In an ancient plea.

VOICE 1:

Measure for measure!

CHORUS: (ECHO)

Retaliation!

(REPEATED BEHIND NARRATOR)

NARR:

Along the corridors of time,
The victims are mute,
Gazing in speechless wonder
At man,
In his infinite ignorance.
For a mistake, once made,
Has an immortality of its own.
Placed upon a pedestal
It is dressed with dignity
By the passing years,
Until at last..
It is offered as a lesson in wisdom,
Or at least...
The sacred word of God.

VOICE 2:

A corpse for a corpse!

CHORUS: (ECHO)

Retribution!

(ADD TO ABOVE)

NARR:

Ah, the veil of history parts..
And there..
In the light of revelation,
Shines the road to fulfillment,
Virtue and justice.

VOICE 3:

An eye for an eye!

CHORUS: (ECHO)

Revenge!

As the story builds, we find that the Congress of the United States has voted to retaliate for the killing of the American prisoner of war by taking the life of a British prisoner. In this next excerpt, General Washington wrestles with his conscience. Notice the echo effect employed to differentiate the inner from the outer voice.

MUSIC: TURNS INWARD, EXAMINING, PROBING,
BACKING:

NARR:

When he was still a child
He looked into a mirror

And found his twin—
Locked in silvered glass.
The image was as real
As any child's companion of the mind.
But through the creeping years
That lead to manhood,
The reflection became less a duplicate.
No longer does it speak
Only when spoken to,
Or echo every sound or shrug,
Or mimic every curve of lip
And lift of eye,
Or the choking laughter of a mouth
Made ugly by distending fingers.
It is now a voice,
Grafted to his mind
And yet—
It is from beyond his body
Or control.
A voice that seems to question,
The sound of a special friend,
But no one that tells him
Only what he wants to hear.

MUSIC: OUT

WASH:

I won't do it! Under no conditions.

WASH 2:

(LIGHT ECHO)

Most understandable.

WASH:

You agree with me?

WASH 2:

Of course I do. You don't think I'd advocate a break with your view of morality.

WASH:

That settles it. I'll send my refusal this very night to the congress. There's no...

WASH 2:

(BREAKING IN)

You are naive.

WASH:

I know that tone. Just what are you getting at?

WASH 2:

The congress will not accept your refusal. You're a soldier, and you report to the congress.

WASH:

They'll have to accept. I will not do something that violates every principle of behavior. I may wear a uniform, but it doesn't mean I've given up my humanity.

WASH 2:

Still, just suppose they refuse to recognize the principles by which you live, and then...

WASH:

(BREAKING IN)

In that case, I'll resign my commission!

WASH 2:

Now there's an ingenious way out of a dilemma. Pack your things and drive off to Mount Vernon and back to planting trees, shrubs, grass and wheat, eh?

WASH:

What of it? The war is practically over, anyway.

WASH 2:

What's it all been about, George, winning a war?

WASH:

You know very well that it's only a first step.

WASH 2:

How are you going to avoid 13 individual areas of selfishness, greed and belligerency when peace is a fact?

WASH:

We'll make one nation out of 13 states. We'll do it!

WASH 2:

What a dream. Thirteen individualists are going to submerge themselves for the common good. Don't make me laugh!

WASH:

I'll admit that it won't be easy. Probably more difficult than winning the war.

WASH 2:

The only possibility of success if for the states to rally around a leader whom they trust. Otherwise....

WASH:

Fortunately, there are many who are available for the task of forming a...

WASH 2:

(BREAKING IN)

Why do you persist in giving substance to illusion? You know full well there is only man who can hold them together! Mount Vernon will have to wait. To go back now is to deny everything you've accomplished these last six years!

On the surface, General Washington follows the dictates of the congress. A prisoner, Captain Asgill, is chosen by lot to be the victim. However, Washington is determined not to take the captain's life and hits upon a scheme to thwart the congress. In poetic narrative, the playwright weaves the threads of the plot.

NARR:

There is a pause while he considers:
Is the life of a boy
Worth the life of a nation?
One life.
Just one.
Forgotten in the oncoming tide of years.
But the general will remember
Through a parade of sleepless nights,
Of nagging nightmares
And rabid regrets.
How many tears, he wonders,
Equal the life of one man?
How many more are added
For an innocent man?

MUSIC: IT LEAKS

NARR:

This he knows for certain:
Even if his plan does not work..
And right now
That plan is little more
Than a hope—
Should his part in it be known,
There will be loosed upon him
The wild emotions of those
Who would burn down the orchard—
And then bemoan the lack of fruit
At the dinner table.

226

Washington speaks to Asgill and in a sympathetic approach, disguising any devious meaning, the general sets the plan in motion.

WASH:

Your family..do you have any brothers or sisters?

ASGILL:

None.

WASH:

I have no children of my own.

ASGILL:

I was told you did have.

WASH:

They were were inherited with my marriage, and I consider them mine, of course. One of your friends volunteered the information that your father is Lord Mayor of London.

ASGILL:

Was. He's dead.

WASH:

I'm sorry.

ASGILL:

Why? You didn't know him.

WASH:

Is it necessary to have an intimate acquaintance with someone before condolences may be offered? (BEAT) Your mother—is she well?

ASGILL:

I assume she is.

WASH:

Have you written her of late?

ASGILL:

No, but I intend to compose a last letter before the..the..

WASH:

Why not write to her now..today?

ASGILL:

(BEAT)...Does that mean you've received word? It must. When is it to be?

WASH:

Oh no, no. You're misin—

ASGILL:

(BREAKING IN)

Why else the sudden concern with my writing habits? When do I die, General? I think it's my right to know.

WASH:

Listen to me, you young fool! I had you brought here to pass on some good news, and you're acting with the kind of impetuosity and misdirected assumptions more fitting of a man in the ranks! I thought you might want to ease your mother's worry, and dammit she is your mother!

Captain Asgill takes the bait and writes to his mother. She, in turn, reacts as General Washington had foreseen. To heighten suspense, there is a sequence in the play where anonymous voices representing concerned citizens comment on the issue which has many Americans divided. The time element is underscored: ..."there's a committee writin' up the order for the hangin' t'send Washington right this very minute." This is played in counterpoint to the narration which describes the ship's problems in reaching its destination with the all important letter from the King of France.

NARR:

The gray hair is a gentle glow
In the flickering light of candles.
Outside, the London night deepens.
In her hands
The quill is a passionate partner,
Pouring out a mother's love
And anguish—
Sharp, lean words that beg for a life
She can still recall
From its fetal beginnings
So many memories ago.
Lady Asgill's letter is hurried back
Across the white-capped waters
To France.
And finally to a room
In the palace at Versailles,
Where the King reads
Of the agonies of war

As felt by a mother
Whose only son is about to die
A relay of horsemen carry the King's dispatch
And soon
A ship puts out for America,
Crowding sail to catch and hold
Every errant puff of wind.
Destination: Philadelphia.

VOICE 1: (FADING IN)

...And the way I figure it, he's got maybe a day or two at the most.

VOICE 2:

Who?

VOICE 1:

Asgill.

VOICE 2:

Yer sister again?

VOICE 1:

Is there a meanin' in that remark I'm supposed to recognize?

VOICE 2:

Nothin'.

VOICE 1:

She says the congress is gonna make a statement later this week—after the execution. In fact, there's a committee writin' up the order for the hangin' t'send to Washington right this very minute. (FADING)..That means he'll have to do it right after he receives the...

NARR:

The ship wallows in a heavy sea.
Only two more days to port
When the mainmast splinters like a matchstick.

VOICE 2:

(FADING IN)

Drink up and this time I'm the one with the news. It's Jeremy Woods who's t'ride to Washington with the order for execution.

VOICE: 1

You don't say. Old Jeremy. When's he goin'?

VOICE 2:

He doesn't know. Soon though.

VOICE 1:

Let's us invite him to a drink.

VOICE 2:

Good idea. (FADING)...That way we'll be the first t'get all the news when he comes back.

NARR:

The mast is bandaged like a broken arm.
The sails are trimmed to lighten the load,
And almost on schedule
The lookout screams...
Land Ho!

Jeremy Woods is the messenger who is to deliver Captain Asgill's death warrant and date of execution to General Washington. He fortifies himself for his journey by stopping at a tavern and drinking with some friends.

SOUND:   ALL THREE BREAK INTO LAUGHTER,
THEN INTO ANIMATED CONVERSATION AS
BACKGROUND TO:

NARR:

The messenger is deep in his beers
And the delectable taste of flattery,
While the ship from France
Is tied to a creaking dock.
The King's letter to the congress,
Establishing his claim
To the living body
Of one Charles Asgill
Is written in French,
Which must be translated—
Which, of course, takes time,
During which Jeremy Woods leaves the tavern
And sets out on his errand of death.

SOUND: OUT

MUSIC: SNEAK: TIME IS RUNNING OUT

NARR:

There once was a tortoise
Who raced a hare
And won.
But not this time.
Jeremy Woods pursues a turtle's pace,
His perception of time and space
Blurred...
By tankards of foaming brew.

MUSIC:  TRAILING

JEREMY:

There y'are, Gen'ral. I was supposed t'give it inter yer
hands and I did it. This feller kept sayin' he'd take it to yer,
but my instructions was to do it m'self.

WASH:

The major is my assistant and he usually receives papers
meant for me, but I do understand, Mr. Woods. You obeyed
your orders well.

JEREMY:

There's a bit of favor y'could do fer me, Gen'ral. I'd like a
good place t'see everythin'.

WASH:

See what?

JEREMY:

Why, the hangin'.

WASH:

There will be no hanging, Mr. Woods.

JEREMY:

But the orders...

WASH:

Another dispatch rider from Philadelphia reached me
almost six hours ago. His orders supersede the papers you
were carrying.

JEREMY:

Tell yer the truth, I don't foller yer none.

WASH:

The prisoner was fortunate that you were somehow
delayed getting here, Mr. Woods.

231

JEREMY:

Them fellers in the congress changed their minds, is that what yer sayin'?

WASH:

Yes, and they were helped along by the King of France.

JEREMY:

Wal, what am I gonna tell my friends? This was the only chance I ever had t'be in the middle of somethin' 'portant.

WASH:

Why don't you tell them that if it had not been for your **deliberate** tardiness, an innocent man would have died. It's a story you can be proud of. And it is true, isn't it?

JEREMY:

True? Why yeah, it's the truth, certainly. It's a thing I did 'cause I felt 'twas the thing t'do.

WASH:

There's a certain young man who will be most thankful.

JEREMY:

Y'told him?

WASH:

I sent him word.

WILSON:

Sir, he's here... Captain Asgill.

WASH:

You will excuse me, Mr. Woods?

JEREMY:

Yeah, sure, sure.

SOUND: DOOR OPENS & CLOSES

ASGILL:

Is it so?

WASH:

Happily.

ASGILL:

And now?

WASH:

You are free. I am authorized to provide transportation to England.

ASGILL:

When may I leave?

WASH:

Today, if you wish. With the first tide.

ASGILL:

I wish it. My sole desire is to leave this place, this country, and most of all, the sight of you.

WASH:

I had hoped our relationship could have been a little different.

ASGILL:

(BITTERLY)

If it hadn't been for my letter, you'd be preparing this minute to see me dead on that gallows outside.

WASH:

I'm a little bewildered, though pleased of course, with what has happened. Perhaps you'd pity an older man by telling him what was in that letter you sent to your mother. I have a feeling it all began there.

ASGILL:

I'd rather not waste my time.

WASH:

Then...I hope you have a good voyage.

ASGILL:

I'll always wonder if you mean words like those...or are they the amenities of the moment that gentlemen are expected to say to each other.

WASH:

They are sincere, Captain.

ASGILL:

I won't forget you, sir. Never.

WASH:

I salute you.

ASGILL:

I cannot return it.

WASH:

I did not expect you to. Goodbye, Captain.

MUSIC: SNEAK

NARR:

It has been said
That each of us is obsessed,
Driven to leave some monument
To our moments here on earth—
Some frantic scribblings
On the walls of our time,
To mock, in desperation,
The onslaught of oblivion.
In 1783
George Washington scratched his mark.
It is clear and legible
And will not be worn away
By the sands of time.

MUSIC: TO CURTAIN

Dialog, sound and music have made the play come alive. Actually, there is a minimum use of sound effects: laughter in the background; a door opening and closing. Panitz has placed the burden on the music to maintain the mood. Since this is a play of ideas rather than rampant action, there was not much call for a variety of sound effects. Transitions were accomplished by the narration. A blend of good writing and effective use of the aural medium has made "A Walk with Two Shadows" a successful radio drama.

# Chapter 7

# Religious Programs

The quantity of religious programs of all types provided to radio stations total almost half a million in a year. Network television productions number in the hundreds. The programs produced by the churches are designed for distinct audiences: children, youth, foreign language groups, and mixed audiences. Formats used include cartoons, documentary, drama, drama followed by discussion, interviews, spots, talk, preaching, music—the gamut. The Broadcasting and Film Commission of the National Council of Churches states that most of the network shows with which it cooperates deal with one of four major concerns of the churches:

1) Preservation of individual and institutional freedom
2) New forms of ministry
3) Technology of human values
4) Major behavior concerns of society (use of drugs; sex problems).

Programs dealing with the above themes portray real-life situations where problems are being solved.

Some of the radio dramas presented by the religious broadcasters include "Guideposts," "Stories of Great Christians" and "Big Jon and Sparkie" for children. Major television productions are presented in cooperation with the networks which have their own religious program directors such as Doris Ann at NBC and Pamela Ilott at CBS. Although biblical themes are encompassed in the networks series, most of the subjects deal with contemporary situations. We have drawn excerpts from several of the CBS religious programs which will illustrate their varied approach.

For the program, "The 7th Day," Israeli soldiers recall the Six Day War and express their innermost emotions. The announcer's introduction gives you the key to the program's content.

## ANNOUNCER

In the summer of 1967, groups of young Israelis, kibbutz members, met to record the effects of the Six Day War on their generation. What emerged of the moral dilemmas, the political differences, and the deep humanitarian reactions was published and is now translated. This testimony speaks not only to Israel but to the world.

In a like vein, CBS presented a religious special, "There Shall Be Heard Again." It is a most unusual presentation. It concerns a Jewish ghetto in Czechoslovakia which transcended its circumscribed and fearful existence by creating musical masterpieces. The narration, written by Arnold Walton, tells the story of the ghetto and gives the background for each composition. The opening of the program  sets the scene.

MUSIC—We hear, and segue from one to the other, about 15 seconds each of GAVOTTE, MORAVIAN THEME, BRUNDIBAR, and PIANO SONATA.

### HOST (VO)

A brightly lighted room... a little pleasant laughter...gay music, and much dancing. Further down the long corridor, a string quartet remembering last spring, and waiting for the next. Up the stairs, and a little in the distance, the children sing the latest song from the city. And in a corner of the large hall below, a young man plays his new sonata to his new young lady. Ah...such sounds! Sounds that come only from a dance orchestra in Vienna...or a string quartet at an outdoor recital in the Moravian Hills....or from youngsters from a choir school in Prague enjoying their latest piece...or from a young man from the Berlin Conservatory meticulously playing on a grand piano in a grand ballroom...Are these the sounds of Vienna? NO! Of the green hills of Moravia? NO! Of the Prague school of the Berlin Conservatory? NO! These are sounds from the Gateway to Hell...the Wayside Station to Death. These are sounds...the MUSIC OF TEREZIN!

MUSIC: Comes to an abrupt stop.

### ANNOUNCER & CREDITS

The following excerpt is a good illustration of this script's technique.

### HOST

Now, you may think that with all this music and entertainment, life was easy in this "ghetto village"...but this place, built to hold 7,000 people, never had less than 70,000 at one time. Men and women were separated and so were the children. And for **them** it was the worst, for they could never understand what they had done wrong...to live like this. And they were right. They had done nothing wrong—except to be born a Jew. A young couple named Taube wrote EIN JUDISCHER KIND, but it could have been written by every man and woman in Terezin, for it was about their most cherished and protected possession...their children...a Jewish child.

MUSIC: EIN JUDISCHER KIND

Another type of religious program presented by CBS uses a documentary approach to the ideas of great religious thinkers. Here is the introduction to "Road Signs On A Merry-Go-Round," written by Joseph E. Clement and Al Cox.

### MAN

Hello, Hello, Hello, Can you hear me? Can you hear me? Hear me? Hello, Hello. Hello, Hello, Can you hear me? It was always the same dream, the same nightmare. A huge prison with millions of inmates. Everyone had forgotten why we were prisoners. No one cared any more. No matter how I tried, I could never find the walls or the gates. No matter how I screamed for help, no one paid any attention. (VOICES IN BACKGROUND) It was a place without meaning, without hope and everyone was isolated and alone. We were forced to make things to amuse ourselves. And we had to play games to fill up the emptiness.

### GIRL'S VOICE

Did you hear that?

### ANOTHER VOICE

Yes, great—

### MAN

I was always conscious of a madness and I fought it as long as I could.

### VOICE (OVER LOUDSPEAKER)

Mr.————————, please come to the information booth——(CROWD NOISES)

### MAN

Hello, can anybody————

### (STREET NOISES)

### (MUSIC, ROCK AND ROLL SINGING)

### VOICE (OF DISC JOCKEY)

Oh yeah, that's great; they got a lot of grab don't they? That's great. Number 15 is——————

(MUSIC, POPULAR SINGING)

MAN

When I became exhausted I looked for something that would kill the worst pain, the awful loneliness.

VOICE (CONTD)

And then I would forget about the struggle and I wouldn't remember about the prison anymore.

WOMAN

When I was a girl I was taught to escape by hiding from all the agony. And in the boarding school I learned that if I closed my eyes and didn't touch anything and didn't let anything touch me, I would never be corrupted. I obeyed all the rules and performed all the duties and kept my thoughts to myself.

(MUSIC IN BACKGROUND)

I loved to be near the unspoiled things. The trees and flowers, the clouds and birds, and even the candle flames. In this solitude I could reach out and touch the infinite; it was so peaceful, so pure and free. I prayed for a death that would finally set me free and I practiced dying a little bit day by day. But death was a far-off stifling promise and here at least there was a semblance of life. So I ran away and I learned to survive by distracting myself so I didn't have to listen to the fear inside. Sometimes I have to remind myself I really am a person, a somebody, and that there's really something terribly important in what that means.

MAN

You're a person to me and I know you know it. We share even the painful elements of truth, in all the ways we have of looking at ourselves and the world. The question is what do we gain by it and where is it taking us. I think we really have an addiction to the way things are. It's all we ever bring home to the children. We give them the same games and the same technology and science and we tell ourselves we're giving them everything and in the end we haven't given them anything.

WOMAN

I am a believer, a passionate believer, a desperate believer. I have a terrible fear of not believing. I'm not sure where a belief leads or what I believe in. But not believing is too much like not existing. There's something about living that demands believing. But I live on the edge of a terrible doubt and despair. If you really love me, help me live my belief.

## MAN

I can try and help you live, but what do I know of believing? What does anybody know of believing. It's not just her or me. It's the same groping in the dark that is everywhere nowadays. The 20th century, the absence of any answers. If we would learn anything in this modern age we could learn that that's one thing that's just not available. That's not saying that I'm not willing to do what I can. We may look at things a little differently but we're out on the same limb, together. And the way I see it, anyone in tune with the times—even if he wants to talk about God—is out on the same limb with us. A lot of questions rooted in doubt. The thing to do is to check the frontier together and listen for any new sounds of belief.

## (MUSIC)

## ANNOUNCER

CBS News presents a special program. "Road Signs on a Merry-Go-Round," an impressionistic look at the ideas of Dietrich Bonhoeffer, Martin Buber, and Teilhard de Chardin.

## (MUSIC PLAYING)

The remainder of the hour script is devoted to excerpts from the widsom of the philosophers with interpositions by the symbolic man and woman, as in this sequence.

## BUBER

The effort to establish relation comes first. The actual relation, a saying of Thou without words comes next. In the beginning is relation, a category of being, readiness, grasping form, mould for the soul. Through the Thou, a man becomes I. Only then can the other primary word be assembled. The man who has become conscious of I, that is, the man who says, I-it, stands before things but not over against them in the flow of mutual action. With the magnifying glass of peering observation he bends over particulars and objectifies them. He isolates them in observation without any feeling of their exclusiveness. Or he knits them into a scheme of observation without any feeling of universality. He sets things in time and space in casual connection, each with its own place and appointed course. It's measurability and conditioned nature. The word of it is set in the context of space of time. The word of

Thou is not limited by these. Without it, man cannot live. He who lives with it, alone, is not a man.

WOMAN

It's difficult for me to unlearn so much of what I was taught and how I grew up. It creeps into my attempts to give our children the experience of being full persons. Yet I feel we must learn to breath a different air. It is essential to be open to relation and dialog with the whole world. That's such a rich way to be free and to live with the presence of God.

MAN

I'm not sure what presence you seek. Although perhaps I am being drawn to a new awareness of our world. There seems to be some basically similar discoveries in these various approaches. Martin Buber starts with the relationship between persons and their world, Tielhard de Chardin carries this through the whole history of life and man and the universe. Is that how you discover presence?

## "Sit Down, Shut Up or Get Out"

One of the finest examples of a drama written for a religious program series is Allan Sloane's "Sit Down, Shut Up or Get Out." It was produced by the National Broadcasting Company in association with the National Council of Churches and presented on the NBC Television Religious Program. It is a study in human relationships, specifically between teacher and student, and child and parents. Based on an experience of the author's own child, it portrays, poignantly and perceptively, the lack of understanding that can destroy the inquiring young mind. It is not a religious drama, in the narrow sense, but it is a drama of the human spirit. Let us savor it in the following excerpts.

We discover our protagonist, Christopher Bright, as a student at Stone Junior High School.

SCENE TWO

INTERIOR: DAY: A CORRIDOR

DOWN A WAYS, A DOOR OPENS ABRUPTLY. CHRISTOPHER BRIGHT, 13, BUT LOOKING YOUNGER, TYPICAL IN CHINOS, PLAID SHIRT AND NO TIE, WITH LONGISH IMPOSSIBLY COMBED HAIR, COMES STORMING OUT, SLAMMING THE DOOR BEHIND HIM. HE GOES TO A ROW OF LOCKERS IN THE IMMEDIATE VICINITY, STRUGGLES WITH THE HANDLE AS WE GO IN FOR A CLOSER SHOT TO

REVEAL THAT HE IS FIGHTING BACK TEARS. HE
CANNOT GET THE LOCKER OPEN SO HE GIVES IT A
VICIOUS KICK—AND IT OPENS.
CHRIS CROUCHES. HE RUMMAGES THROUGH A
MARE'S NEST OF BOOKS, PAPERS, CLOTHES, A
FOLDING CHESSBOARD, AND FINALLY COMES UP
WITH ONE BOOK: A COLLEGE-LEVEL BIOLOGY
BOOK. WE MIGHT ALSO SEE VARIOUS OTHER
BOOKS, LIKE "OLIVER TWIST," SCHIRER ON THE
THIRD REICH. CHRIS THEN HUNKERS DOWN TO HIS
BUTT IN FRONT OF THE LOCKER AND BEGINS TO
READ. THE SQUAWK BOX SPEAKS UP, AND HIS
ATTENTION IS MOMENTARILY DISTRACTED FROM
THE BOOK, BUT THE MOMENT HE HEARS
"DRAMATIC CLUB" HE RETURNS TO HIS READING.

PRINCIPAL (VOICE OC P.A.)

Attention, please. I have been asked by the Dramatic Club
to announce that the rehearsal of "The Emperor's
Clothes" will be held in the girl's gym instead of the
auditorium. And may I take this opportunity to remind all
homeroom teachers that mid-year progress reports may
be picked up at the administration desk at the close of the
school day. Thank you.

GOING TO A CLOSER SHOT OF CHRIS, WE SEE THE
PAGE HE IS READING. TIMED RIGHT AFTER THE
WORDS "THE EMPEROR'S CLOTHES," WE SEE AN
OVERLAY ILLUSTRATING THE HUMAN BODY,
VEINS AND ALL. WE ALSO SEE SOMETHING ELSE.
CHRIS IS USING A CIGARETTE AS A BOOKMARK. AS
THE SQUAWK BOX, AFTER A MOMENT, CONTINUES,
CAMERA LEAVES CHRIS TO REVEAL, DOWN THE
HALL, **THE COACH** CROSSING CORRIDOR TO HIS
OFFICE. HE NOTICES CHRIS. COACH WALKS DOWN
THE HALL (HE IS WEARING SWEATER AND
SNEAKS) AND COMES UP TO CHRIS, NOW LOST IN
HIS BOOK. HE STIRS CHRIS WITH A SNEAKERED
FOOT. CHRIS LOOKS UP.

COACH

What're you doing out here?

CHRIS

Reading.

COACH

Reading what?

CHRIS HOLDS UP THE BOOK. COACH SHAKES HIS
HEAD IN "HE'LL NEVER LEARN" MODE.

                              COACH

Reading sir.

                     A BEAT: NOT UNKINDLY

On your feet, Bright.

               CHRIS SCRAMBLES TO HIS FEET
                              COACH

Where you supposed to be?

                              CHRIS

Science—but Mister Bolton said——

                              COACH

Uh-uh——no hassle. You wanna read——read in the
library.

                              CHRIS

But——

                              COACH

On the double! Or would you rather take a detention?

CHRIS TURNS AND HEADS FOR THE LIBRARY.
COACH WATCHES AFTER HIM A MOMENT, JUST
SHAKING HIS HEAD. CHRIS APPROACHES DOOR TO
LIBRARY. A NICE YOUNG TEACHER—MR.
WADLEY—COMES OUT WITH A LOAD OF BOOKS. HE
NODS TO CHRIS AS THEY PASS. CHRIS SAYING——

                              CHRIS

Hi.

               BUT WADLEY STOPS AND TURNS
                            WADLEY

Hold it, Chris.

HE BECKONS TO THE BOY, WHO COMES OVER.

What're you doing wandering around the halls?

                              CHRIS

Well, it's somewhat complicated. I was sitting over there,
and the coach came over——

                            A BREATH

242

You see, we were studying distillation in science, and Mr. Bolton——

WADLEY

Look, I didn't ask for the history of the wheel. One thing at a time. Let's see your pass.

CHRIS

I don't have one. You see, I was in science ——

WADLEY

No pass.

HE SHAKES HIS HEAD: **SINCERE**

Chris—listen to me. Once and for all. What do you think I'm trying to get over in social studies?

CHRIS

The structure of society——
but in **science**, just now——

WADLEY

Hear me out. This is a society with certain rules. There are reasons for those rules. Without rules—we'd have disorder. Without order—we can't run the society, the school. Without school—you can't get an education. Without an education—you can't make it in the larger society. Now— is asking for a pass like everyone else so big a price to pay for getting an education?

CHRIS

(AFTER A BIT)

You know, sometimes you're just as unfair as the Feds——

WADLEY

The what?

CHRIS

The monitors. They never give you a chance to explain either.

WADLEY

The Feds. That's one for the book.

( A BEAT: NOT UNGENTLY )

Go on, Chris. Go to the office and get a pass before the Feds grab you.

(A BEAT)

You're in enough trouble already.

CHRIS TURNS TO GO. WADLEY ADDS———

And I'll still see you after school!

WADLEY CLEARS. CHRIS CONTINUES BACK DOWN THE CORRIDOR.

COACH JUST COMING OUT OF AN OFFICE OFF CORRIDOR. HE SEES CHRIS, PLANTS HIMSELF RIGHT IN THE BOY'S WAY. **CAMERA HOLDS** IN FOREGROUND AS THE SCENE PLAYS OUT SILENT. CHRIS CONFRONTS COACH IN CORRIDOR, COACH POINTS BACK IN DIRECTION FROM WHICH CHRIS HAD COME; CHRIS STARTS TO PROTEST, TRIES TO PASS COACH, COACH REACHES OUT AND GRABS THE BOY, TRYING TO TURN HIM BACK IN OTHER DIRECTION; BOY STRUGGLES TO GET LOOSE, AND THEN, AS WE **ZOOM** IN TO CLOSE SHOT, CHRIS GETS HIS FREE HAND LOOSE AND GIVES THE COACH A TERRIFIC BELT RIGHT IN THE STOMACH. SOMEWHAT WINDED, THE COACH SIMPLY PICKS THE KID UP, FLAILING AND PROTESTING GRIMLY AND THE **BOOK** DROPS OUT OF THE BOY'S HAND. STILL HOLDING THE BOY, THE COACH STOOPS TO PICK IT UP — AND THE CIGARETTE DROPS OUT OF IT. THE COACH RECOVERS THE CIGARETTE. COACH CARRIES CHRIS BACK INTO HIS OFFICE.

And so Chris is summoned to the principal's office where a group of teachers and the guidance counselor, Mr. Newman, meet to sit in judgment on him.

**SCENE NINE:**

PRINCIPAL'S OFFICE

AS IT IS IN ACTUALITY: A LARGE DESK TO ONE CORNER, NEXT TO WHICH IS THE PANEL-BOARD AND MICROPHONE FOR THE PUBLIC ADDRESS SYSTEM. THERE IS A ROW OF CHAIRS ALONG ONE WALL OF THE ROOM, AND IN THESE ARE SEATED THE PERSONAGE SUMMONED EARLIER: MR. WADLEY, MISS TENDAL, THE COACH, MR. BOLTON, MRS. SANTANGELO. WE COME INTO THE ROOM — WITH ITS OTHER APPURTENANCES SUCH AS PICTURES OF LINCOLN, JEFFERSON, WASHINGTON, NIXON, THE AMERICAN FLAG, THE CONSTITUTION,

ETC. ETC. — WITH NEWMAN, WHILE MEEHAN IS JUST HANGING UP THE TELEPHONE. MEEHAN PICKS UP A PAD AND A MIMEOGRAPHED FORM AS NEWMAN COMES INTO THE SHOT. AS MEEHAN, THE PRINCIPAL, COMES AROUND HIS DESK HE MOVES A TYPEWRITER INTO POSITION IN FRONT OF AND TO ONE SIDE OF HIS DESK (I.E., ABOUT WHERE A CLERK OF COURT WOULD SIT)

### PRINCIPAL

I think we're about ready to... proceed...

TO MISS TENDAL, WHO RISES AND COMES FORWARD

Betty, as Chris's homeroom teacher, would you type up a draft——

BUT AS SHE TAKES HER SEAT AND PUTS THE FORM INTO THE TYPEWRITER, PRINCIPAL NOTICES NEWMAN STANDING THERE.

Sam?

**NOTE**: THE ATMOSPHERE IS VERY RELAXED. EVERYBODY IS QUITE NATURAL AND COOL. NO TENSIONS.

### NEWMAN

Just a suggestion. I think Chris might be helped if he had some part in this process. I'd like to bring him in before anything's committed to paper.

### WADLEY

I agree.

### MRS. SANTANGELO

I think it's only fair.

### BOLTON

You're setting a precedent. You do it for one—you have to do it for all of them.

### PRINCIPAL

That's true.

IMMEDIATELY, MISS TENDAL STARTS TO TYPE.

### NEWMAN

### (SHARPLY)

Just a minute!

SHE STOPS

I promised him I'd try. He values our relationship——and so do I. This is one way to reinforce it.

PRINCIPAL

No problem.

HE SMILES

Just keep him off the soapbox.

NEWMAN STARTS FOR THE DOOR, BUT STOPS.

NEWMAN

On second thought—there **is** a problem.

NEWMAN IS CHOOSING HIS WORDS WITH EXTREME CARE.

Without going into clinical details, Chris sometimes sees things—sees **the world**—differently from other children. To a certain extent, he lives in a world of his own.

WE PAN ALONG THE FACES OF THE TEACHERS. THEY ARE CONCERNED AND PAYING ATTENTION INTENTLY, EVEN THE COACH.

NEWMAN

Sometimes, in fact——and I'm sure you've all had experience of one kind or another in this area—sometimes his way of dealing with situations is to ————well, "tune out" on reality. You may call it daydreaming...you may call it inattention...you may call it forgetfulness...you may call it fantasy————but whatever it is, there are times when we can't tell how Chris sees things. Or us.

HE IS AT THE DOOR. HIS HAND ON THE KNOB. VERY QUIETLY

Or this.

HE OPENS THE DOOR. HE GOES THROUGH.

The play takes on the aura of a courtroom with "charges" leveled at the defendant. The flashback technique is used throughout the "courtroom" scenes.

PRINCIPAL

(READING)

Whereas, Christopher Bright, eighth grade, has, over the first marking period, been the center, occasion, and cause of various and sundry disciplinary problems——

## WE PAN ALONG THE "JURY"

### PRINCIPAL

And whereas, said Christopher Bright has been disruptive, dissenting at every possible opportunity, accordingly occupying the valuable and limited time of his teachers to the detriment of their attention to curriculum and class— And whereas, said Christopher Bright seems determined, in short, upon turning the school upside down to his **own** detriment——now, therefore, it becomes incumbent upon this assemblage by the powers vested in it by the Board of Education to arrive at a just and significant communication concerning said Christopher Bright suitable for inscription upon Form 227 dash W, Report to Parents, Pupil Progress, for their perusal, signature, and return to Stone Junior High School. Do you understand that,Chris?

### CHRISTOPHER NODS

### PRINCIPAL

Do you have any questions?

CHRISTOPHER LOOKS TO NEWMAN. NEWMAN SHAKES HIS HEAD NO. HE SHAKES HIS HEAD NO. BUT OVER THE SHOT, WE HEAR——

### CHRIS

VOICE OVER, FILTER

Yes. Why don't we have the right to judge **you**, and write reports about you?

Miss Tendal, Christopher's English teacher, cites an example of his erratic behavior.

### MISS TENDAL

As for vocabulary... I'm sure you'll agree that the language in this example of Christopher's creative writing is—— well, you can judge for yourself.

SHE PASSES THE SHEET UP TO THE PRINCIPAL. HE FROWNS AT IT.

### PRINCIPAL

Do you think such words belong in something to be read to other children?

### CHRIS

Well, they've heard them on the school bus. You ought to—

NEWMAN PUTS A HAND ON HIS ARM BEFORE HE
CAN GO ANY FARTHER.

PRINCIPAL

(READING)

Quote, I can't take any more of this censored, screamed
Pruneface, the bus driver. If you censored censored
monsters don't stop your censored censored racket, so
help me censored I'll stop the censored censored censored
bus and the whole censored bunch of you little censored
can walk to the censored school. Thus began Pruneface's
daily nightmare.

HE PUTS THE PAPER DOWN

Do you call this creative writing?

SCENE SIXTEEN:  CLASSROOM

MISS TENDAL, BACK TO CAMERA, IS WRITING ON
THE BLACKBOARD. AT THE TOP OF THE WRITING
WE CAN READ

**THE SHORT STORY**

SHE HAS ALSO WRITTEN

BE IMAGINATIVE! BE FREE
BE DESCRIPTIVE! BE ACCURATE
BE REALISTIC! BE TRUTHFUL

AND NOW WE WATCH AS SHE WRITES,
UNDERLINING——

WRITE WHAT YOU KNOW!

CHRIS

VOICE OC, FILTERED

Write what you know. And when you do——**they** know
people talk like that, **they** know people behave like that——
why do they say one thing and mean another?

The testimony continues; this time the witness is Mr.
Wadley, Christopher's social science teacher.

WADLEY

However, in terms of behavior—for some reason, he seems
to have a compulsion, you could call it, to take positions in
opposition to the general trend of any given discussion, any
given assignment. You say it's white——Chris jumps up
and says it's black!

## SCENE EIGHTEEN: CLASSROOM

WE OPEN ON A PICTURE OF A. LINCOLN, COME DOWN TO REVEAL A GIRL LEAVING A BULLETIN BOARD AS CHRIS COMES UP TO POST A SHEET OF PAPER PRINTED IN HIS OWN HANDWRITING.

#### WADLEY

#### VOICE OVER

For example—this morning, the assignment being to bring in a relevant clipping or quotation for the bulletin board—

WADLEY COMES INTO FRAME AND EXAMINES THE SELECTION.

#### WADLEY

Just a minute, Chris.

#### CHRIS COMES BACK IN

#### WADLEY

Where'd you find that?

#### CHRIS

In a book.

#### WADLEY

Read it.

#### CHRIS

#### (EYES CLOSED)

This country, with its institutions, belongs to the people who inhabit it. Whenever they shall grow weary of the existing government, they can exercise their constitutional right of amending it, or their revolutionary right to overthrow it.

#### WADLEY

That's very interesting. Do you think we have the right to overthrow the government?

#### CHRIS

Well——I thought we could **discuss** it.

#### WADLEY

In junior high school?

                    CHRIS

Well——

                   WADLEY

Just a minute. What's your source? Who said that?

CHRIS POINTS. CAMERA TILTS TO SHOT OF A. LIN-
COLN.

                    CHRIS

He did.

CAMERA COMES DOWN: CHRIS AND WADLEY.

First Inaugural Address. I thought everybody knew **that**.

                   WADLEY

                   QUIETLY

We'll discuss **that** after school.

                    CHRIS

I can't. I have to——

                   WADLEY

                   QUIETLY

If you want another detention for tomorrow——just keep it
up.

SCENE NINETEEN: "COURTROOM"

WE ARE ON CHRISTOPHER BUSILY WRITING
ANOTHER NOTE, AS WADLEY WINDS UP.

                   WADLEY

Now, frankly, I think a great many of Christopher's
opinions and ideas aren't his own...I feel he's influenced,
perhaps, by an overpermissive family situation...so his
acting out isn't totally his own fault...I don't know what the
rules are at home—but he certainly disregards them in
class.

We find an understanding teacher in the person of Mrs.
Santangelo.

               MRS. SANTANGELO

I would like to say that Chris seems to be a **gifted** child.
And like most such children—he has his own little ways...

CHRIS PUTS HIS CHIN DOWN IN HIS HANDS AND
SMILES AT HER AS SHE SMILES AT HIM.

MRS. SANTANGELO

(VERY SOFTLY)

Chris...

HE IMMEDIATELY STRAIGHTENS UP

Now, Chris and I had **many** problems from the start——
but we talked about them——

A LATIN SHRUG

and we argued about them——

CHRIS IS GRINNING

MRS. SANTANGELO

and we **fought** about them.

CHRIS IS ACTUALLY CHUCKLING

MRS. SANTANGELO

For example, the very first day, Chris announced firmly
that he hated Spanish, that the language was illogical, the
pronunciation was impossible——

SHE SMILES

Why should a house be feminine? Why should a tree be
masculine? I'm only taking it because I **have** to!

SCENE TWENTY: CLASSROOM: BLACKBOARD NOW
HAS SPANISH ON IT.

MRS. SANTANGELO

Chris...understand me. I know you can do excellent work—
if you want to.

(SOFTLY)

But if you wish, you may drop out of my class. I will help
you choose another subject.

(VERY SOFTLY)

But I wish you would stay.

CHRIS

Why?

MRS. SANTANGELO

Because I think you need a friend in school, joven. Don't
you?

CHRIS BITES HIS LIP AND NODS. SHE TOUCHES HIS
HAIR.

MRS. SANTANGELO

You see—who are you as a person is more important to me
than anything, Chris. Even the marks you get.

SHE LIFTS HIS CHIN WITH HER HAND

Please stay in my class. Just so you can have somebody to
whom you are important as a person—not just a pupil.

But Christopher's science and math teacher, Mr. Bolton,
an avid disciplinarian, testifies to the boy's intransigence. Mr.
Bolton does attempt to rationalize Christopher's behavior, but
his testimony is interrupted by an accusation from the coach.

SCENE TWENTY-FIVE: "COURTROOM"

COACH STANDS UP. HE IS VERY TESTY.

COACH

Let's stop wasting time. You all keep making excuses for
him because he's so smart. WELL—I can't see it. Far as
I'm concerned, this kid is playing with half a deck. Rules?
He doesn't even recognize they exist!

HE HOLDS UP A CIGARETTE

There isn't a kid in this school who doesn't know the rules
against smoking——but I took this from him right in the
halls. Now I ask you!

BOLTON

Coach—I was getting to that. But first—we **have** to make
allowances for Chris. If you really knew his I.Q.—if you
had any conception of his previous psychological
problems——within this school system, and outside——

NEWMAN

(TENSELY)

May I ask how you're so certain of that?

BOLTON

You have your files—I have my sources.

NEWMAN

CLOSE SHOT WITH CHRIS

I swear, as God is my witness, Chris——not from my
files.

BUT CHRIS THROWS HIS HAND OFF

BOLTON

(CONTINUING, OVER)

I know, in fact, that Chris ranks in the top percentile of academic potential—well above the school norm, 'way above the national norm——

AND NOT WITHOUT PASSION OR COMPASSION, BY THE WAY.

That's why I started out to——well, give him a little more leeway than the others. But it didn't take me long to realize discipline was what he needed. And by golly, if nobody else was going to give it to him—I was. Because I'm determined that he'll be a credit to the school—a worthy product of our system. But Chris—we're only human, you know. Teaching isn't easy; none of us can run a classroom for one kid out of 33. We've got to have rules, we've got to have order.

SCENE TWENTY-SIX: SCIENCE CLASSROOM

BOLTON STANDING NEXT TO CHRIS'S DESK.

BOLTON

So put that away and let's go on from distillation to atomic particles——

CHRIS

But Mr. Bolton—

BOLTON

(WEARILY)

Please—no more of your interminable questions. I'm beginning to think they're just an excuse for launching on a long irrelevant lecture——

CHRIS

But this is relevant!

NOW WE SEE HE IS HOLDING UP A CIGARETTE.

I think we ought to do a distillation on **this**. A real experiment. We can measure the tars and the carcinogens, and we can write it up for our parents, and for kids who're stupid enough to smoke—

TO BOLTON. TIGHT-LIPPED. END OF HIS ROPE.

CHRIS

If you don't call **that** relevant to science—what is?

### BOLTON BLOWS—QUIETLY

Chris—I'm giving you five seconds to close your mouth—get back in your seat—or leave the class.

### (A BEAT); HE CALLS

Chris.

### HE SHOUTS

Chris!

### SCENE TWENTY-SEVEN: "COURTROOM"

### BOLTON

At that—Chris chose to leave the class. But that explains the cigarette, Coach—

### CHRIS

### LEAPS TO HIS FEET

### OUT OF CONTROL

That's not what you said!

A HUBBUB ENSUES, DURING WHICH NEWMAN TRIES TO CALM CHRIS DOWN, CHRIS REPEATING

It's not what he said, he never said that! He's a liar!

### NEWMAN

Chris, control yourself. There's a right way and a wrong way—

### CHRIS

### (ESCAPING NEWMAN)

Why don't you tell **him** that?

### HE POINTS QUIVERINGLY AT THE "JURY"

Why don't you tell them **all** that!

### HE POINTS AT BOLTON

Why don't you tell the truth? You told me to sit down—shut up—or get out!

HE CLOSES HIS EYES AND PUTS HIS HANDS IN FRONT OF HIS FACE. NEWMAN PUTS AN ARM AROUND HIS SHOULDERS, BUT CHRIS THROWS IT OFF. THE COACH COMES OVER AND TAKES OVER. IN A MAN-TO-MAN FASHION, HE PUTS BOTH HANDS ON THE KID'S SHOULDER.

COACH

I'm sorry, fella. Why didn't you explain?

CHRIS

Why didn't you give me a chance to?

COACH

Okay—but is that any reason to belt me?

CHRIS PULLS AWAY FROM THE COACH'S HANDS.

You can't go around belting teachers. Don't your parents teach you respect?

HE TURNS TO THE OTHERS.

You think **you** got problems? Let me tell you—when you've got **two hundred** kids in P.T.—and every day, day after day, the same problem with the same kid!

SCENE TWENTY-EIGHT: A LOCKER ROOM

THERE IS A DOOR TO ONE SIDE, SAYING BOYS' GYM, FROM BEHIND WHICH COMES THE SOUNDS OF HAPPY BOYS AT PLAY. CHRIS IS SITTING IN FRONT OF HIS LOCKER IN SKIVVIES, GRIMLY AND DOGGEDLY UNTYING KNOTS IN A GYMSUIT, THEN WITH HIS TEETH TRYING TO UNTIE THE KNOTS HIS SNEAKER LACES HAVE BEEN TIED TOGETHER WITH. COACH COMES INTO FRAME.

COACH

Come on, Bright—get the lead out.

CHRIS SIMPLY HOLDS UP THE TIED-TOGETHER SNEAKERS.

COACH

Why don't you carry your stuff around so the other guys can't get at it?

CHRIS

I lose it.

COACH

Cause you're always dreaming, kiddo.
Always got your nose in some oddball book.

HE LOOKS AT HIS WATCH

You got one minute to be out on the floor—or you'll do laps.

AS COACH HEADS FOR THE DOOR TO THE GYM—
                    CHRIS
                 (MUTTERING)
What am I supposed to learn from that?
                    COACH
What was that last crack?
                    CHRIS
Nothing.

                    COACH
Okay—30 seconds. Forget the suit. Skivvies and socks.

HE CLEARS. CHRIS LOOKS DOWN AT HIMSELF IN
UNDERWEAR AND SOCKS. HE WALKS TOWARD THE
DOOR. AS HE APPROACHES IT, THE SOUND OF
CHILDREN PLAYING GROWS LOUDER. CHRIS PUTS
HIS HAND TO THE DOOR AND OPENS IT A CRACK—
BUT THE SOUND CHANGES TO THE ROAR OF WILD
ANIMALS. HE LETS IT CLOSE AGAIN. AS WE MOVE IN
FOR THE EXTREMELY CLOSE SHOT, CHRIS CLOSES
HIS EYES AND PUSHES THE DOOR OPEN. THE
SOUND OF WILD ANIMALS BECOMES DEAFENING.

SCENE TWENTY-NINE: NEWMAN'S OFFICE

CHRIS IS SITTING FACING NEWMAN, HIS CHIN ON
HIS ELBOWS.
                    NEWMAN
Forty-five minutes of laps. That's pretty rough.
                    CHRIS
Being in my underwear was worse. Everybody laughed.
                    NEWMAN
Coach isn't a bad guy. Want me to speak to him?
                    CHRIS
I think the more you talk to them about me——the more
they blame me for everything.

NEWMAN STUDIES THE KID. THEN—
                    NEWMAN
Chris—if the kids understood you better, do you think
you'd get along better?
                    CHRIS
Maybe.

NEWMAN

Have you thought about trying to make them understand you—in their own terms?

CHRIS

What do you mean?

NEWMAN

Well—take, for example, the names they call you. Bookworm—.

CHRIS

(BITTERLY)

Creep. Mental. **Re**-tard.

NEWMAN

But what do **you** do? You hit back with words they have to look up. Neanderthal—troglodyte—sadist—

CHRIS

**Sad**-ist.

NEWMAN

A GRIN

Always correcting.

SERIOUSLY

Chris, I can take it. But you automatically get their backs up. You have to be so different all the time.

CHRIS

Well—aren't I?

NEWMAN

(VERY, VERY QUIETLY)

So was I.

CHRIS STUDIES HIM

But one day—I decided I was not going to submit to violence forever—

CHRIS

Did they push you around too?

NEWMAN

With the worst kind of violence—the kind they throw at anybody who's different.

HE UNREELS THE LITANY OF HATE

Jewboy. Kike. Sheeny. Hebe.

HE TAKES A DEEP BREATH, GOES ON

Nigger. Spade. Dago. Wop. Spic. Hunky. Polack. Jap. Kraut. Chink. Mick.

ANOTHER PAUSE

Wasp. Pig. Cracker. Fag. Snob. Spaz. Bum.

(BITTERLY)

Names on the land.

CHRIS

You left one out.

A PAUSE

Gook.

NEWMAN

HE COMES BACK FROM WHERE HE HAS BEEN

True. Anyhow—the next time it happened—I answered back in the language they understood best. Pow. I was lucky. I caught him flush on the schnozz. And it took three of them to pull me off.

CHRIS

You mean—use violence?

NEWMAN

I mean as guidance counselor and psychologist, I cannot countenance fighting—

CHRIS

Well, then—

NEWMAN

But man to man——I'm suggesting that you might gain some respect on their terms, if you didn't just stand there and take it.

CHRIS

AFTER A PAUSE

What happened to you?

NEWMAN

HE GRINS

I got clobbered. But the kid I belted—well, he didn't exactly turn into my best friend. But they stopped pushing me around.

CHRIS

I——I'm not afraid to get hurt. It's just that—

NEWMAN

(VERY QUIETLY)

I know the insults to your personal dignity, Chris—and there isn't a damn thing I can do to stop it. But I also know there comes a time when you have to stand up and say—no more.

(A BEAT)

I know nonviolence is your way. But it isn't working very well, is it?

CHRIS SHAKES HIS HEAD NO

I'm not telling you to turn into a tiger.
Just to let them know you won't be pushed around. Think about it, Chris. Think—be ready—be first—be fast—and POW. Try thinking like **they** do for a change.

CHRIS

As they do.

NEWMAN

What do you want—good grammar—or advice? The very next one who pushes you around—Pow.

SCENE THIRTY: "COURTROOM"

NEWMAN

It was **my** mistake, Coach—and I'll take complete responsibility for the incident. I was dead wrong.

COACH

Oh no. For once, Doc—you were on the ball.

(TO CHRIS)

Tiger—I didn't know you had it in you. But next time—come to me, and you and the other guy can put on the gloves. By the rules.

Whaddayasay?

CHRIS JUST LOOKS AT HIM

CHRIS

It's still violence. It's still wrong.

COACH SPREADS HIS HANDS

COACH

There y'are, Doc.

(SARCASTICALLY)

So much for—all that gobbledegook about relating appropriately to crisis situations within the peer group.

(A BEAT)

No way.

After the "trial," Mr. Newman hands Chris the "verdict": his report card. Notice the technique Allan Sloane uses in conveying the report to the viewer.

SCENE THIRTY-FIVE: ADMINISTRATION OFFICE

CHRIS IN HIS CHAIR. DOOR TO PRINCIPAL'S OFFICE OPENS, AND THE TEACHERS STREAM OUT. AS CHRIS WATCHES, THEY SEEM TO BE MOVING IN A CURIOUSLY MECHANICAL MOTION, AS EACH TURNS TO THE COUNTER AND TAKES FROM IT A BUNDLE OF ENVELOPES. THEY PASS HIM, AND CHRIS WATCHES AS EACH, IN TURN, TAKES A TIMECARD OUT OF A RACK AND "PUNCHES OUT." LAST TO LEAVE THE ROOM IS NEWMAN, WHO CLOSES THE DOOR BEHIND HIM AND HANDS CHRIS AN ENVELOPE.

NEWMAN

Here you are. Don't forget to have your parents sign it and respond.

CHRIS

I won't.

NEWMAN

Got a ride?

CHRIS

Uh-huh. My mother's coming.

NEWMAN

Fine.

(A BEAT)

If they want to call me, I'll be in tomorrow.

CHRIS

Okay.

HE WATCHES AS NEWMAN GOES TO THE TIMECLOCK AND PUNCHES OUT. CHRIS EXAMINES THE ENVELOPE. HE STARTS TO OPEN IT.

ASSISTANT

Hey——you can't do that!

CHRIS HOLDS UP THE ENVELOPE

CHRIS

Why not? It's got my name on it.

WE MOVE IN ON CHRIS AS HE BEGINS TO READ. AS THE FOLLOWING ENSUES, THE CHANGES IN HIS FACE REGISTER CURIOSITY, CONCERN, RESISTANCE, DISAPPOINTMENT, SHOCK AND JUST-SHORT-OF-TEARFUL ANGER. AS HE READS, THE ENSUING VOICES ARE HEARD OFF CAMERA, LIGHTLY FILTERED.

PRINCIPAL

Study habits—

MISS TENDAL

Needs improvement.

PRINCIPAL

Respect for others—

BOLTON

Needs improvement.

PRINCIPAL

Participation in group—

COACH

Needs improvement.

PRINCIPAL

Self-discipline—

NEWMAN

Needs improvement.

PRINCIPAL

Uses classroom time to advantage—

Needs improvement.

PRINCIPAL

VOICE OVER, FILTER

Christopher continues to make his own problems, and to make things more difficult for himself. He has been frequently disruptive, often disobedient, and his constant dissent in many social situations contributes to the difficulties noted above.

CHRIS STUDIES THE PAGE. HE TAKES THE SHEET THAT IS STAPLED TO IT AND PLACES IT ON THE BACK OF A BOOK FROM HIS BOOKBAG, WHICH HAS A COVER FASHIONED OUT OF THE PAGES I HAVE SUBMITTED ALONG WITH THIS—THE HIGH SCHOOL BILL OF RIGHTS. WE SEE ENOUGH OF THIS COVER TO IDENTIFY IT, AS CHRIS BEGINS TO WRITE WITH THE STUB OF A BROKEN PENCIL. WE SEE THE OPENING WORDS OF WHAT HE WRITES, BEFORE THE DISSOLVE.

Now there is a transistion to Christopher's room. And the playwright's description of the room is another insight into the boy's character.

SCENE THIRTY-SIX:

NIGHT: CHRISTOPHER'S ROOM

THE ROOM IS OPERATIVE IN UNDERSTANDING THE CHILD. IT IS NOT A TYPICAL BOY'S ROOM. THERE ARE NO MODEL AIRPLANES, FOR EXAMPLE.

THERE ARE, ON THE OTHER HAND, BOOK, BOOKS, BOOKS—ON SHELVES, PILED ON A BATTERED DESK, STREWN ABOUT THE FLOOR. THERE IS A SMALL MICROSCOPE, A PORTABLE TYPEWRITER, A CHESSBOARD—AND A BULLETIN BOARD WHICH IS A MELANGE OF CLIPPINGS OF CURRENT EVENTS, INCLUDING MANY ON "ECOLOGY"—AND A GALAXY OF PICTURES CUT OUT OF NEWSPAPERS AND MAGAZINES, INCLUDING PICTURES OF MARTIN LUTHER KING, MAHATMA GANDHI, THE BERRIGAN BROTHERS...THERE ARE PEACE BUTTONS AND SYMBOLS STUCK INTO THE CORKBOARD. THERE ARE ALSO QUITE A FEW POSTERS. ONE SAYS YOU HAVE NOT CONVERTED A MAN BECAUSE YOU HAVE SILENCED HIM. ANOTHER SAYS WAR IS NOT HEALTHY FOR CHILDREN AND OTHER LIVING THINGS. ANOTHER IS THE POSTER OF JESUS CHRIST.

MOTHER IS — TENSELY — STRAIGHTENING UP THE ROOM. PICKING UP BOOKS HERE, STACKING THEM THERE, FINDING A SOCK UNDER SOMETHING. FATHER IS READING THE SHEET OF PAPER. HE FINISHES. HE IS SPEECHLESS. ALL HE CAN DO IS SHAKE IT FOR A MOMENT — THEN CLOSE HIS EYES. HE IS TREMENDOUSLY MOVED.

### FATHER

Wow.

### A PAUSE: HE CAN HARDLY TALK

That kid can write rings around both of us.

### HE ALL BUT BREAKS

Do you realize how much he knows about himself, how well he knows himself?

### MOTHER

More than a child should know. You're proud—and he's shattered.

There follows a discussion between the father and mother about the views of the younger generation and about Chris, in particular. When Chris walks into his room and sees his parents there, the discussion centers about the manifesto Chris has written in response to the school's report. The question arises whether or not the boy's reply should be sent to the principal.

### FATHER

To send or not to send, that is the question.

### CHRIS

I don't think so. I think the question is — am I going to do what you've always told us to do.

CAMERA REVEALS PICTURE OF THE FAMILY OF BOYS, WITH CHRIS GRINNING AMONG TWO OLDER BROTHERS. CAMERA NOW PANS TO HIS POSTERS.

What they did.

### CHRIS

### (VERY SOFTLY)

When you talked with my brothers about the war, didn't you say—

### FATHER

If you want to volunteer for the Marines—I will honor you, and I will respect you. If you want to go C.O.—or go to

Canada — or go to jail — I will respect you, and I will honor you. Whatever you do, I will back you up all the way—

                    CHRIS

but be sure you do what you **have** to do.

                    (A PAUSE)

Or do you want me to think one thing — and say another, just to play it safe?

          FATHER STANDS UP ABRUPTLY

                    FATHER

There you have it.

HE REACHES OUT TO HIS WIFE FOR THE PAPER. RELUCTANTLY, SHE HANDS IT OVER. HE STUDIES IT, SHAKING HIS HEAD.

                    CHRIS

Tell you what. I'll consent to a compromise. Why don't we let Mr. Newman see it first?

                    (A PAUSE)

I trust him.

GRAVELY, THE FATHER AND SON SHAKE HANDS.

Father and son go to see Mr. Newman.

    SCENE THIRTY-SEVEN: NEWMAN'S OFFICE

NEWMAN IS AT HIS DESK, FATHER IN BUSINESS GARB, TAKING CHRIS'S REPORT OUT OF HIS BRIEFCASE. HE IS ABOUT TO HAND IT OVER TO NEWMAN, BUT CHANGES HIS MIND AND HANDS IT TO CHRIS, WHO'S STANDING BY WITH HIS BOOKS AND STUFF.

                    FATHER

Read it to him, Chris.

                    CHRIS

Aw...

                    FATHER

Come, do your thing.

AS CHRISTOPHER READS, YOU CAN PLAY HIS DECLARATION OF INDEPENDENCE ALTERNATELY AGAINST NEWMAN AND HIS FATHER. I WOULD STILL, HOWEVER, LIKE TO SEE IN THE PSY-CHOLOGIST'S OFFICE THAT POSTER DEPICTING

AMERICA AS IT IS TODAY. IT IS CALLED "AMERICA THE BEAUTIFUL."

CHRIS

Well...

HE TAKES A DEEP BREATH

I find that you have been too negative about my progress as expressed in your comments. I find that the Is in learning skills and habits are correct, but I am inclined to disagree about the I in respect for others.

I also think that I made meaningful contributions, but that I do have to improve in participation.

Your notes suggest that I am a rude boy, and out of whack. Well, as to being out of whack — I am, because I think differently. But as to being rude, I feel that you are somewhat mistaken. You see, I am a loner, and should learn to participate, but I loathe being in a group, because they have a tendency to crowd me out, as I disagree on things in a way that seems offensive to them. So I have gotten checks on self-discipline, respect for others, and in participation. Now, I am being absolutely truthly.

HE CORRECTS HIMSELF

I meant "truthful," I guess.

HE TAKES A LONG BREATH, TURNS THE PAGE, AND PLUNGES ON

The only way I can improve is to agree to everything. But I am not like that, because I have the nerve to tell a person that he is wrong. I think you have been shortsighted about me making it hard for myself. I am not the equal of anyone—I am inferior to some people, and I am superior to some. But here, everything is like a jigsaw puzzle. And anything that doesn't fit in is socially excluded—like the untouchables of India.

SILENCE FOLLOWS THE READING. THE FATHER IS AT THE WINDOW, BACK TO CAMERA. SUDDENLY, A BELL RINGS OC, THEN—

PRINCIPAL

VOICE OC, FILTER

Good morning. Here is our word for today. A teacher affects eternity. He can never tell where his influence stops. Henry Adams.

Have a good day, one and all.

FATHER
(TO NEWMAN)

Well——what do you think?

NEWMAN

I think Chris had better take off — or he'll be late for home room.

FATHER CRUMPLES CHRIS'S HAIR. AS THE BOY TURNS TO GO—

NEWMAN

Wait, Chris. What do you really want out of school?

CHRIS

Well...if I could just——just learn things I'd **like** to learn, as well as what I **have** to learn——no. If I could just be a **person**——instead of a kickball——or a product?

NEWMAN

Good enough. Hit the road.

CHRIS TAKES OFF. NEWMAN PICKS UP THE PAPER. HE SHAKES HIS HEAD.

In the final scene, Chris resolves his dilemma.

**SCENE THIRTY-EIGHT:** A LONG LONG CORRIDOR

CHRIS WALKS AWAY FROM CAMERA ALONG THE ABSOLUTELY EMPTY HALL. AS HE PROCEEDS, GETTING SMALLER AND SMALLER DOWN THIS CORRIDOR WHICH IS LIFE——

VOICE

ROBOT-LIKE, ON ECHO

SIT DOWN...sit down...sit down...sit down...

CHRIS

VOICE OVER TAILOFF OF ECHO

I will stand up to you.

VOICE
(AS BEFORE)

SHUT UP...shut up...shut up...shut up...

CHRIS

(AS BEFORE)

I will speak out.

VOICE

(AS BEFORE)

Or GET OUT...get out...get out...get out...

CHRIS

(AS BEFORE)

I will not be driven out.

CHRIS

VOICE OVER

I will accept their science, and their math, and their history, and their phys ed, and their English Lit — but I will live my life **my** way. I would rather lose on my own terms than win on theirs. Like all the others who were different.

IN FLASHES: HIS HEROES: MARTIN LUTHER KING, MAHATMA GANDHI, AND THE WANTED POSTER OF JESUS CHRIST.

LONG LONG CORRIDOR SHOT. THE TINY BOY IN THE DISTANCE.

CHRIS

VOICE OVER

I bet they were scared too.

The Broadcasting and Film Commission of the National Council of Churches in its annual report summarized Allan Sloane's drama: "The purpose of the program was to deal with the threat to freedom involved in the suppression of dissent, through the story of a young child who is 'exceptional' with his struggle for survival in a school system that depends on 'rules' for its survival."

How effectively the author accomplished this purpose is attested to by the thousands of letters received by NBC after the program's presentation.

# Chapter 8
## Children's Programs

Even after 30 years, debates are still raging about the pervasive influence of television on the young mind. Congressional committees investigate violence on the TV screen. Voluntary organizations, such as "Action for Children's Television" (ACT), maintain a constant vigil of children's programming. ACT publishes a news letter for its members and other interested people; its officers appear on pertinent symposia; and it petitions Congress and the Federal Communications Commission. ACT has put forth a proposal that children's programs should not be sponsored, that they be declared a public service area so that "producers can design creative and constructively entertaining programs for children."

There is no question that television influences children; the problem is, to what degree? The small screen is often categorized as an electronic babysitter and some surveys have purported to show that there are preschool children who watch TV eight hours a day! And these surveys indicate that children spend more time viewing TV today than they did a decade ago.

A distinguished committee of behavioral scientists made a 2-year study for the surgeon general, United States Public Health Service, on "The Impact of Televised Violence." The committee stated, "The experimental studies bearing on the effects of aggressive television entertainment content on children support certain conclusions. First, violence depicted on television can immediately or shortly thereafter induce mimicking or copying by children. Second, under certain circumstances, television violence can instigate an increase in aggressive acts. The accumulated evidence, however, does not warrant the conclusion that it has an adverse effect on the majority of children. It cannot even be said that the majority of the children in the various studies we have reviewed showed an increase in aggressive behavior in response to the violent fare to which they were exposed. The evidence does indicate that televised violence may lead to increased aggressive behavior in certain subgroups of children, who might constitute a small portion or a substantial proportion of the total population of young television viewers. We cannot estimate the size of the fraction, however, since the available evidence does not come from cross-section samples of the entire American population of children.

"The experimental studies we have reviewed tell us something about the characteristics of those children who are most likely to display an increase in aggressive behavior after exposure to televised violence. There is evidence that among young children (ages four to six) those most responsive to television violence are those who are highly aggressive to start with—who are prone to engage in spontaneous aggressive actions against their playmates and, in the case of boys, who display pleasure in viewing violence inflicted upon others."

Why all this violence in television programming? Is it a distorted mirror of life? Unfortunately, the brutal reality is that the violence shown on TV is often tame compared to the actual terrors perpetrated by man. When you read a novel like "The Painted Bird" by Jerzy Kosinski, it may turn your stomach and your first reaction may be that the violence of man against his fellow man is completely exaggerated. On second thought, you realize, with a shudder, that so many of us are "painted birds" set upon by our fellow creatures.

The fact is that man is the most violent of all animals. A prominent anthropologist once remarked that man is the missing link between the ape and the human being. Our fervent hope is that someday shortly we will evolve into humans!

The tragedy is that man has the capability of living at peace with his fellows, of tremendous creative achievements, of making a world that is not only habitable but lovable. To install those goals, education for positive values should begin in the early years and that, in the long run, is the aim of one of the most innovative of children's programs, "Sesame Street."

Nevertheless, some psychologists have quibbled with "Sesame Street" productions on the premise that they are completely nonviolent and, therefore, not truly representative of life. But if it is true that violence on television can influence young viewers to antisocial behavior, should not the reverse be equally valid? "Sesame Street," besides teaching the preschooler his alphabet, tries to present social behavior in a meaningful pattern; for example, cooperation accomplishes good results. The Children's Television Workshop, which produces "Sesame Street," set out to prove "that television has the potential to reach and teach virtually every preschool child in this country regardless of his background; that television can provide him with the constructive entertainment and intellectual stimulation he critically needs to begin growing up with a sense of accomplishment, pride, and dignity."

Despite the fact that children are a very large and vulnerable segment of our population and very avid viewers of TV, this is an audience that has been largely catered to in quantity rather than quality. Whenever there has been a body of protest about the overload of violence on children's programs or the proliferation of mindless cartoons, then the networks have taken remedial action. However, CBS, for one, could counter that its "Captain Kangaroo" program is educational, albeit sponsored, and that it has been on the air for more than 16 years and has been cited by ACT for "a significant step towards upgrading children's television."

In adult programming, the networks have always rationalized that they are giving the public what it wants. But can they employ the same justification for children's programs? Do preschool children have preconceived notions of what they want to see?

The surgeon general's Scientific Advisory Committee on Television and Social Behavior observed that "Generally, infants and young children are less able than older persons to distinguish stimuli which are products of fantasy from those which are products of reality. Most children are more apt than older people to respond emotionally and physically, as well as ideationally, to their own fantasies and to the fantasies presented to them as if they were reality."

Nonetheless, the commercial networks have made attempts at quality programming for children. Westinghouse stations have their "Earth Lab" programs, which we discuss further on in this chapter. NBC has "Take a Giant Step" and its long run "Mr. Wizard," and a dramatization of the Babar stories. ABC presents "Curiosity Shop" and "Make a Wish." CBS revived "You are There" as a young people's version of its news series which offers reenactments of historic events such as Paul Revere's Ride, the Pony Express, and the Siege of the Alamo. Another CBS venture is "In the News," designed to give young people the whys and wherefores of what's happening in the world.

However, most of the input for quality programming has come from public television. Presentations such as as "Misterogers Neighborhood," "Masquerade," "Zoom," "What's New," "Hodge Podge Lodge," have been highly commended. "Sesame Street" may not be the best of all possible worlds for children's television, but it is an imaginative, exciting, entertaining, and informative world. The staff of the Children's Television Workshop is constantly searching for more dynamic ways of reaching the preschool child and now, with "Electric Company," the elementary school child. Some educators have differed with the "Sesame

Street" approach, particularly John Holt ("Big Bird Meets Dick and Jane," **Atlantic,** May '71). Holt offered some very constructive criticisms. Of course, it is a healthy sign when a television program arouses controversy and receives recognition in national magazines. It is prima facie evidence of the program's impact. **Time** magazine acclaimed "Sesame Street" as "not only the best children's show in TV history, it is one of the best parents' shows as well." Commissioner Lee of the Federal Communications Commission stated that there had been "no single educational television program on a national level that had tried to borrow the most effective contemporary television techniques for preschool instructional programming. Then came "Sesame Street," perhaps the most important series ever to be shown on American television."

According to Les Brown ("Television, the Business Behind the Box," Harcourt Brace Jovanovich) "Sesame Street" had been offered to the commercial networks but had been rejected. It was then that Mrs. Joan Ganz Cooney was able to enlist the aid of several foundations and thus began "Sesame Street's" outstandingly successful career on public television. "Within months," Les Brown says, "it became the model for excellence in programming for the very young and it drove all three networks to the creation of series for children that would be cultural or educational—and at the same time entertaining and commercial."

In the matter of technique, the presentation of a children's program depends on the age group to be reached. But there is a great deal of overlap, in the sense that many youngsters enjoy watching the same programs adults do, particularly action-type programs such as westerns and science fiction dramas. In an article in **Educational and Industrial Television** (May, '72), Jack Lyle and Heidi R. Hoffman noted that, based on a survey they were working on, it is apparent that bright children are not necessarily attracted by intellectually stimulating programs. They, like adults, are also given to watching highly popular programs, although they were quite critical of those programs. The difference between the bright and nonbright children is that the bright also find time for reading and other activities, including athletics, while the nonbright spend most of their free time watching the small screen.

Since programming on television is so highly competitive for its share of audience, it becomes a question of how palatable do you make children's programs. There may be some educators who react against sugar coating. We are reminded of the pioneer work of Theodore Thomas in educating people musically. Thomas was probably the most famous conductor in America during the latter part of the 19th century and early 20th century. Almost singlehandedly, he made the symphony orchestra part of our culture and, undoubtedly, introduced more new classical music to this country than any other conductor. However, he found that audiences of the day did not respond to symphonic music. They preferred gay waltzes and quadrilles. Therefore, he set out to educate them. He would carefully choose a movement from a symphony that had the vivacity of the music that was in popular vogue. He would play only the one movement and then follow it with a waltz or quadrille. At the next concert, he would include two movements of the symphony and so on. Very shortly, his audiences were requesting more symphonies. Before his death, Theodore Thomas was able to see a dream come true: where there had been only one symphony orchestra in the United States (the New York Philharmonic) now there were dozens.

Surely, Theodore Thomas had used sugar coating in educating the public; the device was eminently successful. There is no reason why the method should not have wider application. If the Cookie Monster and Big Bird of "Sesame Street" are a joy to the preschool child, they are also devices to enhance the learning process.

### "Sesame Street"

For the writer, the following paragraphs, describing how "Sesame Street" is put together, will be especially instructive.

"A Sesame Street program may contain as many as 50 separate segments, and with five original, hour-long shows being broadcast each week, there is a painstaking job of coordination among producers, writers, directors, performers, filmmakers, researchers and technicians.

"Every moment of Sesame Street deliberately integrates education and entertainment. Therefore, the Workshop team of experienced staff writers must prepare an hour of comedy for each program, building in lessons based on weekly curriculum guides set by the Workshop's research department.

"To complete this combination of laughs and lessons, the writers first prepare the live action scenes on Sesame Street which will include the Muppet puppets, the four regular hosts who appear daily on Sesame Street, and visiting celebrities who make guest appearances on the show.

"Music for these sections are composed and scored by the Workshop musical staff.

"Writers then draw upon an ever-growing bank of live-action and animated films, which are commissioned from about 40 of the country's top filmmakers. Day in and day out, the Workshop teams must decide the type, number, and order of segments that will go to make a completed program.
"Sesame Street is video-taped at studios in New York City. Once an individual program is fully assembled, it is viewed by Workshop officials, altered if necessary for optimum impact, and then fed each morning over the Public Broadcasting System network to the nearly 200 noncommercial stations carrying the series. An additional 50 stations, commercial and noncommercial, receive the program on video tape."
Now let us examine some excerpts from a "Sesame Street" script. The opening sequence comingles humor with an exercise routine. Humor is an integral element of every "Sesame Street" script.

Film: Show Identification

Film: Opening Sesame Street Theme

GREETING — EXERCISES (UP-DOWN, FAST-FASTER, BODY PARTS)

TOM IS LEADING DAVID, SUSAN AND SOME KIDS IN THE JUMPING JACK EXERCISE. THEY GREET AND SUGGEST THAT THE AUDIENCE JOIN IN.

Tom: Up...down...up...down...etc.

BIG BIRD ENTERS YAWNING...HE IS VERY TIRED.

BB: Hi everybody...(YAWNING)

Susan: Hi BB....boy you sure look tired. Don't you usually take a nap at this time?

BB: A nap? Naw. (BIG YAWN) I'm not tired today. (YAWN).

David: I don't know BB. I think you should take your nap.

BB: I don't need a nap I tell you. What are you doin'? (YAWN)

Tom: Exercises BB...but I think you're too tired to do them.

BB: I'm not too tired. I can do them. (YAWN)

ALL ARE SKEPTICAL

BB: No no... I'm all right. Go ahead.

Tom: Well, all right (LEADS 10 SECS OF JUMPING JACK..10 SECS OF TOUCHING TOES...AND FINALLY

RUNNING IN PLACE WHICH SHOULD GET FASTER, AND FASTER).

**BB**: (YAWNS AND IS QUITE LETHARGIC...AND FINALLY DURING RUNNING IN PLACE SLOWS DOWN AND FALLS ASLEEP STANDING UP)

**Susan**: (TAPPING BB) BB. Wake up!

**BB**: What...What? (STARTS RUNNING IN PLACE)

**David**: We're finished BB. You can stop.

**BB**: Oh yeah...boy that was fun. (BIG YAWN)

**Tom**: I dunno BB. I think you should take your nap.

**BB**: A nap? Are you kidding? Don't be silly. (BIG YAWN. LAYS HEAD ON SUSAN'S SHOULDER)

In the following scene, the play on Big Bird's sleepiness is continued; this time we have a lesson in subtraction interwoven.

BB HELPS TOM (SUBTRACTION)

BB AND TOM ARE NEAR THE ARBOR. THERE ARE THREE LARGE CARTONS STACKED ON THE GROUND.

**BB**: (YAWNING) Okay, now what do you want me to do Tom?

**Tom**: Gee I dunno. Are you sure you're not too tired?

**BB**: No, Tom...I'm fine.

**Tom**: All right if you say so. Now what I'd like you to do is count these cartons for me before I bring them into the store.

**BB**: Count the cartons? Sure, okay.

**Tom**: Thanks. (EXITS INTO STORE)

**BB**: Okay, now...one, two, three. Three... Tom has three cartons here. I'll go tell him. (BIG YAWN) On second thought I'll just wait till he comes out. (SITS DOWN ON A STOOL AND FALLS ASLEEP.)

TOM ENTERS WITH A HAND TRUCK

**Tom**: Well BB, how... (REALIZES BB IS SLEEPING) And he wasn't tired. Oh well...I'll just take one of these cartons inside cause thats all that will fit on my wagon here. (PUTS ONE CARTONS ON HANDTRUCK WITH SOME DIFFICULTY; SAYS) "3 take away 1 is 2" (AND THEN WHEELS THE CART INTO THE STORE, MAKING A LITTLE NOISE JUST AS HE GOES INSIDE)

**BB.:** (AWAKENED BY NOISE) What ? Huh? Oh I must have fallen asleep. Mmmm? Now what was I doing? Oh yeah, counting cartons. Let's see now, there are one..two, two cartons. Two cartons...(YAWNING) Two...(FALLS ASLEEP AGAIN)

TOM ENTERS WITH HAND TRUCK AGAIN

**Tom:** Still sleeping huh? Humph! Now let's see I'll take away one more carton. (LOADS CARTON ON TRUCK; SAYS) "2 take away 1 leaves 1" (AND EXITS INTO STORE AGAIN)

**BB:** (WAKES) Two! Huh? (LOOKING AT CARTONS.) Mmmm? There aren't two cartons there. There's only one..one carton. (FALLS ASLEEP AGAIN)

TOM ENTERS WITH HAND TRUCK

**Tom:** And now I'm gonna take this one away, which leaves none. (LOADS TRUCK AND EXITS, THEN RETURNS AFTER A SHORT PAUSE) Well I'm finished.

**BB:** (WAKES) Huh? What? Oh, hi Tom. I'll be finished counting in a minute.

**Tom:** But...

**BB:** (LOOKING AROUND WHERE CARTONS WERE) Tom...I counted your cartons...and you don't have any. (YAWNS & FALLS BACK TO SLEEP)

**Tom:** (REACT)

About midway through the program, the Big Bird episode is concluded. There are a few film inserts including a three-and-one-half minute story on bridges. Then the next sequence illustrates the meaning of cooperation.

THREE BRIDGE TABLES SET UP, EACH WITH A CHAIR.

ONE CHILD COMES IN CARRYING A LARGE STACK OF PAPER FOR DRAWING (LARGE). PUTS IT ON TABLE NO. 1 AND SITS DOWN. IS ABOUT TO DO SOMETHING BUT REALIZES SHE HAS NOTHING BUT PAPER TO WORK WITH. PIXILLATES AROUND.

**VO:** Here's Joanne. She wants to do some paintings. Why isn't she painting? She certainly has lots of paper...

CHILD NO. 2 COMES IN WITH THREE POTS OF PAINT. PIXILLATES AROUND AND PUTS PAINT ON TABLE NO. 2 AND SITS. OPENS THE PAINT BUT CAN'T DO ANYTHING EITHER. BOTH KIDS LOOK AT EACH OTHER.

**VO**: And here is Artie...he'd like to do some painting too. Why isn't he painting? He has a lot of paint.

KID NO. 3 COMES IN, CARRYING THREE BRUSHES. PIXILLATES AROUND AND ENDS UP AT TABLE NO. 3.

**VO**: And Denise wants to paint too. Why do you suppose she's not painting? She has a lot of brushes.

THREE KIDS GLARE AT EACH OTHER, PIXILLATE AROUND IN FRUSTRATION AND PLOP BACK INTO THEIR SEATS.

**VO**: These three kids don't seem to be having much fun. Say, kids?

THE KIDS LOOK UP.

**VO**: You're not getting much painting done, are you?

KIDS ALL SHAKE THEIR HEADS NO.

**VO**: Supposing you were to....cooperate? Huh?

KIDS LOOK AT EACH OTHER, LOOK AT THE EQUIPMENT...THE PIXILLATE AROUND, DISTRIBUTING THE STUFF TO EACH OTHER SO THAT EACH ONE ENDS UP WITH PAPER, PAINT AND A BRUSH.

**VO**: Ah...that's better. Now **everybody** can have fun.

FADE OUT ON KIDS PAINTING AWAY HAPPILY.

Another sequence, preceded by a video tape of the Golden D story and the Lou Rawls Alphabet Song, presents a brief exposition of words with the letter d.

**David**: d...dribble! (DRIBBLES A BASKETBALL)

MATTE: **d**ribble

(He stops dribbling, holds ball to camera. There is a "d" on it.)

**David**: Dribble. D

CUT TO: OSCAR IN CAN.

**OSCAR**: d...dust! (THROWING HANDFULS OF DUST IN THE AIR)

MATTE: **d**ust.

**Oscar**: Heh, heh, heh! (THROWING DUST)

CUT TO: TOM IN FRONT OF STORE

**Tom:** d...dance! (STARTS SCAT SINGING AND SILLY TAP DANCE)

Matte: dance.

Scenic: construction door—basketball hoop

Talent: Tom, David, Oscar

Props: dust for Oscar, basketball with "d" on it.

Matte: **d**ribble, **d**ust, **d**ance

And this sequence illustrates the use of farce in projecting a learning experience.

VTR: OLD WEST—DOC HOLIDAY (ROLES AND FUNCTIONS: MAILMAN, FIREMAN, DOCTOR)

OLD WEST SALOON SET...RINKY TINK PIANO IS PLAYING. COWBOY MUPPETS SAUNTERING AROUND. ONE MUPPET HAS A MAILBAG OVER HIS SHOULDER, ONE HAS A PIECE OF HOSE IN HIS HAND, AND ANOTHER HAS A STETHOSCOPE AROUND HIS NECK AND A ROUND DOCTOR MIRROR UNDER THE BRIM OF HIS COWBOY HAT.

A COWBOY COMES RUNNING IN

**Cowboy:** Sinister Sam, the meanest hombre west of the pecos, is coming!

PIANO STOPS PLAYING

**Cowboy:** (WHISPERING AND SHAKING WITH FEAR) Sinister Sam? Oh no! Lookout...Oh...etc.

SINISTER SAM BURSTS THROUGH SWINGING DOORS

**SAM:** (OMINOUSLY) I'm looking...for...Doc...Holiday!

MUSIC STING

**Doc:** Ohhh! (RUNS AND HIDES UNDER A TABLE)

**Sam:** (GOES UP TO MAILMAN) Let's see now. I'll bet you're the doc.

**Mailman:** (NERVOUSLY) No, Mr. Sinister Sam. I'm not the doctor. I'm the mailman. I deliver the mail. See my mailbag?

**Sam:** Yeah, I guess you're not the Doc. (MOVES QUICKLY TO THE FIREMAN) But I bet you are.

**Fireman:** Nnnnno Mr. Samister Sin...I mean Sinister Sam. I'm the fireman. See my hose? I put out fires.

**Sam:** Well then, where is the doctor?

**A.M.'S:** We don't know.

**Sam:** Well you hombres better find him because...I've got...an... itchy...trigger finger.

**A.M.'S:** (RUN TO TABLE WHERE DOC IS HIDING) Here he is.

**Doc:** (STARTS TO LEAVE) Excuse me...I have a house call to make...

**Sam:** Hold it...don't move. Like I said I have an itchy trigger finger.

**Doc:** Oh okay. But what do you want with me?

**Sam:** I want you to stop it from itching. It's driving me crazy. I'm always scratching it. What do you think it's a mosquito bite or something? Got some calamine lotion?

**Doc:** (FAINTS)

### "Earth Lab"

Another outstanding children's program is the "Earth Lab" series produced by Group W (Westinghouse Broadcasting Company) and written by Howard Jaffe. The programs are intended for upper elementary school children and teenagers (8 to 14 years old) and cover a wide variety of subjects: "Getting the Story Straight," which deals with the communication of news; "Sock it to Whom?", which delves into the problems of violence and agression; "You're A Magnet, Too," which explores the power of magnetism; and so forth.

"Earth Lab" uses the same narrator for each program; he is, in a sense, a teacher who guides the participating youngsters along the path of the subject matter the script is examining, as in this sequence from "You're A Magnet, Too."

REX IS SEATED IN THE MIDDLE OF EMPTY CYLINDERS. HE'S DEEP INTO "DEPTH PERCEPTION" TEST: ONE EYE SHUT, ARMS EXTENDED WITH INDEX FINGERS POINTED, TRYING TO TOUCH FINGERTIPS. WHILE HE'S DOING IT, THREE KIDS ENTER BEHIND HIM, REGARD HIM, SMILE AT EACH OTHER, ONE "SH SH'S" THE OTHERS.

**KID:** Yep, there's **always** something exciting happening in Earth Lab.

**REX** (SURPRISED): Oh, uh...I was just trying that old stunt...you've done this haven't you?

KIDS RESPOND

**REX**: You know, you stick your arms straight out (KIDS FOLLOW INSTRUCTIONS)...point your index fingers, close one eye, and try to bring your fingertips together.

KIDS REACTIONS

**REX**: If you have trouble, try it with both eyes open, and you'll see how we use **two** eyes to judge distance.

**KID** (NOT TRYING): That's pretty good, Rex...but what does it have to do with magnetism?

**REX**: I thought you'd never ask. (PICKS UP THREE PAIRS OF DOWELS WITH CERAMIC MAGNETS ON ENDS. SHOULD BE PAINTED DIFFERENT COLORS SO REX CAN TELL DIFFERENCE BETWEEN TWO PAIRS THAT HAVE OPPOSITE POLES — SO THEY STICK — AND A THIRD PAIR THAT HAS LIKE POLES, SO THEY REPEL) I knew you'd be around sooner or later, and I wanted to try a similar stunt with these magnets. Just close one eye, hold them at arms length with your arms spread apart, and try to bring them together. GIVES OUT THREE SETS. TWO KIDS WITH "GOOD" SETS DO IT EASILY. KID WITH "PHONY" SET HAS TROUBLE.

**REX** (TO KID WITH "PHONY"): Maybe you'd better try it with both eyes.

KID TRIES AGAIN, STILL N.G.

OTHER KIDS THINK IT'S FUNNY. ONE OF THEM TELLS OTHER...

**KID**: I have a feeling that this trick has nothing to do with eyesight...

**REX**: All right, I'll admit it...but you **did** sneak up on me, you know.

**KID** (SAME ONE WHO ASKED BEFORE): Then I'll ask the same question... what does it have to do with magnetism?

THEY ALL SIT ON CYLINDERS

**REX**: Well, let's see...did you ever hear the expression, "opposites attract?"

KIDS RESPOND

**REX**: Okay, that **attraction** has to do with the "poles" of a magnet.

**KID**: Like, north and south poles?

To introduce a humorous flavor, "Earth Lab" presents "Magneto the Magnificent" who acts as a pleasurable co-instructor with Rex, as in this scene.

**KID**: How do you know where east is?

**MAGNETO**: That's where the sun comes up, of course. Except on cloudy days, then I don't do my exercises. But, when I **am** doing my circles, see (MAKES CIRCLES WITH OUTSTRETCHED ARMS)...I know that since I'm facing east, my left hand — that's the red glove — is pointing north, and my right hand — the green — is pointing south.

**KID**: Did you ever think about using a compass?

**MAGNETO**: How much exercise can you get from a compass?

KID GIVES HIM LOOK THAT MIGHT EXPRESS THE OPINION, "FREAK!" MAGNETO GETS OUT THREE PAIRS OF GLOVES FOR KIDS

**MAGNETO** Now, bear with me for a moment, if you will...and I will get, as they say, to the point. (HANDS OUT GLOVES) Rex, where is north around here? (REX INDICATES A DIRECTION) The sun, of course, I left outside. So, let us all be magnetic compasses, and point, as so...red hand **always** to the north, green to the south. (THEY STRETCH ARMS OUT, SCATTERED AROUND). But now, suppose we happened to join together. How would our poles line up? Let's see...(kid), you shake hands with me, and you, (kid), shake hands with (other kid).

MAGNETO SHAKES HANDS WITH ONE KID: 2 OTHERS SHAKE SEPARATELY)

**REX**: Wait a second, Magneto. You've got a problem here. When you shake hands like that, your "green poles" are **together** and your "red poles" are at opposite ends. A compass can't have both ends pointing north.

**MAGNETO**: Exactly, Rex. I knew **you** would see that.

**REX** (TO KIDS): So, what are you going to do about it? How can you join up so that your "red poles" can still all point north?

KIDS FIGURE IT OUT ("Let's try this", etc.) GET IN A STRAIGHT LINE, THREE KIDS HOLDING HANDS, ALL

FACING FRONT. MAGNETO STEPS INTO LINE, AND RAISES KIDS' HANDS IN TRIUMPH.

**MAGNETO:** Ah, bravo! Perfect! You see, in order for us all to keep our magnetic direction, we've got to join a north pole with a south pole with a north pole, all the way down the line.

REX GETS "PHONY" SET OF DOWELS FROM BEFORE

**REX:** And since all magnets have a north pole and a south pole, when you try to put two norths and two souths together, they "repel" each other. (PICKS UP "GOOD" SET) But, when you match one north and one south, the opposites attract.

MAGNETO AND KIDS DO A LITTLE "LEG-OVER-LEG" ROCKETTES ROUTINE. (**PIANO**)

**MAGNETO:** Tall-short, left-right, white and black, opposites attract!

It's a fact! Opposites attract!

Where "You're A Magnet, Too" examines aspects of physical science, "Sock It To Whom?" delves into the realm of social science. The teaser develops the theme of the program.

OPEN ON FOUR KIDS HITTING THE KIND OF "SCHMOO-SHAPED" INFLATABLES THAT POP UP WHEN YOU KNOCK THEM DOWN. ONE KID IS A "BARKER" WITH STRAW HAT AND CANE.

**BARKER:** Are you angry, mad or potentially violent? Step right up to our punching gallery, and sock it to 'em. Knock 'em, rock 'em and let it all hang out. A nickel for five minutes...a quarter gets you a half-hour.

REX ENTERS TO BARKER

**REX:** Wait a second. Are you serious with this business? I mean, do you think it's healthy?

**BARKER:** It's better than taking it out on your baby brother.

REX TO OTHER KIDS

**REX:** Possibly. After all, getting angry is pretty natural behavior. And if you can let out your angry feelings without hurting anybody, maybe this works.

ASKS KIDS IF THEY'RE THINKING ABOUT ANYTHING IN PARTICULAR WHEN THEY'RE

PUNCHING...IF PUNCHING THE "BAG" REMINDS THEM OF ANYBODY THEY'D LIKE TO HIT OR A SITUATION THAT MADE THEM MAD. KIDS COMMENT.

**REX** (TO CAM): I guess at one time or another, we all want to "sock it to 'em." And today on Earth Lab we're concerned with how often and "how come" we get that feeling. And since, we could all just as easily be on the receiving end, we might also want to know, "Sock It To Whom?"

**OPENING TITLES, ANIMATION**

The technique of this episode of "Earth Lab" is to present examples of everyday aggression followed by a discussion of the problem, as in this situation:

TWO KIDS AT TV SET (ADOLESCENT AND PREAD.). BIGGER KID GETS UP AND SWITCHES CHANNELS. LITTLE ONE SAYS, "No!," BUT BIGGER ONE SAYS "Shaddup" AND PUSHES LITTLE ONE OFF HIS CHAIR (STOOL). LITTLE ONE STARTS CRYING. TERRY STORMS IN AND DEMANDS TO KNOW WHAT HAPPENED ("What's all the bawling about?") BIGGER KID SAYS LITTLE ONE'S UPSET BECAUSE HE (OLDER) SWITCHED PROGRAMS.

LITTLE ONE SUGGESTS, THROUGH THE SOBS, THAT HE GOT HIT.

TERRY ASKS OLDER KID IF THAT'S TRUE.

BIGGER KID ADMITS IT, RELUCTANTLY ("Aw, it was only a shove").

TERRY GRABS BIGGER KID BY SHIRT FRONT.

**TERRY**: "I've had about enough of your bullying him around" I don't know where you picked that stuff up!!! (PAY OFF LINE)

HOLD SHOT OF LITTLE KID CRYING FOR STUDIO TRANSITION ____

REX AND THREE KIDS WATCH FILM END ON PHILO (WALL) OUTPUT.

**REX**: They're not exactly the most mild-mannered family in town are they? Do you think that parents like that are aware of the influence they have on their kids' behavior? (KIDS COMMENT) Do you ever find yourself unconsciously imitating the people around you? (KIDS REPLY, CROSSING TO INTERVIEW AREA, JOINING OTHER KIDS, DR. SNYDER, MONKEY AND BRAIN

IMPLANT INSTRUMENTS) Maybe that angry father would understand a little about how he behaves if he'd study the way his family acts. Dr. Daniel Snyder here and his colleagues at the Yale University School of Medicine are doing that, in a way, with some of (monkey's) cousins. They think they might be able to understand what happens to our bodies and our brains in violent situations by studying animals. And a lot of it **does** have to do with environment, doesn't it?

DR. SNYDER RESPONDS RE IDEA OF PHYSICAL CONFINEMENT: CAGES, GHETTOS, PRISONS.

KIDS ASK WHAT KIND OF EXPERIMENTS THEY DO.

SNYDER DESCRIBES, WITH POSSIBLE FILM TO LAY OVER.

**KIDS' Q'S:** Why are some people more violent than others? Does the way we're "built" have anything to do with how we act? Can you control people or animals who are most violent? Can "violent" people control themselves?

The final sequence of the program follows the same pattern with Rex summing up.

REX AND KIDS SEATED, WATCHING TV. WE SEE BACK OF MONITOR.

SOUND EFFECTS: A GUN FIGHT.

REX ASKS KIDS IF THEY'VE SEEN ENOUGH. THEY HAVE. HE ASKS ONE KID TO SHUT OFF SET. KID DOES. REX ASKS KIDS IF THEY EVER GET TIRED OF WATCHING PEOPLE SHOOT AT EACH OTHER ON TV. KIDS ANSWER (YES OR NO).

**REX:** You know, a few organizations have counted the number of people that get killed during a week's worth of night-time television dramas, and it averages between 70 and 80 and that doesn't count war scenes. Do you think watching that much violence can effect your behavior, or is it just harmless entertainment?

(KIDS COMMENT) (REX TAKES OUT NEWSPAPER CLIPPING FROM A FOLDER)

Well, when I knew we were going to be talking about violence on Earth Lab, I started saving some newspaper articles, and this one's kind of interesting. It says "Ex-Convict Testifies Against Teacher in Slaying." Supposedly, this teacher was in love with her principal, and she tried to hire a professional killer to "take care of" the principal's wife. It sounds a little like a movie story, doesn't it? (KID'S REPLY) What do you think is most likely: do people get ideas for committing crimes from movie plots, or do most crime "stories" come from real life? (KIDS RAP) Do you think a person who watches a lot of television or sees a lot of movies can confuse the make-believe and the real worlds and begin to think that problems can be worked out as easily as they are on the screen? (MORE RAP)

(REX CLOSES WITH THESE RHETORICAL QUESTIONS)

It's sort of like asking "which came first, the chicken or the egg?", isn't it? Do we enjoy watching violent behavior because it reflects the way we really are, or does seeing so much of it give us new ideas. How much of the 'fight' in our human nature could be avoided by breeding a little human understanding?

CREDITS OVER SIAMESE FIGHTING FISH

(MUSIC: MARCH OF THE SIAMESE CHILDREN, KING AND I)

The ideal children's programs are those which combine sufficient action to hold the youngster's attention and sufficient information to influence them for the good. As we have seen, there is generally an overabundance of action and a minimum of information on the airwaves. But there are many programs which fulfill the ideal and others that come very close. The series of documentaries presented by the National Geographic and the Jacques Cousteau underwater spectacles are exemplars of fine programming for both a juvenile and adult audience. The films produced by the Disney organization on insects, flowers, and animals are remarkable for their photography. The "Wonderful World of Disney" presents commendable action stories, many of them adaptations of juvenile classics. CBS has produced several original dramas for young people which have been very well written and critically acclaimed, but they are too few.

The point is that given the opportunity, writers can create the first rate vehicles for young people which can hold attention without resorting to an overload of violent action.

# Chapter 9

## The News Program

A news writer at a local radio or television station is more likely to be a jack of all trades, combining the duties of a reporter, film editor, and photographer. At the network level, he is more precisely a writer. J.W.Roberts, bureau chief, Time-Life Broadcast, Inc., summed up the requirements for a radio or TV journalist:

An inquisitive mind.

A large does of dissatisfaction with the quick answer.

A strong measure of skepticism about form.

A deep hunger to get to the real guts of any problem.

A firm belief that every event has at least two sides to it, and quite often more.

A large trust in the human ability to work out disagreements without violence.

All the knowledge of human history and experience you can absorb.

A real determination to tell it like it is, not like you think it should be, or want it to be—like it is. That's the hardest job in the world. But it's also the most satisfying.

In a statement before the Subcommittee on Constitutional Rights of the Committee on the Judiciary of the United States Senate, one of our most prestigious newsmen, David Brinkley, expressed his opinions on television news:

"The first point is that television news every night reaches people who are not reached by any other news medium, and never have been. It reaches people who may buy a daily newspaper, but who often read only the sports pages or the comics, who skim the front pages lightly and almost never read the editorial pages.

"People who, therefore, do not fully understand what the function of journalism is.

"I have learned this over the years by a careful reading, often between the lines, of vast quantities of mail from the millions of people at the other end of the tube.

"And what I have found are profound misconceptions about the purpose of a news broadcast. Great numbers of people resent the fact that much of what we put on the air is unattractive, disturbing, depressing and even ugly. And a great many somehow have the idea that when we put this stuff on the air — campus riots, urban riots, violent demonstrations, and so on — that we put it on because we approve it, endorse it, or advocate it.

"Every time we have an ugly or depressing public event — say, a spasm of urban arson and looting — I get letters by the hundreds saying, in effect, 'why do you glorify and dignify this kind of unspeakable conduct?' The answer, of course, is so obvious it's almost embarrassing to have to make it. It is that we put this stuff on because we think the audience would like to know about it, or ought to know about it — certainly not because we like it or approve it or advocate it.

"Second is that on television, journalism takes on a personal dimension. On a newspaper, the reporter is not seen. His work is in the form of cold type on paper. On television, of course, he's there in living color complete with haircuit and necktie.

"And people can always detect, or think they can detect, a raised eyebrow — but only when they don't like what he's saying.

"A third point is that a news broadcaster comes out of the same tube, the same box, as a succession of entertainers — comedians and actors, jugglers and so on. Following all that, when a face comes on that is not wearing a toothpaste smile and says there's been another riot and more war casualties and taxes are going up and so on .. pouring out a turgid stream of depressing news, it looks even worse by comparison with the light entertainment before it and after it."

And, in summation, Brinkley said:

"And finally, on the general subject of how well television news does its job and how much it merits the criticism it now gets. I believe the network news programs — the only ones I am familiar with — are pretty good.

"Their limitations are quite severe, imposed as they are by the nature of the medium itself. They obviously are not comprehensive, much of what they do is excessively brief. But a half-hour is a half-hour and there is no way to stretch it. A newspaper can add pages. We can't.

"I do believe them to be honest, and I know there is no conspiracy or plot to undermine the right or the left. I think the proof is the fact our bitterest critics are the far right and the far left. The far right generally thinks we are radicals, while the far left thinks we are conservative members of the establishment.

"We have, indeed, been guilty of some sins and made our share of mistakes, particularly in the earlier years of television news, the years when new kinds of American history were being made and being reported by new people using an entirely new medium.

"Now, today, we still have a number of faults. But the rampant political bias charged by our critics simply does not exist. What happens mainly is that people project their own political biased on us.

"A biased opinion simply is an opinion you do not agree with.

"If we are accused of bias by both sides — far right and far left — we must be doing something right."

David Brinkley is one of the few network newscasters who writes all of his own copy. Other topnotch newsmen at the networks write a good deal of their copy, but much is also prepared for them by news writers.

So much for philosophy. Now, to the practicalities. There have been many books devoted solely to the subject of radio and television news writing. We have listed some of them in our bibliography. We particularly recommend David Dary's "Radio News Handbook" (TAB BOOKS). In this one chapter we shall try to define some basic elements of news writing.

## CLARIFICATION

If there is one factor of most importance to guide the embryo news writer, it is clarity. In an article in the **Writer's Digest**, Sandy Goodman, a TV news writer and producer, praises Brinkley as the "best television news writer of them all...master of the simple declarative sentence."

There is much more leeway in newspaper journalism; sentence structure may be more involved; the writing more literary. But simplicity is the keynote for broadcast news: so much has to be conveyed in so little time. We are reminded of the cartoon showing a TV news producer towering over a reporter and irately exclaiming, "Can't you learn to sum up the world situation in less than 30 seconds!"

There has been, to be sure, an extension of news time. TV network affiliates often present an hour of combined local and national news followed by a half-hour of network news. And the all-news station is now a factor in large cities.

For all that, listeners or viewers must have an immediate grasp of the news item. They cannot ask the newscaster to repeat the statement; they can reread an item in the newspaper. Therefore, the following principle is applicable to broadcast news writing: present only one thought in each sentence.

Here, for example, is a sentence as it appeared in a daily newspaper:

"Instead of refusing to accept a compromise senate plan to restrict the bussing of school children, house members voted overwhelmingly to insist on legislation outlawing bussing altogether and the vote is sure to produce a long fight between the two houses of congress."

This is how the item was written for broadcast on the Mutual network:

"The house of representatives has refused to accept a compromise senate plan to restrict the bussing of school children. Instead, house members voted overwhelmingly to insist on legislation outlawing bussing altogether. The vote is sure to produce a long fight between the two houses of congress."

As you can see, each sentence in the above copy expresses one thought.

## VARIATION

Varying the length of your sentences permits more effective pacing. In order to maintain the principle of one thought to one sentence, there may be a disposition to keep all sentences brief. But if all sentences were short, the effect would be too staccato and difficult to listen to. Notice the variation in this excerpt from the "CBS Evening News with Walter Cronkite."

"In Charleston, South Carolina, hospital and union officials reported tonight that a settlement has been reached to end a strike against two hospitals there. Negro nonprofessional workers walked out 13 weeks ago, charging their union with discrimination. Part of the settlement reportedly includes the release from jail without bail of the Reverend Ralph Abernathy, jailed last Saturday on charges of inciting to riot."

## ALLITERATION

Avoid tongue twisters. Be sure to read your copy aloud. If you stumble over a phrase, then it may have to be reworded. Alliteration, especially of the 's' sounds, may set up a potential fluff. As a general rule, it is best to avoid alliteration of any type.

## IDENTIFICATION

In identifying someone in the news, it is preferable to have his title, if applicable, precede his name. For example, this news item from a WRC-TV telecast:

"School superintendent Hugh Scott today honored the city council's subpoena"...."School board president James Coates told the council that the majority of the board does not blame the fiscal crisis on Superintendent Scott."

The above type of identification is both a time saver and provides good reading flow. If you wrote, "James Coates, president of the school board," you would have a tendency to slight pauses before and after the identification. This may result only in the lapse of a second or so, but when you may have a dozen or more identifications in, let us say, a 3½-minute newscast, you could be wasting precious time.

The trend today is to use the live quotation: sound on film for TV or audio tape for radio. Naturally, it is much more effective to hear directly from the newsmaker than to have him quoted. But attributing quotations can be handled by simply naming the quoted person followed by the verb, said; "Secretary of State Rogers, in his news conference, said..."

Another guideline is to be sure to clarify your antecedents, otherwise misunderstanding may arise on the part of the listener. Suppose you were to write, "John Doe, assistant to the Secretary of Labor, resigned today." A late tuner or someone not listening too closely might only catch, "Secretary of Labor resigned today." In this case, brevity could be confusing. The news item might better be written, "John Doe resigned today. He was assistant to the Secretary of Labor."

## LEADS

Newspaper editors have long contended that newcasts have no front page and, therefore, every item on a newscast appears to carry the same weight. Whether this is so or not, it is the general practice in radio and television for the producer to place what he considers the most important news item at the beginning of the newscast.

Many newscasts open with teaser items as in the case of this telecast over WRC-TV:

"The president talks about some form of national sales tax.

"And a hijacker, who parachuted, is captured.

"Details next on News 4 Washington."

A newscast by a local station may defer a lead item of national import if an incident of transcending impact occurs locally: a strike of sanitation workers, a hurricane, an explosion in a local factory, or results of a local election.

## GENERAL CONSIDERATIONS

It is a simpler assignment to write news for radio than television largely because of the stringency involved in writing to film. The TV news writer faces the difficult challenge of having to tailor copy to precise time segments. A film insert may run only 26 seconds; the copy will have to match exactly. It cannot run over into the next news item which may have no relation whatever to the preceding story. It is not an easy task. But it does teach you to make the most of your words.

Because of the emphasis on the "eyewitness" type of news, much of the newswriter's copy becomes merely a lead-in; e.g., "On capitol hill, another development in the I T & T issue...Mutual's Bill Greenwood is there..."

For television news, the picture and sound should tell the bulk of the story. The copy should add material that is not discernible from the visual:

| Scene | Copy |
|---|---|
| LS airliner at far end of airport | The hijacker of a Hughes West airliner was captured this evening after he parachuted from the plane with 50 thousand dollars ransom money. He |
| MS wheat field | broke a leg when he landed in a Colorado wheat field about one hundred thirty miles northeast of Denver. |

In the above sequences, the viewer can identify an airport and probably recognize a wheat field, but the copy gives him details that could not be learned from just seeing the visual.

## ON THE LOCAL LEVEL

Local radio and television stations broadcast a good deal of community news. The definition of community depends on the power and location of the station. WBT, Charlotte, North Carolina happens to be on the state line and, therefore, reaches both North Carolina and South Carolina. It faces a problem of news balance between its primary metropolitan area and the outside area of about 40 countries. Fortunately, outlying countries are generally interested in urban affairs.

Most local stations encourage their staff to enter into community activities. The news writer at the local level is usually also a reporter and so it is a valuable asset to be community conscious. The chief news source may be the local newspaper. The station, also, will subscribe to one or both of the wire services whose function we will discuss further on in this chapter.

The following are excerpts from a typical local newscast presented by radio station WVMC in Mt. Carmel, Illinois.

NEWSCASTER: NORTH MIDDLE SCHOOL AND MT. CARMEL HIGH SCHOOL STUDENTS, WITH LANCASTER SCHOOL AS THEIR GUESTS, HEARD PERFORMANCES BY THE EVANSVILLE PHILHARMONIC'S LITTLE SYMPHONY YESTERDAY. MUSIC DIRECTOR MINAS CHRISTIAN CONDUCTED THE ORCHESTRA IN VARIED PROGRAMS RANGING FROM BACH AND MOZART COMPOSITIONS TO JESUS CHRIST SUPER STAR. THE FIRST PERFORMANCE WAS AT NORTH AT 9:15 AM AND THE HIGH SCHOOL CONCERT WAS AT 10:15. APPEARANCE OF THE ORCHESTRA WAS MADE POSSIBLE BY PATRONAGE FUNDS RAISED FOR THE ORCHESTRA BY A LOCAL COMMITTEE HEADED BY E. J. TALLEY AND JOHN HURLBUT, PRESIDENT OF JEL-CO RADIO. IN MARCH, STRING ENSEMBLES FROM THE PHILHARMONIC APPEARED AT SOUTH AND ST. MARY'S SCHOOL. SOME 60 PERCENT OF THE ORCHESTRA'S MAINTENANCE FUND COMES FROM TRI-STATE PATRONAGE CONTRIBUTIONS.

-0-

LAST NIGHT'S MOONLIGHT MADNESS SALES IN DOWNTOWN MT. CARMEL BROUGHT RECORD CROWDS DESPITE A PERSISTENT DRIZZLE. CHARLES WILDERMAN, CHAIRMAN OF THE WABASH COUNTY RETAIL MERCHANTS ASSOCIATION, SAID THAT CROWDS ARE ESTIMATED AT ABOUT 10 PERCENT HIGHER THAN LAST YEAR. HE ANNOUNCED WINNERS IN THE NIGHT ATTIRE COSTUME CONTEST. FIRST PLACE — ARTHUR SMITH, OWNER OF THE HOUSE OF FURNITURE. SECOND, DON DANIEL, MANAGER OF P N HIRSH WITH MRS. JESSIE BURKE, OWNER OF MODE-O-DAY WINNING THIRD AWARD.

-0-

GEORGE W. WOODCOCK, WABASH COUNTY STATES ATTORNEY, ANNOUNCED THAT RAYMOND L. WOODS, 73 OF ROUTE 3 MT. CARMEL, APPEARED IN CIRCUIT COURT YESTERDAY BEFORE CIRCUIT JUDGE CLARENCE E. PARTEE AND ENTERED INTO A NEGOTIATED PLEA OF GUILTY TO THE CHARGE OF CONTRIBUTING TO THE DELINQUINCY OF A CHILD. WOODS WAS PLACED ON PROBATION FOR ONE YEAR, WITH THE FIRST 60 DAYS TO BE SERVED IN WABASH COUNTY JAIL.

SALLY J. FRENCH, DAUGHTER OF MR. AND MRS. UEL FRENCH OF RURAL ROUTE 3, MT. CARMEL, IS THE WINNER OF A UNIVERSITY OF ILLINOIS SCHOLARSHIP, ACCORDING TO BILL DENHAM, SUPERINTENDENT OF EDUCATIONAL SERVICE REGION. THE SCHOLARSHIP IS AWARDED ON THE BASIS OF SCORES MADE ON THE A-C-T EXAMINATIONS GIVEN EARLIER THIS YEAR. IT PROVIDES MISS FRENCH WITH A TUITION-FREE SCHOLARSHIP FOR FOUR YEARS AT ANY OF THE U OF I's CAMPUSES — URBANA-CHAMPAIGN, CHICAGO CIRCLE OR MEDICAL CENTER.

-0-

AFTER TWO WET SATURDAYS IN A ROW, THE MT. CARMEL LITTLE LEAGUE WILL ATTEMPT TO HOLD LITTLE LEAGUE TRYOUTS AGAIN THIS SATURDAY AT ED WALTERS FIELD. TIMES ARE 8:30 FOR 10 YEAR OLDS, 10:30 FOR THE 11 and 12 AGE GROUP: 1:30 FOR 9 YEAR OLDS AND 3:30 FOR THE 8 YEAR OLDS. PARENTS ARE REQUESTED TO HAVE THEIR LITTLE LEAGUERS AT THE TRYOUT SITE AT LEAST 20 MINUTES BEFORE THE SCHEDULED TIME FOR EACH AGE GROUP. APPLICATIONS ARE AVAILABLE FOR THOSE WHO MISSED THE PRIOR SIGNUP DATE.

## COMMENTATOR

Unlike the newscaster who presents a straightforward recital of the news, commentators choose one major news event and give their views on the subject. They may be compared to the columnist on a newspaper, but there are far more newspaper columnists of every variety than there are broadcast analysts. We would venture to say that the situation exists because the networks and local stations approach controversy, to say the least, gingerly.

One of the outstanding news commentators is NBC's David Brinkley. The commentary below is typical of his approach.

"In this new session, congress will spend a lot of time on welfare, annual incomes for the poor, and Social Security.

"From reading our mail, it is clear there is one small change they could make in Social Security that would hurt nobody and benefit millions of people.

"Now, when a person retires at 65 and collects his meager pension . . barely enough to keep him from starving . . he is discouraged from working to earn more . .

292

even if he's able to and wants to. Because if he does work, and earns more than about 30 dollars a week, he starts losing his pension.

"His pension is not a gift, not charity and not welfare. He paid for it, in advance. So there is no reason in fairness to make any rules on what he can do with it when he gets it.

"A wealthy person can retire at 65 and collect any amount in dividends, interest, rents and so on and still get all of his Social Security. One who is not wealthy . . and who wants to work and is able to . . even part-time . . is discouraged from doing so.

"Private retirement plans make no rules. They see it as a straight cash deal — you pay while you work and they pay you back when you retire.

"There is no reason why the federal government can't do the same. In simple truth ... when a person retires, whether he works or not is none of Washington's business."

## EDITORIALS

Editorializing is a Johnny-come-lately to the broadcasting industry. The so-called Mayflower Decision proved a turning point. Although the Federal Communications Commission ruled in 1939 that a radio station could not editorialize, its ruling brought such a wave of protest that the Commission subsequently qualified its decision permitting broadcasters to editorialize, provided equal opportunity for rebuttal was given.

In 1972, a survey for the **Broadcasting Yearbook** showed that almost 65 percent of AM stations, 46 percent of FM stations and over 50 percent of TV stations are now editorializing at least occasionally. The NAB operational guide, **Broadcasting The News**, states that "Many stations broadcasting editorials believe their editorials should be restricted to local issues and stands should be taken on national issues only insofar as those issues directly affect the station's own community. Other stations take a broader view, editorializing on national and international questions.."

At radio and television stations in the large metropolitan areas, usually one of the more experienced newsmen is given the assignment of editorialist. He both writes and voices the editorials. At WRC-TV, Bryson Rash is manager of editorial services. As such, he is responsible for the formulation of subject matter for editorials. Many of the themes, however, may come from colleagues at the station or from concerned citizens. The subject matter is presented to the editorial board at the station and, if agreed upon, the script is then written by Rash and the final copy is again presented for a censensus, since the editorial will become an expression of the station's position. Four or five different editorials are aired each week, generally three times daily. When requested, opposing views are given equal time. A typical WRC-TV editorial is reproduced below:

### OPENING

This is an expression of editorial opinion by WRC-TV. Speaking for the station is Bryson Rash.

### RASH

No one is happy about the welfare program — those who pay for it or those who are on it. In the District of Columbia, the welfare budget has risen from 6.8 million in 1962 to $36 million this year.

If that figure startles you — it should, for the rate of growth of welfare recipients in the District is the highest in the nation. Apparently it also staggered congress, for it overreacted by cutting $5 million from the city's welfare budget which it thought represented fraud and over-payment. Now funds to aid those on welfare are running out.

The city's new Human Resources Director, Joseph Yeldell, has accepted the challenge of finding the needed money. WRC-TV feels his proposals are comprehensive and deserve support. Under the new system, if approved by the City Council, all welfare recipients will have to report every three months for case review and registration for training programs and work. Action is being taken to set up better inspection procedures, more day care centers, and a flat grant payment system. A real effort also is being made to find jobs for thousands of recipients who are unemployed but able to work. Safeguards against government abuse are promised, and must be observed to assure that in this new process the honest poor are given the dignity and respect that is due them.

The District of Columbia has shown good faith to its welfare recipients and to its taxpayers. Congress must too —by supporting the District government in its attempts to move or add the additional funds needed to carry the city's poor through the fiscal year.

### CLOSING

This has been an expression of editorial opinion by station WRC-TV, presented by Bryson Rash. This station welcomes comments on its editorial opinions and recognizes its obligations to provide spokesmen for significant opposing viewpoints a reasonable opportunity for reply.

Address your response to WRC-TV, 4001 Nebraska Avenue N.W., WASHINGTON, D.C. 20016. This editorial was prerecorded.

WRC is located in a metropolitan area of almost three million population. As another example of editorial opinion, here is an as-broadcast editorial from WVMC in Mt. Carmel, Illinois, population less than 10,000 (city proper).

"Dear friend consumer. And who of us ISN'T a consumer? Would you believe that a brand new, super regulatory agency is about to be created in Washington? How we've managed without it, we'll never quite understand. Somehow we have, but the house has already passed a bill which implies we're bad off without this proposed Consumer Protection Agency. The Senate Government Operations Committee has a bill before it, S 1177, which goes even farther than the house version.

"If this comes to pass in the shape of the senate bill, friend consumer, you'll be surrounded with protection! Not only that, the new agency would determine what you the consumer wants...even what you SHOULD want! It would dominate various agencies which have been in existence to protect you and me from fraud or whatever. But apparently these bureaus aren't enough. There has to be a super agency to keep the agencies in line.

"This new agency — get this — would be able to represent consumer interests (as determined by the agency) before any other government agency. It would determine what is in your best interests, with no surveys of what you or I think necessary. It's big daddy all over again — big daddy knowing better than you or I. This proposal rates you and me with about kindergarten level intelligence.

"The new Consumer Protection Agency would have teeth, legal means...in short, would have sweeping authority never before granted another agency in government. The house committee that gave birth to one version of this sorry and frightening charter commented, 'It's new and unusual.' This has to be the understatement of the year in a town given to superlatives.

"It is a frightening proposal in the name of protection which has sweeping implications for your freedom and mine. Today we have choice in the market place. If one brand doesn't particularly fit our needs, we turn to another. But suppose some super agency can set the standards — suppose we don't like them. Where do we then turn? As imperfect as our system is — we'll take today's competition in exchange for complete government domination — and this new Consumer Protection Agency...as outlined in both the house and senate bills...is a giant step toward virtual government control.

"The words of Secretary Connally, made in Chicago recently, come to mind. He said, and we quote — "Our system in general is being challenged...it is time, though, to pause and reflect and give credit that something has been accomplished in this country. Better schools. Better food..." And we might add — it is the world's highest standard of living...a standard never achieved in any government-dominated society.

"Do we need a czar-type agency to protect the consumer? Who'll then protect the consumer from the czar? We urge you to tell your congressmen and senators that you do not buy this concept of overprotection. Remind them that regulatory agencies now write rules with the same force of law as acts passed by elected officials. It is time to call a halt to — regulation without representation. Thank you."

## THE WIRE SERVICES

Almost all radio and television stations which present daily newscasts subscribe to either or both of the major wire services: Associated Press (AP) and United Press International (UPI). It was not always so. In the 30s, newspapers, fearing the competition of radio news, pressured AP and UPI to deny their service to radio stations. However, by the early 40s, these restrictions were completely eliminated. Radio was not only recognized as a potent force for the dissemination of news, but many newspapers discovered that radio news reports actually helped their circulation. The necessarily brief items on radio led the listener to his newspaper to obtain fuller details.

With the advent of radio and later, television, as powerful news media, the wire services developed special copy to meet the audio-visual requirements. Interestingly enough, the tight, precise writing required for the broadcast media has had its impact on writing for newspapers so that many of the dailies now have crisper copy.

We are juxtaposing, for your study, comparable items as sent on the UPI press wire and its radio wire.

| Press Wire | Radio Wire |
|---|---|
| ....SAO PAULO, BRAZIL (UPI) — A BRAZILIAN | ....(SAO PAULO, BRAZIL) — VARIG AIRLINES PAID A 254- |

VARIG AIRLINES TURBO-PROP AIRLINER ON A DOMESTIC FLIGHT WITH 87 PASSENGERS ABOARD WAS HIJACKED ON TUESDAY AND FORCED TO RETURN TO SAO PAULO, WHERE THE HIJACKERS DEMANDED ABOUT $300,000. THE FOUR-ENGINE ELECTRA WAS HIJACKED WHILE EN ROUTE TO CURITIBA NINE MINUTES AFTER TAKE OFF FROM SAO PAULO'S CONGONHAS AIRPORT, A VARIG SPOKESMAN SAID. HE SAID IT CARRIED 78 PASSENGERS AND NINE CREW MEMBERS.

"WE THINK THERE ARE THREE HIJACKERS," SAID THE SPOKESMAN.

THE ELECTRA LANDED AT CONGONHAS AND TAXIED TO THE FRONT OF A RAMP NEAR THE AIR-PORT FIRE STATION. POLICE AND AIR FORCE TROOPS IMMEDIATELY SEALED OFF THE AREA.

VARIG SAID IT WOULD AWAIT FEDERAL GOVERN-MENT INSTRUCTIONS REGARDING PAYMENT OF RANSOM. IT WAS REPORT-ED THE HIJACKERS ALSO DEMANDED PARACHUTES. THE HIJACKING OCCURRED AT 3:44 P.M. THE FIRST OFFICIAL WORD WAS THAT THE HIJACKERS HAD ASKED FOR 1.5 MILLION CRUZEIROS, SOMEWHAT LESS THAN $300,000.

THOUSAND DOLLAR RAN-SOM TONIGHT FOR THEIR PLANE HIJACKED EARLIER TODAY WITH 87 PERSONS ABOARD. ONE OF THE PASSENGERS IS WASHINGTON D-C DISC JOCKEY FELIX GRANT.

And here is an example of the sound-on-film (SOF) service offered to television subscribers by UPI.

| NARRATION | SECS-SCENE |
| --- | --- |
| PRESIDENT NIXON'S TOP ADVISERS ON ECONOMIC AND TRADE RELATIONS GATHERED AT THE WHITE HOUSE TUESDAY TO | 15; ANNCR ON CAMERA |

DISCUSS THE "NUTS AND BOLTS" OF AGREEMENTS REACHED AT THE MOSCOW SUMMIT MEETING AND ITS EFFECTS ON THE U.S. ECONOMY. COMMERCE SECRETARY PETER PETERSON SOUGHT TO COUNTER REPORTS

THAT THE ABSENCE OF A SOLID AGREEMENT ON TRADE WAS THE WEAKEST LINK IN THE SUMMIT AGREEMENT BY SAYING THE TALKS HAD "CLOSED THE GAP" ON COMMERCIAL ISSUES THAT HAVE TROUBLED THE TWO NATIONS FOR TWENTY YEARS. MEETING WITH NEWSMEN AFTER THE CABINET ROOM CON-FERENCE, PETERSON DESCRIBED SOME OF THE PROBLEMS THAT WILL HAVE TO BE SOLVED IN INCREASED TRADE WITH RUSSIA...

25; WHITE HOUSE— CABINET ROOM, MEETING

1:43; PETERSON SOF

(SOUND UP FOR 1:18)

(PARAPHRASING)
PETERSON SAYS: AT THE PRESENT TIME, OUR TRADE WITH THE SOVIET UNION IS ON THE ORDER OF A COUPLE MILLION DOLLARS. COMPARE THAT WITH OUT TOTAL EXPORT-IMPORT OF AROUND $90 BILLION. CONSIDER ALSO THAT WE ARE DEALING WITH A NONMARKET NATION. WE, OF COURSE, ARE A MARKET EN-TERPRISE NATION. WE HAVE TO WORK OUT SUCH THINGS AS HANDLING ARBITRATION PROCEDURES, PATENTS AND COPYRIGHTS. WHILE THERE ARE OP-PORTUNITIES AHEAD, THERE IS SOME OF THIS FOUNDATION LAYING THAT

MUST TAKE PLACE. WE
EXPECT TO MAKE MAJOR
PROGRESS IN THE JOINT
COMMERCIAL COMMISSION
(END CUE: "THAT MEETS
IN JULY.")

UPI has prepared a **Broadcast Stylebook** for its writers and the following excerpts will be of benefit to potential news writers.

**Measuring Copy:** Time is precious to a broadcaster. Learn to measure it in terms of the written word. Don't waste it by overwriting. When the desk asks for an 8-line story, tell it in eight lines, not ten. Naturally, no two announcers read at the same speed. But there is a rule of thumb in translating lines of copy into air time. Count the number of full typewritten lines. If margins have been set properly, the average full line will contain ten words. The average newscaster reads approximately fifteen lines (or 150 words) of copy per minute.

**Accuracy:** The most important ingredient of any story you ever will hand to a United Press International desk is accuracy. Never forget it. Check and recheck all facts, figures and names. In radio or television, nine out of ten corrections reach an entirely different audience. The time to make one is BEFORE the copy hits the wire.

**Broadcast News Writing:** How does it differ from newspaper writing? What are the techniques...the problems ...the aims? Broadcast news copy is good if it is accurate, authoritative, entertaining and "listens" well. It must inform and please the ear, not the eye. Since people speak more informally than they write, a newscast is more informal than page one of a newspaper. It must not, however, be so informal it fails to win listener respect. The newspaper writer has his Five Ws; the broadcast news writer his Four Cs—Correctness, Clarity, Conciseness and Color. At the risk of oversimplification, the ability to write for the ear could be defined as:

"Selection and placement of story detail on paper in such a way as to create listener illusion that the announcer is 'back-fence talking' the facts in an authoritative yet entertaining way."

And let's not look down our journalistic noses at that word "entertaining." A good newscast must have sparkle. If yours is dull, the listener will turn to another. He has plenty from which to choose.

The reader makes his choice at the newsstand. The listener tunes in what pleases him...and at no cost or inconvenience. Your words have one fleeting crack at the man with the finger on the dial. Select them carefully.

One reasonably sure way to interest the listener is to be interested in the story yourself...not just a writer, but as a person. You must feel the urgency, the pathos, the excitement or the humor that makes an event newsworthy. And you must make the listener feel it, too.

**Transitions:** It's important to have each paragraph flow into the next one. Do it with ideas and skillful organization of facts...not "crutch" words or phrases. Perhaps the most overworked words in radio copy are MEANWHILE, MEANTIME and INCIDENTALLY. Forget them, especially "incidentally." If something is only "incidental" it has no place in a tight newscast.

**Overwriting:** Nothing pegs a beginner so quickly as a flowery, verbose style. Write with enthusiasm but flavor with dignity. The best adjective or adverb invented is no match for an active verb.

**Numbers:** To ensure clarity, broadcasters have their own style for figures.

From one to nine, write out: one, two, three, etc., unless used to indicate sports scores, time or dates.

From 10 to 999—use numerals, e.g., 14, 35, 989, etc.

Hundred, thousand, million, billion—write it: 15-hundred (not 1,500); five-thousand (not 5,000); 12-thousand-500 (not 12,500); eight-million (not 8,000,000); and nine-billion-220-million (not 9,220,000,000).

Round out figures unless the exact one is necessary to the story. For all practical purposes $1,613 becomes "16-hundred dollars." Bracket in exact figure where desired, e.g. "16-hundred dollars ($1,613) etc."

Never say "a million." The "a" is heard as "eight," making the figure sound like "eight million." Write it "one million."

Never begin a sentence with a figure unless you spell it out.

In writing dates, it is December 1st, 9th, 31st, etc.

**Meaningless Words:** Never use LATTER, FORMER and RESPECTIVELY when referring to persons, places or things already mentioned. Since the listener can't refer back to a previous sentence or paragraph, those words are meaningless.

News writing, coupled with reporting, can provide a challenging and exciting career. What the market is like can be described by some of the variety of station news operations outlined in the National Association of Broadcasters pamphlet, **Broadcasting the News.** An optimum situation is a top-power radio-TV outlet in a midwestern metropolitan area which employs 16 staff news writers. At the opposite end is a low-power radio station on the east coast which operates with a one-man news staff. Another radio-TV operation in the northeast has a 6-man reporting-rewrite staff. The better news operations carefully edit and frequently rewrite national and international copy received from the wire services.

Salaries vary considerably, depending on the size and location of the radio and television stations. A beginner at ABC or CBS may start at about $155 a week. Some network news writers average above $25,000 a year. Many of the larger, individual stations offer news writers salaries ranging from $195 to $265 weekly. Salaries, of course, fluctuate with union demands, inflation, deflation and other economic ills. Of course, the star gazing embryo news writer may dream of emulating a David Brinkley with a basic yearly income of $250,000.

With the younger generation's rebellion against the materialistic values of their parents, perhaps we should leave money matters and conclude with the idealistic principles as expounded by the NAB in its Preface to **Broadcasting the News.**

"The broadcaster's highest duty is to inform the public. This also is his greatest challenge and opportunity. The public stature of a single station or of the entire broadcasting profession can be no higher than the level at which it serves the public's need for information."

# Chapter 10

## Commercials

The commercial, as we know it, will probably be with us into the foreseeable future. Public television exists without commercials, but even here we have to draw a fine line. When the statement appears on the screen that this program was make possible by a grant from, let us say, Mobil or General Electric or some other large industrial corporation, is this not, in essence, a commercial, subliminal as it may be? Of course, it can be argued that the credit line is involuntary since the FCC requires it. Nevertheless, the name of the organization that sells numberless quantities of consumer products is there and, as Madison Avenue would put it, enhancing the corporate image.

Cable television systems (CATV) not only sell community antenna service but also consumer products. The chances are that even if CATV were to become the broadcast medium of the future, it would probably support itself largely by a form of commercial sponsorship.

Pay TV? Some of the early starts were abortive. New starts have been encouraged by the rise of cable television. Pay TV would have to provide subscribers with a service they cannot obtain on free TV. First-run movies? Broadway plays? Exclusive sporting events? Possibly. There is one danger we can foresee. If pay TV will have to strive for a very large audience in order to realize extensive profits, it will eventually be pulled into the same whirlpool of mediocrity that now characterizes free TV: the necessity for appealing to the lowest common denominator. Perhaps pay TV may succeed with highly specialized audiences who are willing to pay fees for programs which presumably the networks cannot supply. However, our concern is with the commercial as we now know it.

Commercial copywriters for a large agency such as Ted Bates, Inc. or Benton & Bowles, Inc. have a creative department and a research department to help them in the formulation of their ideas. They have time to develop their copy within the scope of a well planned campaign. They deal with huge sums of money and, therefore, can give their ideas full scope.

On the other hand, if they start, as many copywriters do, at a radio or TV station, or a small advertising agency, they may find themselves writing many commercials each week. Hard-sell and volume will be their guidelines. Terry Galanoy in his racy book on making television commercials, "Down the Tube" (Henry Regnery Company), reveals, "I once had a job writing 12 live television commercials for Dodge cars every morning and then producing them on live television shows in the afternoon and evening—five days a week." But no matter where they are situated, copywriters must think in terms of creativity. Granted, a far cry from any literary achievement, but nonetheless a writing assignment to which they should apply all their talents.

We recommend that potential copywriters familiarize themselves with the basics for advertising procedure, and an excellent start is to study the book by the name "Advertising Procedure," Otto Klepner (Prentice-Hall), the "bible of the industry." There are several other fine volumes noted in our bibliography.

Shirley F. Milton in "Advertising Copywriting" (Oceana Publications) points up the attributes of an advertising writer: "An interest and facility in handling words, an ear for the speech of today, a more than idle interest in people and an understanding of basic motivation and, finally, some experience in selling."

In writing commercials for TV, writers at the top advertising agencies may find that they are engaged in full-scale productions that employ the services of actors, artists, director, producer, scene designer, camaramen and other personnel. They have a story to tell but very little time to tell it in: 60 seconds. But in that time, if it is a national account, they must convey a message that impacts on millions of viewers.

Rosser Reeves in "Reality in Advertising" (Alfred A. Knopf) emphasizes, "Each advertisement must make a proposition to the consumer. Not just words, not just product puffery, not just show-window advertising. Each advertisement must say, 'Buy this product and you will get this specific benefit.' " Mr. Reeves postulates an advertising law: "If the product does not meet some existing desire or need of the consumer, the advertising will ultimately fail." Here he comes to a parting of the ways with the famous economist, John K. Galbraith. Reeves believes that Galbraith has his theory in reverse: "Advertising does not synthesize desires," Reeves insists. "Desires instead synthesize advertising."

The concepts for your commercials will depend on the audience you are reaching: Is your product for everyone? Teenagers? Children? Women? Men?

The writer who wants to make a career of advertising will benefit by a study of psychology. What motivates people? What arouses desires? Conversely, what turns people off? Shirley Milton defines buying motives as the "drives within the individual which influence action, determine choice and provide the conscious reason for buying."

## COMMERCIAL CATEGORIES

For the purposes of study, we can classify commercials into ten categories. None of these categories is immutable. There may be overlapping of technique and some categories can probably be subdivided.

1. Monolog: utilizing one voice.

2. Dialog: generally, two voices: the announcer and a participant; two women; a husband and wife; a simulated salesman and a client.

3. Dramatized: a playlet with two or more characters involved in an episode built around the use of the product.

4. Jingle: extolling the virtues of a product in song; the goal here is to create a very catchy tune which the listener will recall readily.

5. Institutional: the commercial as an instrument of public relations; selling an image rather than a product.

6. Testimonial: a celebrity testifies to the quality of a product.

7. Demonstration: showing the viewer how an appliance operates.

8. Cartoon: the use of animation to capture attention; particularly effective for children's products.

9. Production: most expensive and ambitious of commercials; may employ singers, dancers and an eye appealing set.

10. Integrated: the type in which the star of a program participates in the commercial which flows out of the program dialog or is popped in like a "Laugh-in" one-liner.

### Examples

Reproduced below are several commercials for study.

| PICTURE | SOUND |
|---|---|
| 1. CU PIANO ROLL IN PLAYER PIANO. CAMERA TILTS UP TO MS CHILD'S BOTTOM SITTING ON TOP OF PIANO. | ANNCR: (VO)<br><br>Ah yes, the good old days... |

| | |
|---|---|
| 2. MS CHILD SUCKING ON BOTTLE. | bathtub formula... |
| 3. MS CHILD GETTING INTO AND OUT OF STUTZ BEAR CAT. | the flashy Stutz Bear Cat and... |
| 4. GROUP OF CHILDREN DANCING (A). | everyone was doing the wet bottom rag. |
| 5. GROUP OF CHILDREN DANCING (B). | Wet cloth diapers, that's what did it. |
| 6. M2S CHILDREN DANCING (A). | Kept your bottom wet... |
| 7. M2S CHILDREN DANCING (B). | kept you moving around. Ah, yes, ... |
| 8. GROUP OF CHILDREN DANCING (C). | I remember it well, and then.. |
| 9. SPINNING "END OF AN ERA." CAMERA LIFTS DOWN, SIMULTANEOUSLY ZOOMING IN ON THE LETTERS AS THEY BECOME STACKS OF PAMPERS BOXES. | the end of an era. |
| 10. (CUT.) ZOOM CONTINUING INTO MCU BOXES. | The day they invented Pampers ... |
| 11. SEQUENCE OF SHOTS OF BABIES DANCING THAT DISSOLVE CONTINUOUSLY INTO ONE ANOTHER (A). | and started making wet bottoms drier. Pampers... |
| 12. DEMO: MS CHILD'S BOTTOM SITTING ON FLATTENED PAMPERS AS HAND FROM O.S. POURS DYED FLUID ON TO PRODUCT. | put in a special stay dry lining. Moisture goes through it and is trapped down below. Next to baby's bottom, the lining stays drier so baby's bottom stays drier. Outside, its waterproof. No plastic pants. |
| 13. SEQUENCE OF MS'S CHILDREN DANCING THAT CONTINUOUSLY DISSOLVE INTO ONE ANOTHER. (B) | Progress, my little chicadees, progress. A new era is upon us. My friends... |
| 14. PRODUCT SHOT. | I give you Pampers. |

The above commercial was developed by Benton & Bowles, Inc., for Procter & Gamble. It runs one minute and can be classified as a production commercial. The copy runs smoothly, adds a touch of humor; a good idea when dealing with a subject like diapers. Rosser Reeves maintains, "The consumer tends to remember just one thing from an advertisement—one strong claim or one strong concept." In this Pampers commercial, the one strong claim is that this diaper stays drier. For what it is worth, the copywriter has used some familiar lines, "Oh, yes, I remember it well" and "The day they invented...," both from the highly successful movie "Gigi." With so many replays of that film on TV, the chances are those lines are familiar to the viewer and the pleasant association adds to the humor and listenability of the commercial.

| PICTURE | SOUND |
|---|---|
| | SOUND EFFECT: (SNEEZE) |
| OPEN ON ECU HAROLD. | HAROLD: |
| | Another cold, honey. |
| CUT TO CU WIFE. | WIFE: |
| | You look terrible, Harold. |
| CUT TO ECU SIDE VIEW HAROLD. | HAROLD: |
| | I feel terrible. Been sneezin', coughin', got a scratchy throat, I'm achey and I need some rest. |
| CUT TO MS WIFE. POURS NYQUIL. | WIFE: |
| | Here Harold, take Nyquil. |
| RACK FOCUS AS HAROLD DRINKS NYQUIL. | ANNCR: (VO) |
| | Vicks Nyquil, night-time cold medicine...relieves more major cold symptoms than the leading capsules. Relieves 'em for hours. So it helps you get the rest you need. |
| CUT BACK TO CU HAROLD. | HAROLD: |
| | I'm lucky to have you, Mildred. |
| CUT TO ECU WIFE. | WIFE: |
| | I know. |
| DISSOLVE TO HAROLD ASLEEP. | ANNCR: (VO) |
| MATTE IN NYQUIL BOTTLE. | You got a cold tonight? Put Nyquil to work. |

The Nyquil commercial (Benton &Bowles, Inc., for Vick Chemical Co.) runs 40 seconds and is an illustration of the use of dialog and dramatization. Notice the production technique of bringing in the announcer's voice offscreen while Harold is drinking the Nyquil and again when Harold is asleep. In the matter of repetition of product name, both the Nyquil and Pampers commercials repeat the trade designation three times, which is enough for identification without being overbearing. Remember, too, that the visual shows you the product.

| PICTURE | SOUND |
|---|---|
| CU PEOPLE WALKING. CAMERA PULLS BACK— REVEAL PEOPLE WALKING | (MUSIC)<br><br>ANNCR: (VO)<br><br>One answer to the air pollution problem would be to eliminate the cars and trucks and buses. But try to imagine a world without them. |
| WALKING LIKE CARS—IN LANES ETC. | At Texaco we're working on better answers. Overall, Texaco is spending an average of one million dollars each week on controlling pollution. |
| PEOPLE SIMULATE BUS, ETC. | The new Texaco gasolines are designed to help cut pollution and improve your car's performance. And they're only a part of our efforts.<br><br>Sure, we might get around without the cars, but we think a better answer is **better** cars and **better** gasolines. |
| HEX OF TEXACO. | We're working to keep your trust. |
| SUPER: WE'RE WORKING TO KEEP YOUR TRUST. | (MUSIC OUT) |

This one-minute commercial (Benton & Bowles, Inc., for Texaco, Inc.) is an example of the institutional category or as the commercial itself is labeled: public relations. It is also an illustration of the monolog treatment. It stresses Texaco's awareness in an area—air pollution—which has aroused great public concern and is a frank statement of good will: "We're working to keep your trust."

| VIDEO | AUDIO |
|---|---|
| JOEL ALDRED IS ON CAMERA. HE IS SEATED IN A 1912 CADILLAC, AND TURNS ON THE HEADLIGHTS. | One of the first "safety" features on a car was this electric headlamp — quite a revolution when it was brought out by General Motors in 1912. |
| HE GETS OUT OF CAR, AND MOVES FORWARD. THE CAMERA PULLS BACK TO REVEAL EACH CAR AS HE IS MENTIONING IT, ONE AT A TIME. (1924 Buick) | In 1924, four-wheel brakes appeared on GM cars, and GM opened its own proving ground to test cars. |
| (1925 CHEVROLET) | In 1925, GM turned on power windshield wipers. |
| (1928 CADILLAC) | In 1928, GM introduced safety plate glass in automobile windows. |
| (1935 MODEL PONTIAC OR OLDS) | In 1934, GM pioneered the steel turret top. |
| JOEL MOVES PAST 3 or 4 CARS REPRESENTING 1940 to 1970 ... | Safety is not new at General Motors. |
| THE LAST CAR TO BE REVEALED IS A 1971 CHEVROLET IMPALA 2-DOOR. | Year after year, GM has built safety into their cars ... into the frame, the interior, the wheels, the brakes. Let's look at a few recent GM innovations ... |
| JOEL MOVES AWAY FROM THE CAR, OFF CAMERA. | |
| DIAGRAM OF ENERGY ABSORBING ASSEMBLY IS SUPERED ONTO ACTUAL CAR. THE DIAGRAM "COLLAPSES" TO DEMONSTRATE THE AC-TION. | (VO) In 1966, General Motors pioneered the energy absorbing steering column. It compresses on severe impact ... to help protect the driver in a collision. |
| STEERING WHEEL DIAGRAM OFF, AS SAME TREATMENT OF SIDE-GUARD DOOR BEAM IS SUPERED ON DOOR. ANIMATED LINE IMPACTS | In 1968, General Motors developed the side-guard door beam ... for added protection against side impacts. |

| | |
|---|---|
| IT FROM A 45-DEGREE ANGLE, AND IS DEFLECTED REARWARD AND AWAY. | |
| SIDE-GUARD BEAM OFF, SAME TREATMENT OF NEW ROOF CONSTRUCTION IS SUPERED ON CAR, SHOWING CONTOUR OF INNER LINER IF POSSIBLE. | For 1971, GM improvements include a new<br><br>double-shell roof construction with a contoured inner panel to help reduce the possibility of head and neack injuries. |
| ROOF DIAGRAM OFF, JOEL COMES ON CAMERA AT FRONT OF CAR AND KNOCKS ON WINDSHIELD GLASS WITH HIS KNUCKLES. | The windshield glass is new, too.<br><br>More resistant to impact from stones, and less likely to produce lacerations if broken. |
| CLOSE ON JOEL AS HE MOVES TOWARD DOOR OF CAR ... | National Safety Council statistics show that auto travel today is three times as safe as it was about 40 years ago. And today, GM is working to make tomorrow even safer. |
| JOEL GETS INTO CAR (STILL CLOSE IN). | But you have to do your part, too. Don't drive if you've been drinking. Maintain your car in safe operating conditions. Observe traffic laws. |
| BUCKLES LAP AND SHOULDER BELTS. | And always wear lap and shoulder belts. |
| SUPER GM MARK OF EX-CELLENCE AND WORDS "GM IS DOING IT." | Everybody wants to find ways to make driving safer. General Motors is doing it. |

This safety commercial was prepared by MacManus, John & Adams, Inc., for General Motors Corporation. It runs two minutes and can be generally classified as a demonstration commercial, although it also includes public relations aspects. Its theme is safety: the one strong claim. Each demonstrated feature underscores this safety theme. And the generous repetition of the sponsor's name apparently leaves no doubt in the viewer's mind of General Motors' concern with safety. It is a definite thrust, in light of numerous callbacks, to assure the potential buyer of the efforts being exerted for safety on the part of the sponsor.

| PICTURE | SOUND |
|---|---|
| GOLF COURSE PUTT GOING IN. | SFX: (CLUNK!) ...Yeah! |
| YOUNG GIRL COMES RUNNING TOWARD GREEN. | JODY: |
| FREEZE-FRAME JODY; CONTINUE ACTION. | Dad...dad... |
| | DAD: |
| | Jody??? |
| | JODY: |
| | Our checkup. Jimmy only had two cavities and I didn't have any. |
| | DAD: |
| | Terrific! ...We did it. |
| | OTHER GOLFER: |
| | How'd ya do it? |
| | JODY: |
| | We brush with Crest now. |
| | DAD: |
| | Crest has fluoride...the others we tried didn't have it. Great for fighting cavities. |
| OTHER GOLFERS ALL WALK OFF. ALL WALK OFF TO NEXT TEE OFF. CUT TO PRODUCT CLAIM. | ANNCR: (VO) |
| | Crest can't promise everybody results like this. But we can promise most people good checkups. Fighting cavities is the whole idea behind Crest. |

We have chosen this Crest commercial by Benton & Bowles, Inc., to illustrate how much can be encompassed within 30 seconds. It also demonstrates, to a degree, the dramatized commercial.

Another example of the amount of copy and production that can go into a 30-second TV spot is this commercial for Pontiac LeMans created by D'Arcy-MacManus-Intermarco, Inc. It illustrates the technique of using animation.

| VIDEO | AUDIO |
|---|---|
| | MUSIC IN AND UNDER |
| OPEN ON DOTTED OUTLINE OF FAMILY GROUP. | ANNOUNCER: Once ... |
| HUSBAND AND WIFE ANIMATE TO FILL PART OF GROUP OUTLINE. | there was ... |
| KIDS ANIMATE TO FILL PART OF GROUP OUTLINE. | a typical ... |
| DOG ANIMATES TO FILL REST OF GROUP OUTLINE. | young family ... |
| DOG LEANS ON WIFE'S SHOULDER. IS SMOKING PIPE. | who didn't want to ... look typical. |
| SMOKE OF DOG'S PIPE ANIMATES INTO ABSTRACT PATTERN. CLEARS AWAY TO REVEAL PROFILE OF LeMANS. | They dreamed of owning ... a mid-size car ... |
| WORD "VALUE" APPEARS OVER LeMANS. | with value ... |
| WORD "PIZZAZZ" FLASHES OVER CAR. | and pizzazz! |
| PIZZAZZ PULSES WITH MUSIC. | (SINGERS): Pizzazz! |
| FAMILY MOVES BACK AS ABSTRACT; "TYPICAL" CARS ANIMATE AROUND THEM. | But every mid-size car they saw ... looked so ... typical. |
| CU OF DOG LOOKING DISTRAUGHT. | Alas, no pizzazz. |
| ANIMATED WORD "PIZ-ZAZZ." | (SINGERS): Pizzazz! |
| HUSBAND AND WIFE LOOKING GLUM. | They almost gave up hope ... |
| HUSBAND AND WIFE BEGIN TO SMILE. | when ... there it was ... |
| HUSBAND AND WIFE BECOME ABSTRACT PATTERN. | ....... |

| | |
|---|---|
| ABSTRACT PATTERN BECOMES LIVE LeMANS. | their dream car. |
| MOVE UP ON ¾ RIGHT FRONT OF LeMANS. | A wide-track Pontiac LeMans ... loaded with ... value and ... |
| ANIMATED WORD "PON-TIAC." | (SINGERS): Pizzazz! |
| BOOM DOWN ON FRONT OF LeMANS. | Most untypical! |
| DISSOLVE TO PROFILE OF LeMANS. | If you don't want to look typical...look into... |
| WORDS "PONTIAC LeMANS" COME IN FROM EITHER SIDE. | an untypical Pontiac LeMans. |
| DOG ENTERS BOTTOM OF FRAME SCREEN RIGHT FOLLOWED BY LARGE BANNER | MUSIC UP AND OUT. |
| SAYING "PIZZAZZ" | |

## RADIO

Although radio lacks the impact of the visual, it can call on the full power of a listener's imagination. David G. Lyon in his book "Off Madison Avenue" (G.P. Putnam & Sons) states that the radio listener is not merely a passive recipient but can be active in creating a scene. "The writer merely specifies the sound effects. The listener himself calls into being the streets through which the screaming fire engine careens and the frightened faces at the tenement windows." Devices such as sound effects and music can give radio a competing vibrancy.

Radio has an advantage in its low cost. As David Lyon puts it, "The idea, not the dollar, determines the quality of the commercial presentation." Many small advertisers who find TV rates prohibitive can launch successful campaigns in radio.

Although costs may be lower in radio, audiences are still very large. TV has taken over the 7-to-11 prime-time evening hours and radio now finds its prime time in "rush" hours. Millions of car radios all over the country are turned on between the hours of 6 and 9 in the morning and 4 to 6 or 7 in the evening.

Many radio commercials open with a sparkling musical note or an intriguing sound effect to capture attention. The guideline of one strong claim is as applicable to radio as it is to

312

TV. However, the radio commercial writer, particularly at a small station or a small advertising agency, may find that sponsors, such as a local furniture store, insist on loading their commercials with every item they have on sale. You can illustrate a dozen articles of furniture on a printed page or list a hundred items, but this kind of listing only serves to confuse the listener and literally turns him off.

Since radio has no visuals, picture words are essential to create an image. Always make it a rule to read your copy aloud so that you may avoid tongue twisters such as alliterative statements which look good in print but cause stumbling blocks in reading.

The following are two radio commercials for Ventura of the Pontiac Motor Division prepared by D'Arcy-MacManus-Intermarco, Inc. The first is a 30-second jingle whose keynote, literally, is the automobile model, Ventura. Its theme: economy.

MUSIC: RHYTHM CHORUS

CHORUS: (CHANTING) V-E-N-T-U-R-A

CHORUS: Ventura

CHORUS: Ven-tur-a

CHORUS: It's an economy car.

CHORUS: It's a prestige car.

CHORUS: Ventura's an economy car...with prestige.

CHORUS: Pontiac Ventura.

CHORUS: Right!

CHORUS: From Pon-ti-ac.

CHORUS: (SINGING) PON-TI-AC.

ANNCR: Ventura is the low-priced economy car from Pontiac.

CHORUS: (CHANTING) V-E-N-T-U-R-A

ANNCR: Ventura's a cut above.

CHORUS: VENTURA.

The second is a one-minute dialog commercial with a humorous approach which also stresses economy.

SFX: STREET NOISE.

ANNCR: And here we are again asking more questions about Pontiac's Ventura II. Young lady...

BRENDA: Oh, hi.

ANNCR: I'd like to ask you some questions.

BRENDA: Oh yes, my name's Brenda, I live at 454 Lincoln Avenue, my number is 543-8910 and you can pick me up about 8:00.

ANNCR: No, no, no. You don't understand...

BRENDA: Oh, but I do.

ANNCR: No, I want to ask you about Ventura II.

BRENDA: Ventura II?

ANNCR: Yes—what is a Ventura II?

BRENDA: (Giggle) Well, it comes after Ventura I.

ANNCR: Well, not exactly...try this. A Ventura II is (a) an Italian sewing machine, (b) a small Pontiac, or (c) a famous monarch?

BRENDA: Oh, I'd say B.

ANNCR: B is correct. It's a small Pontiac, how did you know?

BRENDA: I picked B because it's the first letter of the alphabet.

ANNCR: Amazing!

BRENDA: Well, did I win anything?

ANNCR: Brenda, you're always a winner with Pontiac's Ventura II. Because Ventura II is the economy car that gives you more than just economy. It gives you Pontiac style, room and prestige at a small-car price.

BRENDA: Wow! Well you learn something new every day.

ANNCR: You sure do.. (FADE)

## CATCH PHRASES

Advertising copywriters are always racking their creative energies to produce a catch phrase that will capture the fancy of viewers and listeners; a word, a sentence that will become part of the vocabulary, at least for a time. Copywriters would be happy to become such phrase makers at least once during their career.

In contemporary advertising, we have a situation where the team of Howard Cohen and Bob Pasqualina, copywriter id art director, respectively, for Wells, Rich, Greene, Inc., ve made it two in a row for their client, Alka-Seltzer. The tch phrases, "Try It, You'll Like It" and "I Can't Believe I e That Whole Thing" took on the status of inside jokes. ven Senator McGovern, after having won four primaries in a ting day, could not refrain from paraphrasing: "I can't lieve I won the whole thing."

There is actually no formula nor any rational explanation what makes an extraordinarily successful catch phrase. erhaps the basic humor of the copy; the familiarity of the tuation. But there have been innumerable advertisements gged on humor and most of them treat a familiar situation. hey have to be commonplace to produce empathy: com-elling cliches.

The storyboards of two of the highly successful Alka-eltzer commercials are reproduced below; a happy note on hich to conclude this chapter.

1. (SFX) MAN: Came to this little place.

2. Waiter says, "Try this, you'll like it."

3. "What's this?"

4. "Try it, you'll like it." "But what is......?"

5. "Try it, you'll like it."

6. So I tried it. Thought I was gonna die. Took two Alka-Seltzer.

7. (SFX) ANNCR: (VO) Alka-Seltzer neutralizes all the acid

8. For your upset stomach and headache, take Alka Seltzer, and feel better fast.

9. MAN: Alka Seltzer works. "Try it, you'll like it."

1. HUSBAND: I can't believe I ate that whole thing.

2. WIFE: You ate it Ralph.

3. HUSBAND: I can't believe I ate that whole thing.

4. WIFE: No Ralph, I ate it!

5. HUSBAND: I can't believe I ate that whole thing.

6. WIFE: Take two Alka-Seltzer. (SFX)

ALKA-SELTZER NEUTRALIZES ALL THE ACID YOUR STOMACH HAS CHURNED OUT.

7. ANNCR: (VO) Alka-Seltzer neutralizes all the acid your stomach has churned out.

8. For your upset stomach and headache, take Alka Seltzer, and feel better fast.

9. WIFE: Did you drink your Alka Seltzer?

10. HUSBAND: The whole thing.

316

# Chapter 11

## "In The Public Interest"

When the Advertising Council was originally established in 1942, one of its goals was to demonstrate that "advertising is a powerful force for public service." It has continued to maintain that precept.

Advertising agencies donate their creative talent to public service campaigns which are rotated among them. Organizations, such as the National Safety Council, the American Red Cross, United Funds, CARE, United Negro College Fund, or governmental agencies, request assistance. The American Association of Advertising Agencies is then asked to nominate one of its members to handle the project on a voluntary basis. Time on the air is donated by the broadcasting industry. The requesting public service or governmental agency, although it receives free creative assistance and free time on radio or television, does assume the cost of such materials as prints or slides that may be used for the presentation and distribution of the announcements.

There are basic similarities between public service announcements and commercials. The same copywriters who turn out the commercials lend their creative energies to announcements in the public interest. And both types of announcements are geared to sell: in the first instance, a product, in the second, an idea. We might say, to stretch a point, that both types of announcements deal with personal welfare. A deodorant makes you a more pleasant person to be with; as a Red Cross volunteer, you are a good neighbor. Aspirin may help dispel your headache; a visit to your doctor may ease your mind about a cancer symptom.

Script formats are the same as commercials. Generally, the public service announcement follows a simple production technique for television because of the expense involved. However, in order to bring the message home with greater impact, many public service announcements are more elaborate productions such as the 60-second film for the National Institute on Alcohol Abuse and Alcoholism appearing in this chapter.

1. (Sfx: party sounds throughout of people talking, glasses clinking, etc. We hear Harry's voice as if far off-mike)

2. (Anncr VO) Meet good old Harry. The best host on the block.

3. Everybody has a good time at Harry's parties. Everybody.

4. And nobody ever goes away sober, either.

5. A drink in your hand puts a smile on your lips, that's Harry's motto.

6. And he'll get you to smile if it takes him all night.

7. There's just one thing though.

8. If Harry's such a good host, how come he makes you feel so bad?

318

9. How come when you wake up tomorrow...

10. ...your head will pound and you'll feel rotten all day long? How come?

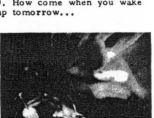

11. Because Harry's a pusher... the neighborhood pusher.

12. There are nine million problem drinkers in this country--and most of them have a friend like Harry.

13. Good old Harry.

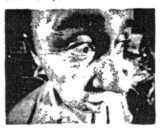

14. With a friend like him, who needs enemies?

15. (Silent fadeout)

An announcement for Easter Seals to help crippled children may use a split screen device, or some announcements employ animation, which is a costly process. But the production expense may be justified particularly for a fund raising campaign. The more attention the announcement gains, the greater the possibility for increased contributions.

The following television announcements for the American Red Cross merely use slides and an offscreen announcer. This is a one-minute spot.

| VIDEO | AUDIO |
|---|---|
| SLIDE:<br><br>Lady getting out of car. | Nowadays, people assume that most problems can be solved with money. From the government. Or from private charity. But there are some problems that money can't solve. Problems that only people can help. Recovery from an accident — or surgery — often requires blood. From healthy people. A blind child, learning how to swim, needs a pool. And the helping hands and hearts of ... people. For a serviceman overseas to hear when he becomes a father, there are Teletype machines to carry the message. But running the switchboards which feed the machine are...people. |
| SLIDE:<br><br>Super: Red Cross Logo "The Good Neighbor" | People who **really** care are sharing their love, energy and time. People are **there** when trouble strikes.<br><br>Today, there are nearly two million such people who are Red Cross volunteers — America's best neighbors. People like you ... helping people like you. |

The above announcement was used as part of the campaign theme: **People.** That explains the repetition of the word, people, in the announcement, actually repeated nine times. A basic premise of advertising, as we have noted, is repetition.

Copywriters are always striving for catch phrases, the thrust of a sentence, the play on words. Observe the closing line: "People like you ... helping people like you."

Writing for the broadcast media presents a great challenge to writers. They must be miserly with words and yet these words must be expansive with meaning. And writers are always up against an arbitrary time limit. It is instructive to discover how the same message in the Red Cross "People" campaign can be told in 20 seconds and in 10 seconds.

| VIDEO | AUDIO |
|---|---|
| Lady getting out of car<br><br>Super: Red Cross Logo and "The Good Neighbor." | Nowadays, people assume that most problems can be solved with money. But there are some problems that money can't solve. Problems that only people can help. People who **really** care are sharing their love, energy and time. As Red Cross volunteers. People like you ... helping people like you. |

| VIDEO | AUDIO |
|---|---|
| Lady getting out of car—<br><br>Super: Red Cross Logo and "The Good Neighbor." | People who **really** care are sharing their love, energy and time. As Red Cross volunteers. People like you ... helping people like you. |

In the above examples, the theme is "People who really care," buttressed by the concluding catch phrase.

## RADIO

Radio spots are comparatively simple and inexpensive to produce. Usually, there is a straightforward one-voice (monolog) approach. Many times the public service agency will obtain the cooperation of entertainment stars to voice the message. The following announcements are typical of a radio campaign:

### ONE-MINUTE RADIO SPOT

#### ANNOUNCER

Franklin Delano Roosevelt ... Toulouse-Lautrec ... Sarah Bernhardt ... Lionel Barrymore ... Peter Stuyvesant ... Beethoven. Each of these people had a handicap ... but they didn't let it stop them. Today there's a program to see that five million Americans with physical or mental handicaps aren't stopped by them either. It's called "HURRAH" — and the letters H-U-R-R-A-H stand for "Help Us Reach & Rehabilitate America's Handicapped." The purpose of HURRAH is to provide the job training, the medical services and the guidance that can make the difference between living a handicapped life and really starting to live. If you've got a handicap ... or if you know someone who does ... we'll send you the address of the rehabilitation agency in your state. Write HURRAH, Box 1200, Washington, D.C. 20013. Life doesn't have to stop because of a handicap ... and HURRAH can prove it. The State-Federal program of rehabilitation services.

30-SECOND RADIO SPOT

### ANNOUNCER

Franklin Delano Roosevelt ... Peter Stuyvesant ... Beethoven ... Toulouse-Lautrec. Each had a handicap ... none let it stop him. Today there's a program to see that five million Americans with handicaps aren't stopped either. It's called "HURRAH" — H-U-R-R-A-H — and it means "Help Us Reach & Rehabilitate America's Handicapped." If you've got a handicap, write to HURRAH, Box 1200, Washington, D.C. 20013, for our booklet on vocational rehabilitation.

20-SECOND RADIO SPOT

### ANNOUNCER

Franklin Roosevelt ... Toulouse-Lautrec ... Beethoven. Each had a handicap ... none let it stop him. Today there's a program to help five million handicapped Americans. It's called "HURRAH" — for "Help Us Reach & Rehabilitate America's Handicapped." For information, write HURRAH, Box 1200, Washington, D.C. 20013.

....The wording of the radio and television spots for the HURRAH campaign are identical. The only difference is that the TV spots use slides.

Another variation for radio is the jingle. This requires that the writer be a good versifier. It also entails a production budget to pay for the choral group and other musicians. A typical example is this jingle for U.S. Savings Bonds.

> "There's more fun in your future
> With a nest egg tucked away,
> So start the payroll savings
> And you'll be on your way.
> You build for tomorrow
> A little bit each time.
> Take stock in America,
> Buy U.S. Savings Bonds."

## IMPACT

How effective are public service announcements? The Advertising Council conducts more than 20 major campaigns a year. The spots are often seen and heard at prime time. As a matter of fact, the announcements may be sold for commercial sponsorship and presented "in the public interest" by a business concern which wishes to enhance its public image.

The National Safety Council credits its public service advertising campaign with helping to save more than 750,000 lives in the last 25 years. The campaign for financial aid to education has increased contributions from 738 million dollars to approximately 1.8 billion dollars annually.

# Chapter 12

## Government Information Programs

The whys and wherefores of government information programs have been the butt of controversy, particularly during the Vietnam War. The specific target has been the Defense Department, although the United States Information Agency (USIA) and the Voice of America (VOA) have had their share of criticism. The crux of the controversy is whether a federal agency is dispensing information or propaganda. The word **propaganda** is in ill repute, although its origin stems from the Roman Catholic Congregation for Propagating the Faith. But, as Webster's dictionary tells us, propaganda is "now often used in a derogatory sense connoting deception or distortion."

Some years ago, the House Committee on Expenditures in the Executive Departments issued its own definitions of information and propaganda. "Information: The act or process of communicating knowledge; to enlighten. Propaganda: A plan for the propagation of a doctrine or system of principles." Dr. Charles S. Steinberg in "The Communicative Arts" (Hastings House) observes that "the meaning of propaganda has various shades and emphases, and even a functional definition has become obscured by meaningless differentiations between destructive versus constructive propaganda." He further notes that the "campaign which attempts to convince the public that cigarettes may cause cancer is as much a propaganda effort as is the advertising of popular cigarettes as a way toward romantic fulfillment."

What it boils down to is that one man's information is another man's propaganda. If the Army Corps of Engineers were to present a film on television showing that organization's activities in helping to clean up rivers, one viewer might accept it as information; another might pronounce it propaganda to justify the Engineers' budget.

Probably few programs have stirred as much controversy in recent years as "The Selling of the Pentagon." This documentary film, produced by CBS, attempted to demonstrate that the Defense Department was issuing proestablishment propaganda to influence the public. We will not delve into the positives and negatives of the film. It has won many awards; its content and approach have been thoroughly dissected and it has been the subject of congressional investigation. However, there is one aspect which the program barely touched, a most important element and one that any student, who may by chance or choice become a government writer, should be aware of.

In the United States, unlike most other nations, broadcasting facilities are privately run, even though the airways are public domain and there is some governmental control through the Federal Communications Commission. In the realm of broadcasting, it would be almost impossible to propagandize the public without the cooperation of the media. Government agencies may produce numerous quantities of radio and television programs, but they cannot reach the public unless the broadcasters schedule them and, fortunately there is no power to force them to do so.

Broadcasters may state that they carry federal government programs in order to fulfill their public service requirements, but there are many other sources which could be utilized nationally and locally. On the other hand, it would be difficult to assert that a radio or TV program produced by the Department of Agriculture on soil conservation or the Department of Health, Education and Welfare on progress in assisting retarded children could be construed as propaganda. Still, a film describing the devastating effects on the air we breathe caused by fumes from automobiles might be derided as propaganda by the automotive industry. There are, as we know, many areas of disagreement between environmentalists and industrialists.

As a matter of record, the USIA is expressly forbidden by law from showing its films on TV stations in the United States unless congress permits an exception as in the case of "Years of Lightning, Days of Drums." The rationale is that the USIA films could be construed as propagandizing the public in favor of the current administration.

Another fact of government life the would-be federal writer must face is learning to take a positive approach to programming output. If a film or radio program or spot announcement is written about the agency's activities, it will always attempt to demonstrate the positive accomplishments of the agency.

Propaganda is only anathema to the opposition and its role changes with each situation. Granted that an overwhelming number of Americans became, to put it very mildly, disenchanted with the war in Vietnam, and, therefore, were willing to decry any films stemming from the Pentagon as propaganda. But in 1942, when the Office of War Information produced the "Why We Fight" series, they were hailed as masterpieces of their type, though there was no question of their propaganda value.

The positive approach is a public relations tenet, although here again we come upon a semantic controversy. Public relations is verboten in federal executive agencies, but public information and public affairs are acceptable. The implication is that public relations connotes high-powered press agentry and there is a public law, dating back to 1913, which forbids "publicity agents" in federal departments. The federal writer is categorized as an information specialist or a technical liaison officer.

Writers should take into consideration that if they were to work for a radio or television station they would be expected to put forth their best efforts for their employer. As documentary writers, they may produce films or radio programs critical of conditions in their city. But it is highly improbable that they would produce and have aired a program critical of the station that employs them. Federal agencies are particularly vulnerable to criticism. Their writers are expected to present the activities of the agency in a favorable light. Pragmatically, if the agency is not serving a useful public service, it should have no reason for existence. Conversely, the public should be informed of the agency's activities. There will be many a time when thoughtful writers will be wrestling with their conscience. They will have to decide whether discretion is actually the better part of valor, or is discretion merely a copout.

Perhaps the role of the civil servant was best expressed by M. Chatenet, when, as Director of the French Civil Service, he observed in a perceptive statement applicable to our own country: "In France, the taste for logic and the tradition of statute law have resulted in an appeal to a more abstract notion, that of the state. Yet it may well be asked if this notion of the state is really so abstract. For it was begotten by the jurists of the Capetian kings, imposed by the strong will of the absolute monarchs, fused with the idea of nationhood by the Jacobins, codified by Napoleon I and humanized by liberal democracy, so that the continuity of the state is identified in France with the history of the French people. As a result, it legitimately serves as a foundation for the search by civil servants of the necessary conciliation between a rigorous respect for the permanent interests of the nation and a loyal obedience to those whom the rules of democracy appoint to lead it."

Paul Rotha, the famous documentary film producer, summed up the role of the creative worker in government: "The creative worker must not, however, simply denounce this limitation and dissociate himself from government service. If he is a practical operator and a practical reformer, he will take the sanction for what it is and do his utmost within the limitations set, and this is one of the disciplines which the creative artist must learn in this period of society." ("Documentary Film," Faber and Faber Ltd.)

As a civil servant, the writer becomes part of a huge bureaucracy; but, in all fairness, before contemplating the negative connotations of the term **bureaucracy**, some thought should be given to the following analysis by Professor William A. Robson of the London School of Economics: "Bureaucracy is clearly indispensible to modern government. This is not merely because it is far more efficient than the older methods of working and of management which it has superseded, but also because it is a leveling, rationalizing force. It uses objective methods of recruitment in place of nepotism and patronage; it seeks to promote according to merit rather than for political or personal reasons. It administers on the basis of rules, precedents and policy rather than on grounds of personal feelings, influence or favoritism. It aims at consistency of treatment in its dealings with the public. These and many other advantages are derived from modern bureaucratic administration."

Every large organization is, in essence, a bureaucracy: government, industry, religion. Bureaucracy, in itself, is not evil. It is good or bad, depending on how strong willed the public is in controlling its own government.

What emoluments can the federal writer expect? The drive towards comparability with industrial rates of pay has raised the scale of government salaries considerably. A beginning writer, entering at the professional level of GS-7, would start at $9,053 annually (Compensation Schedule, January 1972). If he advances to a GS-13 level, the maximum rate is $24,362. It is possible for a writer to become a special assistant to a cabinet officer and receive the top compensation of $36,000.

The above rates compare very favorably with staff writers at independent stations or networks. Free-lance writers, of course, have no limitations on their earnings. But there is nothing to prevent federal writers from "moonlighting," depending on their creativity and energy. After all, writing can be done at any time.

## DEPARTMENT OF DEFENSE

The writing and production techniques for federal programs are similar to those used by commercial producers.

As a matter of fact, many of the government programs are produced by commercial contractors, and even when the government agency has production facilities of its own, free-lance writers are hired to write scripts.

Stemming from World War II, the Defense Department has always had an active radio and film program. The concentration has been largely on internal programs. The budget for training films, orientation films, Chaplain's Guidance films, instructional and medical films, and radio and TV programs for the American Forces radio and television stations overseas runs into the millions of dollars.

In the Defense Department, there are agencies within agencies. The upper echelon, the Office of the Secretary of Defense, has its Office of Information for the Armed Forces with its own motion picture branch which produces films encompassing all the military services. It also supervises the activities of the American Forces Radio and Television Service, its arm for communication via the broadcast media with troops stationed overseas. In addition, each military service has its own information division which produces radio programs and motion pictures. Programs are not only produced at department levels, but various agencies within each department also produce programs to meet specific needs, as for example, the Army Medical Center at Walter Reed.

Those military bases which possess audio-visual capabilities present programs on a local level generally in cooperation with the neighboring radio and television stations. Local radio and television programs usually consist of news about the military installation or concern themselves with community relations activities.

## The United States Army

On a departmental level, the Army, until the end of 1971, had been producing a half-hour film series, "The Big Picture." Production facilities were located at the Army Pictorial Center in New York City until its closure in 1970. The Big Picture films were cleared for presentation on television stations in the United States and had a remarkably long run of 20 years. Prints of this series are still available in Army film libraries for public showing.

The Big Picture documentary film series illustrates the point we have discussed previously concerning the government-media relationship. Some 300 or more commercial TV stations gave free time to the half-hour programs, as did approximately 40 educational TV stations. The Big Picture films were informational documentaries as distinguished from training films and were produced under Command Information (internal) auspices to inform the widespread Army publics of worldwide Army activities.

With the demise of the series, the Army's Command Information Unit turned its attention to special internal problems such as drug abuse and race relations. Free-lance scripter Paul Caster was contracted to write a documentary film on the subject of drug addiction. Since so much had been written on the drug scene, the writer had to be aware of the many film scripts previously produced and to try to avoid a rehash of what had already been said.

His script was ambitious. It called for nine exteriors and eleven interiors. We have chosen some excerpts to illustrate the writer's approach.

FADE IN...

1. EXT. LAKE OR RIVER—DAY—**UNDERWATER**

FULL SHOT: RIVER (OR LAKE) BED

The camera is moving forward slowly through the water. It is a shallow area, perhaps some ten feet deep, so that the sunlight penetrates from above, in shafts of flickering light. The camera, however, avoids the surface. It concentrates on the bed, and moves among the plant life. The effect is peaceful, serene, with the camera movement matching the almost slow-motion effect of movement in the water.

MUSIC: WE SUPPORT WITH MUSIC THAT IS AS "COOL" AS THE VISUAL. NO MELODY, JUST RHYTHM, PROVIDED BY A SLOW BASS, AND PERHAPS SOME GUITAR CHORDS, PACED TO MATCH THE MOVEMENT ON-SCREEN.

We watch for a beat, and then the narrator's voice is heard. (We will refer to him as the narrator throughout the script, though he will appear live on-screen in several sequences.) His delivery is soft, easy. He **speaks** to the audience — he does not "narrate" in the formal sense.

NARRATOR     Welcome...to the Cool World.

2. MEDIUM SHOT: THE WATER

As before, but now with a longer lens, to change the perspective. The camera continues its forward glide through the water, and we watch in silence for a beat or two.

MUSIC: CONTINUES...

DISSOLVE TO

328

3. CLOSE SHOT:  THE WATER

As before, but with an even longer lens that tightens the perspective once again.

MUSIC: CONTINUES...

Again we watch for a beat, and then...

NARRATOR        If you lived here, you'd probably look like this...

Now suddenly the camera shifts for a BIG CLOSEUP of a fish—as tight a shot as we can get, so that the fish's head LOOMS LARGE and GROTESQUE.

(NOTE: If the above scene is too difficult to achieve, we can substitute a STRAIGHT, SUDDEN CUT to the CLOSEUP of the fish).

4. SERIES OF SHOTS:  THE FISH

We watch (and follow) the fish as he glides through the water. His pace is leisurely — we avoid shots that show his jerky, sudden movements, and offer those in which he waltzes "at ease."

MUSIC: CONTINUES...

NARRATOR        No sweat, no pressure, no problems, no rules, no red lights. You wouldn't be too bright — but you wouldn't care. You'd set your own pace, and follow your own nose, heading straight toward anything that looked good to you.

5. ECU: FISH'S HEAD

A semiprofile. The fish seems to be "looking" off screen toward something. (Or, ideally, we would be PANNING WITH HIM and then see him come to an abrupt halt, or perhaps backing a few inches.) This is a QUICK CUT.

MUSIC: ENDS WITH A SLIGHT STING.

6. LONG SHOT: OBJECT (LURE)

A subjective shot — presumably what the fish "sees." (Ideally, made with some sort of a fish-eye lens, or other wide-angle lens that will give us the deliberate distortion we need to visually support the idea that this is the fish's viewpoint.)

In the distance, highlighted by a shaft of sunlight, there is an object we cannot identify, but which looks bright and colorful — a hazy blob of bright color that stands out against the greenish blur of the underwater terrain. It moves back and forth lazily.

MUSIC: A STING — SHIMMERING AND MAGICAL.

NARRATOR  And, if you WERE a fish, THIS would look good to you. Very good.

### 7. CLOSEUP: THE FISH

He moves forward, suddenly — a dart of action. He goes OFF SCREEN RAPIDLY.

### 8 THROUGH 13: SERIES OF SHOTS:

A: Shots of the fish moving forward toward the objective. These are all CLOSE. Some are with moving camera, as the fish approaches the camera; some are perhaps behind the fish, following him closely. We might also include one or two side angles as he darts quickly across the screen, entering and exiting.

B. Shots of the objective (the lure). These are ALL made with the fish-eye (or other wide-angle) lens. All are made with a moving camera, as it constantly approaches the object, getting closer and closer. None of these shots make the object identifiable— it is kept soft and hazy, and it moves constantly, almost dancing in the water. We get the impression of bright color and rhythmic motion.

The A and B series is intercut to build a sequence that details the fish's progress through the water, toward his objective. The individual shots are cut rhythmically, so that they get shorter and shorter as the fish gets closer and closer — moving faster and faster.

MUSIC: IDEALLY WE STING EACH SHOT OF THE OBJECT WITH THE SAME SHIMMERING, MAGICAL "ZING."

NARRATOR  So you'd move right on out — the simple, direct action. In your Cool World, every creature is his own boss, and you'd take orders only from your own impulses. Freedom? Your world is full of it — and it's total, and it's unrestricted.

The on-screen pace is quickening, and the object is getting quite close as the narrator continues:

NARRATOR  Free to move, free to live, free to swing. Man, would you swing!

As he says "swing" there is an instantaneous STRAIGHT CUT TO:

### 14. CLOSE SHOTS: OBJECTIVE (LURE)

Now, for the first time, we see the objective "in the clear." It is shot with a normal lens, the shot crisp and clear. We see that it is a fisherman's lure, on the end of a line. It is clearly visible ON SCREEN just long enough for it to be identified — a SPLIT SECOND — and then, suddenly and abruptly, it is snagged by our fish, who darts into view and bites hard on it.

(NO MUSIC HERE).

15. MEDIUM SHOT: FISH & LINE

A QUICK CUT as the fish is yanked, hard, up toward the surface, the movement fast and brutal.

16. MEDIUM SHOT: FISH & LINE

Another QUICK CUT, the camera nearer the surface, as the hooked fish flashes upward, continuing his rough trip up toward the surface. (He should just flash up from bottom to top of the frame, hooked and helpless).

17. MEDIUM SHOT: SURFACE (FROM BELOW)

Still underwater, the camera looks up toward the surface as — in another QUICK CUT — the fish is zipped up and we see his body break through the surface of the water.

18. MEDIUM CLOSE SHOT: SURFACE, FROM ABOVE

The camera looks down at the surface of the water as the fish is snapped up out of the water, flying up and away, going off screen.

SOUND EFFECTS: THE SPLASH AS HE EXITS, AND GENERAL OUTDOOR NOISE.

(NOTE: Scenes 14 through 17 are ALL QUICK CUTS — a montage of flash cuts, in which the violent movement is continuous and jarring; contrasting with the earlier languid, rhythmic, and peaceful scenes.)

19. CLOSE SHOT: FISH & HANDS

The fish is in the big, burly hands of the fisherman. The hands work quickly and brutally, ripping the hook from the fish's mouth. This scene is deliberately "rough" — we want the audience to shudder at its callous, unfeeling brutality.

SOUND EFFECTS: WE HEAR THE RIPPING NOISE AS THE HOOK IS TORN FROM THE FISH'S MOUTH.

20. EXT. RIVER (OR LAKE( BANK—DAY MEDIUM CLOSE SHOT: BASKET

(Or, possibly, just a patch of ground.) The fish is thrown casually onto the ground, or into the basket. It lies there, flopping futilely, gasping out its life. The camera MOVES IN SLOWLY for a CLOSEUP of the dying fish, watching as it slowly dies. We watch this in silence for a beat, and then...

(QUIETLY, UNEMOTIONALLY)

NARRATOR        Meet a swinger. (PAUSE) You know, even the dumbest human being is smarter than a fish. We have to be — 'cause we live in a more complicated, demanding world. Rules, regulations, problems, responsibilities, limitations, restrictions — we've got a planet full of them...

### 21. ECU: FISH

An extremely tight shot, concentrating on the head and mouth, as the mouth opens and closes once or twice, feebly — a last movement before death. (NOTE: This shot to be used under the narration for previous scene, for a little visual variety).

### 23. CU: TACKLE BOX

The camera is tight on a selection of lures. The fisherman's hands poke around, finally selecting one and bringing it forward so that it fills and dominates the screen, with the hook prominent.

NARRATOR        ...and of hooks. Today, more than ever before. Bigger and better hooks — bigger and better "lures," dangling in front of our eyes, promising all sorts of joy, pleasure and dreams come true. But that sharp point is always there, too — and very few of us can manage to bite without feeling their sting.

### 23. ECU: TACKLE BOX

The camera PANS SLOWLY ACROSS the array of lures in the tackle box. Ideally, the hooks will be highly visible, arcs of gleaming metal, glittering with highlights. (If we cannot get the effect we want via sunlight and star filters, this shot should be STUDIO MADE — there MUST BE bright "kicks" off the hooks, and the lures MUST LOOK colorful and attractive.)

NARRATOR        Okay, then — this is a movie about hooks. And we want to say right now that, with the kind of hooks WE'LL be talking about...WE're the fish.

As soon as the narrator says "fish," we make a STRAIGHT CUT to:

### 24. ECU: FISH

Concentrating on the head, showing at least one dead, glazed eye. The torn mouth is open, the fish has "had it." Dead, gray, cold — as grim as we can make it look.

MUSIC: A STING, OR CHORD — SOMETHING FINAL AND OMINOUS.

Then a STRAIGHT CUT to:

25. MONTAGE: ARMY REPORTS TITLE.

The writer suggests a 20-second montage that details the production of a film with a series of flash cuts. Specific shots for the montage are alphabetically listed:

A. CLOSE SHOT: An Arriflex camera being threaded, the film running through.

B. CLOSE SHOT: The camera turret being turned, with a long lens clicking into taking position.

C. CLOSE SHOT: Camera with soldier's eye at the rubber eyepiece, his hand working the lever of a zoom lens.

D. MEDIUM SHOT: An Army cameraman in a field, Arriflex on his shoulder, shooting while bracing himself against the turbulence created by a helicopter.

The script portrays, in graphic detail, the availability and the consequences of such drugs as heroin, LSD, amphetamines, barbiturates: the gamut. Here is a sequence midway in the program.

76. CU: DRIVER

ANOTHER ANGLE, shooting directly toward the driver, as if through the windshield. The CAMERA PANS LEFT to show the back seat of the car, and we see that the narrator is seated to the left rear of the driver. As he talks we MOVE IN for a CLOSE SHOT of the narrator.

He talks to the audience, but keeps looking forward nervously toward the now offscreen driver and the road ahead. He reacts occasionally, as if praying that he will survive the drive, and once or twice he is thrown to one side by a sharp turn.

NARRATOR     The feeling of pep and confidence a stimulant provides can make a guy push a tired body too far. He'll take risks — (HE IS THROWN TO ONE SIDE AS, SIMULTANEOUSLY, THERE IS A SQUEAL OF PROTESTING TIRES) — NOT because he's brave, but because he can't recognize them.

SOUND EFFECT: A LOUD, BLARING HORN, COMING CLOSER QUICKLY.

We hit his face with a light that gets stronger — as if from a rapidly approaching auto — and we ZOOM IN QUICKLY for a BIG CLOSEUP of the narrator as he winces, closes his eyes tight and holds up his hands protectively in front of his face...as if expecting a head-on collision within the next instant. Then we make a STRAIGHT CUT to:

77. INT. DRUG DISPLAY
BIG CLOSEUP: NARRATOR

To MATCH THE END OF PREVIOUS SCENE, with the same expression on his face — eyes tight shut, shoulders hunched, hands up protectively.

SOUND & MUSIC: THE LOUD NOISE AND MUSIC STOP ABRUPTLY WITH THE CUT TO THIS SHOT. THE TRACK IS SILENT.

He opens one eye, then the other, and looks about. He breathes a sigh of relief, and lowers his hands, and we PULL BACK QUICKLY for a MEDIUM SHOT that reveals that he is once again standing behind the drug display. He wipes some imaginary sweat from his brow, then looks once again at the stimulant pill, which is still held in one hand. (He is also still holding the depressant pill in his other hand).

(LOOKING AT STIMULANT PILL)

NARRATOR          Stimulants. (NOW AT CAMERA): There's another thing they say about one of them, and by "they" I **don't** mean doctors, or the "establishment." It's the younger generation that said it: Speed kills.

He lowers the stimulant, and now raises the depressant pill up for observation.

78. CU: NARRATOR

And the depressant pill that he holds up before him.

NARRATOR          Depressants don't "stop the world" so that you can get off, but they do slow it down quite a bit.

The CAMERA MOVES IN for an EX TIGHT SHOT of the depressant pill he holds aloft. It is round, and forms a circle that FILLS THE SCREEN.

NARRATOR          You might call the depressant a "tune-out" device...

DISSOLVE TO

79. INT. LIVING ROOM NIGHT
EX CLOSE SHOT: TV SET ON-OFF KNOB

The room is small, and somewhat grubby. There is a TV set, a few lamps, a recliner and a cheap sofa. Next to the recliner is an end table with a drawer. On the table is a lamp, which throws a tight circle of light and leaves surrounding areas in darkness. The lighting is LOW KEY, dreary.

The CAMERA STARTS FULL on the TV's on-off knob, which FILLS THE FRAME (matching the depressant pill's screen position and proportions as seen at the end of the previous scene).

SOUND EFFECTS: THE SOUND OF A TV PROGRAM, FILTERED FOR A TINNY EFFECT.

Timed to directly follow the narrator's statement that the depressant is a "tune-out" device, a man's finger reaches in and presses the knob. There is...

SOUND EFFECTS: A CLICK, AND THE TV PROGRAM NOISE FADES OUT QUICKLY.

80. CLOSE SHOT: NAT

The CAMERA SHOOTING OVER the TV set. He is a young man, early 20s. He wears a sport shirt and denims, and mocassins. His hair is disarrayed, his eyes foggy. He looks half-asleep, and his movements are halting and stumbling.

He is still leaning over the set, with one hand extended toward the knob, but now he straightens up slowly, yawns and stretches. His expression, though foggy, is somewhat blissful. It is a happy fog of indifference and serene detachment.

He turns, walks away from the set (and the camera) and flops into the recliner. He has some difficulty as he tries to place the chair in the reclining position, and there is some fumbling and bumbling.

NARRATOR    You forget your troubles, and move into a slow-motion, sleepy and relaxed world.

81. MEDIUM CLOSE SHOT:   NAT

HOLDING the top of the end table in the foreground. He has fallen into an uncomfortable, awkward position in the chair, but it doesn't seem to bother him. He looks at his watch, but obviously cannot read the small numbers. He then reaches forward, opens the drawer in the end table and, fumbling and clumsy, he takes out a bottle of pills.

NARRATOR    Problems, worries, anxieties? All forgotten. And so is the hook.

82. EX CLOSE SHOT:   PILLS

As Nat's hands clumsily flip off the plastic lid, he drops the bottle on the tabletop, and six or seven pills spill out onto the tabletop. He attempts to pick up one pill, but his groping attempts make him drop it—it is too small for his inept fingers to grasp.

NARRATOR    Ordinarily, you might be well aware of the dangers that go with an overdose — but the same chemicals that have tuned out your troubles have also tuned out your judgment.

Unable to pick up a single tablet, Nat's hands try a different technique: He holds one open palm against the table's edge, and brushes all the loose pills into it with his other hand — at least six of them.

83. MEDIUM CLOSE SHOT: NAT

SIMILAR TO SETUP FOR SCENE 81, also holding the upper surface of the table. He looks at the pills in his hands, as if trying to focus on them — and apparently unable to. Finally, he shrugs, and then tosses the whole handful into his mouth. Now he starts looking about on the table's surface — he needs something with which to "wash them down." He picks up a water glass, but it is empty.

NARRATOR     Confusion is the order of the day on Cloud Nine. Your brain doesn't think — it's too busy floating.

His mouth stuffed with dry pills, Nat's need for liquid is now urgent. He gropes around in the dark area on the table, and brings out a bottle of liquor. His actions still thick and clumsy, he pours some of the alcohol into the glass, and then gulps it down — choking slightly, coughing, spilling some liquid on his chin.

But he gets it down — pills and all — and then flops back onto the chair. We DOLLY IN SLOWLY for a CLOSEUP of his face as he falls into an instant, heavy sleep. His mouth is open, his chin is wet. He is an ugly sight.

NARRATOR     Depressants plus alcohol. That's the formula for a big, sharp, ugly...and frequently fatal...hook.

We look at Nat's somewhat repulsive image for a beat, and then TILT DOWN to the tabletop, and MOVE IN QUICKLY for a CLOSEUP of one pill, which still rests on the tabletop.

Then a description of the effects of hallucinogens and narcotics.

104. INT. DRUG DISPLAY
CU:       HALLUCINOGENS  &  NARCOTICS
SECTION

On the left, a display of hallucinogens, including dosage forms of LSD: peyote cactus buttons and ground buttons; illicit dosage form of LSD, PCP, DOM, PSILOCYBIN: sugar cubes, etc. (REF: Page 15 of DRUGS OF ABUSE booklet).

On the right, a display of narcotics: Opium poppy and derivatives; morphine base; morphine; heroin; addict's equipment including cord, spoon, matches, hypodermic. (REF: Page 3 of DRUGS OF ABUSE booklet).

The narrator's hand reaches in and points to each area in turn as he mentions them.

NARRATOR        Hallucinogens...narcotics.

We DOLLY IN and CENTER ON the hallucinogens, excluding the narcotics.

NARRATOR        There are a wide variety of hallucinogenic drugs. They've got long, formal names like "Lysergic Acid Diethlamide," abbreviated names like S-T-P, D-M-T, L-S-D...and the usual array of slang names like acid, cubes, royal blue, sugar, Chief, Howk, Serenity, Instant Zen and — believe it or not — Businessman's Special.

## 105. CU: DISPLAY & NARRATOR

The hallucinogens in the low foreground, the narrator standing directly behind them.

NARRATOR        Nearly all of them are outlawed, except for approved research. They are most dangerous because they are unpredictable. Oh, they can pretty much guarantee illusions and hallucination — you know: a trip. But what form that trip will take...is anybody's guess.

He looks down, and we ZOOM IN as he picks up a small white pill, HOLDING IT UP for the CAMERA.

## 106. ECU: THE PILL

At first occupying about one-third of the frame, but then there is an immediate ZOOM IN so that it FILLS THE FRAME.

NARRATOR        Some guys have been lucky...

At this point, we SUPER an EXPLOSION OF RED, that BURSTS OUTWARD and fills the SCREEN with color.

(We can probably achieve this by a superimposition of an extreme close shot of an explosion, in color. We will HOLD IT ON SCREEN for just an instant, and then cut away to:)

## 107. SPECIAL EFFECTS: COLOR DISPLAY

We can probably achieve the effect we want here by multiple-exposures of a KALEIDOSCOPE. Each shot should be star-filtered; some undercranked, some overcranked. One might be deliberately out of focus. The effect should be a spectacular display of colors in motion.

(We might also include a SUPERIMPOSED image of a young man's face, distorted by an extreme wide-angle lens, lit from below with colored lights — his eyes wide, his mouth open.)

Or, possibly, we might SUPER a FULL FIGURE of the man — perhaps a **WHITE** silhouette, with bleeding edges, that floats through the frame (shot in slow motion) at a 45-degree angle.

Obviously this shot cannot be "spelled out" in a shooting script. It must be achieved via a bit of camera and optical bench experimentation.

MUSIC & EFFECTS: WE MATCH THE WEIRD IMAGES ON THE SCREEN WITH APPROPRIATELY WEIRD SOUND EFFECTS, AND SOME WAY-OUT MUSIC THAT IS DOCTORED ELECTRONICALLY.

NARRATOR    They claim to have SEEN music...and HEARD colors...to have visited a fantasy land that Walt Disney never dreamed of.

We watch and listen to the images and the soundtrack for a beat. Then...

NARRATOR    But others...

The instant the narrator completes "but others," we STRAIGHT CUT TO:

108. **REVERSE** REPEAT OF SCENE 106

The same action shown in Scene 106 (zoom in full on pill, then fill the frame with an explosion), but now SHOWN IN REVERSE — so that the EXplosion becomes an IMplosion, and then we see the pill, full frame.

MUSIC & EFFECTS: STOP ABRUPTLY WITH THE CUT TO THIS SCENE.

We HOLD the pill on-screen, as:

NARRATOR    ...using the same pill—the same "trip ticket"— have found themselves crawling through nightmares more horrible, and more real, than any dream ever delivered.

MUSIC: DURING THE NARRATOR'S PRECEDING PARAGRAPH, WE BUILD UP AN OMINOUS KETTLEDRUM BEAT, AND, UNDER IT, WE ALSO SLOWLY FADE IN AN EXTENDED, CONTINUOUS MALE SCREAM. (WE EXTEND IT ARTIFICIALLY VIA A LOOP). AS HE COMPLETES HIS NARRATION, WE SUDDENLY INCREASE THE VOLUME ON THE SCREAM SO THAT IT IS AT FULL GAIN. SIMULTANEOUSLY, WE...

...BATHE the on-screen pill with a SPLASH OF VIVID RED LIGHT.

(We are building the audience to a feeling that they're going to be hit with something horrible — some hideous images on the screen, some shock visuals. But instead of delivering on the promise, we simply make a STRAIGHT CUT TO:)

## 109. CLOSE SHOT: NARRATOR

SAME SETUP as SCENE 105: The narrator to the rear of the display of hallucinogens. He is still holding the small pill, but his attitude is light and relaxed. He is smiling.

EFFECTS & MUSIC: STOP ABRUPTLY WITH THE CUT TO THIS SCENE.

NARRATOR
(CASUAL)

Relax. We're not going to beat your eyeballs in with our version of a nightmare trip. We couldn't do it justice. A "bad trip" outclasses any horrors a movie can put together...and that can be only the beginning. It's not all bad dreams...

## 110. ECU: PILL

The CAMERA FULL ON THE PILL once again.

NARRATOR

Hallucinogens can also cause a total freakout — panic...in stereo.

The closing is a pitch to the soldier's better judgment.

## 150. INT. BARRACKS **OR** BEDROOM—NIGHT—FULL SHOT: "GUARD"

(NOTE: This can be shot either in a civilian bedroom or a barracks — or BOTH, if desired, for a choice of endings.)

We see the same young man — enlisted man — seen earlier on guard duty and in the shower. He is in the last stages of getting dressed. (And here, too, we can shoot him either in uniform or civvies, or both).

As he gets dressed, he will be deep in thought. He puts on his clothing without thinking about what he is doing, his actions automatic.

the CAMERA MAKES A LONG, SLOW DOLLY IN—

"closing in" on the man, in a sense.

NARRATOR

In today's world, problems are plentiful, and miracles are in very short supply. There is no quick, easy solution to real problems...just some gimmicks that offer temporary relief — a few moments of escape, that NEVER turn off tomorrow, and can never tune out reality. Some of these gimmicks are harmless; others are harmful...and some are deadly. Laws and regulations have been designed to protect you from those with the sharpest hooks, but that protection is never total. In the final analysis, the only foolproof protection must be provided by your own intelligence...your own ability to recognize and avoid the dangers...your own free choice, working to your own best advantage.

At this point, the CAMERA IS CLOSE on the young man. When the narrator says "your own intelligence," and from that point on, the CAMERA CENTERS on the man's image as reflected in a wall mirror, which he turns to, to survey his own image. For the balance of the paragraph of narration, he is looking directly into his own reflected image — eyeball to eyeball, still thoughtful. He is still looking, still thinking, as we...

FADE OUT

FADE IN...

151. INT DRUG DISPLAY

CLOSE SHOT: : NARRATOR

He looks and talks directly at the audience, his attitude straightforward, his delivery straight. No business, no sales pitch — the only feeling we want is one of total sincerity.

NARRATOR      Army regulations prohibit the use of drugs of abuse — but the Army also recognizes that the problem is one requiring more than simple solutions. If you are involved with drug abuse, you can't solve your problem instantly, or miraculously. But your best course of action is to seek help — voluntarily, of your own accord. Your C-O, your chaplain, the doctor — they're ready to help. Do yourself a favor and avoid bigger problems tomorrow. Go see them. Get off the hook.

FADE OUT

Radio programs were produced by the Army, sporadically, before World War II, largely for recruiting. During World War II, the then War Department's Radio Branch went very heavily into radio production, particularly, "The Army Hour" series. That program in an abbreviated 25-minute version is still being broadcast. Interestingly enough, in this decade—the 70s— radio has taken an upsurge in the Army with special disc jockey programming for closed-circuit systems within Army installations, a half-hour series entitled "Contempo" for broadcast on American Forces radio stations overseas, a 5-minute series, "World-Wide" and a weekly news show called "Army News Notes." The following script is typical of the "Army Hour" series.

MUSIC: "THE ARMY GOES ROLLING ALONG," THEN UNDER

ANNCR: This is The Army Hour...the program that keeps you up to date on what's happening in the Army around the world. From Ft. Hood, Texas — an Army wife views Today's Army:

(TEASER: Mrs. Gwen Stewart)

(CUE: "...for instance, if you're.....from the things that is offered to you now..."

ANNCR: And our guest stars are Victor Borge and The Kings Men...in an excerpt from — COMMAND PERFORMANCE!

MUSIC: "YA TA TA, YA TA TA," THEN UNDER

ANNCR: COMMAND PERFORMANCE, U.S.A. — a priceless collection of the greatest entertainers in America...who made this perhaps the best variety show in the history of radio. On this edition we bring you the man who combines his classic skill as a pianist with his amazing talent as a comedian....and with him, one of the finest singing quartets. Now, on to Hollywood....where our Master of Ceremonies, Spencer Tracy, is standing by to introduce Victor Borge....and The King's Men....on — COMMAND PERFORMANCE!

(Victor Borge and The King's Men)

MUSIC: SYNCOPATED BONGOS AND AIRBEAM

ANNCR: Our reporters recently have been querying enlisted men and officers in widely scattered posts on what they think of the new Modern Volunteer Army. And their opinions, as you've heard, have varied from enthusiastic to so-so, and all degrees in between. Then it occurred to us — why not try to find out what an Army wife thinks...after all, she too is devinitely a part of today's Army. So, here's Army Hour reporter MSG Jerry Clark talking to Mrs. Gwen Stewart at the Junior NCO Wives Club — Ft. Hood, Texas.

SPOT

MUSIC: DOCUMENTARY PLAYOFF

MUSIC: "POT LUCK," THEN UNDER (2:36)

ANNCR: And here's the Studio Band inviting you to join them for some — "POT LUCK,"

MUSIC: UP TO CLOSE

MUSIC: "LOVE'S BEEN GOOD TO ME," THEN UNDER (2:39)

ANNCR: The united States Army Chorus...backed by the Studio Orchestra....and — "LOVE'S BEEN GOOD TO ME."

MUSIC: UP TO CLOSE

      (COMMERCIAL: recruiting)

MUSIC: "COUNT OF MONTE TWISTO," THEN UNDER (3:00)

ANNCR: Coming on now to wind up this session...the Army Dance Band with — "THE COUNT OF MONTE TWISTO."

MUSIC: UP TO 23:30, THEN FADE OUT

MUSIC: "THE ARMY GOES ROLLING ALONG," THEN UNDER

ANNCR: The Army Hour, prerecorded for broadcast at this time, is produced by the Office of the Chief of Information, Department of the Army. Music by the Studio Band of the Army Field Band, conducted by Lt. Jack Grogan...the Army Chorus and Studio Orchestra, by Col. Samuel Loboda...and the Army Dance Band, directed by MSG Lonnie Wilfong. Our guest performers ONSTAGE were Victor Borge and The King's Men from Command Performance. Script and production by David B. Eskind. This is Ed Caputo speaking.

MUSIC: "DOG FACE SOLDIER"

## The United States Navy

The Navy produces a great many information and training films and maintains its own production facilities at the Naval Photographic Center in Washington, D.C. An example of one of the scripts for the Navy's film programs is "The ASWEPS Story," written by George Brenholtz.

| PICTURE | SOUND |
|---|---|
| FADE IN | |
| 1. SHOW OPENS with a HOLD on the LETTERS A S W E P S. CAMERA ZOOM OUT and HOLDS on the LETTERS as they stack vertically. SPELL OUT... SUBMARINE WARFARE ENVIRONMENTAL PREDICTION SERVICES. | |
| FADE TO BLACK | |
| FADE IN: | MUSIC: ANTICIPATORY, slightly SUSPENSEFUL. BUILDING TOWARD the UNDERWATER SEQUENCE and the discovery of the |

2. And HOLD on a LONG SHOT of a PACIFIC BEACH. We see a sweeping curved surf line with trees in the BG. The water washing gently on the shore.
No. 30074

3. CUT TO CLOSE SHOTS of the SURF and SFX: BREAKERS. At one point a wave smashes up against a flat ROCK in the FG.
No. 30074 and No. 36429

DISSOLVE TO:

4. FROM A DEEP WATER SHOT, the CAMERA PANS RIGHT to WAVES dashing against rocks. CUT TO SEMIHIGH ANGLE SHOT on a ROCK as it is inundated by a wave.
No. 36428

5. A SIDE-ANGLE SHOT on a SMALL COVE. A few WAVES slide gently on to the beach, reaching their peak.

6. A HIGH-ANGLE SHOT PAST a SMALL GROUP of SEAGULLS with SURF breaking on the BEACH in the BG.
No. 36428

7. MED CLOSE SHOT on SEAGULLS as they drift across the surface of the water.
No. 34529

8. CUT TO AN EXTREME HIGH-ANGLE TRAVELING SHOT (AIR TO GROUND) as our CAMERA SWEEPS along a stretch of BEACH.
NO. 36338—

9. DIRECT CUT TO A LOW-ANGLE SHOT with OUR CAMERA FACING the incoming SURF. WAVES WASH OVER CAMERA. As a SECOND wave inundates our CAMERA POSITION WE..

DISSOLVE TO:

SUBMARINE. It is important that the MUSIC in this section of the film is NOT MELODRAMATIC or loaded with STINGERS. Avoid a TRAVELOG QUALITY.

The SOUNDS of an OCEAN SURF; WAVES dashing against ROCKS. The LONELY MEWING of a handful of SEAGULLS.

SFX: SHARP SLAP of the BREAKERS as they head in toward shore. FOLLOW WITH the MUFFLED, BUBBLING QUALITY of an UNDERWATER PRESENCE.

10. A SHORT MONTAGE SHOWING a WIDE EXPANSE of OCEAN. A LONG LINE of CLOUDS appear ready to blot out the sun. We catch SUN's RAYS as they glitter iridescently on the surface of the water. SHAFTS OF LIGHT ARE seen coming through the clouds.

NARRATOR:

(ON DISSOLVE) The sea... Timeless...Terrifying...Beautiful...Endless and deep. A supreme wonder and paradox of man's natural world.

DISSOLVE TO:

11. SHOT from the STARBOARD SIDE of a SHIP (probably a DD) in a gathering fog. We are moving straight into it now.
No. 42395

Throughout history, the sea has served mankind as a barrier and a highroad, uniting and dividing the peoples of the earth.

The narration continues to describe exploration of the sea and then there is a transition to the role of the submarine.

PICTURE

SOUND:

39. CUT TO SUBMARINE PULL-AWAY SEQUENCE (using the 434 stock footage series). We are caught off guard by the SUBMARINE'S sudden movement.

a. From an EXTREME CLOSE ANGLE the SAIL MOVES PAST CAMERA, clanging into the GUY WIRE being used by the DIVERS.

b. CUT TO a SECOND CLOSEUP on the SAIL as it moves through FRAME. The CAMERA, through a flood of bubbles, TILTS DOWN and HOLDS for a SHOT on the body of the SUB as it passes by.

c. FROM A CANTED ANGLE we see one of the DIVERS swimming near the GUY-WIRE AREA. It is alive with the swirl of bubbles caused by the SUB'S PROP WASH. FROM CHANGE of ANGLE we STUDY a SECOND SHOT on the GUY-WIRE AREA. As the SOUND of the SUB FADES INTO THE DISTANCE we again hear the NARRATOR.

NARRATOR:

In World Wars One and Two, America's combat submarines operated...for the most part...in the thin upper layer of the ocean environment. And even there they enjoyed only restricted periods of true submergence.

| | |
|---|---|
| 40. CUT BACK TO SHOTS on the SUBMARINE as it MOVES PAST CAMERA for a SECOND TIME. These are CLOSE LOW-ANGLE VIEWS of the SAIL and AFTER SECTION of the SUB. This time around, the name NARWHAL can be clearly made out on the side of the sub. | The nuclear submarine is the first true submersible; the first naval craft since the sailing ship able to stay at sea indefinitely. |
| 41. LONGER SHOT on the SUBMARINE as it moves into the gathering gloom. | The combination of their far-reaching weapon systems, and their great speed and depth have made them a challenge seriously affecting the political, economic and military well-being of the free world. |
| | SFX: The PINGING of SONAR on the OPEN SEA. |

The next sequence deals with tracking submarines, and the narrator describes the submarine hunt. Then the writer delves into the mission of ASWEPS.

| PICTURE | SOUND |
|---|---|
| | NARRATOR: |
| 90. Shot along the DECK of the DD SHOWING A CARRIER IN THE DISTANCE. At the moment, the CVS is also sending out light signals. | To help the Navy solve the problems of these invisible barriers, and to aid in the gathering of broad synoptic views from its many possible ASW hunting grounds...the Naval Oceanographic Office developed ASWEPS....the ASW Environmental Prediction Services. In 1966, after years of perfecting the system, the Oceanographic Office turned the Prediction Services over operationally to the Naval Weather Service. |
| 91. CUT TO NEW LIVE-ACTION PHOTOGRAPHY. CLOSE SHOT on the EN-VIRONMENTALIST as he stands in front of his working CHARTS in the CVS BRIEFING ROOM. | |
| 92. QUICK SIDE-ANGLE COVER SHOT of the V.S. SQUADRON COMMANDER, OPERATIONS OFFICER, AIR GROUP COMMANDER, in the BRIEFING ROOM. They are dressed in flight gear, taking notes, etc. | |

93. BACK TO CLOSE SHOT on the .. ENVIRONMENTALIST.

94. TWO SHOT (NEW PHOTOGRAPHY) on the TWO AEROGRAPHERS MATES. They are working at a weather display table. CAMERA IN for a CU on their material.

95. CLOSE SHOT on the MAP FACSIMILE RECEIVER as one of the aerographers takes a fresh map off of the receiver's roller.

NARRATOR:

A typical ASWEPS team consists of an Environmentalist or Oceanographic forecaster...and two aerographers mates working out of the flagship weather office.

The environmentalist's job is to produce a working package of oceanographic data that accurately reflects the environmental conditions over thousands of square miles of ocean.

The final scenes are a summing up.

|  PICTURE | SOUND |
|---|---|

120. CUT BELOW DECK TO the DD'S CIC AREA. CAMERA IN CLOSE FOR QUICK VIEWS of the SITUATION and PLOTTING BOARDS. This, too, should be the best as far as our CIC FOOTAGE is concerned.

NARRATOR:

Linked as it is to so many uncertainties, the hunt for a submarine is quite possibly the deadliest game of hide and seek ever played by modern man.

121. CUT TO CLOSE REAR-ANGLE OR SIDE-ANGLE SHOT on a HELICOPTER PILOT as he flies BIRD.

SFX: In the BG and BUILDING, the FILTERED VOICES of the PILOT and his CREW talking during hunt...- VOICES ALSO OVER THE HELICOPTER SCENES.

122. CUT TO A CLOSE SHOT on a HELICOPTER as it dips its HYDROPHONE. A SECOND BIRD flies through the SCENE. We PAN with it and hold as it lowers its HYDROPHONE. This SEQUENCE should convey CONSTANT MOVEMENT on the part of the HUNTERS. Many helicopters are evidently on the scene. No. 40697

It's time consuming and it calls for courage, patience, technical skill and...quite often...a little bit of luck.

123. CUT DIRECTLY to a CLOSE TWO SHOT on TWO HELICOPTERS HOVERING together ON SCREEN. No. 40697

SFX: SOUNDS OF BIRDS, UP FULL. FOR NARRATION.

124. CUT TO MED SHOT on an S-2 TRACKER. We favor the NOSE AREA of the PLANE. Follow with an INTERIOR SHOT on the S-2's RADAR MAN and his SCOPE which is pinging away in the darkness. No. 42625 and No. 40700

NARRATOR:

What the hunter needs is an edge...

125. From the pinging SCOPE we CUT DIRECTLY to a SHOT of the ENVIRONMENTALIST at work (NEW PHOTOGRAPHY).

And men like the Environmentalist, who can translate seemingly odd bits and pieces of scattered oceanographic information into quick and useful tactical tools, are the men who can supply that need.

126. CUT BACK TO THE SCOPE PINGING in the darkness.

127. CUT TO A LONG VIEW of the OPERATION showing the CVS in the BG. Perhaps here we CUT TO a DD running SHOT, as well as a MED LONG SHOT on a SMOKE POT floating on the water's surface.

128. CUT TO a CLOSE SHOT on a SPINNING COMPUTER TAPE. (NEW PHOTOGRAPHY).

129. CUT TO ZOOM SHOT on a PERISCOPE RUNNING THROUGH the WATER. As our AERIAL CAMERA swings in an arch around the SCOPE, we CUT TO....
No. 40702

130. A HAND REMOVING PHOTOFAX COPY from its COPY REEL on the CVS. (NEW PHOTOGRAPHY.)

131. SHORT HOLD on a SUB UNDERWATER, CLOSE.

132. CUT TO MED SHOT on a HELICOPTER as it drops a PARACHUTED EXPLOSIVE CHARGE. We PAN DOWN for the EXPLOSION.
No. 40702.

133. ON CUE WITH the EXPLOSION, we CUT TO a

SHORELINE LOW-ANGLE
SHOT. A WAVE washes OVER
OUR CAMERA. A SECOND
WAVE STARTS IN as we CUT
TO...

NARRATOR:

134. A BEAUTIFUL SHOT across a PATCH of OPEN OCEAN. FOLLOW with other beauty SHOTS of the sea.

DISSOLVE TO:

Throughout history, the sea has served mankind as a barrier and highroad...uniting and dividing the peoples of the earth.

135. AN UNDERWATER SHOT on TWO DIVERS as they MOVE PAST CAMERA. We HOLD and THEN FOLLOW THEM as they move further into the deep.

136. As we HOLD ON THE TWO DIVERS, OUR CAMERA SCENE FADES TO BLACK.

FADE TO BLACK

Now in the final moments of the 20th Century...surrounded by increased scientific and technological skills...and reaching for an increased awareness of the universe ...man has finally come to recognize the sea for what it truly is...a miracle.

THE END

The U.S. Air Force has a motion picture facility at Norton Air Force Base in California. The U.S. Marine Corps also produces radio programs and films. The military services, unlike other executive agencies, have a pool of musical talent available in the military bands and choruses which are used extensively in the production of their programs.

## THE UNITED STATES INFORMATION AGENCY

The most active government agency in the audio-visual area is the United States Information Agency (USIA). "The role of the Agency is to support the foreign policy of the United States by explaining it to people in other countries; to build overseas understanding of United States institutions and culture; and to advise the U.S. Government on public opinion abroad and its implications for U.S. policy. The Agency also administers the Department of State's cultural and educational exchange program overseas."

The USIA produces and acquires about 500 film and TV documentaries annually for distribution in 130 countries. In addition, 2,700 targeted news programs and 20,000 news clips are made for use on foreign television. Audiences for these add up to one billion for direct projection showings and to a potential television audience of 500 million in the 100 countries with TV.

To give you an idea of the varied subject matter of some of these documentaries, here are brief outlines of previously produced films:

"The Infinite Journey": a portrayal of man's aspiration to reach the moon; a 90-minute color film narrated by Gregory Peck.

"Selamat Datang and Welcome": a 15-minute color film on the state visit of Indonesian President Suharto to the United States.

"Some Beautiful People": a series of four 30-minute programs on young Anerican musical groups.

"Africa Will Be": a documentary on African nations working in many fields to develop the continent's human and natural resources.

"American Sketches": a series of films produced mainly for television stations in the Middle East, depicting various aspects of American life.

## "Voice of America"

The USIA's radio arm, the Voice of America (VOA) broadcasts over 800 hours of programs weekly of which about 180 hours are in English and the remainder in some 35 different languages.

In its "Guide for Writers and Editors," the VOA sets forth its aims: "Our constant aim and effort is to tell the news as it is. That means accurately. It means also that we report the facts showing the whys and the context of events. And we try to put these facts in a way that'll be understood by people of political and cultural backgrounds much different from ours."

VOA correspondents in the U.S. and abroad file reports, news inserts, features, news analyses, interviews and occasional documentaries. The Current Affairs Division produces the commentaries, news analyses and longer features, including documentaries. These are written in the same radio style used for the news. Short sentences and simple words are preferred. However, these scripts do serve to explain sensitive political subject matter and may when necessary fall back on exact official language. Commentaries and news analyses are three to three and a half minutes long. Features which use tape inserts or call for two or more voices may run longer.

In addition to its direct broadcasts, VOA services foreign radio audiences through the placement of taped package programs, thousands of which are sent each year to USIA offices in foreign countries. USIA offices overseas also originate radio programs in approximately a dozen languages for use on local stations. Parts of these programs are based on VOA supplied tapes or scripts.

## DEPARTMENT OF AGRICULTURE

From the time the Department of Agriculture was established in 1862, one of its prime missions has been to assist the nation's farmers by informing them of developments to aid productivity. Recently, there has been a great deal of emphasis placed on consumer concerns.

In 1961, the Department began a weekly television program, "Across the Fence," hosted by Layne R. Beaty, Chief of the Radio and Television Service. The program is produced for the Department of Agriculture by WRC-TV in Washington and is seen on some 100 TV stations across the nation. The following opening of a typical "Across the Fence" program will give you some idea of its scope.

| VIDEO | AUDIO |
|---|---|
| Tease | |
| SLIDE 1 | MUSIC: (Selected background music, "Spaced Out," establish, then under for Beaty's narration.) |
| | BEATY |
| | COMING UP NEXT ON ACROSS THE FENCE...A NUTRITION EXPERT WILL SHED SOME LIGHT ON ORGANIC FOODS. |
| CAMERA: CU Smith | JAMES V. SMITH, ADMINISTRATOR OF THE FARMERS HOME ADMINISTRATION WILL EXPLAIN WHY HE IS OPTIMISTIC ABOUT RURAL DEVELOPMENT TRENDS. |
| SLIDE 2: Tractor | AN AGRICULTURAL ENGINEER WILL DISCUSS TRACTOR SAFETY. AND...- |
| CAMERA: CU Eggs | WE'LL HAVE A REPORT ON THE INSPECTION OF EGGS. ALL THIS TODAY ON ACROSS THE FENCE. |

Since the program consists largely of interviews, the interviewees portion is generally ad-lib to provide an unstaged conversational response. An example is this portion of an interview with Dr. Ruth Leverton, Science Advisor for the Agricultural Research Service.

Segment No. 3: Layne Beaty and Dr. Ruth Leverton in living room set; two chairs, coffee table.

VISUALS:

SUPER: Dr. Ruth Leverton, Science Advisor, Ag. Research Service

CAMERA: CU Beaty

BEATY

HOW MANY FRIENDS DO YOU HAVE WHO ARE ON A DIET? IT MAY BE A HIGH FAT DIET...OR HIGH PROTEIN...OR LIQUIDS...OR FRUIT...OR MAYBE HUMMINGBIRD TONGUES. AND EACH FRIEND PROBABLY HAS A BOOK TO PROVE HIS DIET IS **THE** ONE AND ONLY ONE FOR HEALTH, BEAUTY, ENERGY OR WHATEVER. THEN THERE'S YOUR FAMILY...EXPECTING MEAT, POTATOES, PIE OR ICE CREAM AT JUST ABOUT EVERY MEAL. ALL THIS DIET TALK HAS YOU WORRIED. OUR NEXT MAY HAVE SOME WORDS OF COMFORT FOR YOU...MAYBE SOME PRAISE, TOO. SHE'S DR. RUTH LEVERTON, SCIENCE ADVISOR, AGRICULTURE RESEARCH SERVICE, USDA.

DR. LEVERTON...WHAT DO YOU DO IF SOMEONE HAS FOUND A WONDERFUL BOOK RECOMMENDING SOME STRANGE DIET, THAT MADE HIS LIFE OVER. DO YOU LAUGH IT OFF...OR TRY THE STRANGE DIET?

LEVERTON

(New life not because of diet, but because maybe got enough sleep, or felt better because believed they'd been helped, etc. Organic food people feel better because they eat more fruits and vegetables than they ever did before. Attribute health to wrong thing.)

351

BEATY

ALMOST EVERY DAY SOMEBODY MAKES HEADLINES BY KNOCKING SOME FOOD AS BEING UNHEALTHY OR UN-WHOLESOME. MAYBE BECAUSE OF SPRAYS OR PROCESSING OR NUTRIENT CONTENT OR WHATEVER. HOW SERIOUSLY SHOULD THE PUBLIC TAKE THESE CRITICISMS?

LEVERTON

(Reassures homemakers of wholesomeness of food supply)

BEATY

HOW MUCH MISIN-FORMATION IS THERE ABOUT FOODS AND NUTRITION...AND WHO ORIGINATES IT? SURELY NOT NUTRITIONISTS?

LEVERTON

(Misinformation from people not qualified to teach nutrition...only qualification is eating, etc.)

On the radio side, the Department of Agriculture prepares a monthly series of spot announcements for use by disc jockeys. Two sample spots are reproduced below:

**BRINGING THE MOUNTAIN TO JUNIOR**     Approx. :50

One of the best places to teach a child a respect for his environment is in an outdoor classroom. Such a classroom would be on the school grounds or nearby. It could be an acre or more...or a small hilly spot...or a swampy spot...or, as in one city school, a few square feet of soil under a fire escape. In an outdoor classroom, a child learns how people use and care for the soil, and how water and air can alter their environment. He can study soil, plants, rocks, and various wild creatures that may move in, such as rabbits, birds and insects. If you're interested in bringing nature to the children in your school, drop a card for a free booklet from the U.S. Department of Agriculture, full of ideas for developing and using outdoor classrooms on school sites of any size wherever they are located. Drop a card to OUTDOOR CLASSROOMS, Agriculture Radio, Washington, D.C. 20250

## MONEY SAVING PROTEINS                    Approx. : 18

Even if you're budgeting, you can still serve your family good protein meals. The U.S. Department of Agriculture suggests you improve the protein value of the meal by combining cereal and vegetable foods with a little animal protein. For example, combine cereal with milk, rice with fish, spaghetti with meat sauce, vegetable stew with meat. Or simply serve milk with foods of plant origin.

## NATIONAL AERONAUTICS AND SPACE ADMINISTRATION

One of the newer federal agencies, NASA, is responsible for man's greatest adventure in exploration. By the end of the 20th century, trips to the lunar orb may become commonplace, but when the first astronauts landed on the moon, it was a feat that set the whole world marveling; and its magic, danger, and awesomeness were there for everyone to contemplate through the electronic wonder of television.

NASA produces both radio and television programs as a sort of progress report to the public on space and aeronautic developments. Here is an example of the weekly radio series, "The Space Story."

WILLARD: FROM WASHINGTON, D.C. ...........COMMENTS ON PLANS FOR A REUSABLE SPACE SHUTTLE SYSTEM!

FLETCHER: : 18 Perhaps the most dramatic impact of the shuttle will be that it will completely change the nature of how we operate in space. Because of the low cost, because we can use simpler payloads and repair and refurbish them, the whole nature of the program will change—it'll be a different kind of space program.

THIS IS WILLARD SCOTT REPORTING ... IN A MOMENT, MORE FROM NASA ADMINISTRATOR, DR. JAMES C. FLETCHER .... ON THE REUSABLE SPACE SHUTTLE.
   THEME: IN AND UNDER

THIS IS THE SPACE STORY, A WEEKLY SPACE AND AERONAUTICS REPORT, BROUGHT TO YOU BY THIS STATION AND NASA, THE NATIONAL AERONAUTICS AND SPACE ADMINISTRATION.
   THEME:    UP AND OUT

THE RESUABLE SPACE SHUTTLE...HALF AIRPLANE, HALF SPACECRAFT. IT WILL BE ABLE TO

CARRY A FULL RANGE OF PAYLOADS INTO EARTH ORBIT, THEN RETURN HOME TO A GROUND LANDING...UNDERGO A BRIEF REFURBISHMENT, THEN BE READY FOR ANOTHER MISSION.

FLETCHER:    :22 Conventional methods throw away the booster, so to speak. And this has always bothered a great many of us. We go to all the trouble of building these expensive launch vehicles, as we call them, and then dump them in the ocean. This way, we'll be able to reuse essentially all of the boosters.

WILLARD:    NASA ADMINISTRATOR, DR. JAMES FLETCHER, CONTINUED THAT THE SPACE SHUTTLE, TO BE FLOWN INTO ORBIT BY A MINIMUM CREW OF TWO MEN, WILL REPRESENT A MERGING OF MANNED AND UNMANNED SPACE ACTIVITIES.

FLETCHER:    :25 Of course, the thing that's talked about the most is that it will replace our existing launch vehicles. But perhaps the most spectacular cost savings will be in the payloads themselves...in the reuse of the payloads, and the repair of the payloads, because, by and large, when you get into the space program a ways, you find that the payloads are the most expensive part of the mission — and so there's a big gain to be had there.

WILLARD: VIRTUALLY THE ENTIRE RANGE OF UNMANNED SPACECRAFT THAT WE KNOW TODAY — INCLUDING SCIENTIFIC, COMMUNICATIONS, WEATHER, AND NAVIGATION SATELLITES — CAN BE CARRIED ALOFT BY THE REUSABLE SHUTTLE INSIDE THE LARGE CARGO BAY. MEN CAN CHECK OUT THE CRAFT BEFORE PLACING THEM INTO THEIR PROPER ORBITS. PERIODIC VISITS BY SHUTTLE CREWS FOR MAINTENANCE AND REPAIR OF ORIBITNG UNMANNED VEHICLES COULD MAKE SATELLITE FAILURES A THING OF THE PAST. ON BOARD THE SHUTTLE, THERE WILL BE ROOM TO CARRY NONASTRONAUT SCIENTISTS AND ENGINEERS INTO SPACE TO CONDUCT EXPERIMENTS IN A PRESSURIZED, "SHIRTSLEEVE" ENVIRONMENT. SHUTTLE CAPABILITIES WILL OFFER A NUMBER OF MILITARY ADVANTAGES TO INSURE OUR NATIONAL DEFENSE. AND THE OPPORTUNITIES FOR INCREASED INTERNATIONAL COOPERATION IN SPACE WILL BE GREATLY ENHANCED.

FLETCHER:    :35 Yes, it certainly will in many senses. For one thing, as you reduce the cost per flight, many other countries become interested suddenly in the use of space. So there's a tremendous interest on that basis alone. The President is very interested in this aspect of it — it is a way of getting people from other countries into space doing useful things.

WILLARD: REUSABILITY...FLEXIBILITY...COST REDUCTION...ASIDE FROM THESE OBVIOUS ADVANTAGES OF A SPACE SHUTTLE TRANSPORTATION SYSTEM, NASA ADMINISTRATOR, DR. JAMES FLETCHER POINTED OUT THAT IN HIS MIND, THE SHUTTLE PROGRAM REPRESENTS THIS COUNTRY'S ONLY MAJOR NEW THRUST IN TECHNOLOGY IN COMING YEARS....THE KIND OF TECHNOLOGICAL THRUST CONSIDERED ESSENTIAL TO A NATION'S GROWTH AND PROGRESS IN TODAY'S WORLD.

FLETCHER: :26 Oh, I don't think there's any question about it. We were exposed to a study just today which shows that technology is the life force in this country. That's the thing that moves the country ahead in many hidden ways — this was an economic analysis. This country has got to proceed to a new technology if it wants to progress.

WILLARD: FROM WASHINGTON...DR. JAMES C. FLETCHER, AND COMMENTS ON THE REUSABLE SHUTTLE — SPACE WORKHORSE OF THE FUTURE.

THEME: IN AND UNDER

THIS HAS BEEN THE SPACE STORY, A WEEKLY SPACE AND AERONAUTICS REPORT, BROUGHT TO YOU BY THIS STATION AND NASA, THE NATIONAL AERONAUTICS AND SPACE ADMINISTRATION. WILLARD SCOTT REPORTING.

For television NASA produces two monthly programs; both are entitled "Aeronautics and Space Report." One series runs 4:30; the other, 14:30. The shorter series is a minidocumentary covering subjects such as moon spacewear and microminiaturization for space. The longer series is subtitled "Special Reports" and includes in a December issue a roundup of the past year's highlights in space activities and a preview of things to come. Or the series may include a film on an upcoming moon flight such as that of Apollo 16.

APOLLO 16...MISSION TO THE MOON'S HIGHLANDS

Apollo 16 Rollout    LAUNCH VEHICLE NUMBER 511 IS ALL TOGETHER NOW...12-DAY ROUND-TRIP TRANSPORTATION FOR APOLLO SIXTEEN...THIS COUNTRY'S NEXT FLIGHT TO THE MOON.

| | |
|---|---|
| Quick intercuts of spacecraft assembly mating scenes | IT TOOK FOUR YEARS, TENS OF THOUSANDS OF PEOPLE, AND SIX MILLION PARTS TO BUILD THIS SATURN ROCKET AND APOLLO SPACECRAFT. THESE ARE BUT A FEW OF THE MAJOR STEPS ALONG THE WAY. |
| Cut to three-shot of the Apollo-16 crew | |
| Cut to John Young sync sound | **Young Sync. :34** |
| | I think Apollo 16 has the potential to be the greatest mission yet... |
| | **Sync under narrator** |
| | THIS IS JOHN YOUNG...COMMANDER OF APOLLO 16. FORTY-ONE-YEAR-OLD YOUNG WAS BORN IN SAN FRANCISCO, AND IS A VETERAN OF THREE PREVIOUS GEMINI AND APOLLO SPACEFLIGHTS. |
| Dissolve to GT-10 recovery scenes | |
| Dissolve to Young on camera | **Young Sync Back Up Full** |
| | ...we have a lot of capability to learn a very great many things about the moon and about spaceflight in general. I think it will add to our knowledge, and any time we can take some of the "un" out of the unknown we've done a lot. |
| Cut to Duke on camera sync sound | **Duke Sync. :27** |
| | "There are three geologic units which we hope to sample in our landing area..." |
| | **Sync Under Narrator** |
| | SHARING THE LUNAR SURFACE EXPLORATION CHORES WITH YOUNG WILL BE THIRTY-SIX-YEAR-OLD CHARLES DUKE...A NATIVE OF NORTH CAROLINA. |
| | **Duke Sync. Back Full** |
| | ...one is called the DESCARTES Mountain formation, which makes up the Southern and Central highlands |

356

of the moon. Neither one of these units has been sampled before, and they comprise 11 percent of the front surface of the moon. So they will be two fairly significant samples.

Cut to Mattingly on camera
VO sync

MATTINGLY Sync :28 under Narrator

CHICAGO-BORN KEN MATTINGLY, THIRTY-SIX, IS COMMAND MODULE PILOT FOR APOLLO 16. IT IS MATTINGLY WHO WILL WORK IN ORBIT AROUND THE MOON WHILE YOUNG AND DUKE CARRY OUT THE SURFACE EXPLORATION.

The technique in this film is simply to write the narration as lead-ins for statements by the astronauts participating in the flight.

Dissolve to LRV training

WHAT'S IT LIKE TO DRIVE THE LUNAR ROVER? CHARLES DUKE DESCRIBES IT.

Duke Sync Sound

Duke Sync. :43 VO

Since the rover does not have a steering wheel, we steer and apply throttle through one stick, if you will, that sits between the two crewmen. To go forward, you just tilt the controller forward. To steer right or left, you tilt the controller right or left, and the wheels respond. It is a very sporty little vehicle in steering because with a 4-wheel steering you can turn around 360 degrees within your own radius of the rover. So you get a very tight turn out of it, which is useful for navigating around craters. But at top speed, it makes it a sporty proposition to drive.

Mattingly floats at zero "G"

ASTRONAUT KEN MATTINGLY WILL HANDLE THE ORBITAL SCIENCE AND PHOTOGRAPHY FOR THE APOLLO SIXTEEN FLIGHT.

The conclusion of the film is a montage in which all three astronauts participate.

Montage

THE MEN AND MACHINES THAT WILL MAKE APOLLO SIXTEEN POSSIBLE ARE NEARLY READY, WITH THE LAUNCH NOW SCHEDULED FOR MID-APRIL. AGAIN, THE THREE ASTRONAUT CREWMEN, **AND**, SOME PERSONAL REFLECTIONS.

Continue action

**John Young sync.** :16 **VO**

Super title: Voice of John Young

The knowledge that we gain about the origin and the evolution of the moon, is one of these days going to help us right here on earth. Of course, it's only one area, but I believe it's an important area, and I guess I'm betting a lot on it.

Continue action

**Duke Sync.** :30 **VO**

Super title: Voice of Charles Duke

By us taking these first few small steps into space, we have broken the ground, so to speak, of a new frontier, and much like the old frontier of the west or the challenge of the oceans, from accepting these challenges and going forward, man has benefited from those and history tells me, anyway, that there is no question about benefiting mankind from space.

Continue action

**Mattingly sync.** :47 **VO**

Super title: Voice of Ken Mattingly

I prefer to believe that challenges, things that are stimulating, are the kinds of things that make societies healthy. I think that you cannot retain a healthy society without giving yourself some kind of a challenge to draw the best out of you. I think Apollo, or the space program in general, is a particularly unique opportunity to do this. This is the first highly technically charged scientific adventure ever to be undertaken in peacetime. There are other large efforts. There are other things like medicine that involve people, but never before have we had a chance to draw together so many people, in so many different walks of life, on a common endeavor, and Apollo is surely the epitome of that group action for a peaceful endeavor.

Montage and NASA seal forms

THIS SPECIAL REPORT BROUGHT TO YOU BY NASA, THE NATIONAL AERONAUTICS AND SPACE ADMINISTRATION.

## HEALTH, EDUCATION AND WELFARE

The sprawling agency known as HEW comprises such diverse components as the Office of Education, the Food and Drug Administration, the National Institutes of Health, the Social Security Administration and a host of other satellites. All of the divisions of HEW produce audio-visual programs from radio spot announcements to film documentaries.

An example of a film documentary produced for the Office of Education by Airlie Productions is "A Light for Debra," written by Don Peterson. It concerns a ten-year-old girl who is mentally retarded. This is the teaser opening.

1 YOUNG BLONDE TEACHER WITH CLIPBOARD GREETING LINE OF RETARDED CHILDREN WAITING TO BEGIN DAY'S ACTIVITIES. DEBRA, WHO WILL BECOME THE FOCAL POINT OF MUCH OF OUR FILM, APPROACHES THE TEACHER.

TEACHER (To Debra): "Debbie, what color is your shirt? What did you eat for breakfast, etc."

NARRATOR BEGINS:

2 SAME; CU OF DEBRA TRYING TO RESPOND — DROOLING, LOOKING PATHETIC.

This is the beginning of Debra's day. Like most children, Debra has breakfast...gets dressed...and goes to school.

3 SAME; DEBRA AND ANOTHER CHILD LEARNING TO SET A TABLE. AN INSTRUCTOR WATCHES FROM BACKGROUND; HE

But there the similarity ends. For Debra lives in an institution and she is part of a progressive research program. Much of what she says and does is

359

| | |
|---|---|
| HOLDS A STOPWATCH AND CLIPBOARD. | precisely monitored. Her actions and responses are timed; her behavior documented. |
| LET ACTION PLAY UNTIL NARRATION ENDS. | |
| 4 SAME. INSTRUCTOR CRITIQUES THEIR TABLESETTING PERFORMANCE AND HANDS OUT TOKENS. | INSTRUCTOR SYNC: (to boy) "Very good, you get 4 tokens — and Debra, you were slower — you get one token." |
| 5 SAME. INSTRUCTOR FILLING OUT CLIPBOARD ON DEBRA'S PERFORMANCE. | NARRATOR RESUMES: Debra was born severely retarded — and like many others sharing her condition — suffers from impaired hearing and speech. |
| 6 DEBRA AT TEACHING MACHINE LEARNING NUMBERS. | INSTRUCTOR SYNC: "What number do you see?" DEBRA: "One." INSTRUCTOR: "What number do you see now?" DEBRA: "Two." NARRATOR RESUMES: A few years ago, children like Debra would have been given little hope for improvement. They would have, at best, lived out empty lives in the isolation of a state—or private—institution. |
| 7 PROJECT ROOM WITH DEBRA AND OTHER CHILDREN AT TABLE. ATTRACTIVE WOMAN INSTRUCTOR SEATED BETWEEN DEBRA AND ANOTHER GIRL. | Today, **research**, in a variety of specialized areas, has given Debra and her classmates a chance to develop to their maximum potential — to grow physically, emotionally, and academically. |
| 8 SUPER TITLE OVER APPROPRIATE FREEZE FRAME FROM SCENE 7 — ENSURING THAT DEBRA IS FEATURED IN THE FRAME. | MUSIC UP FOR TITLE. |

"A LIGHT FOR DEBRA"

The script is written basically for an offscreen narrator with interspersed statements by medical practitioners.

| | |
|---|---|
| 18 DEBRA OPERATING PLUNGER MACHINE WHICH REWARDS PROPER RESPONSE WITH CANDY. | NARRATOR: Other researchers investigate the child's **behavioral** characteristics — theorizing that students in any structured program should be grouped according to behavior competence...rather than IQ — sex — or age. |
| | Simple plunger machines are one method behavior researchers are using to measure the child's potential. Response is precisely documented — with solid-state logic eliminating human error or professional prejudice. |
| 19 SAME; COMPUTERIZED MACHINERY DOCUMENTING DEBRA'S RESPONSES — PRINTOUTS, NEEDLES OR PENS MARKING PAPER, FLASHING LIGHTS. INTERCUT WITH SC 18. | |
| 20 SAME; PORTABLE PLUNGER MACHINE IN REC AREA. BOYS IN EARLY TEENS PULL LEVERS TO GET MUSIC. THEY LAUGH, SHAKE, AND SNAP FINGERS TO MUSIC. | This portable plunger machine stationed in the institution's recreation area offers candy...colored slides...and music. The child, through exercising a sustained preference, lets the staff know what kind of reward — or reinforcement — will be most effective in the classroom. |
| | MUSIC UP; (Plunger machine) |
| | A child who prefers music over pictures...or candy...may work better and actually learn more rapidly when music is structured into his training program. |
| 21 TEENAGE BOY LISTENING TO MUSIC OVER SPECIALLY RIGGED SPEAKER. HE SELECTS THE MUSIC OF HIS CHOICE BY KEYING SMALL DEVICE. | Some researchers, in applying this data, refine it further. What **kind** of music does the child like best? This simple device permits the child to select from a variety of music categories. |
| | MUSIC UP, AS BOY MAKES SEVERAL SELECTIONS — USE EXTREME CONTRASTS — ROCK, CLASSICAL, POPULAR VOCAL, ETC. |
| 21 SAME BOY OPERATING MATH TEACHING MACHINE. | Thus, basic behavior research finds full application in a |

MUSIC REWARDS CORRECT RESPONSES. INTERCUT CU'S OF BOY PUSHING BUTTONS — GETTING RIGHT AND WRONG ANSWERS.

structured training program. In this case, music — a specific type of music — becomes the payoff for programmed mathematics instruction. As long as the child answers the questions correctly, the music continues.

Bridging the gap between basic research in the laboratory and practical applications in the classroom is receiving more and more emphasis in the well organized research program.

22 DR. LENT.

DR. LENT SYNC: "I believe that historically we have been most deficient in this respect. The discoveries that we've made, the techniques that we've contributed haven't been really useful to the people who work with children. There are too many gaps between laboratory discovery and classroom usage. We are attempting to rectify this problem by providing the missing steps — the in-between processes. And, in doing this, we are making heavy use of media personnel to arrange the teaching materials in such a way that they will help the children, and that, after all, is our most important job."

Another example of this technique is the concluding segment of the script.

54 84-86. DEBRA OPERATING TEACHING MACHINE OR PLUNGER MACHINE RECEIVING CANDY OR OTHER REWARDS.

ECU BACK OF MACHINE, SHOWING CANDY MOVING ON ENDLESS BELT.

INSERT CUTS OF COMPUTERS, PRINTOUTS, FLASHING LIGHTS, MAG TAPES. THIS MUST GIVE IMPRESSION THAT DEBRA

NARRATOR:

The institution where Debra lives — as well as a few other progressive centers — serves as a living laboratory for research-minded staff members of nearby universities. The institution encourages them to pursue their thinking **inside their walls** — where the retardates live, work, and play...in short, **where the action is!**

IS FOCAL POINT OF RESEARCH — VIRTUALLY "PLUGGED IN"

55 DR. BAKER ON CAMERA.

"Essentially, I came into Farrel Hall looking for a good placement for my Harvard graduate students...a place where they could learn something about mental retardation. And, was immediately struck the first time I came in with the fact that many of the children weren't learning as much as I felt they could be. And this seemed to me, to us, to be a very ideal kind of setting to see how we could change the institution and essentially set up a new kind of institution that would function better for the kids."

56 SIGN "67TH STREET" — THEN CU'S OF CHILDREN WORKING PUZZLES, FORM BOARDS, ETC.

BACK BAKER VOICEOVER: "Project 67 was our first project. We began that in May of 1967 and it took 6 of our worst behavior problem children in the building and moved them into a small structured environment where we concentrated on some of the kinds of things that we thought were getting in the way of learning."

EMPHASIZE CHILDREN RECEIVING REWARDS FOR CORRECT BEHAVIOR.

DR BAKER SYNC: "Since that time, the tenants in the building became very interested in our behavioral techniques which essentially use rewards for the children and asked that we come into the wards and restructure the wards. What's really happening is that we first came into the place expecting to find a place for a couple of student placements out of my course and have now essentially taken over and are running the entire building along behavior modification lines."

57 CUTAWAY FROM DR. BAKER TO SHOW FERNALD RESIDENT MAKING BED UNDER WATCHFUL EYE OF ATTENDANT.

58 ANY CLASS, ANY INSTRUCTOR — SHOWING STUDENT BEING

NARRATOR RESUMES:

This pooling of professional curiosity — innovative thinking

MONITORED AND
RESPONSES DOCUMENTED
ON CLIPBOARD — STOP-
WATCH TIMING, ETC.
REINFORCEMENTS.

59 GIRL STRAPPED INTO
REFLEX-MEASURING
DEVICE.

60 CHILDREN GETTING
DRESSED, OR HELPING IN
THE KITCHEN.

61 ARCHITECTURAL IN-
NOVATION — SHOWING
BRIGHT COLORFUL EN-
CLAVES WITH SEVERAL
RETARDATES ENGAGED IN
ACTIVITIES, SEATED ON
WHITE "DIRECTOR
CHAIRS" — BRIGHTLY
COLORED CANVAS CONES.

62 BOY BEING LIFTED INTO
SPECIAL CHAIR THAT AC-
COMMODATES HIS
DISABILITY

63 OLDER FOLKS IN LARGE
TILE ROOM — ROCKING,
SITTING IDLY, STARING AT
WALLS.

64 MONTAGE OF SCENES
FEATURING HIGHLIGHTS
OF WHAT WE HAVE SEEN SO
FAR — BRIGHT MODERN
"SHOWCASE" SCENES,
ILLUSTRATING MODERN
RESEARCH — FRUITS OF
RESEARCH — CHILDREN
WITH HOPE AND HAP-
PINESS ON THEIR FACES
INTERCUT WITH SHOTS OF
THE CLINICAL LAB — RATS
BEING PLACED IN CIR-
CULAR MODEL — COM-
PUTER TAPES AND

— pure and applied research —
often has impact upon the institution itself. It may con-
tribute to...

...new diagnostic procedures;

...new techniques in managing
the wards and organizing activities; ...

...new concepts in architectural
design
that actually stimulate and
enhance
the retardate's development;

...and new devices that ac-
commodate the handicapped's
disabilities...allowing him to
function more comfortably,
more productively.

Many institutions, until only
recently, based their operation
upon an isolation model —
offering their charges little
more than protective custody —
and, of course, some still do! In
practical terms, this means a
lifetime of staring at tile walls
from the vantage point of a
state-procured rocking chair.

Today, through research on
many fronts — basic and applied — this pattern is slowly
changing. Old barriers are
coming down. Hope is replacing
despair.

And, the focal point of all the
dedication and the energy is
Debra — a human being whose
horizons were once tragically
limited — but who now faces a
future in which research is
gradually pushing back the
darkness...and, for the first

FLASHING LIGHTS —
CHILDREN GETTING OUT
OF WHEELCHAIRS AND
ATTEMPTING TO WALK.

END FILM ON APPEALING
ECU OF DEBRA ENGAGED
IN ANY ACTIVITY—
R E S P O N D I N G    T O
TEACHER—PUTTING
TOKENS IN POCKET, ETC.

SUPER END TITLES OVER
KEY SCENES FROM FILM.

time, is revealing the pathway
ahead.

There are many other federal agencies which offer opportunities to writers in the audio-visual media. One of the newest agencies, the Environmental Protection Agency, contracts for many films to demonstrate what is being done now and what is being planned for the future in combatting pollution in all its aspects. The Department of Housing and Urban Development is also active in the audio-visual field. The Treasury Department has its continuing campaign for U.S. Savings Bonds. The Veterans Administration prepares a series of radio spots to reach all veterans concerning benefits available to them.

Agencies, such as the Department of Commerce, Labor, Interior, are generally print oriented and their audio-visual output is comparatively little. This is true also of the smaller agencies. Often, it is a matter of budget; films are very costly to produce.

Obviously, there are many opportunities for writers with the federal government either as information specialists under civil service or as free-lancers for film or radio production agencies which have government contracts.

# Chapter 13

## Public Broadcasting

This chapter is a very brief overview of what was until recently known as educational television and radio. However, we feel that a concise summation of noncommercial broadcasting and the role of the writer may prove useful.

We now use the qualifier "public" which perhaps more accurately describes these noncommercial stations. The connotation of education to many people is a formalized learning process. Programs on public television and radio stations may be classified as educational in the broadest sense, but they may be entertaining also. Public broadcasting stations spend a good part of their daytime hours in purely instructional activities geared to actual classroom requirements. In fact, the noncommercial stations play a dual role: instructional programming in coordination with school systems and public programming for a varied juvenile and adult audience.

We know that advertising pays the bills for commercial broadcasting. Where, then, does the money come from for noncommercial stations? Broadcasting magazine offered the following breakdown of sources of income for public broadcasting during 1970: $30 million from state governments or boards of education; $20 million from local sources including schools and various boards of education; $10 million from state universities and colleges; $8 million from intraindustry, including the Corporation for Public Broadcasting; $5 million from the federal government; $8.5 million from national foundations, primarily the Ford Foundation; $8.8 million from subscribers, individuals and industry. There are other sources which brought the total to above $100 million for that year.

In October 1970, National Educational Television (NET) and Channel 13 in New York City (WNET) merged into the Educational Broadcasting Corporation. From 1953 on, NET has been the principal producer of outstanding cultural, public affairs, science and children's programs for the national chain of public television stations. Its programs, such as "The Great American Dream Machine," "Black Journal," "NET Playhouse," "Soul!", and "NET Opera Theater," have won national and international awards. NET has been responsible for bringing important dramas to the public airwaves including Clifford Odets' "Paradise Lost" and Arthur Miller's "A Memory of Two Mondays."

National program production is underwritten jointly by the Ford Foundation and the quasi-governmental Corporation for Public Broadcasting. The latter was authorized by congress in the Public Broadcasting Act of 1967 to "Promote the growth and development of the nation's public television and radio systems." CPB does not produce programs but provides grants to production centers. Its funds come from the federal government and private sources. Its board is appointed by the President with the advice and consent of the senate.

The CPB finances National Public Radio (NPR), the noncommercial radio network which went on the air April 20, 1971. Donald Quayle, NPR president, set forth its goals: "In its cultural mode, NPR will preserve and transmit the cultural past while encouraging and broadcasting the work of contemporary artists, to provide listeners with an aural esthetic experience to enrich and give meaning to the human spirit. In its journalistic mode, NPR will actively explore, investigate and attempt to interpret issues of national and international import. In this way we hope to enable the individual to better understand himself, his government, his institutions, and his natural and social environment."

NPR's initial series was a weekly hour-and-a-half audio magazine called "All Things Considered..." NPR microphones have become a regular fixture at the National Press Club, bringing to the radio network the complete statements of some of the world's most prominent newsmakers.

The CPB believes that public broadcasting has an obligation to experiment and innovate; therefore, it supported the National Center for Experiments in Television at KQED, San Francisco, and the National Center for Audio Experimentation at WHA, Madison, Wisconsin. The TV Center's work includes research on imminent technological changes such as home playback devices and on the psychological, educational and behavioral effects of television. The operations of the Audio Center resemble that of its video counterpart, but carry a greater emphasis on applied, as opposed to theoretical, research. A major focus has been on increasing the use of "binaural" sound, a method of recording that stimulates reception of sound by both ears and has the effect of putting the listener in the midst of an event. Using this technique, the Center produced six radio dramas and a series of "eco-dramas." miniplays with environmental themes. A number of the latter were aired through National Public Radio. In addition, the Center has experimented with "compressed" sound and has been active in encouraging writers to utilize the new techniques to new effect. Because of the excellent productions presented by NET and the establishment of CPB, public broadcasting has taken a monumental upward surge and it has offered American viewers a choice. As Terence O'Flaherty, television critic of the San Francisco Chronicle, pointed out in an article for American Education (PBS—The Cinderella Network"), public broadcasting offers "the only regularly scheduled dramatic series on the air, the only grand opera program on TV, the only book series, the only program devoted to international opinion, the only regular series devoted to rock music, the only regular network programs aimed at the black audience, and the only series devoted to experimental filmmakers."

It is obvious that public broadcasting is essential to a viable future for our most important medium of communication. Les Brown in "Television" (Harcourt Brace Jovanovich, Inc.) suggests that "PBS become a full-fledged noncommercial correlative of the commercial networks — a head-on competitor without the cash motive. I am not recommending that it join the Philistines, only that it give commercial TV a run for its influence on society."

With more than 200 TV stations and over 500 radio stations and more in the offing, public broadcasting is reaching an even greater share of the American audience. It is hampered because many of its TV stations are UHF and a good percentage of its radio stations are low-powered. If public broadcasting is to reach an equivalent status with England's BBC, obviously the Corporation for Public Broadcasting will require a substantial budget and greater autonomy. It will need to provide funds for both the creative and technological improvement of public broadcasting stations. Public programming must be of the highest quality or it will not attract audiences no matter how specialized. Very few viewers or listeners will excuse amateur programming on public broadcasting because the stations plead poverty. It is much too simple to turn the dial. The hard facts are that television productions are extremely costly. The Children's Television Workshop requires an eight million dollar annual budget to maintain the quality of its programs.

NPACT

In July 1971, the National Public Affairs Center for Television was created as the primary national producer of

368

news and public affairs programs for noncommercial TV stations. The Center, based in Washington, D.C., has produced three major weekly series: "A Public Affair — Election '72," offering a comprehensive look at the political process during a presidential year; "Thirty Minutes With..." featuring Elizabeth Drew, Washington editor of Atlantic Monthly, interviewing noted newsmakers; "Washington Week in Review" with moderator Robert MacNeil, a panel of four Washington correspondents and a guest reporter analyzing the major news events of the week.

## INSTRUCTIONAL BROADCASTING

The wealth of first-rate programming from network sources has been of inestimable value in improving the service of noncommercial radio and television stations to their respective publics. On their part, individual stations and state networks are constantly improving their transmissions. The Kentucky Educational Television Network (KET), for example, offers a "range of programs uniquely aimed at that state's viewers, working closely with other state agencies." KET has the largest closed-circuit two-way TV system in the country for a state educational television network, and its executive director, O. Leonard Press, is striving to make it the best. The network provides programs in the classroom for almost 500,000 of the Commonwealth's 700,000 public school students.

More than 30 hours of regular college instruction each week are fed to Kentucky's community colleges by closed circuit. Courses such as "The Revival of the Two-Party System" were seen by college students across the state. One of the most effective and popular series presented by KET is devoted to Kentucky's history. "The Hills Resound" portrays the folk music of the state. A few excerpts will illustrate the production and writing technique of this informative and entertaining program.

FILM: SUPER TITLES OVER SHOTS OF MOUNTAINS, TREES                    :20

SONG: "Come My Little Roving Sailor" (Merle and guitar or banjo; melody only BG, very hauntingly; (music prerecorded)

(DISS)

MERLE SINGS: (Verses 1 & 2) "Madam, I have gold and silver, Madam, I have house and land,

|  | |
|---|---|
| :20 | Madam, I have a world treasure, All shall be at your comman |
| :20 | Madam, do not stand on beaut Beauty is a fading flower; The reddest rose in yond garden Will fade away in half an hour (Cont'd. melody under NARR |

MERLE:

(VO except where noted)

| FILM: SUSTAIN FOOTAGE OF MOUNTAINS, OLD CABIN :20 | Music is people. The hills a valleys of Kentucky ha resounded with the distincti songs of a hardy folk for ov three centuries. |
|---|---|
| FILM: PAN TO MS MERLE ON LOCATION IN WILDERNESS, RED RIVER GORGE :20 | The music of Kentucky drawn from the sinews of pioneer people and their cient heritage. From beginning, music has been bright thread, spun through homespun fabric of their liv What is their music? They ha |
| :25 | sung tales of all the basics existence — of birth and dea of love and hate, of courting betrayal, of battles loneliness, of sorrows and f of work and loss. |

(DISS)

MERLE:

| FILM: MONTAGE OF MUSICIANS FROM GREENUP FESTIVAL, RENFRO VALLEY | Youthful or aged, wealthy poverty stricken, educated without learning, Kentucki have been true troubado preserving and crafting music of their lives in a mele fever. Where did their m come from? (Music Out) |
|---|---|
| (BLACK) :01 | |
| :23 FILM: PICS — PIONEERS, EXPLORERS, HUNTERS, EARLY KENTUCKY | (Up Music) Dan & Lo Brock — with J.DCrowe SONG: "The Cumberl Gap" (very upbeat) |

MERLE: (Melody BG)

With their truck lashed to wagons or longboats, these early Anglo Saxon minstrels trudged through the gaps from Virginia or poled downriver in rafts and longboats on the waters of the Ohio.

FILM: HORSE FARMS, TOBACCO, OLD KY. HOME, ETC.

SONG: BG "Old Kentucky Home"

MERLE: Voice Over Music

:40

Finally the Bluegrass regained its bloom and Kentucky prospered in its fame for good tobacco, sippin' whiskey, fast horses, lovely women, and plaintive music. Even Stephen Foster gave the state a song.

(Music Out)

4:00

SONG: "Dark As A Dungeon" — Merle first few bars thru MERLE BG, melody only

MERLE: (SOF)

FILM:

In the name of progress, the roads pushed further into the hollers, and coal mines slashed across the green mountains. The land and its people endured a new kind of ravishment.

(DISS)

FILM: MS MERLE, LOCATION OLD MINE TIPPLE, JACKSON COUNTY

FILM: VARIOUS SHOTS OF OLD MINE TIPPLE, MINERS

And still the people sang, their voices telling new tales in a new way. They sang of moonshining and feuding and hard times and high passions. There were young voices now, raised in protest. (MERLE SINGS)

"Come all ye young fellows so young and so fine
And seek not your fortune in a dark, dreary mine;
It blackens your faces and darkens your soul

**371**

| | Till the blood in your veins runs as black as the coal." |
|---|---|
| VTR: VARIOUS SHORT SEGMENTS FROM GREENUP FESTIVAL, CONTEMPORARY SOUNDS | MERLE: VOICE OVER BG — SOF (DIRECT EDITS) |
| | The new sound now echoes the old folk ballads as the people still sing on of their lives and times. |
| 3:00 | SONGS AND MUSIC IN QUICK INTERMINGLED SEGUES: BILLY WILLIAMS, EN- TERTAINMENT COM- MITTEE, LEE PENNINGTON |
| VTR: OLD FIDDLE PLAYER (DOC WHITE) 1:18 | MERLE: (Voice over second verse below): What do all these songs mean? That music is people and that folk is the music of the people giving music back to the people. And that is the sound of KENTUCKY. |
| SUPER CREDITS | |

Not all subjects lend themselves to the inherently interesting treatment of "The Hills Resound." KET has to tackle such prosaic subjects as informing teachers of the necessity for properly filling out professional staff data forms. The script assignment was undertaken by staff writer Ann Hebson who wisely decided on a light motif for so ponderous a subject. The title itself is a play on words: "Filling Out Your Form." This excerpt illustrates the approach.

| SANDY'S HANDS PICK UP PENCIL — CU LABEL "NO. 2" PENCIL | |
|---|---|
| CU OF SANDY TURNING PENCIL TO SHOW LABEL | SANDY: (She looks very neat and crisp at first and then becomes increasingly frazzled — till hair is twisted, shirt collar open, etc. — shoes off) |
| SHOW STAFF DATA FORM | Well, it's time to fill out our staff data forms again. First of all, a regular Number 2 soft lead pencil is a necessity because all these forms will be processed by an optical scanner. I cannot use a ballpoint, or a pen, or a colored |
| SHOW NUMERAL GUIDE CU ON FORM WITH SANDY'S PENCIL POINTING AT IT | pencil. This also stresses the fact that the numerals must be formed exactly as shown by the guide on the form. |

| MCU OF SANDY SITTING DOWN TO DESK, LOOKING STUDIOUS | Since Kentucky is pioneering a first in compiling all its professional data, I want to make sure I do it right — so I'd better carefully check the in- |
|---|---|

MCU OF SANDY SITTING DOWN TO DESK, LOOKING STUDIOUS

TURN FORM OVER TO SHOW INSTRUCTION

SHEET CU — CU OF PARTS I, II, AND III WITH SANDY'S PENCIL POISED AT EACH IN TURN

SHOW SANDY'S HANDS CORRECTING MISTAKE PROPERLY

Since Kentucky is pioneering a first in compiling all its professional data, I want to make sure I do it right — so I'd better carefully check the in- struction sheet on the back of the form first. Since Parts I, II, and III are already preprinted, I need to check them only for accuracy. So I'll check the school district number and name, and the school number and name in Part I. They're okay. My social security number is correct in Part II. Oops, they misspelled my name in Part III, so I'll correct it on the second line.

WETA in Washington, D.C. is, naturally enough, the origination point for many of the NPACT programs. But as an individual station, it presents instructional programs to the schools in the metropolitan area. An enrichment type of program for primary literature is "Celebrate a Book." The objectives of each program are outlined as a preface to each script.

CELEBRATE A BOOK
BIOGRAPHIES (PEOPLE BEHIND THEIR FACES IV)
PRIMARY LITERATURE
BRENDA HOLMES

Nonbehavioral Objectives

—to get the students to read the books presented
—to introduce the concept of "biography"
—to introduce the image of people succeeding in spite of difficulties
—to slightly introduce methods of communication used by deaf, dumb and blind
—to impress upon their minds that there are lots of biographies they can choose from and read.

Behavioral Objectives

After viewing the television lesson:

—the student should read one or more of the books presented or others in the same category.
—the student should be able to identify what a biography is.
—the student should be able to express what is meant by

people accomplishing goals or things in spite of difficulties or problems.

—the student should be able to express (in some creative way) one or more of the ways Laura learned to communicate.

The script itself combines narration and dialog. The visuals are simple. The language of the script is readily comprehensible for primary grades, but there is never any "talking down." These excerpts will show how the program handles a learning experience in an informative and palatable manner.

| VIDEO | AUDIO |
|---|---|
| CAMERA IN ON BRENDA AND HUGO, AT TRUNK, WORKING WITH CHEMISTRY SET. | |
| BRENDA LOOKS AT CAMERA | BRENDA: HELLO! Excuse us for being so busy, but Hugo and I are trying to be scientists today, aren't we, Hugo? |
| HUGO NODS; SUDDENLY THERE IS A SMALL PUFF OF SMOKE, AND THEY BOTH JUMP | Oh dear! I guess we aren't such good scientists, Hugo. |
| HUGO IS TREMBLING | You look all shaken up. |
| HUGO NODS | Why don't you go lie down for awhile. |
| HUGO NODS, WAVES TO CAMERA | You really have to be very careful when you're conducting scientific experiments—there are so many things that can go wrong. But science has always interested me (she laughs) even if I'm not very good at it. But I know there are lots of people who are. Here, wait! |
| SHE CROSSES TO BOOKSHELF | Here's a book about a man who was a famous doctor and conducted many experiments. His name was Charles Drew, and he lived right here in Washington about 40 years ago. This book is a special type of book called a biography—which is the story of a man or woman who actually lived. A biography |

| | |
|---|---|
| IN ATTIC: (ACTION TO SUIT DIALOG) | is a book an author writes about someone else's life. If someone writes a story about his own life, that's called an autobiography. But this book, **Charles Drew** by Roland Bertol, is a biography. |
| PULLS MICROSCOPE TOWARDS HER | Do you know what this is? It's called a microscope, and when you look at things through this tube with a series of lenses inside, the things you see through the tube are magnified to thousands of times their original size. Dr. Drew worked with this microscope because he was working on the problem of preserving blood for transfusions (blood spoils just like food if it's not properly stored). But Dr. Drew had another problem, a problem that made it hard for him to get into medical school, and meant that he made lots of enemies because he was strong enough to stand up for what he believed in. He was a black man, and back in the 1920s, it was even more difficult for a black man or woman to get certain opportunities than it is today. |
| IN ATTIC: (ACTION TO SUIT DIALOG) | GEORGE: Hi, Brenda, this is **(name)**<br><br>BRENDA: (to camera) This is my friend, George, and his friend **(name)** |
| HANDS HER A BOOK | GEORGE: I brought you something, Brenda. |
| | BRENDA: **Child of the Silent Night,** by Edith Fisher Hunter. What's this book about? |
| | CHILD: It's a biography. |
| | BRENDA: No kidding! |
| | CHILD: Yeah, it's about a little girl, Laura Bridgman, who was deaf and dumb and blind. She couldn't hear or talk or see. |

GEORGE: But she learned words, she learned how to read using braille or raised letters, and she learned how to talk, using sign language, or what is called the manual alphabet.

BRENDA: My goodness! How did she learn that?

CHILD: George and I will show you, okay?

BRENDA: Okay!

GEORGE TAKES OUT A BLINDFOLD AND EAR PLUGS, PUTS THEM ON CHILD

PUTS HAND OVER MOUTH

CHILD: Now I can't hear or see—and I'll pretend I can't talk.

TAKES KEY FROM POCKET

TAKES SPOON FROM POCKET

GEORGE: Laura's doctor, Dr. Howe, took things that Laura knew, like a key and a spoon and put raised letters on them that spelled out their names. Then he had Laura feel the letters and the things the letters splled and after awhile, she started to understand that those letters spelled the names of things.

GUIDING CHILD'S FINGERS

CHILD REACHES FOR A BOOK, PICKS UP LETTERS GEORGE HAS BROUGHT AND SPELLS OUT B-O-O-K

BRENDA: Why don't you read about Laura Bridgman, too? Now we've seen two biographies where real people who had problems managed to do things in spite of them. Here, let me show you some other biographies you can read.

CAMERA PANS ALONG BOOKS SET UP ON SHELF AS IN DISPLAY.

There's a book about Benjamin Franklin, one about George Washington Carver, a little pioneer girl, Sarah Noble, Henry Morgan, a pirate and lots of others.

IN ATTIC: (ACTION TO SUIT DIALOG)

GEORGE: Brenda, I want to teach you something.

CHILD: No, let me!

GEORGE: Okay.

(CHILD and BRENDA spell)

GEORGE: Now, let's all do it together!
(They do)

BRENDA: What are we saying?

GEORGE AND CHILD: Goodbye!

BRENDA: Okay (laughing) Goodbye (they wave). See you next week.

(Ad-libs and spelling through credits)

Another type of program presented by WETA is "From Nine to Five," a series designed for use by employers to upgrade the skills of office personnel. Typical of the series is this episode depicting the many roles of the secretary. At the opening, the "hostess" defines the many kinds of secretaries.

HOSTESS: (AT HOME BASE) We hear many people talking about many kinds of secretaries, private secretaries, secretary-girl Friday, secretary assistant, pool secretary, secretary-typist...there are almost as many names and descriptions as there are secretaries. Maybe it's important to define just what it is we're talking about when we say secretary. For our purposes, the word secretary is a generic term. It means all types of people, male or female, who comprise the office team, from the file clerk, typist, office machine operator to the stenographer-transcriber or private secretary. All of the people who handle and are responsible for the routine and efficiency of the office and whose collective personalities and behavior make up the office personality that is so obvious to the people who work in the office and even more so to those who have casual or frequent contact with the office.

The "hostess" elaborates on the various parts the secretary must play.

VIGNETTE SERIES (ROLES OF SECRETARIES)

HOSTESS: VO

MEMORY EXPERT: First thing in the morning she's a memory expert...organizing all the appointments for the day, we well as the work that has to be completed...this morning ...later in the day. Then there's the followup correspondence and the telephone messages remaining from yesterday.....

TEACHER: Then there's the new employee...she has to be taught how she fits into the office routine...what her duties and resonsibilities are, where she will find the things and information that she'll need...and of course there's the office procedure to be learned.

AUTHOR: Correspondence is always a time-consuming job...and frequently she's the author of the letter, confirmations, reservations, arrangements, invitations....

In addition, the secretary is also linguist, psychologist, editor and public relations specialist. And she faces recurring office crises, as this sequence shows.

ESTABLISH THAT IT'S ALMOST QUITTING TIME. BOSS GIVES JOBS TO SECRETARY...AND SUPERVISOR GIVES SOME TO OTHER GIRLS (TWO) IN OFFICE AND ALL BEGIN HARD AND FEVERISH

BOSS: (To SECRETARY) Sorry to give you this so late in the day, but it's a rush job and it just reached my desk...(GIVES HER SEVERAL PILES OF PAPER AS HE ISSUES INSTRUCTIONS) This has to be proofed and each page that has corrections must be redone and

WORK. CLOCK SHOWS OVERTIME

five copies of the whole package made. This is the record section and has to be brought up to date as of last Friday. This part has been edited and several parts are being deleted. You can retype the corrected pages and fit it all together. I need the whole thing for a meeting at 9:00 tomorrow morning. I'll be here if you need me. .....and thanks very much...

SECRETARY LOOKS AT CLOCK...SUPERVISOR LOOKS AT CLOCK AND THEY LOOK AT ONE ANOTHER... THEN SMILE AND SEPARATE...SECRETARY SITS AT HER DESK AND BEGINS TO WORK...

To add realism, filmed interviews are held with actual secretaries and, at the conclusion, the "hostess" sums up the secretary's place in industry.

FILMED INTERVIEW WITH TWO SECRETARIES TO WELL KNOWN MEN. FILM SHOULD BE SHOT IN CASUAL WAY WITH WOMEN RESPONDING TO OPEN-END QUESTIONS. QUESTIONS SHOULD BE EDITED OUT AND TWO INTERVIEWS INTERCUT. SOME QUESTIONS:

How does your day begin?
What's the first thing the senator asks for in the morning?
Why do you feel your job is interesting? Unusual? Not unusual?
What happens when you goof?
What kinds of deadlines do you work to?

STATEMENTS WILL HOPEFULLY EXPRESS INITIATIVE, TACT, THOUGHTFULNESS, KNOWLEDGE OF HERSELF, READINESS TO SERVE, SELFLESSNESS.....

HOSTESS: SUMMARY: For a long time women had no place in business at all...and it took a long time for them to earn the right just to be in the office. Once in, their value was not to be denied and the busy businessmen soon found that, in terms of office efficiency and business profits, the ladies were nice to have around. The secretary, by proving that she could play a variety of roles in the office, proved also that she was not expendable. By perfecting her skills and by taking a vital interest in the work of the office, she earned professional rank. Historically, that's what has happened. You are not history, but you're part of it and right now, at this point in time and at this point in your career, is the best possible time to ask yourself a few extremely pertinent questions:

Where are you now? Professionally that is.
Where do you want to go?
What do you need to get there?

There's an old joke about the man who stopped out in the country to ask directions of a farmer. The farmer heard him out, then said, "You can't get there from here." Well, you can get there from here, anywhere there is...but you have to know where you're going....and what it'll take to get there.

We have merely touched the surface of public and instructional broadcasting. To cover the subject adequately would require a book in itself and there is already a vast body of literature available. The principles of writing we have enunciated in previous chapters should serve as guidelines for writers in public broadcasting. They will find themselves somewhat handicapped by small budgets at individual stations, but this may prove a spur to their imagination, for they will have more opportunity to experiment at a noncommercial station. As William H. Siemering summed it up (**Educational/Instructional Broadcasting**, Nov. 1969): "If we are to be true to our name and high hopes, we must provide a program service meeting human needs: esthetic, intellectual and effective. Rather than a mass medium which tries to unite us in a common banality, public broadcasting must unite us in our common humanity."

# Chapter 14

## Copyrights And Markets

The Library of Congress defines a copyright as "a form of protection given by the law of the United States (Title 17, U.S. Code) to the authors of literary, dramatic, musical, artistic, and other intellectual works." The owner of a copyright is granted by law certain exclusive rights in his work including:

(1) The right to print, reprint and copy the work.

(2) The right to sell or distribute copies of the work.

(3) The right to transform or revise the work by means of dramatization, translation, musical arrangement or the like.

(4) The right to perform and record the work.

Published or unpublished dramatic works such as the acting versions of plays for the stage, for filming, radio, television, and the like, as well as pantomines, ballets, operas and operettas, can be copyrighted. Also, published or unpublished motion pictures that are dramatic in character such as feature films, filmed or recorded television plays, short subjects and animated cartoons, musical plays, and similar productions having a plot may be copyrighted. And copyrights may be obtained for published or unpublished nondramatic motion pictures: newsreels, travelogs, training or promotional films, nature studies, and filmed or recorded television programs having no plot.

Titles, names or slogans cannot be copyrighted. However, the title of a program can be protected by registering it as a trademark with the U.S. Patent Office. It is also possible to obtain protection by continual use of the title which identifies it with a program.

Applications for copyrights may be obtained by writing to the Copyright Office, The Library of Congress, Washington, D.C. 20540. The fee is $6.00 for each work. The copyright is good for 28 years with one renewal. Renewals are not automatic and the copyright will lapse after 28 years if the author or his assignee does not renew. The renewal fee is $4.00

Works copyrighted by U.S. citizens can receive protection in all countries that are parties to the Universal Copyright Convention. However, you should be aware that copyright legislation has been pending for some time in the congress and new regulations may be resolved after publication of this text.

How necessary is it for beginning writers to copyright their unpublished scripts? If you were writing a play for the legitimate stage, it would be essential. However, there is little need for copyrighting a television or radio drama. In the first place, very few, if any, TV producing organizations will accept an unsolicited manuscript unless it comes from an agent. Therefore, the writer will have to find an agent first and the correspondence between yourself and the agent and the potential producer may furnish some concrete evidence or prior claims.

Scripts may also be registered with the Writer's Guild of America, East, 1212 Avenue of the Americas, New York, New York 10036 or Writer's Guild of America, West, 8955 Beverly Boulevard, Los Angeles, California 90048. Write to either of those addresses for information.

If you have an idea for a series, you certainly do want to protect it. Ideas, per se, cannot be copyrighted. Nevertheless, you can protect the idea by writing an outline of it and mailing a copy to yourself, registered. The postal stamp on the flap of the envelope will establish the date. It is important that the envelope remain sealed. Therefore, you ought to write the title of the idea on the envelope so you will know what it contains. After working on several ideas and finding that very much time elapses between conception and inception, you will find this simple instruction invaluable.

If you have ever had any dealings with the law, then you must be aware of all the ifs, ands, buts, whereases and wherefores. For a thorough clarification of your literary rights we recommend you read Philip Wittenberg's "The Protection of Literary Property" (The Writer, Inc.).

## Markets

We will have to confine this section to a general purview of the television and radio markets for free-lance writers. When we speak of markets, we are referring mainly to dramatic scripts. Documentaries, news, commercials are written either on assignment or by staff writers.

To be specific about individual programs is not very feasible because by the time you may be reading this book, the program in question may no longer be on the air. It will be necessary for you to watch your current program schedules, especially at the beginning of the fall season. If you are interested in a particular type of program: situation comedy, western, mystery, science fiction, then make note of the ongoing characters, because scripts must be tailored to their specifications. If you have an idea for a series, you will need to write a sample episode plus several outlines of additional episodes. All your television scripts, as we mentioned previously, will have to be submitted through an agent. You can obtain a list of agents from the **Literary Marketplace**, which is available in most libraries. Or a good list of TV agents may be obtained by writing to the **Writer's Digest.**

Magazines like the **Writer's Digest** and **The Writer** are helpful in keeping up with current market availabilities. Other sources are the trade publications: **Variety** and **TV Guide.** These publications are also useful to the beginning writer in listing open contests. The contests may be few, but they are of great value in that a free-lance writer may submit a script without having to go through an agent, and some of the prizes are substantial. WBAL-TV in Baltimore sponsored a TV script contest for which the first prize was $3000. EARPLAY, Radio Hall, Madison, Wisconsin, received a grant from the Corporation for Public Broadcasting for purchase awards of 20 scripts each year during the life of the grant. There are also to be five awards of $1000 each and five at $500 each in open competition for radio scripts of 15 minutes or less and an identical set of awards for scripts 30 minutes or less. Hopefully, this will be a continuing project and, therefore, an excellent market for literary radio dramas.

The Cooperative Broadcast Ministry of Connecticut sponsors an annual competition for TV plays of 20 to 25 minutes illustrating themes and issues of concern to the contemporary church. Plays must be suitable to in-studio video-tape production on the local level. Detailed information on prizes and deadline for submissions may be obtained by writing to Religious Video-Drama Competition, 120 Sigourney Street, Hartford, Connecticut 06105.

Undoubtedly, other competitions are or will be available over the years, and if you intend to become a free-lance playwright, it will be advisable for you to search all sources for these opportunities.

# Assignments

## The Documentary

1. Write a treatment for a proposed documentary film on a social problem of national significance.

2. Write a half-hour TV documentary on local pollution problems; use inserts of imaginary interviews with public officials.

3. You are assigned to produce and write a series of radio documentaries on local historic sites; write one half-hour episode.

4. Study one of the documentary programs on TV; write a critical analysis of the program.

5. Write an hour TV informational documentary on either a scientific or medical development.

6. Prepare a scene-by-scene synopsis for an hour TV documentary on natural disasters: hurricanes, floods, earthquakes.

7. Your local TV station is honoring its hometown astronaut by producing a series of half-hour documentaries on the moon landings. Write the first episode, which is a biography of the imaginary astronaut.

## The Drama

1. Develop a scene-by-scene outline for an hour TV drama.

2. Write a 2-page biography of the protagonist of your proposed TV drama.

3. Write a 4-minute teaser for your TV drama.

4. Develop a sequence in your TV drama which requires the use of the flashback; write the scene.

5. Watch a TV drama, preferably in an anthology series, and write a constructive criticism of the play, including development of characters, impact of dialog, plot construction.

6. Write the plot outline for an hour TV western or crime or adventure play.

7. Develop characters for a half-hour TV situation comedy series and write brief biographical sketches of the main characters.

8. Write a half-hour religious drama based on a Biblical theme or contemporary mores.

9. Write a half-hour radio drama based on a problem of civil rights.

10. Choose a short story of your liking and adapt it for an hour TV drama.

## Children's Programs

1. Watch several programs for children on TV; write a critique of the programs with particular emphasis on the extent of violence, if any.

2. After your evaluation of children's programs currently on the air, develop an outline for what you would consider an effective series.

3. Write a half-hour historical TV drama for a juvenile audience patterned after the "You Are There" technique.

4. Develop several synopses for a "how-to" series for youngsters; e.g., "How to Keep Healthy," "How to be a Good Swimmer," "How to Make the Most of Your Library."

5. Write a half-hour TV documentary on a topic that would be of interest to elementary school children.

## News

1. Using the front page of a daily newspaper, rewrite the copy for a 5-minute radio newscast.

2. Rewrite the same copy for a 15-minute TV newscast.

3. Write a one-minute editorial on a local problem.

4. You are a reporter-writer for a local radio station; write a 5-minute newscast on community events.

5. Write a 3-minute commentary on a subject of national import.

## Commercials

1. Write a one-minute **dialog** radio commercial for a national account.

2. Convert the above copy into a TV commercial.

3. Create a slogan or catch phrase for an actual or imaginary product.

4. Create a jingle for a soft drink bottling company.

5. Write a monolog commercial for radio: (a) 20 seconds (b) 10 seconds.

6. Lay out a storyboard for a TV commercial planning a full-scale production.

7. Write a TV testimonial commercial for voicing by an actual or imaginary screen star.

8. Write a one-minute radio institutional commercial for a public utility.

9. Write a TV commercial for demonstrating a home appliance.

10. Write a multivoiced radio commercial for an automobile manufacturer making full use of sound and music.

### Public Service Announcements

1. A local civic organization is sponsoring a book fair; write a 30-second radio announcement.

2. The United Givers Fund is running its annual campaign; prepare a one-minute TV announcement asking for contributions.

3. There is a shortage of nurses in your state hospitals; write a one-minute radio announcement stressing the need.

4. Lay out a storyboard for a one-minute production spot for the cancer campaign.

5. Create a one-minute TV spot underlining the dangers of drug abuse.

# Glossary

**ACROSS-THE-BOARD:** A program which is scheduled daily at the same time.

**AD-LIB:** Speaking without script; improvising speech.

**ANIMATION:** Creating an illusion of movement usually with cartoon figures.

**ANSWER PRINT:** A composite print of a film; generally the final form in which the film will be released.

**ATMOSPHERE:** In radio, the background sounds of an event; in TV, shots to create a mood.

**AUDIO:** The sound part of a TV program.

**BACKGROUND:** In radio, sound effects or music. In TV, the rear portion of a set.

**BILLBOARD:** Opening or closing credits of talent involved in the program.

**BOOM:** A metal arm used for suspending a microphone or a camera in midair.

**BREAK:** Commercial insertion in a program.

**BRIDGE:** A transitional device.

**BUSINESS:** Stage action such as answering a telephone.

**CAMERA ANGLE:** Placement of the camera for a specific shot.

**CAMERA CHAIN:** Refers to the camera's power supply, video controls and cables.

**CLOSED CIRCUIT:** Radio or TV transmission within a confined area to a limited number of receivers.

**CLOSEUP:** A camera shot taken very close to an object or an individual; a big closeup may detail a single feature of the individual or the object.

**COLD:** Beginning a program without an introduction.

**CONTINUITY:** The written part of a program, particularly referring to nondramatic programs.

**CRAWL:** A scroll moving horizontally or vertically and containing program credits; generally used at the conclusion of a program.

**CREDITS:** Names of the personnel involved in the production of a program.

**CROSSFADE:** In radio: fading out dialog, sound, or music while fading in other sound, music, or dialog.

**CUE:** Narration, dialog, music, or sound effect which calls for response.

**CUE CARD:** A prompting card, off camera, to assist a performer.

**CUT:** (1) To stop action; (2) to switch instantaneously from one camera to another; (3) to delete a line or a scene of a script.

**CYCLORAMA:** A curved curtain or screen used as a background for a TV setting.

**DIALOG:** Conversation between characters.

**DIORAMA:** A miniature scene wholly or partially 3-dimensional.

**DISSOLVE:** Fade out of one picture and fade in of another; lap dissolve: a slow dissolve.

**DOLLY:** A trolley on which a camera is set, permitting it to be mobile; to "dolly in" means to move the camera forward; "dolly out," to move back.

**DRY RUN:** Rehearsal prior to production.

**DUB:** A copy made from a master tape, video or audio.

**ESTABLISHING SHOT:** Usually a long shot at the opening of a program to picture the locale.

**EXPOSITION:** Explanation of details essential to the progression of a program, generally accomplished through dialog or narration.

**EXTERIOR:** An outdoor set.

**FADE IN:** Audio: gradual increase in volume of sound, voice, or music; video: picture appearing on screen from black.

**FADE OUT:** Audio: gradual decrease in volume of sound, voice or music; video: picture slowly going to black (fade to black).

**FILTER:** Lens screen to reduce intensity of light.

**FILTER MIKE:** Microphone to achieve special noise effects.

**FLASHBACK:** Device for recreating scenes from the past.

**FLUFF:** An error.

**FOOTAGE:** Length of a part of film.

**FRAME:** Single rectangle of film; one 24th of a second.

**FREEZE FRAME:** Continuous reprinting of single frame to give the illusion of stopped motion.

**GAIN:** Increase in power of a signal in an amplifying system.

**GIMMICK:** A device; an idea.

**GOBO:** A nontransparent black screen.

**GRIP:** A stagehand.

**HITCH-HIKE:** Brief commercial advertising another product of sponsor in addition to main commercial.

**IDIOT CARDS:** Cue cards.

**IN THE CLEAR:** Narration without background accompaniment.

**INTERLOCK** Picture and sound on separate film running in synchronization.

**INTERCUT:** Cutting from one camera to another.

**KILL:** To eliminate a scene or a line of dialog; to extinguish lights on the set.

**KINESCOPE:** A film print made from a video tape.

**LEAD:** Principal character in a play.

**LIMBO:** Shots usually taken with a black background so there is no definable frame of reference.

**LIP SYNC:** (1) Singing or dialog mouthed to prerecorded audio; (2) picture and sound recorded simultaneously.

**LIVE:** Presentation of a program at the time it is actually seen, as differentiated from filmed or video taped presentation.

**LOCATION:** Scenes to be filmed away from the studio.

**LOGO:** A visual identification symbol.

**LONG SHOT:** (LS) A full view of a scene to encompass the background.

**MEDIUM SHOT:** (MS) In between closeup and long shot.

**MONITOR:** (1) A TV receiver; (2) to evaluate a TV or radio program.

**MONTAGE:** Radio: a rapid succession of voices relating to a connected idea; TV: a series of brief scenes in quick succession.

**OFF:** Radio: music, voice or sound at a distance from the microphone; TV: voice off screen (OS).

**ON THE NOSE:** On time.

**OPTICALS:** Effects used in a film after shooting, such as dissolves.

**OPTIONAL CUT:** Dialog or action which the writer has indicated may be deleted.

**OUT OF SYNC:** Lack of synchronization between audio and video.

**OUTTAKE:** Portion of film or video tape not used in final print.

**PACKAGE:** A complete program presented by a producer.

**PAN:** Abbreviation of panoramic. Horizontal movement of camera across a scene.

**PANTOMIME:** Expression by action or gesture without use of words.

**PILOT:** An episode of a proposed new series.

**PLATTER:** A disc recording.

**PROPS:** Abbreviation of properties; objects used on a set.

**RATING:** A method of audience measurement.

**REACTION SHOT:** A camera shot to show emotional response.

**REAR-SCREEN PROJECTION:** A device in which a still picture or a film clip is projected onto a semitransparent screen placed at the back of a set.

**RELEASE PRINT:** Approved print for distribution.

**REMOTE:** A program or portion thereof broadcast at a location different from the originating studio.

**RESOLUTION:** (1) Denouement of a play; (2) clarity and definition of a picture.

**ROUGH CUT:** First showing of a film without opticals or without music or final narration.

**SEGUE:** The flow of one musical selection into another.

**SET:** The physical surroundings of a scene.

**SINGLE SYSTEM:** A film camera which records picture and sound simultaneously.

**SLIDE:** A picture or title on a single frame or film transparency.

**SNEAK:** To fade in sound or music very softly.

**SOAP OPERA:** A daytime serial.

**SPECIAL EFFECT:** A device to create illusions.

**SPLIT SCREEN:** A special effect to present two or more scenes on the screen simultaneously; e.g., telephone conversation with both participants visible.

**STET:** A notation to let stand a previously deleted line in a script.

**STING:** A musical chord to punctuate a highly charged scene.

**STOCK SHOTS:** Film sequences available from a film library or repository.

**STRETCH:** To slow the pacing of a program.

**SUPER:** Abbreviation for superimposition; overlapping of the picture on one camera by the picture on another camera.

**SUSTAINING:** Unsponsored.

**SYNC:** Abbreviation for synchronization; audio and video portions matching.

**TAG LINE:** The final statement of a program.

**TAKE:** (1) An individual sequence of camera action; (2) an acceptable shot.

TELEPROMPTER: A mechanical prompting device.
TILT: Vertical movement of a camera.
TRANSITION: To move smoothly from one scene to another.
TRUCKING: Movement of camera beside a character or object in motion.
TWO SHOT: A shot of two individuals.
UNDER: To bring music down and keep behind dialog.
UP: A direction to raise the volume.
VIDEO: The visual portion of a program.
VIDEO TAPE: A form of magnetic tape for recording sound and picture.
VOICE OVER: Narration over silent footage.
WILD TRACK: To record sound or music separately for possible later use in a program.
WORK PRINT: An edited print which is not a composite and which is used for judging final revisions.
ZOOM: A special lens which permits going from a wide shot to a closeup without moving the camera.

### Scripting Abbreviations

ANNCR: Announcer
BG: Background
BIZ: Busy; busily
CS: Close shot; closeup (also CU)
C2S: close two-shot (closeup shot of two individuals on single frame)
CU: Closeup
DISS: Dissolve
ECU: Extreme closeup
EX: Extreme; extremely
EXT: Exterior
FAV: Favors; favoring
FG: Foreground
FWD: Forward
FX: Sound effects
INT: Interior
L: Left
LH: Left-hand
LS: Longshot
MC: Medium closeup
MON: Montage

MOS: Moving offscreen
MS: Medium shot
NARR: Narrator
OC: Off camera (also OS, for off screen)
OFX: Optical effects
ON: Cue for video action to follow
OS: Off screen
POSS: Possible; possibly
POV: Point of view
R: Right
RH: Right-hand
SF: Stock footage
SFX: Special effects
SUPER: Superimpose
VO: Voice over
WS: Wide-angle shot
WILD: Multisubject sequencing
X: Cross; crosses
2S: Two-shot
3S: Three-shot

# Bibliography

Barnouw, Erik, **A History of Broadcasting in the U.S.** (3 Vols.), Oxford University Press, 1970.

Bluem, A. William, **Documentary in American Television,** Hastings House Publishers, Inc., 1965.

Bluem, A. William and Manvell, Roger, **Television, The Creative Experience,** Hastings House Publishers, Inc., 1967.

Brown, Les, **Television,** Harcourt Brace Jovanovich, Inc., 1971.

Chapman, John, **Broadway's Best, 1960,** Doubleday and Company, Inc., 1960.

Cubeta, Paul M., **Modern Drama for Analysis,** Henry Holt and Company, Inc., 1955.

Dary, David, **Radio News Handbook,** Tab Books, 1970.

Field, Stanley, **Television and Radio Writing,** Houghton Mifflin Company, 1959.

Friendly, Fred W., **Due to Circumstances Beyond Our Control,** Random House, Inc., 1967.

Galanoy, Terry, **Down the Tube,** Henry Regnery Company, 1970.

Gassner, John, **Dramatic Soundings,** Crown Publishers, 1968.

Gassner, John, **Theatre at the Crossroads,** Holt, Rinehart and Winston, Inc., 1960.

Grebanier, Bernard, **Playwriting,** Thomas Y. Crowell Company, 1961.

Hazard, Patrick D., Editor, **TV AS ART: Some Essays in Criticism,** National Council of Teachers of English, 1966.

Kernan, Alvin B., **Character and Conflict, An Introduction to Drama,** Harcourt, Brace & World, Inc., 1963.

Kleppner, Otto, **Advertising Procedure,** Prentice-Hall, Inc., 1966.

Langner, Lawrence, **The Play's the Thing,** G.P. Putnam's Sons, 1960.

Lyon, David G., **Off Madison Avenue,** G.P. Putnam's Sons, 1966.

MacNeil, Robert, **The People Machine,** Harper & Row, Publishers, Inc., 1968.

McLuhan, Marshall, **Understanding Media: The Extensions of Man,** McGraw-Hill Book Company, 1964.

Milton, Shirley F., **Advertising Copywriting,** Oceana Publications, Inc., 1969.

Morris, Norman S., **Television's Child,** Little, Brown and Company, 1971.

Nicholson, Margaret, **A Manual of Copyright Practice,** Oxford University Press, 1970.

Reeves, Rosser, **Reality in Advertising,** Alfred A. Knopf, Inc., 1961.

Ruch, Floyd L., **Psychology and Life,** Scott, Foresman and Company, 1963.

Small, William, **To Kill a Messenger; Television News and the Real World,** Hastings House Publishers, Inc., 1970.

Steinberg, Charles S., **The Communicative Arts,** Hastings House Publishers, Inc., 1970.

Stone, Vernon A., **Careers in Broadcast News,** Radio Television News Directors Association, 1972.

Taylor, Sherril W., Editor, **Radio Programming in Action,** Hastings House Publishers, Inc., 1967.

**Television and Growing Up: The Impact of Televised Violence;** Report to the Surgeon General of the United States Public Health Service, 1972.

**Television and Social Behavior;** Report to the Surgeon General's Scientific Advisory Committee on Television and Social Behavior, 1972.

**Television News, Anatomy and Process,** Wadsworth Publishing, 1961.

Trapnell, Coles, **Teleplay, An Introduction to Television Writing,** Chandler Publishing Company, 1966.

Tyler, Poyntz, Editor, **Television and Radio,** H.W. Wilson Company, 1961.

Wainwright, Charles A., **The Television Copywriter,** Hastings House Publishers, Inc., 1966.

Wittenberg, Philip, **The Protection of Literary Property,** The Writer, 1968.

**Writing News for Broadcast,** Columbia University Press, 1971.

Wylie, Max, **Writing for Television,** Cowles Book Company, Inc., 1970.

# Index

396